W9-CAD-145

Secret History of the English
Occupation of Egypt

Sheykh Mohammed Abdu

SECRET HISTORY OF THE ENGLISH OCCUPATION OF EGYPT

Being a Personal Narrative of Events

By

WILFRID SCAWEN BLUNT

NEW YORK

Howard Fertig

1967

PUBLISHER'S NOTE

When I first arranged with Mr. Blunt to publish *The Secret History of the English Occupation of Egypt,* I suggested that he write for the American Edition a brief foreword bringing the book into even closer relation to the Anglo-Egyptian situation as it stands today. He thought this idea a good one, and agreed to write such a note. But Mr. Blunt was born in 1840, and has for a number of years been in failing health. In June he wrote me that he was so ill as to be quite unable to finish the foreword, which he had actually commenced to write. He felt furthermore that any advantage the edition would gain by having a new preface by him would be more than counterbalanced by any delay in the appearance of the book "at the present extremely critical moment."

He remarked further: "What could I have said more appropriate today as a new preface than the few words which already stand as the short preface I set to the first edition of my *Secret History* (published in London and which you reprint in this new edition). This and my poem *The Wind and the Whirlwind* (which you also give as an Appendix). Both are absolutely true of the present shameful position of England in Egypt and the calamity so closely threatening her Eastern Empire. What could I say more exactly suited? This is the punishment we are reaping today for our sin of that sad morning on the Nile which saw the first English gun open its thunder of aggression just forty years ago at Alexandria in the name of England's honour. What could I add to my words of grief and shame then uttered and repeated here? Let these stand for my new preface. My day is done. Alas! that I should have lived to see those words come true of England's punishment, more than true."

A. A. K.

(1922)

PREFACE OF 1895

I desire to place on record in a succinct and tangible form the events which have come within my knowledge relating to the origin of the English occupation of Egypt—not necessarily for publication now, but as an available document for the history of our times. At one moment I played in these events a somewhat prominent part, and for nearly twenty years I have been a close and interested spectator of the drama which was being acted at Cairo.

It may well be, also, that the Egyptian question, though now quiescent, will reassert itself unexpectedly in some urgent form hereafter, requiring of Englishmen a new examination of their position there, political and moral; and I wish to have at hand and ready for their enlightenment the whole of the materials I possess. I will give these as clearly as I can, with such documents in the shape of letters and journals as I can bring together in corroboration of my evidence, disguising nothing and telling the whole truth as I know it. It is not always in official documents that the truest facts of history are to be read, and certainly in the case of Egypt, where intrigue of all kinds has been so rife, the sincere student needs help to understand the published parliamentary papers.

Lastly, for the Egyptians, if ever they succeed in re-establishing themselves as an autonomous nation, it will be of value that they should have recorded the evidence of one whom they know to be their sincere friend in regard to matters of diplomatic obscurity which to this day they fail to realize. My relations with Downing Street in 1882 need to be related in detail if Egyptians are ever to appreciate the exact causes which led to the bombardment of Alexandria and the battle of Tel-el-Kebir, while justice to the patriot leader of their "rebellion" requires that I should give a no less detailed account of Arabi's trial, which still presents itself to some Egyptian as to all French minds, in the light of a pre-arranged comedy devised to screen a traitor. It does not do to leave truth to its own power of prevailing over lies, and history is full of calumnies which have remained unrefuted, and of ingratitudes which nations have persisted in towards their worthiest sons.

SHEYKH OBEYD, EGYPT.
1895

PREFACE ON PUBLICATION

Since the first brief preface to my manuscript was written twelve years ago, events have happened which seem to indicate that the moment foreseen in it has at last arrived when to the public advantage and without risk of serious indiscretion as far as individuals are concerned, the whole truth may be given to the world.

Already in 1904 the original manuscript had been thoroughly revised, and in its purely Egyptian part remodelled under circumstances which add greatly to its historic value. My old Egyptian friend, Sheykh Mohammed Abdu, of whom so much mention is made in it, had taken up his country residence at my doors at Sheykh Obeyd, and I found myself in almost daily intercourse with him, a most precious accident of which I did not fail to take full advantage. That great philosopher and patriot—now, alas, lost to us, for he died at Alexandria, 11th July, 1905, the day being the twenty-third anniversary of the bombardment of that city—after many vicissitudes of evil and good fortune had attained in the year 1899 to the supreme position in Egypt of Grand Mufti, and having thus acquired a wider sphere than ever of influence with his fellow countrymen, had it at heart to bequeath to them a true account of the events of his time, events which had become strangely misunderstood by them, and clothed with legends altogether fantastic and unreal.

On this subject he often spoke to me, regretting his lack of leisure to complete the historic work, and when I told him of my own memoir, he urged me very strongly to publish it, if not in English at least with his help in Arabic, and he undertook to go through it with me and see that all that part of it which related to matters within his knowledge was accurately and fully told. We had been personal friends and political allies almost from the date of my first visit to Egypt, and with his garden adjoining mine it was an easy matter for us to work together and compare our recollections of the men and things

we had known.   It was in this way that my history of an epoch
so memorable to us both took final shape, and I was able (how
fortunately!) to complete it and obtain from him his approval
and *imprimatur* before his unlooked-for death closed forever
the chief source of knowledge which he undoubtedly was of the
political movement which led up to the revolution of 1881, and
of the intrigues which marred it in the following year.

   The Mufti's death, a severe blow to me as well as to Egypt,
postponed indefinitely our plan of publishing in Arabic, nor
till the present year has the time seemed politically ripe for the
production of my work in English.   The events, however, of
1906, and now Lord Cromer's retirement from the Egyptian
scene, have so wholly changed the situation that I feel I ought
no longer to delay, at least as far as my duty to my own countrymen is concerned.   We English are confronted to-day in our
dealings with Egypt with very much the same problem we misunderstood and blundered about so disastrously a generation
ago, and if those of us who are responsible for public decisions
are, in the words of my first preface, to "re-examine their position there, political and moral," honestly or to any profit, it is
necessary they should first have set before them the past as it
really was and not as it has been presented to them so long by
the fallacious documents of their official Blue Books.   I should
probably not be wrong in asserting that neither Lord Cromer at
Cairo nor Sir Edward Grey at home, nor yet Lord Cromer's
successor Sir Eldon Gorst, have any accurate knowledge of
what occurred in Egypt twenty-five years ago—this notwithstanding Lord Cromer's tardy recognition of the reform movement of 1881 and his eulogium of Sheykh Mohammed Abdu
repeated so recently as in his last annual Report.   Lord Cromer,
it must be remembered, was not at Cairo during any part of
the revolutionary period here described, and, until quite recently, has always assumed the "official truth" regarding it
to be the only truth.

   For this reason I have decided now finally on publication,
giving the text of my Memoir as it was completed in January,
1905, the identical text of which my friend signified his approval
suppressing only certain brief passages which seem to me still
too personal in regard to individuals living, and which could
be excised without injury to the volume's complete historic

value. I can sincerely say that in all I have written my one great aim has been to disclose the *verité vraie* as it is known to me for misguided History's sake.

If there is at all a second reason with me, it must be looked for in a promise publicly made as long ago as in the September number of the "Nineteenth Century Review" of 1882 that I would complete some day my personal *Apologia* in regard to events then contemporary. At that time and out of consideration for Mr. Gladstone, and for the hope I had that he would yet repair the wrong he had done to liberty in Egypt, I forbore, in the face of much obloquy, to exculpate myself by a full revelation of the hidden circumstances which were my justification. I could not clear myself entirely without telling facts technically confidential, and I decided to be silent.

There is, however, a limit to the duty of reticence owed to public men in public affairs, and I am confident that my abstention of a quarter of a century will excuse me with fair judging minds if I now at last make my conduct quite clear in the only way possible to me, namely, by a complete exposure in detail of the whole drama of financial intrigue and political weakness as it was at the time revealed to me, substantiating it by the contemporary documents still in my possession. If the susceptibilities of some persons in high places are touched by a too candid recital, I can but reply that the necessity of speech has been put on me by their own long lack of candour and generosity. During all these years not one of those who knew the truth has said a confessing word on my behalf. It will be enough if I repeat with Raleigh:

> Go, Soul, the Body's guest,
> Upon a thankless errand.
> Fear not to touch the best,
> The truth shall be thy warrant.
> Then go, for thou must die,
> And give the world the lie.

WILFRID SCAWEN BLUNT.

NEWBUILDINGS PLACE, SUSSEX.
April, 1907.

CONTENTS

APPENDICES

CONTENTS

CHAPTER I

My first visit to Egypt was in the winter of 1875–6, when I spent some pleasant months as a tourist on the lower Nile. Before, however, describing my impressions of this my earliest acquaintance made with the Egyptian people, it may be as well, that, for their benefit and the benefit of foreign readers generally, I should say a few words in explanation of what my previous life had been as far as it had had any relation to public affairs. It will show them my exact position in my own country, and help them to understand how it came about that, beginning as a mere onlooker at what was passing in their country, I gradually became interested in it politically and ended by taking an active part in the revolution which six years later developed itself among them. I was already thirty-five years of age at the date of this first visit, and had seen much of men and things.

I began life rather early. Belonging to a family of the landed gentry of the south of England with strong Conservative traditions and connected with some of the then leaders of the Tory party, I was placed at the age of eighteen in the Diplomatic Service, in the first instance as attaché to the British Legation at Athens where King Otho was still on the throne of Greece, and afterwards, during a space of twelve years, as member of other legations and embassies to the various Courts of Europe, in all of which I learned a little of my profession, amused myself, and made friends. I was thus, between 1859 and 1869, for some weeks at Constantinople in the reign of Sultan Abd-el-Mejid; for a couple of years in the Germany of the Germanic Confederation; for a year in Spain under Queen Isabella; and for another year in Paris at the climax of the Emperor's prestige under Napoleon III; and I was also for a short time in the Republic of Switzerland, in South America, and in Portugal. Everywhere my diplomatic recollections are agreeable ones, but they are without special political interest or importance of any official kind.

Our English diplomacy in those days, the years following the Crimean War, which had disgusted Englishmen with foreign adventures, was very different from what it has since become. It was essentially pacific, unaggressive, and devoid of those subtleties which have since earned it a reputation of astuteness at the cost of its honesty. Official zeal was at a discount in the public service, and nothing was more certain to bring a young diplomatist into discredit at the Foreign Office than an attempt, however laudable, to raise any new question in a form demanding a public answer. We attachés and junior secretaries were very clearly given to understand this, and that it was not our business to meddle with the politics of the Courts to which we were accredited, only to make ourselves agreeable socially, and amuse ourselves, decorously if possible, but at any rate in the reverse of any serious sense. It is no exaggeration when I affirm it that in the whole twelve years of my diplomatic life I was asked to discharge no duty of the smallest professional importance. This discouraging *régime* gave me, while I was in the service, a thorough distaste for politics, nor was it till long after, and under very different conditions and under circumstances wholly accidental, that I at last turned my attention seriously to them. My pursuits as an attaché were those of pleasure, social intercourse, and literature. I wrote poems, not despatches, and though I assisted diplomatically at some of the serious dramas of the day in Europe, it was in the spirit of a spectator rather than of an actor, and of one hardly admitted at all behind the scenes. On my marriage in 1869, which was soon followed by the death of my elder brother which left me heir to the family estates in Sussex, I retired without regret from the public service to attend to matters of private concern which had always interested me more.

Nevertheless my early connection with the Foreign Office, though it was never to be officially renewed, was maintained on a friendly footing as of one honourably retired from the service, and this and my experience of Courts and capitals abroad, proved later of no little value to me when I once more found myself thrown by accident into the stream of international affairs. It gave me the advantage of a professional knowledge of the machinery of foreign politics and, what was still more important, a personal acquaintance with many of those who were working that machinery. Not a few of these had been my intimate friends. Thus at the very outset of my life I had found myself in official fellowship with Lord Currie, who for so many years directed the permanent policy of the Foreign Office, with Sir Henry Drummond Wolff, Sir Frank Lascelles, Sir Edward Malet, Lord Dufferin, Lord Vivian, and Sir Rivers Wilson, all closely connected afterwards with the making of Egyptian history, with Lord Lytton who was to be Viceroy of India in the years immediately preceding the crisis of 1881, and amongst foreign diplomatists with M. de Nélidoff, Russian Ambassador at Constantinople, Baron Haymerly, who died Prime Minister of the Austrian Empire, and M. de Staal, for twenty years Russian Ambassador in London. With all these I was on terms of personal intimacy long before I paid my first visit to Egypt, and it is with a full knowledge of their individual characters that I am able to speak of them and judge them. Having been myself, as it were, of the priesthood, I could not well be deceived by the common insincerities which are the stock in trade of diplomacy, or mistake for public policy action which was often only personal. It is far too readily believed by those who are without individual experience of diplomacy that the great events of the world's history are the result of elaborate political design and not as they are really in most instances, dependent upon unforeseen accidents and the personal strength or weakness, sometimes the personal whim, of the agents employed.

For the first few years of my retirement from the service I occupied myself entirely with my domestic affairs, and, as I have said, it was only by accident that my mind was gradually turned to politics. In 1873, finding myself in indifferent health, and to escape a late spring in England, I made with my wife our first common journey in Eastern lands. We went by Belgrade and the Danube to Constantinople, where we found Sir Henry Elliott at the Embassy and renewed acquaintance with other friends connected with it, among them with Dr. Dickson, of whom I shall have afterwards to speak in connection with the tragical death of Sultan Abd-el-Aziz, and who attended me with great kindness during a sharp attack of pneumonia I had there and for whom I contracted a sincere regard. The Ottoman Empire was then enjoying a period of comparative tranquillity before the storm of war which was so soon to burst over it, and I troubled myself little with its internal broils, but my sympathies, such as they were at that time, were, in common with those of most Englishmen of the day, with the Turks rather than the Christians of the Empire. On my recovery from my illness, I bought half a dozen pack horses at the At-maidan, the horse market at Stamboul, and with them we crossed over to Scutari and spent six pleasant summer weeks wandering in the hills and through the poppy fields of Asia Minor, away from beaten tracks and seeing as much of the Turkish peasant life as our entire ignorance of their language allowed. We were impressed, as all travellers have been, with the honest goodness of these people and the badness of their Government. We judged of the latter by what we saw of the ways of the Zaptiehs, our semi-military escort, whose manner with them was that of soldiers in an invaded country. Yet it was clear that with much fiscal oppression a large personal liberty existed in rural Turkey for the poor, such as contrasted not unfavourably with our own police and magistrate-ridden England. The truth is that everywhere in the East the administrative net is one of wide meshes, with rents innumerable through which all but the largest fish have good chance of escaping. In ordinary times there is no persecution of the quite indigent. I remember telling some peasants, who had complained to me through my Armenian dragoman of hardship in their lives at Government hands, that there were countries in still worse plight than their own, where if a poor man so much as lay down by the roadside at night and got together a few sticks to cook a meal he ran the risk of being brought next day before the Cadi and cast into prison; and I remember that my listeners refused to believe my tale or that such great tyranny existed anywhere in the world. My deduction from this incident is the earliest political reflection I can remember making in regard to Eastern things.

The following winter—that is to say, the early months of 1874—we spent in Algeria. Here we assisted at another spectacle which gave food for reflection: that of an Eastern people in violent subjection to a Western. The war in which France had just been engaged with Germany had been followed in Algeria by an Arab rising, which had spread to the very out-skirts of Algiers, and the Mohammedan natives were now experiencing the extreme rigours of Christian repression. This was worst in the settled districts, the colony proper, where the civil administration was taking advantage of the rebellion to confiscate native property and in every way to favour the European colonists at the native expense. With all my love for the French (and I had been at Paris during the war, and had been enthusiastic for its defence at the time of the siege) I found my sympathies in Algeria going out wholly to the Arabs. In the Sahara, beyond the Atlas, where military rule prevailed, things were somewhat better, for the French officers for the most part appreciated the nobler qualities of the Arabs and despised the mixed rascaldom of Europe—Spanish, Italian, and Maltese as well as their own countrymen—which made up the "Colonie." The great tribes of the Sahara were still at that time materially well off, and retained not a little of their ancient pride of independence which the military commandants could not but respect. We caught glimpses of these nomads in the Jebel Amour and of their vigorous way of life, and what we saw delighted us. We listened to their chauntings in praise of their lost hero Abd-el-Kader, and though we misunderstood them on many points owing to our ignorance of their language, we admired and pitied them. The contrast between their noble pastoral life on the one hand, with their camel herds and horses, a life of high tradition filled with the memory of heroic deeds, and on the other hand the ignoble squalor of the Frank settlers, with their wineshops and their swine, was one which could not escape us, or fail to rouse in us an angry sense of the incongruity which has made of these last the lords of the land and of those their servants. It was a new political lesson which I took to heart, though still regarding it as in no sense my personal affair.

Such had been the preliminary training of my life, and such its main circumstances when, as I have said, in the winter of 1875–6 I first visited Egypt. The only other matter which, perhaps, deserves here a word of explanation to non-English readers, and it is one that in Europe will receive its full appreciation, is the fact that my wife, Lady Anne Blunt, who accompanied me on all these travels, was the grandaughter of our great national poet,

Lord Byron, and so was the inheritor, in some sort, of sympathies in the cause of freedom in the East, which were not without their effect upon our subsequent action. It seemed to us, in presence of the events of 1881–2, that to champion the cause of Arabian liberty would be as worthy an endeavour as had been that for which Byron had died in 1827. As yet, however, in 1875, neither of us had any thought in visiting Egypt more serious than that of another pleasant travelling adventure in Eastern lands. We had on leaving England the plan of entering Egypt from the south, by way of Suakim, Kassala, and the Blue Nile, and so of working our way northwards to Cairo in the spring, but this, owing to the issue, just then so unfortunate to Egypt, of the Abyssinian campaign, was never realized, and the only part of our program which we carried out was that instead of landing at Alexandria, as was then the universal custom, we went on by the Canal to Suez and there first set foot upon Egyptian soil.

My first impression of all of Egypt is of our passage on the last day of the year 1875 through Lake Menzaleh, at that time the unpersecuted home of innumerable birds—a truly wonderful spectacle of prodigal natural life—to a point on the Canal north of Ismailiyah. What a sight it was! Lake Menzaleh was still an almost virgin region, and the flocks of flamingos, ducks, pelicans, and ibises which covered it, passed all belief in their prodigious magnitude. The waters, too, of the lakes and of the Canal itself were alive with fish so large and in such great quantities that not a few were run down by our ship's bows in passing, while everywhere they were being preyed on by fish hawks and cormorants, which sat watching on the posts and buoys. I imagine that the letting in of the sea for the first time on land never before covered with water provided the fish with feeding ground of exceptional richness, an advantage which has since been lost. But certain it is that both fish and birds have dwindled sadly since, and it seems unlikely that the splendid spectacle we saw that winter will be again enjoyed there by any traveller's eyes.

We landed at Suez in the first days of the year 1876, and the news of the great disaster which had overtaken the Egyptian army in Abyssinia was the first that greeted us. The details of it were not generally known, but it appeared that seven ortas, or divisions, of the Khedivial troops had perished, while a tale was in circulation of the Khedive's son, Prince Hassan, having been captured and mutilated by the enemy, an exaggeration which was afterwards disproved, for the prince, a mere boy at the time, had been carried away from the battlefield of Kora early in the day, at the very beginning of the rout, as had Ratib Pasha himself, the Egyptian general in command, who was in charge of him. Loringe Pasha, however, the American, had really lost his life with many thousands of the rank and file, and the misfortune put a final limit to the Khedive Ismaïl's ambition of universal empire on the Nile. In our small way it affected us, as making our thought of a journey to Kassala impossible, and deciding us on a less adventurous one immediately in Lower Egypt.

We were anxious, nevertheless, to see Egypt in a less conventional way than that of ordinary tourists, and, having our camping equipment with us for the longer journey, we hired camels at Suez and went by the old caravan route to Cairo. It is not necessary that I should say much of our journey across the desert. The four days spent in it alone with our Bedouin camel-men gave us our first practical lessons in Arabic—in Algeria we had been dependent wholly on a dragoman—and they laid the basis, too, of those relations with the desert tribes of Arabia which were afterwards to become so pleasant to us and so intimate. On the fifth morning we entered Cairo, greeted on our arrival at Abbassiyeh by the whistling of bullets fired by the Khedivial troops at practice, for we had unwittingly encamped overnight just behind their targets and the aim of the recruits was very uncertain, but no harm was suffered. We little thought at the time that we should ever be interested in the doings of these soldiers as a fighting army, and still less that our sympathies would one day be with them in a war against our own countrymen. I was as yet, though not perhaps even then enthusiastically so, a believer in the common English creed that England had a providential mission in the East, and that our wars were only waged there for honest and beneficent reasons. Nothing was further from my mind than that we English ever could be guilty, as a nation, of a great betrayal of justice in arms for our mere selfish interests.

Neither need I say anything in detail about Cairo, through

which we passed that day without stopping longer than to ask for our letters at the Consulate. Our object was to see the country districts and not to waste time on a city already in part European, and we thought to find camping ground immediately beyond the Nile. So we rode on. We did not understand the entreaties of our camel-men that we should alight and let them and their camels go back, or realize that we were doing them an injustice by forcing them to break the tribal rule which forbade them as Bedouins of the eastern desert to cross over to the west. In spite of their expostulations we held on our way by the Kasr-el-Nil bridge and the road to Ghizeh. We had caught sight of the Pyramids and pushed on eagerly in their direction, and were only stopped by the failing light which overtook us at sunset close to the little fellah village ɔt Tolbiya, the last but one before the Pyramids are reached. It was there that we made our halt and alighted for the first time on the black soil of the Nile, as yet hardly dry from the autumn inundation.

The good people of Tolbiya, in their hearty fellah fashion, received us with all possible hospitality. Though living on the tourist road to the Pyramids and accustomed to treat Frank travellers in some sort as their prey, the fact of our alighting at their village for a night's lodging gave us a character of guests they at once recognized. Of all the Europeans who for many years had passed their way, not one had made a pause at their doors. Thus our relations with them were from the outset friendly, and the accident served us as an introduction in the sequel to other villagers when, after a few days spent among these, we went once more on our way. We had no choice at the time but to stay where we were, for in the morning our Bedouins refused to go a mile farther with us, and, having received their hire, departed with their camels. Other camels then had to be found. So it happened that my first week in Egypt was occupied in going a round of the neighbouring village markets in search of the needed beasts, and making purchases of pack saddles and water skins and all kinds of travelling gear for our further journey.

The fellahin at that time were in terrible straits of poverty. It was the first of the three last terrible years of the Khedive

Ismaïl's reign; Ismaïl Sadyk, the notorious Mufettish, was in power; the European bondholders were clamouring for their "coupons," and famine was at the doors of the fellahin. It was rare in those days to see a man in the fields with a turban on his head, or with more than a shirt to his back. Even in the neighbourhood of Cairo, and still more in the Fayûm to which we took our way as soon as the camels were procured, I can testify that this was the case. The country Sheykhs themselves had few of them a cloak to wear. Wherever we went it was the same. The provincial towns on market days were full of women selling their clothes and their silver ornaments to the Greek usurers, because the tax collectors were in their villages whip in hand. We bought their poor trinkets and listened to their stories, and joined them in their maledictions on a government which was laying them bare. We did not as yet understand, any more than did the peasants themselves, the financial pressure from Europe which was the true cause of these extreme exactions; and we laid the blame, as they did, on Ismaïl Pasha and the Mufettish, Ismaïl Sadyk, little suspecting our English share of the blame.

The villagers were outspoken enough. Englishmen in those days were popular everywhere in Mohammedan lands, being looked upon as free from the political designs of the other Frank nations, and individually as honester than these in their commercial dealings. In Egypt especially they stood in amiable contrast with the needy adventures from the Mediterranean sea-board—the Italian, Greek, and Maltese money-lenders— who were sucking the life blood of the Moslem peasantry. Already there were rumours in the air which had reached the village of a possible European intervention, and the idea of it, if it was to be English, was not unpopular. The truth is that the existing state of things was wholly unendurable, and any change was looked to with joy by the starving people as a possible relief. England to the fellahin in their actual condition of beggary, robbed and beaten and perishing of hunger, appeared in the light of a bountiful and friendly providence very rich and quite disinterested, a redresser of wrongs and friend of the oppressed, just such, in fact, as individual English tourists then often were, who went about with open hands and expressions of sympathy. They did not suspect the immense commercial selfishness which had led us, collectively as a nation, to so many aggressions on the weak races of the world.

In the year 1876 I too, as I have said, was a believer in England, and I shared the common idea of the beneficence of her rule in the East, and I had no other thought for the Egyptians than that they should share with India, which I had not yet seen, the privilege of our protection. "The Egyptians," I wrote in my journal of the time, "are a good, honest people as any in the world—all, that is, who do not sit in the high places. Of these I know nothing. But the peasants, the fellahin, have every virtue which should make a happy, well-to-do-society. They are cheerful, industrious, obedient to law, and pre-eminently sober, not only in the matter of drink, but of the other indulgences to which human nature is prone. They are neither gamblers nor brawlers, nor licentious livers; they love their homes, their wives, their children. They are good sons and fathers, kind to dumb animals, old men, beggars, and idiots. They are absolutely without prejudice of race, and perhaps even of religion. Their chief fault is a love of money, but that is one political economists will readily pardon. . . . It would be difficult to find anywhere a population better fitted to attain the economical end of the greatest happiness for the greatest number. In politics they have no aspirations except to live and let live, to be allowed to work and keep the produce of their labour, to buy and sell without interference and to escape taxation. They have been ill-treated for ages without losing thereby their goodness of heart; they have few of the picturesque virtues; they are neither patriotic nor fanatical nor romantically generous. But they are free from the picturesque vices. Each man works for himself—at most for his family. The idea of self-sacrifice for the public good they do not understand, but they are innocent of plots to enslave their fellows. . . . In spite of the monstrous oppression of which they are the victims, we have heard no word of revolt, this not from any superstitious regard for their rulers, for they are without political prejudice, but because revolt is no more in their nature than it is in a flock of sheep. They would hail the Queen of England, or the Pope, or the King of Ashantee with equal eagerness if these came with the gift for them of a penny less taxation in the pound."

Such were my first thoughts about Egypt in the early days of 1876, not altogether inaccurate ones, though I was far from suspecting the growth already beginning of political ideas in the towns. Neither did I understand the full influence of European finance in the hardships from which the peasantry were suffering. Nevertheless, on our return to Cairo in March I saw something of the reverse of the medal. Mr. Cave's financial mission had arrived during our tour, and was established in one of the palaces on the Shubra Road, and from its members—one of whom was an old acquaintance, Victor Buckley of the Foreign Office, and from Colonel Staunton, our Consul-General—I learned something of the condition of financial affairs; while a little later Sir Rivers Wilson, also my friend, who was to play later so prominent a part in Egyptian affairs, appeared at Cairo and joined the other members of the financial inquiry. What their report was of the condition of affairs I need not here relate in detail, but it will help to an understanding of the matter if I give a very short account of it and how their mission came to be appointed, the first of its kind in Egypt.*

The Khedive Ismaïl's reign had begun in the full tide of a period for Egypt of high material prosperity. His predecessor, Saïd, a man of fairly enlightened views, had had the good sense to give all possible encouragement to the fellahin in agricultural matters. He had abandoned the claim of the Viceroy to be sole landlord on the Nile, had recognized proprietary rights in the existing occupiers of land, and had fixed the land tax at the low figure of forty piastres to the feddān. This had resulted in a general enrichment of the population, and the fellahin, emancipated from their old condition of serfdom to the Circassian Pashas, were everywhere accumulating wealth. Egypt at the close of Saïd's reign had become not only the most prosperous province of the Ottoman Empire, but one of the most progressive agriculturally of the Eastern world. The

* Note. For a fuller and better account of the finance of that time serious students of Egyptian history should consult "Egypt's Ruin" by Theodore Rothstein published by A. C. Fifield, 13. Clifford's Inn, London, in 1910 with an introduction by me.

revenue, though small in comparison to what it is now, probably not more than four millions sterling, was easily collected, and the expenses of administration were insignificant, while the public debt amounted to only three millions.   It is true that in his later years Saïd had granted a number of concessions to European adventurers on terms which were becoming a heavy burden on the state, but the general wealth of the country was so large that this was not more than its light taxation could bear, and the Viceroy had at his disposal, when all yearly claims had been discharged, probably not less that a couple of millions for his free expenditure.   Certainly there never had been an age in Egypt when the mass of the native inhabitants had been so materially prosperous; and to the fellahin especially it had come to be spoken of as, for them, the "age of gold." Ismaïl, when in 1860 he succeeded to the Viceroyalty, was without question the richest of Mohammedan princes and master of the most prosperous of Mohammedan states.

Ismaïl's character, before he became Viceroy, had been that of a wealthy landed proprietor managing his large estates in Upper Egypt according to the most enlightened modern methods.   He was praised by nearly all European travellers for the machinery he had introduced and the expenditure he had turned to profit, and it is certain that he possessed a more than usual share of that natural shrewdness and commercial aptitude which distinguishes the family of Mohammed 'Ali. His succession to the Viceroyalty had been more or less a surprise to him, for until within a few months of Saïd's death he had not been the immediate heir, and his prospects had been only those of an opulent private person.   It was perhaps this unexpected stroke of fortune that from the beginning of his reign led him to extravagance.   By nature a speculator and inordinately greedy of wealth, he seems to have looked upon his inheritance and the absolute power now suddenly placed in his hands, not as a public trust, but as the means above all things else of aggrandizing his private fortune.   At the same time he was as inordinately vain and fond of pleasure, and his head was turned by his high position and the opportunity it gave him of figuring in the world as one of its most splendid princes.   He was surrounded at once by flatterers of all kinds, native and European, who promised on the one hand to make him the richest of financiers, and on the other the greatest of Oriental sovereigns. In listening to these his own cleverness and commercial skill betrayed him, and made him only their more ready dupe. Ismaïl, before his accession, had been an astute money-maker according to the ways in which money was then made in Egypt, and he had had, too, a European education of the kind Orientals acquire on the Paris boulevards, superficial as regards all serious matters, but sufficient to convince him of his capacity to deal with the rogues of the Bourse with the weapons of their own roguery. In both directions he was led astray.

His first act of self aggrandizement was simple and successful. The revenue, which rested chiefly on the land tax, was low, and he raised it by progressive enhancements from the 40 piastres where he found it, to 160, where it has ever since stood. The country under his hand was rich and at first could afford the extra burden. Men gave of their superfluity rather than of their necessity, and for some years did so without complaint. This enhancement, however, of the revenue was only part of his rapacious program. His native flatterers reminded him that in the days of his grandfather the whole land had been regarded as the Viceroy's personal property, and that, moreover, Mohammed Ali had claimed and exercised for some years a monoply of its foreign trade. Ismaïl schemed to revive these rights in his own person, and though he did not dare, in the face of European opinion, to commit any great acts of open confiscation in regard to the land, he gained to a large extent his ends by other means, and so rapidly that in a few years he managed to get into his own hands a fifth of the whole area of the cultivable land of Egypt. His method was by various means of intimidation and administrative pressure to make the possession of such lands as he desired to acquire a burden to their owners, and to render their lives so vexatious that they should be constrained to sell at prices little more than nominal. In this way he had, as I have said, possessed himself of an enormous property in land, and he doubtless thought that this was to prove to him a correspondingly enormous source of personal income. But his very covetousness in the matter proved his ruin. It was found in practice that while under his personal management as a comparatively small owner his estates had been well worked, and had brought him wealth, his new gigantic ownership laid him open to losses in a hundred ways. In vain he laid out enormous sums on machinery. In vain he laid whole villages and districts under contribution to furnish him forced labour. In vain he started factories on his estates and employed managers from Europe at the highest salaries. He was robbed everywhere by his agents, and was unable to gather from his lands even a fraction of the revenue they had brought in taxation when not his own. This was the beginning of his financial difficulties, coinciding as it did with the sudden fall in agricultural prices, and especially of cotton, which soon after set in, and it was the beginning, too, of the ruin of the peasantry, whom, to supply his deficiency, he now loaded with irregular taxation of all kinds. Ismaïl Sadyk, the notorious Mufettish, was his chief agent in this disastrous history.

It was not long, however, before Ismaïl fell into much more dangerous hands, and embarked in much more ruinous adventures than these early ones. To say nothing of the enormous sums which he poured out like water on his own private pleasures, of his follies of palace building, his follies with European women, and his follies of royal entertainment, there were schemes of ambition vast enough to drain the purse of any treasury. It is not known precisely how many millions he expended at Constantinople in procuring himself the Khedivial title, and in getting the order of the viceregal succession altered in favour of his son. But it must have been very many, while still more went in hair-brained schemes of speculation and in liabilities contracted towards European syndicates. Lastly, there was the conquest of the Upper Nile, and the attempted conquest of the kingdom of Abyssinia. To provide for all these immense expenditures loans had to be raised, at first on a small scale with local bankers and Greeks of Alexandria, and presently in more reckless fashion on the European Stock Exchange. Here his worst counsellor and evil genius had been Nubar Pasha, the Armenian financier, who, by a strange inversion of ideas, has come to be regarded by a certain class of Egyptian opinion ignorant of history as an "Egyptian patriot." Nubar was, however, in fact, the one man who, more than any other after Ismaïl himself, was responsible for Egypt's financial ruin. Commissioned by his master to find him money at any cost

Note in correction as to Nubar's wealth *see* Appendix.

to meet his extravagant wants, he raised loan after loan for him in Europe on terms which realized for him hardly more than 60 per cent. of the capital sums he inscribed himself for as debtor, while he, Nubar, pocketed as commission several millions sterling. Of the ninety-six millions nominally raised in this way, it has been calculated that only some fifty-four reached Ismaïl's hands.

At the date which I am writing of the whole of this liability had not yet been incurred, but already the interest on the foreign debt amounted to four millions yearly, and to raise sufficient revenue to meet it and to carry on the administration and pay the huge expense of the Abyssinian war, the peasantry were being fleeced, as I have described, under pressure of the whip, of their last hoarded piastres. Those who talk lightly in these days of Ismaïl as a prince rather unfortunate than guilty, and to be pitied in some sort for the betrayal of the country financially to Europe, know nothing of the truth, nor do they realize the enormity of the ruin inflicted by his selfish folly on his fellah subjects. It has been calculated that the total cost of his reign to Egypt amounted to something like 400 millions sterling, nor is this in my opinion an exaggerated estimate, for it had gathered in the whole of the peasant savings of a number of prosperous years, and nearly the whole of their agricultural stock besides the public debt, and left them, moreover, indebted privately to the amount of something like twenty millions to the Greek and other local usurers.

Such had been the causes of Egypt's misfortunes as I learned them at Cairo in the spring of 1876. With regard to the origin of our financial intervention, it was certainly at that time Ismaïl's own foolish doing, and was not, as far as I know, prompted by any direct political motives in England. He most certainly applied to the English Government for financial assistance through Colonel Staunton in the autumn of 1875, and in a way that almost necessitated the assistance having a political character. His reason for choosing England rather than France as the recipient of his confidences was that at the time England was in a far better position financially to help him. The French Government was still crippled by the expense of the war with Germany of 1870, and was really unable to assist him in any effectual way, while, as I have already said, the friendship

was given in the Viceregal Kiosque at the Pyramids, and was one
of those extravagant entertainments Ismaïl was accustomed to
dazzle European eyes with, nor was there anything wanting to
point the contrast between the wealth of the entertainer and
the poverty of those at whose expense it was really given.   The
table was spread for us literally under the eyes of a starving
multitude of peasants, the very peasants Mr. Cave was there
to save from ruin.   Yet none of us seemed to feel the incongruity of it all.   We feasted elaborately, and drank champagne
of the best, and went our way, and it is only now that, with
a better knowledge of the whole circumstances, I recall the
real character of the scene and recognize it for what it in all
verity was with its waste and surrounding misery, a true presentment of the twin causes of the coming revolution.

CHAPTER II

On leaving Cairo that spring of 1876 we paid our first visit to the confines of Arabia. It was then more the custom with European tourists than it is now to go on from Egypt into Syria by way of the desert, and we took once more to our camels and our tent life, and with the same Bedouins who had escorted us from Suez, crossed the Suez Canal and made a long tour through the Sinai peninsula and on by Akabah to Jerusalem. As we were strange to the country we passed through, and were still very ignorant of Arabic and had with us no dragoman, we got into some rather perilous adventures which are now amusing to recollect, though at the time they were disagreeable enough. It is perhaps worth recording as a curious accident of travel that as we were passing along the shore of the Gulf of Akabah, which is fringed in places with coral reefs, we had stopped to examine these and to admire the wonderful colours, purple, gold, and vermilion, of the innumerable little fishes which live in them. I was standing thus at the sea's edge, my gun, which I always then carried, in my hand, when I saw a great commotion in the water near me and suddenly, before I was well aware of the cause, a large shark, one of a shoal, leaving the rest came straight to where I stood and was already within a few yards of me before I understood what manner of fish it was or that that I was the object of its attack. I had barely time to raise my gun when it turned, as these fishes do, on its side and rose half out of the water to take hold of me, and it was so near me when I fired that my charge of small shot killed it without the need of a second barrel, so that we were able, with the help of a lasso, to bring it high and dry on shore. It was a very large one, nearly ten feet long, and I do not doubt that if I had been a little more careless than I was I might have been carried from the rock into the sea by it. The incident brought home to me the danger which was once so common in Egypt for the fellahin from crocodiles in the Upper Nile, and I have been cautious in the matter of sea bathing ever since.

We fell into trouble, too, with certain Arabs on our way, through our ignorance of the rules and customs of the desert. When camped outside Akabah, we received a visit from Abunjad the well-known Sheykh of the Alawin, a branch of the Howeytat tribe, who had the customary right of escorting travellers to Petra, and whom we managed to offend, with the result that we ended by starting without escort or guides, our only native companions being two Arab boys who had followed us from Mount Sinai, and knew nothing of the northern country. With these we ventured north for Palestine, and presently ran short of water. The wells, when we by fortune found them, proved to be almost dry, and it was only after great hardships under a burning sun that we at last reached an Arab encampment. Things had become so bad for us one night that we had resolved that if at noon on the following day we should have still failed to find water we must abandon our baggage and push on on our best camels for our bare lives to the settled country. An hour, however, before the time agreed on, the happy sound of an ass braying told us that a camp must be near, and presently we spied an Arab child perched on a mound, and from him, under some compulsion of fear, got knowledge of their watering place. It was a beautiful pool of rain water in the hollow of a rock, and here we lay long and quenched our thirst and filled our goat skins. By good fortune it was, the men of the place, Azazimeh Arabs, were away or I doubt if we should have been allowed to take so liberal a share of this "Bounty of God," for they were in possession of the place and had sown a little barley field, as Bedouins often do on the Syrian frontier for the chance of rain, and this was all their drinking store till their corn should be ripe. Nor were they otherwise than justly angry on their return, and we had to watch all night for fear of an attack. It was not till morning that they came with shouts and menaces, but we had already loaded our camels, and being well armed held on our way. Knowing the ways of Bedouins better now, I feel sure that we need not thus have quarrelled with them, and that with a little explanation and payment for our disturbance of their rights they would have received us well. But as it was, we were within a hair's breadth of a serious misadventure, and deserve to be thankful that the following day we at last reached the grass lands between Hebron and Gaza. Here the more settled Arabs gave us a good reception, and having made friends with them the memory of our past danger was soon forgotten. This ended our travels for that year, and from Jerusalem we returned in the early summer by the ordinary sea route to England.

The winter of 1877–8 saw us again in the East, this time with a larger program of adventure. We visited Aleppo, and passed down the Euphrates to Bagdad, and on our return journey made acquaintance with the great Bedouin tribes of Mesopotamia and the Syrian Desert south of Palmyra. We began now to know something of the language, and to understand the customs of the Arabs, and made no more mistakes of the kind I have just described. For this we were largely indebted to the wise counsels of the then English Consul at Aleppo, Mr. Skene, who had had a large experience of Bedouins and their ways, and who taught us to approach them on their nobler side, and putting aside all fear to trust them as friends, appealing to their law of hospitality. The history of this most interesting and successful journey has been very fully written by my wife in her "Bedouin Tribes of the Euphrates," in reality a joint work, in which my first political views in regard to Arabian liberty may be traced by those who care to seek them. My sympathy with the Arabs as against the Turks, with whom they were at chronic war, was the result of no pre-conceived idea, and still less of any political plan, but was caused by what I saw, the extreme misgovernment of the settled districts by the Ottoman officials, and the happiness of the still independent tribes. It was a time of much local disorganization. The Russo-Turkish war was in its last desperate throes at Kars and Plevna, and though our good wishes were all with the Moslem armies as against the invading Muscovites, the sight of the miserable Syrian and Mesopotamian villagers being driven in chains as recruits to the sea coast moved us to anger against the imperial government, an anger which the hatred everywhere manifested by the Arabs against the Turks daily intensified. It was impossible in those days of far worse rule than now for any one with the instinct of liberty to do otherwise than resent the Ottoman misgovernment of its Arabic-speaking provinces. It was a government of force and fraud, corrupt and corrupting to the last degree, where every evil engine was employed to enslave and degrade the people, where the Moslems were worse treated than the Christians, and where all alike were pillaged by the Pashas. The Turk in his own home in Asia Minor has a number of honest and manly virtues, but as a master in a subject land he is too often a rapacious tyrant. Every villayet had been bought with money at Constantinople, and the purchasing Valy was making what fortune he could during his term of office out of those he was given to administer. The land of Bagdad, under Ottoman rule, we had seen turned into a wilderness, Damascus into a decaying city. Everywhere land was falling out of cultivation, and the Government, like a moral plague, was infecting the inhabitants with its own corruption. Can it be wondered at if, in view of these doings, we thought and spoke strongly, and, though our Government at the time was in open alliance with the Porte, our sympathies were with any scheme which might make the Arabian provinces independent of the Empire?

On my return to England I find a record that on the 14th of May, 1878, I was taken by my cousin, Philip Currie (now Lord Currie), who was then his private secretary and one of the highest officials at the Foreign Office, to see Lord Salisbury. Lord Salisbury had just accepted the Ministry of Foreign Affairs, and, though I knew nothing of it, must have been at the point of signing the famous secret treaty with the Sultan known as the Cyprus Convention, and our journey in Arabian lands had excited his interest to learn from me something about them. In answer to his questions I told him all my thoughts very frankly, and I remember especially suggesting to him the possible independence some day of Syria, and that it might join hands with Egypt against the common misgovernment of their Turkish rulers. To this, however, he by no means responded, saying that there could be no political connection between the two provinces of the Ottoman Empire, and that the case of each stood on a separate basis. He was more influenced by me, however, when I spoke unfavourably of the then much talked of Euphrates Valley Railway scheme, under English guarantee, in which I saw a new danger to Arabian liberty, and

I have reason to know that my arguments weighed with him to the extent that he shortly after refused all Foreign Office support to the enterprise, which has remained to this day abandoned.   My conversation on this occasion left me with a high opinion of Lord Salisbury's intelligence on Eastern matters, and, though his view of them has never been mine, I have always preserved a strong feeling of his personal integrity, while it began a connection between us never intimate, but always friendly on his part.   To the last he allowed me to write to him on these subjects, and though seldom agreeing he invariably responded to my occasional letters with more than the usual official courtesy.

Any hopes, however, that I may have had of persuading Lord Salisbury to my views about the Arabs were speedily dispelled by his attitude that summer at Berlin, when his policy was publicly proclaimed of guaranteeing to the Sultan the whole of his Asiatic dominions.   The inner history of the Congress of Berlin as it affected Egypt is so curious, and at the same time so important, that it is necessary I should tell it here as I learned it soon after the events had happened.

It will be remembered that the terrible winter of 1877–8 witnessed the final scenes of the war between Russia and Turkey, and that the spring of the new year found the Czar's army at the gates of Constantinople.   The same period had been one of extreme misery in Egypt.   The Cave mission, whose arrival I had seen at Cairo, had been followed by other financial missions of less integrity, which had resulted in what was known as the Goschen-Joubert arrangement of the Khedive Ismaïl's debts, a truly leonine settlement, according to which the enormous yearly charge of nearly seven millions sterling had been saddled on the Egyptian revenue, an amount which could only be wrung out of the ruined fellahin by forcing them, under the whip, to mortgage their lands to the Greek usurers who attended the tax-gatherers everywhere on their rounds through the villages.   The last two Niles had been very bad ones, and there had been famine in the land from the sea to Assouan. Many thousands of the villagers—men, women, and children— had died that winter of sheer hunger.   There had been nothing like it since the beginning of the century.   Under these circumstances it was clear that either the Khedive must go bankrupt or a reduction be made on the interest of his debts, the Goschen-Joubert arrangement being abandoned. The former course would have been the more equitable and by far the better one for the country, but in the foreign bondholders' interests this was put aside, and a final attempt was made by these, this time successfully, to secure the diplomatic intervention of the great Powers for yet another settlement between Ismaïl and his creditors, The moment was a favourable one as far as England was concerned, for it coincided with the resolve of the English Government, under Disraeli's guidance, to play a forward political game, and take the leading part in the affairs of the Ottoman Empire. Lord Derby, who so far had gone unwillingly with his chief in his new policy of imperial adventure, now would go no further with him and left the Foreign Office, and, as we have seen, was replaced by Lord Salisbury. It was the signal of a general diplomatic advance, not unaccompanied with menace. The British fleet was brought through the Dardanelles into the Sea of Marmora, the Russian army was overawed and prevented from entering Stamboul, and under pressure of the English demonstration a treaty of peace was hurriedly drawn up between the Czar and the Sultan, the treaty of San Stefano. On the side of Egypt, at the same time, an official Commission of Inquiry was appointed, which, though nominally international, was intended at the Foreign Office to be mainly an English one, my friend Sir Rivers Wilson being chosen as English commissioner. His appointment was, I believe, almost the first Lord Salisbury signed on taking the command in Downing Street.

It will also be remembered that two months later a secret convention was negotiated at Constantinople by our then Ambassador, Sir Henry Layard, a man of great ability and knowledge of the East, who had acquired the personal confidence of the still youthful Sultan, Abdul Hamid, in accordance with which the island of Cyprus was leased to England and a guarantee given to the Sultan of the integrity of all his Asiatic provinces in lieu of promises of reform to be enforced by the presence in Asia Minor of certain ambulant English consuls, military men, who were to give advice and report grievances. The idea of the Cyprus Convention, certainly in the minds of Disraeli and Salisbury who signed it and of Layard its true

author, was to establish informally but none the less effectually
an English protectorate over Asiatic Turkey. The acquisition
of Cyprus was in their view to be the smallest part of the bar-
gain. The island was really of very little value to England as
a *place d'armes,* and its selection for that purpose was due less
to its fitness for the purpose than to a fantastic whim of
Disraeli's, backed up by the roseate report of its potential
wealth sent in by one of our consuls who had an interest in the
island. Disraeli many years before, as a quite young man, had
in his novel "Tancred" advanced half jestingly the idea of a
great Asiatic empire under an English monarchy, and Cyprus
was to be specially included in it as recalling the historic fact
that our English king, Richard Cœur de Lion, had once been also
its sovereign. The whole thing was a piece of romantic fooling,
but Disraeli loved to turn his political jests into realities and to
persuade his English followers, whom as a Jew he despised, in
all seriousness to the ways of his own folly. The really important object aimed at by Layard in the Convention—and it
was certainly his rather than Salisbury's, who was new to office
and whose experience the year before at Constantinople had
made him anything but a Turcophile—was to acquire the
strategic control of Asia Minor, which it was thought might be
effected through the ambulant consular posts it created. These
were to supervise the civil administration in the provinces, and
see that the peasantry were not too much robbed by those
who farmed the taxes, and that the recruiting grounds of the
Ottoman army were not depopulated by mismanagement. Thus
the advance of Russia to the Mediterranean might, it was
thought, be checked in Asia as their advance in Europe had been
checked at San Stefano.

Looking back at the position now, with our knowledge of
subsequent events, and especially of the Sultan Abdul Hamid's
character, it seems strange both that the Sultan should have
signed such a Convention which, if it had been carried out, would
have put Asiatic Turkey as much into English military hands as
Egypt is to-day, or that our Foreign Office should have believed in its success, and the epithet applied to it at the time
by Gladstone, who denounced it as an "insane Convention,"
seems more than justified. It must, however, be remembered
that as regards Abdul Hamid he had really no choice, with

the Russian army still at his doors, but to accept the English alliance even if it should mean tutelage, and also that up to that point England had always proved a reliable and disinterested friend.   Layard, on the other hand, was conscious of his personal ascendency at the palace, and he knew how great the prestige was in the Asiatic provinces of the English name. An English Consul in those days held a position of absolute authority with Valys and every class of Ottoman officials, and he may well have thought that this could be indefinitely extended. The honour of England was so great in all Turkish eyes, and her policy towards the Moslem Empire had been so sympathetic that no suspicion existed anywhere of her having selfish plans. Layard, too, was himself a believer in the Turks, and he may have had dreams of playing the part at Constantinople of *Maire du Palais,* which Lord Cromer has shown us an example of since at Cairo.   Now, it is only astonishing that such English dreams should ever have been indulged in, or that by Moslems England's disinterestedness should ever have been trusted.

Lastly, it will be remembered that a month after the secret signature of the Cyprus Convention, the great European Congress of 1878 met at Berlin.   It had been called together principally at Disraeli's instance, and was to be the most important meeting of the Powers since the Congress of Paris.   Like the earlier Congress its special object was to determine the fate of European Turkey and of the Christian subjects of the Sultan, and on England's part to revise the treaty of San Stefano.   On its success in this direction Disraeli had staked his whole reputation as a statesman.   England had intervened, according to his showing, on the highest motives of policy as Turkey's best and most disinterested friend, and it was on her approval as such by the other great Powers that depended his political position at home no less than abroad.   So vital, indeed, to Disraeli did success at the Congress appear, that he went himself to it as chief plenipotentiary, taking Lord Salisbury, who was still new to diplomacy, with him as a second ambassador, while Russia was represented by Prince Gortschakoff, France by M. Waddington, and Italy by Count Corti, Prince Bismarck presiding as host over the whole august assemblage.   I may add that Currie accompanied Lord Salisbury as *précis* writer on the occasion, and Lord Rowton, Disraeli.

The general proceedings of the Congress are of course well known, and I need not here describe them, but what has never been published is the following all important incident, of which, as already said, I learned the particulars some little time after it occurred. The Congress assembled on the 13th of June, and as the matters to be discussed were of the highest moment, and there was not a little suspicion of each other among the plenipotentiaries in regard to a possible partition of Turkey, it was proposed at the outset that a preliminary declaration should be made by each Ambassador affirming that his Government came to the Congress unfettered by any secret engagement as to the questions in dispute. This declaration Disraeli and Salisbury, who seem to have been taken by surprise, and were unprepared to make a clean breast of their secret doings with the Sultan, had not the presence of mind to refuse, and no less than the others formally agreed and gave their word to— it must be remembered that both were new to diplomacy. It may therefore be imagined how high a surprise it was, and scandal at Berlin when a few weeks later, 9th July, the text of the hidden Cyprus Convention was published in London by one of the evening papers. One Marvin, an Oriental traveller and linguist, but who had no official position at the Foreign Office, had been imprudently employed as translator and copyist of the Turkish text by Currie, and had sold his information for a round sum to the "Globe." The publication came as a thunderclap on our Embassy at Berlin, and though the authenticity of the text was promptly denied in London, the truth at Berlin could not long be concealed. Our two plenipotentaries found themselves confronted with the unexplainable fact that they had perpetrated a gross breach of faith on their European colleagues, and stood convicted of nothing less than a direct and recorded lie. The discovery threatened to break up the Congress altogether. Prince Gortschakoff declared himself outraged, and he was joined in his anger on the part of France by M. Waddington. Both gave warning that they would withdraw at once from the sittings, and M. Waddington went so far as to pack up his trunks to leave Berlin. The situation was an ugly one, and was only saved by the cynical good offices of Bismarck, on whom Disraeli, as a fellow cynic and a man of bold ideas, had made a sympathetic impression. The German

Chancellor, as "honest broker," brought about the following compromise, with which M. Waddington declared himself satisfied. It was agreed between the French and English plenipotentiaries:

1. That as a compensation to France for England's acquisition of Cyprus, France should be allowed on the first convenient opportunity, and without opposition from England, to occupy Tunis.

2. That in the financial arrangements being made in Egypt, France should march *pari passu* with England; and,

3. That England should recognize in a special manner the old French claim of protecting the Latin Christians in Syria.

It was in consideration of Disraeli's surrender on these three points that Waddington consented to remain at Berlin and join the other ambassadors in arranging the Balkan settlement, which eventually was come to more or less on the lines of the English proposals. The price thus paid to France by Disraeli of a province belonging to his ally the Sultan, it is curious to reflect, enabled that statesman to return a little later to London and claim a public triumph, with the famous boast in his mouth that he had brought back "peace with honour." A curious history truly, and deserving to be specially noted as marking the point of departure for England of a new policy of spoliation and treacherous dealing in the Levant foreign to her traditional ways. To the Cyprus intrigue are directly or indirectly referable half the crimes against Oriental and North African liberty our generation has witnessed. It suggested the immediate handing over of Bosnia to Austria. It helped to frustrate a sound settlement in Macedonia. It put Tunis under the heel of France, and commenced the great partition of Africa among the European Powers, with the innumerable woes it has inflicted on its native inhabitants, from Bizerta to Lake Chad, and from Somaliland to the Congo. Above all it destroyed at a critical moment all England's influence for good in the Ottoman Empire. It embittered Moslem hearts against her in 1881 and 1882, and, as I will show, was a powerful factor in the more violent events of those troubled years in Egypt. Also it most certainly defeated its own end in Asiatic Turkey if England's co-operation in reform was really contemplated. The doings at the Congress opened the Sultan's eyes to the danger there might be in any English co-operation, and also beyond question hardened his heart to a policy contrary to English advice, and in which he has been only too successful, that of suppressing all liberty and self-government among his own Turkish subjects. To it the Liberal party at Constantinople owes more than to anything else its ruthless persecution, and it is even not too much to say that whatever woes have been inflicted on the Armenians have been caused by the false hopes raised at Berlin of their emancipation by England's moral help, a help her own immorality has made her powerless to give. The immediate effect in Egypt of the compromise come to with M. Waddington was the despatch of a telegram from Berlin to Wilson at Alexandria ordering him, much to his chagrin and surprise, to see that in all the financial appointments made in connection with his official inquiry, France should receive an absolutely equal share. It was, indeed, though unknown to Wilson at the time, the determining cause, a year later, of the Anglo-French condominium. [1]

Public affairs were in this position when in the autumn of that same year, 1878, I found myself once more upon my road eastwards. My journey of the winter before to Bagdad, and especially the success I had had in a matter much more interesting to me than any politics, the purchase and bringing safely home of the Arab mares which were to form the nucleus of my now well-known stud at Crabbet, had roused considerable interest and curiosity in England, and I had spent the summer preparing my wife's journal for publication, and it was now in the

---

[1] I have given the story of the arrangement made with Waddington as I heard it first from Lord Lytton at Simla in May, 1879. The details were contained in a letter, which he showed me, written to him from Berlin, while the Congress was still sitting, by a former diplomatic colleague and have since been confirmed to me from more than one quarter, though with variations. In regard to the main feature of the agreement, the arrangement about Tunis, I had it very plainly stated to me in the autumn of 1884 by Count Corti who had been Italian Ambassador at the Congress. According to his account, the shock of the revelation to Disraeli had been so great, that he took to his bed, and for four days did not appear at the sittings, leaving Lord Salisbury to explain matters as he best could. He said there had been no open rupture wth Waddington, the case having been submitted by Waddington to his fellow ambassadors, who agreed that it was one that could not publicly be disputed, "Il faut la guerre ou se taire." The agreement was a verbal one between Waddington and Salisbury, but was recorded in a dispatch subsequently written by the French Ambassador in London, in which he reminded the latter of the conversation held in Berlin, and so secured its acknowledgment in writing.
See Appendix VI. as to the Berlin Congress.

Press. We were not content, however, with this, and had made up our minds to a new expedition still more adventurous than any we had yet attempted, and were on our way back to Damascus, from which starting point we designed to penetrate into central Arabia and visit Nejd, the original home and birth-place of the Arabian horse. Our sea-voyage from Marseilles would touch at Alexandria, and it so happened that I found on board the Messageries steamer at Marseilles my friend Sir Rivers Wilson who had just been appointed Finance Minister in Egypt, and in his company we made the voyage. During the six days' passage I had ample opportunity to learn from him all that had happened during the past two years at Cairo, and the tale he told me of the condition of the country was a very terrible one. I remember well his account of that most dramatic of the many crimes of the Khedive Ismaïl, his murder of the Mufettish Ismaïl Sadyk, an act of treachery which more than any other alienated from the Khedive the allegiance, I will not say of his Egyptian subjects at large, for that he had already lost, but even of that group of slaves and servants by which he was surrounded.

Ismaïl Sadyk was an Algerian by birth but had come at an early age to Egypt, and had by his abilities risen in the viceregal service, his first connection with the Court having been, I believe, under Abbas I as a superintendent of his stud. Under Saïd and Ismaïl he had served in various official capacities and had made himself, as we have seen, Ismaïl's *âme damnée* in the work of extracting their last piastres from the fellahin. With all his cruelties to them—and he had shown inexhaustible in-genuity in devising means for their spoliation—he had main-tained a certain honourable repute at Cairo as an Arab gifted with the traditional virtue of generosity and a large liberality in spending the wealth he had acquired, and so as an old man was not unpopular. For the last few years of his life he had been Finance Minister, and to Ismaïl had always proved himself a devoted and faithful servant. Ismaïl had nevertheless be-trayed him a few months before the time I am writing of basely to his death, and under circumstances so revolting that the Egyptian world, used as it was to crime in high places, had been shocked and confounded. The Khedive's motive had been the wholly base and selfish one of screening himself by casting upon his too faithful Minister the blame of certain frauds he had himself committed, and he had insured his silence by having the old man murdered almost in his own presence.

The details given me by Wilson were as follows: Ismaïl had been in the habit, in his dealings with the various European commissioners whom he had from time to time invited to inquire into his financial affairs, of concealing as far as was possible from them the extreme truth of his senseless extravagances, and with his Minister Ismaïl Sadyk's help had once more now, as on previous occasions, presented to the new official commission a false statement of his debts. The pressure, however, on him was severe, as the commission had received a hint, if I remember rightly, from Riaz Pasha, that they were being befooled on this point, and he, fearing that the whole truth would come out, and when the matter should be fully gone into by the commission his Minister might tell the facts, determined to be beforehand with him and make of him his scapegoat and victim. He took the execution of the deed into his own hands. It was his custom with his Minister, with whom he was on the closest possible terms of personal friendship, to call sometimes for the old man in the afternoon at the Finance Office and take him for a drive with him to Shubra or to one or another of his palaces; and so on this occasion he did, and, suspecting nothing, the Minister mounted with him and they drove together to the Jesireh Palace and there got down and entered. No sooner, however, were they inside than Ismaïl on some pretext left him alone in one of the saloons and immediately sent to him his two younger sons Husseyn and Hassan and his aide-de-camp, Mustafa Bey Fehmy, when the princes struck and insulted the unarmed Minister and hustled him on board one of the viceregal steamers which was lying with steam up beside the quay, and there, though not without a vigorous resistance, the old man was despatched. According to Wilson, the actual doer of the deed was Mustafa Bey, acting under the Khedive's order, and he added that the truth had been disclosed through the young aide-de-camp falling ill of fever soon after and telling it in his delirium. I have reason, however, to believe that as far as Mustafa's personal act went this was a mistake, though the rest of the facts have been fully confirmed to me, and that the Mufettish was handed over by Mustafa to Ishak Bey, in whose charge he perished, though whether at once or a little later is uncertain. Some say that Ismaïl Sadyk was thrown as many another had been thrown, with a stone tied to his feet into the Nile, others that he was conveyed alive as far as to between Waddy Halfa and Dongola and there strangled. All that is quite beyond dispute is that once on board the steamer he was never seen again alive, and that the steamer having gone up the river, it was some weeks later officially announced that the Mufettish was away in Upper Egypt for a change of air and ultimately that he had there taken to drink and died. It is also certain that Mustafa, a mild young man and unused to scenes of violence, and being himself, as the Mufettish was, of Algerine extraction, was so horrified at the *rôle* he had been ordered to play in it that he had a long and dangerous illness. It was this experience that a year later caused him to take the part he did against his master Ismaïl and utimately to join Arabi in the earlier phases of the revolution of 1881–2. He is the same Mustafa Fehmy who has for so many years filled the office of Prime Minister in Egypt.

Of all these things we talked as we sat day after day on the deck of the Messageries steamer, and, especially, of course, of Wilson's own important mission as Ismaïl Sadyk's successor. Wilson's hopes at that time were high regarding his own administrative success, and he showed a keen appreciation of the responsibility of the charge he had undertaken of restoring Egypt to prosperity and rescuing the fellahin from their financial bondage, but he was also fully aware of the difficulties which lay before him. The Khedive's character he had learned to understand, and he was prepared to find in him an astute and unscrupulous opponent. But he counted on his own *bonhomie,* tact, and knowledge of the world to be able to live on friendly terms with him, and to avoid what personal risks he might run. He relied too on his French education, for he had lived much at Paris, to preserve intact the dual character of the Anglo-French Ministry, of which he formed a part, and above all he relied on Nubar. In Nubar he reposed unlimited confidence, believing him to be a heaven-born Eastern statesman, and one devoted to English interests. He had, moreover, behind him, as he thought, the full support of the London Foreign Office, and what was perhaps even a stronger stay in Europe, the interest and power of the house of Rothschild.　On this last he knew he could rely, for he had just persuaded them on his passage through Paris to advance that fatal loan of nine millions on the Khedivial Domains which was to bind them to the cause of European intervention whenever necessary on the part of the bondholders.　To myself, who knew Wilson well, though I sympathized to the full with his humanitarian hopes and personal aspirations, there seemed to be certain elements of doubt in his position which did not augur altogether well for his success.

We parted at Alexandria in good hope that all would go well with him in a mission so much one of despair to a ruined state, but with misgivings.　The difficulties before him we both guessed would be immense, and in spite of his excellent qualities of heart and head and his great *savoir vivre,* I had my fears for him.　The event more than justified my forebodings, and in a shorter time than either of us could have thought possible.

Sir Rivers Wilson's brief career as Finance Minister in Egypt failed through many causes.　It was of ill omen, I think, at the very outset that it should have commenced with a new and heavy loan, the proceeds of which it is difficult to find were put to any serious purpose.　Errors of administration, too, there certainly were which inflicted great injustice on the people, and which, as will be seen later, prepared the way for a general discontent.　It is not, however, necessary for me to go into these, for they are matters of notoriety to be found in the Blue Books.　Wilson's excuse for them must be found in the fact that in all matters of internal policy he trusted absolutely for guidance to Nubar, and that he greatly overrated Nubar's power to deal with them.　If Wilson had been more of a statesman and less of a financier he would not have blundered as he did into political difficulties which, with a little more experience of the arts of government, might have been easily avoided. Nubar was a weak reed on which to lean.　As a Christian and an alien it was not difficult for one so astute as Ismaïl to rouse Mohammedan opinion against him, and when, thinking only of restoring the financial equilibrium, Wilson began a series of crude retrenchments among the native officials, a discontented class was at once brought into existence which gave the Khedive his opportunity of diverting the popular ill-will from himself to his Christian Ministers. What made it the more easy for him was that in these retrenchments no European salaries were cut down. The agreement with France had made it imperative that each Englishman employed in Egypt should be duplicated with a Frenchman, and Wilson did not dare touch one of them. Wilson, as holding the purse strings, had to bear the odium of all this.

Nor did he, in spite of his good intentions, succeed in relieving the peasantry in any way of their burdens. It was an essential part of his program that the Khedive should remain solvent, and that meant that the interest on the enormous debt should be punctually paid. The nine millions advanced by the Rothschilds went mostly in paying the more urgently immediate calls, and not a tax was reduced or a demand remitted. On the contrary, the *régime* of the whip went on, even more mercilessly than before, in the villages, and an additional terror was introduced into the agricultural situation by the institution, at great expense and most futilely carried out, of a new revenue survey, under English direction, which was interpreted as the prelude of a still enhanced land-tax. Lastly, the project, lightly suggested by Wilson, of rescinding the Moukabalah arrangement, which would have meant confiscation by the Government of landed property representing something like fifteen millions, disturbed every landowner's mind, and led to the belief that even worse things might be expected of the English Minister than any they had suffered from his predecessors. It seems to me astonishing now with my better knowledge of Egypt that any one so intelligent and well meaning as Wilson undoubtedly was should have fallen into such errors, and I half suspect that some of them were suggested to him for his discomfiture by the Khedive himself. The climax of the Wilson-Nubar political unwisdom was reached when, without any arrears of pay being given them, the native army, including 2,500 officers, began to be disbanded. This put the alien Ministry finally into the Khedive's hands, and it was a chance Ismaïl did not throw away.

The history of the *émeute* of February, 1879, which overthrew the Nubar-Wilson Ministry, needs to be recounted here as it really happened, for the truth about it will not be found in any published history. The Khedive was, as we have seen, anxious to divert the popular hatred with which he was regarded in Egypt from himself to his new Ministers, and he was also most desirous of ridding himself of their tutelage. By an Act called the Rescript of 1878 he had abdicated his personal control of the revenue and the administration into their hands, and used as he was for eighteen years to absolute power in Egypt it irked him already to have lost it. He had only signed the Rescript as an alternative to bankruptcy, and this being averted he did not intend to stand by the letter of his bond. Being also an astute judge of character, he had seen at once the weakness of the Ministry, how Wilson and his French colleague, de Blignières, depended, in their foreign ignorance of Egyptian things, altogether on Nubar for their knowledge how to act, and also how helpless Nubar himself was as a Christian to rule a Mohammedan country.

Nubar was known to the Mohammedan official class as an Armenian adventurer, who had enriched himself as agent of the loan-mongers of Europe at the public expense, and to the fellahin as the author of the International Tribunals, an institution extolled by foreigners, but to them especially odious as having laid them more than any other agency had done in bondage to the Greek usurers. As these Courts were then administered in Egypt, a fellah who had once put his signature to any paper for money borrowed could be sued before foreign judges according to a foreign procedure and in a foreign language, without the smallest chance, if he was a poor man, of defending himself, or of showing, as was often the case, that the figures had been altered or the whole paper a forgery, and he might be deprived of his land and of all he possessed before he well knew what the claim made on him rightly was. Nubar was known especially for this, and was without following of any native kind or supported by any opinion but that of the foreign commercial class of Alexandria. It was therefore through Nubar that Ismaïl saw the new *régime* could be most easily attacked, and most surely reduced to impotence. All that was needed to overthrow it was a public native demonstration against the unpopular Christian, and this the discontent of the 2,500 officers cashiered and cheated of pay and pension made it a very easy matter to arrange.

Ismaïl's chief agents in getting up the *émeute* of February were Shahin Pasha, one of his own Court servants, and Shahin's brother-in law, Latif Effendi Selim, who, as Director of the Military College, held a position specially advantageous for the purpose. By these a demonstration of the students of the college was arranged, which at the hour named marched through the streets of Cairo announcing their intention of demanding the dismissal of the obnoxious Ministry, and they were joined by the crowd and especially by such of the cashiered officers as chanced to be upon their way, and it was so arranged that they should arrive at the Government offices at the hour when the Ministers were about to leave it. There they found Nubar Pasha in the act of stepping into his carriage, and they insulted and assaulted him, Nubar's moustache being pulled and his ears boxed. A general popular demonstration followed, and presently the first regiment of the Khedivial Guard under its colonel Ali Bey Fehmy, which had been held in readiness, appeared upon the scene, and a little after the Khedive himself. A few shots were then fired over the heads of the demonstrators, and the Khedive having ordered them to their homes the crowd dispersed. The program, arranged beforehand with Ali Bey, had been successfully carried out, and the Khedive was able to claim of the English and French Consuls, to whom he immediately appealed, the necessity of Nubar's dismissal, and to persuade them that but for his powerful intervention and authority with the people worse things would have happened. Nubar therefore was advised to resign, and a Moslem official of the Khedive's choosing, Ragheb Pasha, was allowed to be named Prime Minister in his place. With Ragheb, a special adherent of his own, at the Ministry of the Interior, Ismaïl knew that Wilson and de Blignières would be powerless to administer the country, and that their fall also must speedily follow.

Nubar having been thus successfully disposed of, Wilson's tenure of office as Finance Minister became, as the Khedive had calculated, all but impossible, and his fall was hastened by extraneous circumstances. Our then Consul-General in Egypt, Vivian (afterwards Lord Vivian and Ambassador at Rome) had been estranged from Wilson by a personal quarrel which had taken place between them, and when in his political difficulties Wilson appealed to him for support, the support was grudg-

ingly given or altogether withheld. Wilson's final discomfiture soon followed; an incident, somewhat similar to that of
February, was arranged in March at Alexandria, on which occasion he and his wife were hustled and hurt by the mob, and
when Wilson laid his complaint before the Foreign Office it
refused him any efficient backing for redress. He was advised,
as Nubar had been, to resign, and, there being no other course
left him, he retired from office and returned to Europe.

I have an interesting letter from Wilson of this date. Writing on 30th April, 1879, he says: "You will I daresay have
heard that I have been upset by that little scoundrel the Khedive.
He didn't quite have me assassinated, as you not without reason
imagined might be the case, but he had me attacked in the street
and very roughly handled, and now he has had the satisfaction
of getting rid of me altogether, H. M.'s Govt., with their usual
loyalty to their agents, having left me to my fate. Crepy
Vivian is the cause and chief abettor of this sudden overthrow
of arrangements which he was instructed specially to protect.
Partly from jealousy, and a good deal from want of intelligence,
with the addition of a great deal of vanity, he went at once into
the Khedive's camp. His Highness, whose highest art of government lies in the disunion of the people he has to deal with,
might reasonably have expected to make a split between Blignières and myself, or between one or both of us and Nubar,
but in his wildest dreams he never could have hoped that the
English Consul-General would become his toady and instrument
for the overthrow of the Ministry imposed on him by an English Government. . . . We leave on the 6th and shall get to
London about the 15th. I am glad to be out of the place now.
The whole thing is going to the devil. The country is pesti-
lential with corruption. The French and English Governments
seem afraid of acting, and for the moment the Khedive rides
rampant and is bleeding the country to death. The smash cannot be delayed, but in the interval it is dreadful to think of the
mischief and misery that are being worked."

CHAPTER III

TRAVELS IN ARABIA AND INDIA

While these important events had been happening in Egypt I had been away, still travelling with my wife on our new adventure in Central Arabia, far removed from all knowledge of them or of the affairs of the outside world.

On our way to Damascus, where we were to begin our serious campaign, we had stopped for some days in Cyprus, being curious to look at the new English possession, just acquired at the cost of so much scandal, which we found receiving its first lessons in English administration at the hands of Sir Garnet Wolseley. The island was still in its summer heat, no rain having fallen, and seemed to us little better than a dusty wilderness. We called on Wolseley at his government house at Nicosia, and found him making the best of a rather forlorn and very isolated position. In his talk with us he put as good a face as he could on the outlook of this latest "gem of Empire," but it was clear that in his professional mind the island had no great merit, and was rather in the nature of that gross of spectacles brought home from the fair we read of in the "Vicar of Wakefield." It was difficult, indeed, to see what use it could be put to, or how it could be made to pay its cost of management. Its acquisition had already begun to bring discredit to the English name, and it was generally spoken of, we found among the Mohammedans of Syria, as a *backshish* taken by England for services rendered to the Sultan.

At Damascus we met several interesting personages, among others the old hero of the Algerian war with France, Seyyid Abd-el-Kader, and that other in some ways hero, the ex-leader of the Turkish constitutional party, Midhat Pasha. My impression of the latter, much as I was inclined to sympathize with Mohammedan reform, was not favourable. Personally he was unimpressive, of no distinguished appearance, and with a certain boastful and self-assertive manner which suggested vanity as a leading characteristic. In a long conversation I had with him on the subject of Ottoman regeneration, I found his ideas shallow and of that commonplace European kind which so often in the East do service for original thought and depth of conviction. His ideas of reform for the Empire, and of the Syrian villayet of which he had just been appointed Valy, as he expounded them to me, were wholly material ones, the construction of railroads, canals, and tramways, all excellent things in their way, but leaving untouched the real necessities of the administration and which, as he had no funds whatever at his disposal for public works, were in his own province quite illusory. Of the larger matters of economy, justice, and protection for the poor, he did not speak, nor did he show himself in the smallest degree in sympathy with the people of the province he had come to govern. Indeed, he was imbued with more than the usual Turkish contempt for everything Arabian, which he took no pains to conceal, and his avowed methods in dealing with the Bedouins were brutal in the extreme. This naturally repelled me. Nevertheless I cannot help regretting now that I did not make some effort at the time of his misfortunes to rouse public feeling in his favour in England, when such might have perhaps saved him from the terrible punishment he suffered at the Sultan's hands. I did not, however, at that time know all the facts, and it was only in 1884 that I learned, from a source on which I could rely, the true history of Midhat's trial on the false charge of murder brought against him three years before. This is so important a matter that I make no excuse for relating it here in detail.

It may be remembered that when I was at Constantinople in 1873 I had been cared for during a serious illness by Doctor Dickson, the then physician of the British Embassy, with whom I had formed a very pleasant intimacy. This worthy old man, who had already at that time been some thirty-five years in Turkey, had become thoroughly orientalized and possessed a wider experience and more complete knowledge of all things Ottoman than perhaps any other Englishman then living. He had, moreover, a loyal sympathy with the people among whom he had so long lived, and had retained with it a very high integ-

rity and sense of old-fashioned English honour, which made
him the most capable and reliable witness possible in regard
to events which had come under his notice. His evidence,
therefore, on what I am about to relate may be considered as
absolutely final on the matter it touches. In 1884 I was again
at Constantinople, and it was then that he gave it me; and it
seemed to me so important as a corrective to history that I at
once on the day I heard it wrote it down. It is textually as follows:

"Nov. 3, 1884. Doctor Dickson was sent by the English
Embassy to investigate the circumstances of Abd-el-Aziz' death;
and he gave us a most precise account of all he had seen at the
palace that day. The party of doctors consisted of a Greek,
Marco Pasha, of an old Englishman who had been Lord Byron's
doctor, and several others. They found the body in the guard
house and examined it carefully. The Sultan was dressed in
a silk shirt, such as the *caïquejis* wear, plain without stripes,
and pink silk trousers. When stripped the body was found
without scratch or bruise, 'the most beautiful body in the world,'
with the exception of the cuts in the two arms on the inside
where the arteries are. The cut on the left arm was deep to
the bone and Dr. Dickson had put his finger into the wound.
That on the right was imperfect and the artery was not severed.
They were manifestly the cause of death. The other doctors
were satisfied with this examination and went away; but Dr.
Dickson and the other English doctor insisted upon taking the
evidence of the Sultan's mother, and this was her account:
Abd-el-Aziz had twice since his deposition tried to destroy himself, once by trying to throw himself down a well, once into
the Bosphorus, but had been prevented; and the Sultana had
been warned to give him no instrument with which he could
effect his purpose. When therefore he had asked her for a
mirror and scissors to trim his beard she had chosen the smallest
pair she possessed, and thought it impossible he should harm
himself with them. She occupied the room next to his, and
there were always one or two girls on watch when she was
not herself with him. It happened, however, that one afternoon
he had ordered the girls out and bolted the door, saying he
wished to be alone; and the girls did not dare disobey. But
when half an hour was passed they came and told her, and at

first she was not alarmed, but bade them wait at the door and listen. Then they came back and said they heard nothing, and at the end of the hour she herself went, followed by her women, and pushed the door open. They found the Sultan leaning on his side on the sofa dead in this position.

[Here in my journal is a sketch.]

"The sofa and the curtains of the room were of velvet, red on yellow ground. And Dr. Dickson's colleague examined the place and found the left arm of the sofa saturated with blood, and a great pool of coagulated blood on the floor beneath; also on the middle of the sofa a small mark of blood corresponding with the wound on the right arm, but though he examined carefully there was not a speck elsewhere than close to the sofa, so that it was impossible there could have been any struggle or murder. As the Sultana said: 'If he was murdered the murderer must have been myself, for I was in the next room and nobody else could have come near him.' At the trial of Midhat and the rest for murder, they produced a linen, not a silk, shirt, with a cut in the side as from a sword thrust, a pair of green or yellow trousers, and a fur dressing gown, not those which were on the corpse, and chintz covers of the sofa and chintz curtains sprinkled with blood, not those of the room where the body was found. Dr. Dickson had thereupon written a protest stating what he knew, and had given it to Lord Dufferin, begging him to have it handed as evidence to the President of the Court. But Dufferin would not interfere without instructions, and while he telegraphed, or pretended to telegraph, Midhat was condemned. Marco Pasha, he says, must have been induced to give the evidence he did. The story of men having been seen climbing in and out of the window was ridiculous, as it was so high from the ground the men must have broken their legs jumping out. Dr. Dickson is a very precise old gentleman, and the sort of witness whose evidence would be accepted by any jury in the world. I therefore entirely believe his account, improbable as at first sight it seems, that a Sultan should not have been murdered and should have committed suicide. Midhat and Damad died in chains at Taïf some months ago, having been starved to death. Midhat's end was hastened by a carbuncle, but he was none the less made away with. The Sheykh el Islam has also recently died tnere, who gave the *fetwa* authorizing Abd-el-Aziz' deposition. This act of terror has given Abdul Hamid the absolute power he now holds."

Another person of importance to my narrative whom we met that autumn of 1878 at Damascus was Sir Edward Malet, at that time Secretary of Embassy at Constantinople, and who was making a tour of Syria partly for his amusement, partly to gather information. During my diplomatic career I had served twice under his excellent father, and had been very intimate with his family and with himself from the days when we were both attachés, and I am therefore able to speak of his character, which has been strangely misunderstood in Egypt, from intimate personal knowledge. Malet was a man of fair ordinary abilities, gifted with much industry, caution, and good sense. Having been born, so to say, in diplomacy and put into the service by his father when he was only sixteen, he had had a thoroughly professional training, and, as far as the traditions and usages of his work went, he was an entirely competent public servant. He could write a good plain despatch, and one which might be trusted to say not a word more than his instructions warranted, and would commit his Government to nothing not intended. He had the talents which are perhaps the most useful under the ordinary circumstances of the service to which he belonged, prudence, reticence and a ready self-effacement, those in fact which should distinguish a discreet family solicitor, —and the duty of a diplomatist, except in very rare cases, is in no way different from that of a solicitor. Imagination, however, Malet had none, nor initiative, nor any power of dealing on his own responsibility with occasions requiring strong action and prompt decision. He was the last man in the world to lead an intrigue or command a difficult situation. Personally he was amiable, without being attractive, and he had retained a certain boyishness of mind which in his unofficial moments was very apparent. His industry was great and his conduct irreproachable. As a quite young man this was very noticeable. He always preferred his work, however little interesting, to any form of amusement, and even when on leave would spend his spare afternoons copying despatches with us in his father's chancery rather than be at the trouble of inventing occupation for himself elsewhere. I record this because he has been credited in Egypt with an ambitious and intriguing restlessness which was the precise opposite of his very quiet character. Neither in pleasure nor in work had he the smallest spirit of adventure. Otherwise it is possible that he might have accompanied us, as I proposed to him to do, to Arabia, but he was not one to leave the beaten track, and, though I interested him as far as I could in my more romantic plan, he preferred to follow the common tourist road, and so went on after a few days to Jerusalem.

Our own journey was a very different one, and proved to be of even more interest than I had anticipated. The full detail of it has been published both in English and in French, under the title "A Pilgrimage to Nejd," and so I will deal with it here briefly. To narrate it in a very few words: we travelled by the Haj Road as far as Mezarib and from thence to the Jebel Hauran, where one of the Druse chiefs of the Atrash family provided us with a *rafyk* or guide, and so passed down the Wady Sirhán by Kâf to Jôf where Mohammed el Aruk, son of the Sheykh of Tudmor, who was with us, had relations. Thence, after some stay with these, we crossed the Nefud; a hazardous passage of ten days through the great sand desert to Haïl and, though we had no letters or introductions of any kind, were received by the Emir Mohammed Ibn Rashid, the then sovereign of independent Nejd, with all possible honour. Our quality of English people was a sufficient passport for us in his eyes, and the fact of our visits made the previous year to so many of the Anazeh and Shammar Sheykhs, rumours of which had reached him. By this time we had learned sufficient Arabic to be able to carry on a conversation, and we found him courteous and amiable, and exceedingly interested to hear all we had to tell him about the affairs of the great world from which Nejd is so completely shut off by the surrounding deserts. On matters which at all concerned Arabia he was curious to learn our opinion, and especially as to the characters of the various Bedouin Chiefs, his enemies or rivals. European politics interested him very little, and hardly more the politics of Constantinople or Egypt, for at that time the Sultan, though Nejd was called at Bagdad a province of the empire, was in no way recognized by the Wahhabi Princes as their sovereign, and the only relations they had had with him for a century had been those of a hostile character. The recollection of Mohammed Ali's invasion of Nejd was still a living memory, and Midhat Pasha's more recent seizure of El Hasa on the Persian Gulf and his abortive expedition to Jôf were much resented at Haïl. It stood us in good stead with Ibu Rashid that we had come to him without the intervention of any Ottoman authority.

The result of this friendly visit to the capital of independent Arabia, with the view I obtained there of the ancient system of free government existing for so many centuries in .the heart of that wonderful peninsula, was to confirm me in the enthusiastic feelings of love and admiration I already entertained for the Arabian race. It was indeed with me a political "first love," a romance which more and more absorbed me, and determined me to do what I could to help them to preserve their precious gift of independence. Arabia seemed to me in the light of a sacred land, where I had found a mission in life I was bound to fulfil. Nor do I think that I exaggerated the value of the traditional virtues I saw practised there.

By nearly all Orientals the Bedouin system of government is looked upon as little else than brigandage, and on the confines of civilization it has, in fact, a tendency to degenerate into such. But in the heart of Arabia itself it is not so. In Nejd alone of all the countries of the world I have visited, either East or West, the three great blessinsg of which we in Europe make our boast, though we do not in truth possess them, are a living reality: "Liberty, Equality, Brotherhood," names only even in France, where they are written up on every wall, but here practically enjoyed by every free man. Here was a community living as our idealists have dreamed, without taxes, without police, without conscription, without compulsion of any kind, whose only law was public opinion, and whose only order a principle of honour. Here, too, was a people poor yet contented, and, according to their few wants, living in abundance, who to all questions I asked of them (and in how many lands had I not put the same in vain) had answered me invariably, "Thank God, we are not as the other nations are. Here we have our own government. Here we are satisfied," It was this that filled me with astonishment and pleasure, and that worked my conversion from being an idle onlooker at the misfortunes of the Eastern world into one filled with zeal for the extension of those same blessings of liberty to the other nations held in bondage. Our journey back to the civilized but less happy world of Irak and Southern Persia, which we visited in turn in the following spring, only confirmed and intensified my conviction. How wretched a contrast indeed to Nejd were the lands of the Lower Euphrates, inhabited by the same Arab race, but a race demoralized, impoverished, and brutalized by Ottoman rule! How still more wretched Persian Arabistan! I cast about in my mind for some means of restoring them to their lost dignity, their lost prosperity and self-respect, and, for a moment, I saw in England's protection, if it could be given, a possible road for them to salvation. It was with ideas of this sort taking shape and substance in my mind that, after a most difficult land journey from Bagdad to Bushire on the Persian Gulf and thence by sea to Kurrachi, I found myself at last in India, where experiences of another kind were awaiting me and a new lesson in the economy of Eastern things.

My reason for going on to India, after the severe journey we had just made, was that on our arrival at Bushire we had found letters awaiting us from Lord Lytton, who had for many years been my most intimate friend, inviting us to pay him a visit at Simla. Lytton, of whose endearing personal qualities I need here say nothing, for I have already paid that tribute to his beloved memory, had been like myself in the diplomatic service, and I had served with him at Lisbon in 1865, and we had written poetry and lived together in an intimacy which had been since continued. Now in 1879 he had been a little over two years Viceroy in India, and at the time we arrived at Simla was just bringing his first Afghan campaign to a successful conclusion, and he signed the Treaty of Gandamak in the first month of our staying with him. Lytton, who was a man of very superstitious temperament, though a rationalist in his religious beliefs, spent much of his spare time during the war, hard worker though he was, in making fire-balloons which he launched at intervals, arguing from their quick or slow ascensions good or bad fortune to his army. Not that he allowed such results to decide his action, for he was a steady worker and sound reasoner, but it soothed his nerves, which were always highly strung, to have these little intimations of a supernatural kind in which he persuaded himself half to believe. He connected my coming to Simla with the good turn the war had taken, and looked upon me as a fortunate influence as long as I was with him. He made me the confidant of all his thoughts, and from him I learned many interesting things in the region of high politics which I need not here particularize, though some of them will be found embodied in this memoir. With my Arabian ideas, as a man of romance and a poet, he at once professed his sympathy, and gave instructions to Sir Alfred Lyall, who was then his Foreign Secretary, to talk the matter over with me and give me all possible information.

The Indian Government was at that time not at all disinclined to make a forward movement in the Persian Gulf. There had been for many years past a kind of protectorate exercised by the Indian Navy of the Arabian seaports, a protectorate which, being rigidly restricted to the prevention of piracy and quarrels between the tribes at sea without any attempt at interfering with them on shore, had been wholly beneficent, and the recent assertion of the Ottoman claim to sovereignty over them was resented at Calcutta. The Sultan Abdul Hamid too had already begun to alarm our authorities by his Pan-Islamic propaganda, which it was thought was affecting the loyalty of the Indian Mohammedans. Ideas, therefore, of Arab independence were agreeable to the official view, and Sir Alfred Lyall reported well of mine to Lytton, so well that there was a plan half agreed to between us that I should return the following winter to Nejd and should be the bearer of a complimentary message from the Viceroy of Ibn Rashid. I am glad now, with my better knowledge of the ways of the Indian Government, that this proposal led to no practical result. I see plainly that it would have placed me in a false position, and that with the best will in the world to help the Arabs and serve the cause of freedom I might have made myself unconsciously the instrument of a policy tending to their subjugation. It is one of the evils of the English Imperial system that it cannot meddle anywhere among free people, even with quite innocent intentions, without in the end doing evil. There are too many selfish interests always at work not to turn the best beginnings into ill endings.

These matters, however, were not the only ones I discussed with Lytton and his subordinates. Sir John Strachey, his finance minister, put me through a course of instruction on Indian finance and Indian economics, the methods of dealing with famines, the land revenue, the currency, the salt tax, and the other large questions then under discussion—Strachey being the chief official advocate of what was called the forward policy in public expenditure—and with the unexpected result that my faith, up to that moment strong in the honesty of the Indian Government, as the faithful guardian of native interests, was rudely shaken. The following extracts from letters written by me at the time from Simla will show how this short glimpse of India at headquarters was affecting me: "I am disappointed," I wrote, "with India, which seems just as ill-governed as the rest of Asia, only with good intentions instead of bad ones or none at all. There is just the same heavy taxation, government by foreign officials, and waste of money one sees in Turkey, only, let us hope, the officials are fools instead of knaves. The result is the same, and I don't see much difference between making the starving Hindoos pay for a cathedral at Calcutta and taxing Bulgarians for a palace on the Bosphorus. Want eats up these great Empires in their centralized governments, and the only way to make them prosper would be to split them up and let the pieces govern themselves." Also to another friend, Harry Brand, Radical Member of Parliament, now Lord Hampden, "The *natives,* as they call them, are a race of slaves, frightened, unhappy, and terribly thin. Though a good Conservative and a member of the Carlton Club I own to being shocked at the Egyptian bondage in which they are held, and my faith in British institutions and the blessings of British rule have received a severe blow. I have been studying the mysteries of Indian finance under the 'best masters,' Government secretaries, commissioners, and the rest, and have come to the conclusion that if we go on *developing* the country at the present rate the inhabitants will have, sooner or later, to resort to cannibalism, for there will be nothing but each other left to eat. I do not clearly understand why we English take their money from these starving Hindoos to make railroads for them which they don't want, and turnpike

roads and jails and lunatic asylums and memorial buildings to
Sir Bartle Frere, and why we insist upon their feeding out of
their wretched handfulls of rice immense armies of policemen
and magistrates and engineers. They want none of these
things, and they want their rice very badly, as anybody can see
by looking at their ribs. As to the debt they have been saddled
with, I think it would be honester to repudiate it, at least as a
Debt on *India*. I never could see the moral obligation governments acknowledge of taxing people for the debts they, and not
the people, have incurred. All public debts, even in a self-
governing country, are more or less dishonest, but in a foreign
despotism like India they are a mere swindle."

On the whole, this brief visit to India at headquarters had
considerable influence with me in the shaping of my ideas on
the larger questions of Imperial policy, and giving them the
direction they afterwards took. I still believed, but with failing faith, in the good intentions, if no longer in the good results,
of our Eastern rule, and I thought it could be improved and
that the people at home would insist upon its being improved if
they only knew.

One of my last recollections of my two months' stay with
Lytton at Peterhoff, as the Viceregal residence was then called
at Simla, was of a dinner at which I sat next to Cavagnari the
evening before he set out on his fatal mission to Kabul. He
was an interesting man, the grandson, so he told me, of a
Venetian merchant who, when the French Republican army
occupied Venice, lent a large sum of money to Bonaparte, which
was never repaid. The Emperor, however, rewarded him by
making his son his private secretary, who became a devoted
adherent of the Imperial family. Lewis Napoleon Cavagnari,
the grandson, was also a strong Bonapartist, and believed himself, on account of his name, to have before him a very high
destiny. He had faith in his "star," and I can testify that in
his talk to me that night—and it was long and intimate—the
last thing he seemed to think of was failure or danger in his
mission. Yet only a few days before he must have had an
admonition in the tragic news, of which we also talked, of the
Prince Imperial's death in South Africa. When we parted it
was with an engagement on my part and on my wife's that we
would go in the autumn to visit him at Kabul. "You must not

come, however," he said, "before the autumn, because I shall
not have got the Residency comfortable or fit to receive ladies."
Of any more dangerous reason he gave us no kind of hint.

Another acquaintance at that time with whom a tragic history
is connected was Colley, then Lytton's military secretary, who
the year following was to die on Majuba Hill. Lytton had the
highest possible opinion of his military talents, and between
them they had in large measure directed the Afghan campaign
from Simla. His fault was, I think, too great self-confidence
and too much ambition. He occupied Majuba because he
could not bear to let the campaign end without gaining some
personal success. Melgund again, who is now Lord Minto,
Pole-Carew, and Brabazon, Lytton's aides-de-camp, were all
three, with Lord Ralph Kerr, among our friends of that time,
and Plowden and Batten, the husbands of their two fair wives.
We made the voyage back from Bombay in Melgund's company
and that of Major Jack Napier, leaving India on the 12th of
July in full monsoon and arriving at Suez on the 25th, and on
the same day by train to Alexandria.

I think it was at Aden, as we passed it to the Red Sea, that
we learned the great news of the day in Egypt, the deposition
of the Khedive Ismaïl, a subject to us of great rejoicing, and
no sooner had we arrived at Alexandria than I learned the full
details of his share in the affair from that other intimate friend
of my diplomatic days, Frank Lascelles, whom I found acting
Consul-General at the British Agency. What he told me does
not differ much from the account of it officially published, and
I need not repeat it here. What, however, is not generally
known is the part played in it by the Rothschilds, which
Lascelles did not at that time know but which I heard later
from Wilson. Wilson, indeed, was able to boast that through
these he had had his full revenge. On his return, he told me,
from Egypt, crestfallen and abandoned by his own Government,
he had gone straight to the Rothschilds at Paris and had represented to them the danger their money was running from
the turn affairs had taken at Cairo and Alexandria. The
Khedive intended to repudiate his whole debt and to shelter
himself in doing so by proclaiming Constitutional government
in Egypt. If they did not prevent this, all would be lost. He
thus succeeded in alarming the Rothschilds and in getting them

to use the immense political influence they possessed in favour of active intervention. At first, however, they had pulled the strings both at Downing Street and on the Quai d'Orsay in vain. The English Government was no longer in an intervening mood, trouble having broken out for them in South Africa; and at Paris, too, there was an equal unwillingness. In despair for their millions the Rothschilds then made supplication at Berlin to Bismarck, who ever since his Frankfort days had extended a certain contemptuous protection to the great Hebrew house, and not in vain. The French and English Governments were given to understand by the then all-powerful Chancellor that if they were unable to intervene effectively in Egypt in the bond-holders' interests the German Government would make their cause its own. This settled the matter, and it was agreed that, as the least violent form of intervention, the Sultan should be applied to to depose his too recalcitrant vassal. To the last moment Ismaïl refused to believe that the Porte, on which he had lavished so many millions and was still appealing cash in hand—for he had hidden treasures—would desert him. The pressure from Europe was too great. Wilson claims to have had the question of Ismaïl's successor submitted to him as be-tween Halim, whom the Sultan much preferred, and Tewfik, and to have decided in favor of the latter as being known to him to be of weak character and so the more convenient political instrument. But be that as it may, the fatal telegram was despatched conveying to Ismaïl the news of his fall, and that his Viceregal functions had passed away from him to his son. It had been Lascelles' disagreeable duty to convey the news to the old tyrant of eighteen irresponsible and ruinous years. True to his rapacious habit, his last act had been to deplete the treasury of its current account and to gather together all the valuables he could anywhere lay hands on, and so retire to his yacht, the "Mahroussa," with a final spoil of his Egyptian sub-jects amounting, it is said, to three millions sterling. Nobody had cared to hinder him or inquire, or bid him stay even for an hour.

CHAPTER IV

ENGLISH POLITICS IN 1880

Cavagnari's tragical death at Kabul, which took place before the summer of 1879 was over, a disaster which involved Lytton in a new war and endless political trouble, effectually ended any projects we had made of fresh travel for that year, either in Afghanistan or Arabia. I spent, therefore, a full twelve months in England, the busiest as yet in some ways of my life. Up to that date, though I was now in my fortieth year, I had not only taken no public part in politics, but I had never so much as made a speech to an audience or written an article for a review, or a letter to a newspaper. Constitutionally shy in early life I had shrunk from publicity in any shape, and the diplomatic training I had had had only aggravated my repugnance to being *en évidence*. Diplomacy, whether it has or has not anything to hide, always affects secrecy and entertains a distrust of public speaking and an extreme jealousy of the indiscretions of the Press. Now, however, having persuaded myself that I had a mission in the Oriental world, however vague and ill defined, I began to talk and write, and even overcame my timidity to the extent of appearing once or twice upon a platform. The first occasion on which I ever thus spoke was at a meeting of the British Association at Sheffield on the 22nd of August, to which I was invited as a distinguished traveller in the company of M. Serpa Pinto, M. de Brazza, and Captain Cameron, all of African fame, and where I opposed Cameron's advocacy of a Euphrates Valley Railroad. I was able to speak on this matter with more authority than he, for, though he had gone out with much beating of drums the year before to explore the route, he had turned back from the difficult part of it—that which lay between Bagdad and Bushire—while we had made the whole route from sea to sea; and I followed up my opposition in an article on the same subject, the first I ever wrote, in the "Fortnightly Review." John Morley was at that time editor of the "Fortnightly," and I had an introduction to him from Lytton, and managed to interest him in my Eastern ideas. Both these little ventures with speech and pen brought me credit and encouraged me to do more in the direction of what was now my propaganda. I was busy too with poetry; and, again, I had my wife's book of travels, "A Pilgrimage to Nejd," to arrange and edit. The multiplied work occupied me fully all the winter.

With home politics I troubled myself not at all, though it was a time of crisis, and Gladstone, with the General Election of 1880 at hand, was in the full fervour of his Midlothian preaching. My sympathies, as far as England was concerned, were still rather with the Tories, and on Oriental questions I looked upon Gladstone, little as I loved the Turks, as an ignoramus and fanatic. My personal friends, with the exception of two or three, Harry Brand and Eddy Hamilton, were all Tories, and my love for Lytton covered in my eyes the worst of Disraeli's Imperial sins. I clung to the thought that England in the East might yet, through the Cyprus Convention properly interpreted, be made an instrument for good, and I was swayed backwards and forwards in regard to her Imperial position by opposing hopes and fears. It was not till I had cleared my thoughts by putting them into print that I gradually came to any settled plan. One great pre-occupation, too, I had that year in the establishment of my stud of Arab horses at Crabbet, about which I was in constant correspondence with the world of sport, including a public one with the Jockey Club. Curiously enough, it was in connection with my views on horseflesh that I first came into epistolary communication with Mr. Gladstone. His well-known hobby about ancient Greece had made him curious to learn my opinion about the horses of antiquity, and especially the probable breeding of those of Greece and Troy; and a message was conveyed to me through Mr. Knowles, the editor of the "Nineteenth Century Review," asking a memorandum on their genealogy. This, and the accident of his naming Edward Hamilton, with whom I was intimate, his private secretary when he took office in April in

succession to Disraeli, were the links which led to our correspondence later on Egyptian affairs.

A few extracts from a fragmentary journal I began to keep
in 1880 will show the chaos of ideas, literary, social, and political in which during that year, I lived. The extracts are only
such as have some relation to Eastern affairs, and I find them
embedded in a mass of notes recording events of private and
ephemeral interest no longer of any value. The first gives a
picture of Lord Stratford de Redcliffe, for so many years our
Ambassador at Constantinople, and who was now living in
retirement and extreme old age with his two daughters on the
borders of Kent and Sussex:

"*March,* 1880.—A visit to Lord Stratford de Redcliffe at
Frant. Lord Stratford has given me a paper on reforms for
Turkey, which he is thinking of sending to the 'Times,' and I
read it in bed. It is an old man's work, rambling and vague,
with hardly an occasional touch of vigour. Old men should
write nothing but their recollections, and Lord S. is ninety-four.
A wonderful old man, nevertheless, with a countenance of
extreme benignity, a complexion of milk and rose leaves, clear
blue eyes, and hair as white as snow. Though rather deaf,
he still talks well. I wrote him in return a memorandum with
my ideas for Asiatic Turkey, and later spent the morning with
him listening to his old-world recollections. He was *Chargé
d'Affaires* at Constantinople when Byron passed through on his
Childe Harold journey, and had ridden with him every day for
six weeks. Byron had been very agreeable, and there was nothing at that time *scabreux* in his conversation. He had also (before that) in 1805 met him at Lord's Cricket Ground at the
Eton and Harrow match, both of them playing in the elevens
on opposite sides. Byron played cricket 'as well as could be
expected considering his infirmity.' He, Lord S., had never
been willing to think there had ever been anything really wrong
between B. and Lady Caroline Lamb. The impression Lord
S. gives me is one of extreme kindness, gentleness, and benignity, quite foreign to his reputation. I had rather sit listening
to these old-world confessions than to the talk of the prettiest
woman in London."

"*March* 16.—Breakfasted with Rivers Wilson and discussed

Colonel Gordon's character. All the world is agreed about his being a very wonderful man. He has ruled the Soudan for four years single-handed, and has repressed the slave trade completely. Now he comes home to England and nothing is done for him. Neither Lord Beaconsfield nor any of the Ministers will so much as see him. He made a mistake at starting (in his relations with them). Passing through Paris (on his way home) he called on Lord Lyons (at the Embassy), and begged him to see to the appointment of a European successor to himself in the Soudan, and in the course of conversation held out the threat that, if the English Government would not do this, he would go to the French Government. Whereupon a correspondence ensued with Lord Lyons, in which Gordon wrote a last very intemperate letter ending in these words: 'I have one comfort in thinking that in ten or fifteen years' time it will matter little to either of us. A black box, six feet six by three feet wide, will then contain all that is left of Ambassador, or Cabinet Minister, or of your humble and obedient servant.' This has stamped him (in official eyes) as a madman. Now he has left Europe, shaking the dust off his feet, for Zanzibar."

This little anecdote is very characteristic of Gordon and is in harmony with much of his correspondence, four years later, with Sir Evelyn Baring. Our officials always detested him, for he habitually violated the rules of their diplomacy and the conventions of their official intercourse. Some thought him mad, others that he drank, and others again that he was a religious fanatic who, when he was in doubt between two courses, consulted his Bible for an oracle, or as a last solution "spun a coin." Not one of them understood or trusted him. At the moment of which I am writing, the early spring of 1880, he was very angry with the English Government for the part it had taken in deposing Ismaïl. Gordon for some reason or other liked Ismaïl, and hated his successor Tewfik, and as soon as he learned at Khartoum what had happened, he had thrown up his Governorship, and was now especially angry because a Turkish pasha, and not a European, had been appointed in his place. Gordon was a man of genius, with many noble qualities, but he was also a bundle of contradictions, and the officials were probably right when they looked upon him as not being at all times quite of a sound mind. This, as will be seen, was the official opinion even at the very moment of his being charged at the Foreign Office with his last mission to Khartoum.

The following, too, of the same date, 16th March, is interesting: "Called on Cardinal Manning. Our conversation was on politics. He asked me which way I should vote at the Elections. I said, 'I should vote only on one consideration, a £5 note,' *Cardinal:* 'You mean you will not vote at all?' *I:* 'I can get up no interest in these things. I look upon European civilization as doomed to perish, and all politics as an expedient which cannot materially delay or hasten the end.' *Cardinal:* 'I take the same view, though probably on different grounds. Europe is rejecting Christianity, and with it the reign of moral law. The reign of force is now beginning again, as in the earliest ages, and bloodshed and ruin must be the result. Perhaps on the ruins the Church may again build up something new.' Talking of Asia, he said that Ralph Kerr had told him that the inhabitants of India attributed the mildness of our rule to fear. They respect the Russians because they govern by military law. *I:* 'The Russians are Asiatics. They govern in the Asiatic way—by fraud if possible—if not, by force. This Asiatics understand.' *Cardinal:* 'The Russians, as you say, are Asiatics; and I will tell you more: their Nihilists are Buddhists. Nihilism is a product not of the West, but of the East.' "

The General Elections, it must be remembered, of 1880 were fought to a very large extent on questions of Eastern policy. Gladstone in his Midlothian campaign had attacked with tremendous violence the whole of Disraeli's scheme of imperial expansion, and had denounced as grossly immoral his intervention at Constantinople and Berlin in favour of the Turks, his acquisition of Cyprus, his purchase of the Suez Canal shares, and his aggression on Egypt—as also Lytton's two Afghan campaigns and the Boer War still raging in South Africa. With regard to Egypt, Gladstone had as long before as the year 1877 made known his views in print, and in an article in the August number of the "Nineteenth Century Review" of that year, "Aggression on Egypt and Freedom in the East," had declared himself in the clearest and strongest terms opposed to the undertaking by England of any form of responsibility

on the Nile.   This article is so remarkable and so wonderfully
prescient of evils he was himself destined to inflict upon Egypt
that it deserves quoting.   He objects in it to such aggression
on various grounds: first, as increasing England's burden of
Eastern rule, already too great; secondly, because extensions
of imperial rule can only be effected by immoral means; thirdly,
as regarded Egypt, that the pretence of protecting the route to
India by occupying the Nile Valley was a false one, the route
by the Cape of Good Hope being England's true line of
communication; and, fourthly, because intervention of any kind,
whether on the Suez Canal or at Cairo, must inevitably lead to
farther and farther adventures in Africa.   "Our first site in
Egypt," he writes, "be it by larceny or be it by emption, will
be the almost certain egg of a North African Empire that will
grow and grow till another Victoria and another Albert, titles
of the lake sources of the White Nile, will come within our
borders, and till we finally join hands across the Equator with
Natal and Cape Town, to say nothing of the Transvaal and
the Orange River on the south or of Abyssinia or Zanzibar
to be swallowed by way of *viaticum* on our journey—and then,
with a great empire in each of the four quarters of the world
. . . we may be territorially content but less than ever at our
ease."   He had made also a plea for the continuation of
Mohammedan self-government at Cairo.   "The susceptibilities
which we might offend in Egypt," he says, "are rational and
just.   For very many centuries she has been inhabited by a
Mohammedan community.   That community has always been
governed by Mohammedan influences and powers.   During a
portion of the period it had Sultans of its own.   Of late, while
politically attached to Constantinople, it has been practically
governed from within, a happy incident in the condition of any
country and one which we should be slow to change.   The
grievances of the people are indeed great, but there is no proof
whatever that they are incurable.   Mohammedanism now
appears in the light of experience to be radically incapable of
establishing a good or tolerable government over civilized and
Christian races; but what proof have we that in the case of a
Mohammedan community, where there are no adverse complications of blood or religion, or tradition or speech, the ends of
political society, as they understand them, may not be passably

obtained." Lastly, he had foreseen the quarrel which an attempt by England to seize Egypt would create with France: "My belief is that the day which witnesses our occupation of Egypt will bid a long farewell to all cordiality of political relations between France and England. There might be no immediate quarrel, no exterior manifestation, but a silent, rankling grudge there would be like the now extinguished grudge of America during the Civil War, which awaited the opportunity of some embarrassment on our side and on hers of returning peace and leisure from weightier matters. Nations have long memories." He had ended his article by a solemn warning and an appeal to the hand of the Most High to confound the intrigues of Cabinets, and secure the great emancipation of the East. "No such deliverance," he concludes, "has for centuries blessed the earth. We of this country (England) may feel with grief and pain that we have done nothing to promote it. Whatever happens, may nothing still worse than this lie at our door. Let us hope . . . that to abdicate duty we may not have to add a chapter of perpetrated wrong."

With these noble declarations, reiterated in a score of speeches during the Election campaign of 1880, I could not but be in sympathy, had it been possible to take them as quite sincere or as representing a policy intended by the Liberal Party to be carried out when they should be in office. But Gladstone did not at that time inspire me with any confidence, and between Whigs and Tories there seemed to me to be but little difference.

"*March* 20.—John Pollen (then private secretary to Lord Ripon) dined with us. We talked of the Elections and agreed there was not much to choose between Whigs and Tories. I shall not vote. Though Lord Salisbury's policy is less contemptible than Lord Granville's or Gladstone's, it is coquetting too much with the Germans to please me. To bring Germany down to Contantinople would be a greater misfortune than anything Russia can accomplish."

"*April* 6.—Paris (the Elections being over and having resulted in a large Liberal majority). Godfrey Webb and I breakfasted with Bitters (my cousin Francis Gore Currie), and I then went to the Embassy. Sheffield (Lord Lyon's private secretary) very important about the new Liberal Government—

what he said to Hartington, and what Granville said to him. Though I abstain from politics, I confess I think the Gladsto-nian triumph a great misfortune. They are so strong now that we shall have all sorts of experiments played with our British Constitution. The game laws, the land laws, and all the *palladiums* will be dismantled. Our policy in Asia will suffer. The Whigs know nothing of the East and will be afraid to reverse the Tory policy, and afraid to carry it logically out. They will try to reform Turkey, and, finding it impossible, will lose their temper and very likely drift into a war. Personally the change is annoying to me, as now Lytton will resign with the Ministry and we shall be baulked of our Indian visit next winter. But all these things are trifles in the march of history."

"*April* 9.—(Still at Paris.) A letter from Anne full of politics. . . . 'Hartington is to be Premier, Goschen Ad-miralty, and Gladstone finance . . . nothing in the foreign policy will be changed! Cyprus kept, Russia thwarted, and Turkey administered from Gallipoli. . . . Lord Ripon does not know his *own* place, if any. I hear Mme. de Novikoff [1] still described as the Egeria of Gladstone.' . . . Dined with Adams (first secretary of the Paris Embassy) and met there Rivers Wilson, who goes to-morrow to Egypt with Dicey, and Arthur Sullivan the composer—all pleasant company." (This was Wilson's final mission in which he arranged the law of liquidation.)

"*April* 26.—Home to England, where Gladstone is the talk of the hour. He has taken office (as Prime Minister) and has surrounded himself with ineptitudes, Childers, Bright, Gran-ville! Hartington, who is a good second-rate man, takes the India Office and Ripon goes to India. This last arrangement is a secret."

Lord Ripon's appointment to India as Viceroy was the only quite sincere attempt made in foreign policy by Gladstone to carry out in office what he had preached when in opposition.

---

[1] Madame de Novikoff, a very charming woman, who was in the confidence of the Russian Government, had come to England for the first time a little before this date, her very earliest English visit being paid to us at Crabbet. She had brought an introduction to us from Madame de Lagréné, a Russian friend of ours living in Paris, and as yet knew no one. She stayed with us a week, but find-ing me unsympathetic with her anti-Islamic views, went on and soon after made a political capture of Mr. Gladstone.

Ripon was a thoroughly honest man, of no very brilliant parts but straightforward and in earnest. He took seriously the mission with which he was entrusted by the new Government of making and keeping the peace on the Indian frontiers, and of inaugurating a new policy having for its object to carry out the Queen's proclamation of self-government among the natives. To the astonishment, and indeed scandal, of the official world, he took with him as his private secretary Gordon, whom all looked upon as mad—than which no better proof could have been given of his *bona fides* towards Native India. Gordon, however, was not of the stuff of which private secretaries, even with a chief like Ripon, are made, and he had hardly landed at Bombay before he resigned. I do not think that Ripon was in fault in this, but rather Gordon's restless chafing against all rules and conventions. I shall have later to describe Ripon's viceroyalty when I come to my second Indian journey in 1884. Now it will be enough to say that, if it achieved comparatively little, it was through the pusillanimity of the Ministry at home rather than his own. He valiantly went on in the course traced out for him at the start, but like boys who sometimes in a race, to make a fool of their companion who is in front of them, hang back and stop, he found out to his confusion after a while that he had been running alone and that the Ministers who had changed their minds without letting him know had long been laughing at him for his persistence. It must have been a bitter moment for him when he, too, had to give in. The other appointments made were all, as far as the highest offices went, given by Gladstone to the Whigs. Lord Granville—the matter which interested me most—got the Foreign Office, an amiable old nobleman with a good knowledge of French, but very deaf and very idle, whose diplomacy was of the old procrastinating school of never doing today what could possibly be put off till to-morrow, or, as he himself was fond of putting it, of "dawdling matters out" and leaving them to right themselves alone. Of such a Minister nothing in the way of a new policy could be expected, and none was attempted either in Turkey, or Egypt, or elsewhere. The Cyprus Convention was neither repudiated nor turned to account for any good purpose, and beyond a little sham pressure put upon the Sultan in the matter of Montenegro and the Greek frontier, things were left

precisely as they were.   The only change made was that
Layard, the author of the Convention, was recalled from
Constantinople and Goschen appointed in his place, the same
Goschen who had made the leonine arrangement for the bondholders in Egypt three years before, his own family firm of
Göschen and Frühling being one of them.   The only act of the
new Foreign Secretary which showed that he remembered Mr.
Gladstone's denunciations of the Turks was that, in order to
prove that Gladstone had been right and Disraeli and Salisbury
wrong about them, he in defiance of the ordinary rule in such
matters at the Foreign Office published a secret despatch of
Layard's which contradicted everything the Ambassador had
written about the situation at Constantinople in his public
despatches.   In this unfortunate document he had laid bare
the secret vices and weaknesses of the Sultan Abdul Hamid, his
personal cowardice especially being insisted on and emphasized
with details then unknown to the world, but now notorious, of
his system of spy-government.   Its publication was a gross act
of treachery to Layard, and was, moreover, an act of folly
from the effects of which our diplomacy at Constantinople has
not yet recovered.   Layard had been, so to say, Abdul Hamid's
bosom friend and had received from him favours of a kind
not usually accorded to European Envoys.   The Sultan had
shown himself to Layard as to a comrade on whom he could
rely, and the disclosure of what he considered Layard's treachery alienated for ever his goodwill from England.

Nevertheless, and notwithstanding the unpromising position
at the Foreign Office, I was resolved in the interests of my
propaganda to make a bid for sympathy for my plans with the
new Prime Minister.   I was encouraged to this by the appointment he had made on taking office of one of my most intimate
friends, Eddy Hamilton (now Sir Edward Hamilton, K.C.B.),
to be his private secretary, from whom I learned that, whatever might be the public exigencies of the moment abroad, Mr.
Gladstone's sympathies with Oriental liberty were no whit
abated.   From Hamilton I had no secrets as to my own views
and plans, and all that he thought necessary to win his master
to them was that I should give them a wider publicity in print.
There were other channels, too, through which it was judged

that Gladstone might be influenced, and some of these are referred to in my journal.

"*June* 12.—Hamilton Aidé took me to call upon Mrs. L, who lives in a big house in M . . . Square, a plump, good-natured Irishwoman of fifty, impulsive, talkative, but without trace either of beauty or anything else. She is one of Gladstone's *Egerias,* and our visit was partly diplomatic, as I want to indoctrinate her with my Arabian ideas, and through her the Prime Minister. She is already enthusiastic about such Arabs as she has seen, and affects a serious interest in the East. She read us with much spirit a drama she had been writing about Herod, Cleopatra, and Julius Caesar—sad stuff, which she assured us Gladstone admired exceedingly.

"Rolland, John Pollen and Lawrence Oliphant to dinner. The last a very attractive man. He has just come back from Constantinople, where he has been trying to get a concession from the Sultan for lands beyond Jordan to be colonized by the children of Israel."

"*June* 22.—The Plowdens to dinner and Eddy Hamilton, who is now Gladstone's private secretary. Plowden goes to Bagdad to-morrow as Resident. I indoctrinated him and Eddy on the Eastern question."

"*June* 26. Lord Calthorpe, Percy Wyndham, and Captain Levitt joined us at Crabbet, and we had a show of horses. Lord C. tells me he has shown my letter about Arab horse-racing to several members of the Jockey Club, and he will bring the matter forward at one of the club meetings next month; so that it is to be hoped we shall succeed. If I can introduce a pure Arabian breed of horses into England and help to see Arabia free of the Turks, I shall not have quite lived in vain. My fourth letter to the 'Spectator' (on the politics of Central Arabia) has appeared to-day, and my article in the 'Fortnightly' ('The Sultan's Heirs in Asia') is advertised. . . . Later to the Admiralty, where Lord Northbrook complimented me on my letters (they were the first I had ever written to a newspaper). Sir Garnet Wolseley was there, a brisk little jerky man, whom it is difficult to accept as a great general. I reminded him of our visit to Cyprus. He said, 'I believe Lady Anne is writing a book.' 'Yes, but we have said nothing about Cyprus in it.'

'Oh, you didn't stay long enough.' 'We thought it best to say nothing."

The article here spoken of, "The Sultan's Heirs in Asia," was, as I have said, a bid for Gladstone's serious attention to my ideas, and through Hamilton's help, who brought it under his notice, it was completely successful, though characteristically the feature of it which interested him most was that which has proved least politically practical, and was to me the least important, namely, the future of the Armenian provinces as an independent state. The idea I propounded was, that in the same way as a large portion of European Turkey had been given its independence, so in the decline of the Ottoman Empire the Asiatic provinces should also be encouraged to form themselves into independent states, according to their prevailing nationalities; and I appealed by name to Mr. Gladstone to make good his words, so freely and so recently uttered in favour of Eastern liberty, by making use of the instrument devised by his predecessors in office, the Cyprus Convention, not for the selfish purposes of English imperialism, but for the good of the peoples of the East. Its publication in the July number of the "Fortnightly" led to my being invited to Downing Street, where I had an opportunity of pressing my views personally on the Prime Minister. It will be seen that I was not on that first occasion much impressed by him; but I was encouraged to develop my ideas, and from that time my opinion, conveyed to him generally through Hamilton, was of some account with Gladstone in regard to Eastern affairs.

"*June* 27.—Called on A. with whom I found Queensberry. He began at once to expound to us his religious doctrines, talking in an excited, earnest way. These doctrines seem to me mere Comtism. There is some sort of Supreme Being, not a personal God, and a conscience by which man is guided in his search of perfection. The principle doctrine, 'faith in humanity,' and the principal duty, 'the perfectioning of body and soul,' especially body. The Marquess is not a very lucid expounder, and proposed to recite us a poem instead—a poem he had written. While we were expecting this in came Philip Currie and a little old man with a long nose and very black eyes, Malkum Khan, the Persian Ambassador. These sat down and listened while Queensberry recited. The poem was in blank

verse, vague, doctrinal, fantastic, beginning with the Matter-
horn and going on to Humanity. When he had finished the
Oriental spoke. He said, 'Perhaps it would interest you to
hear the story of a religion which was founded some years ago
in Persia, and of which I was at one time the head. It will
exemplify the manner in which religions are produced, and you
will see that the doctrine of Humanity is one at least as congenial to Asia as to Europe. Europe, indeed, is incapable of
inventing a real religion, one which shall take possession of
the souls of men; as incapable as Asia is of inventing a system
of politics. The mind of Asia is speculative, of Europe practical. In Persia we every day produce "new Christs." We
have "Sons of God" in every village, martyrs for their faith
in every town. I have myself seen hundreds of Babis suffer
death and torture for their belief in a prophet whose doctrines
were identical with those of Jesus Christ, and who, like Him,
was crucified. Christianity is but one of these hundred Asiatic
preachings, brought into notice through its adoption by the
Greek mind and given a logical form and a material complexion. If it had remained an Asiatic faith it would long ago
have perished, as a hundred moral and mystic teachings have
perished before and after it. When I was a young man I, too,
as I told you, founded a religion which at one time numbered
30,000 devotees. I was born an Armenian Christian, but I
was brought up among Mohammedans, and my tone of thought
is theirs. I was foster-brother to the Shah and when he came
to the throne he made me his Prime Minister. At the age of
twenty I was practically despotic in Persia. I saw the abuses
of government, the decline of material prosperity in the country,
and I was bitten with the idea of reform. I went to Europe
and studied there the religious, social, and political systems of
the West. I learned the spirit of the various sects of Christendom, and the organization of the secret societies and free-
masonries, and I conceived a plan which should incorporate
the political wisdom of Europe with the religious wisdom of
Asia. I knew that it was useless to attempt a remodelling of
Persia in European forms, and I was determined to clothe my
material reformation in a garb which my people would understand, the garb of religion. I therefore, on my return, called
together the chief persons of Teheran, my friends, and spoke

to them in private of the need which Islam had of purer doctrine. I appealed to their moral dignity and pride of birth.
There are in Persian two words, each signifying Man—*insan,*
from the Arabic, and *adhem* (Adam), more strictly Persian in
derivation. The second signifies Man as a genus, a particular
kind of animal—the first man as an intellectual and distinguished being (the *homo* and *vir* of Latin). You all, I said,
pride yourselves that you are more than *adhem;* you are also
insan. And it is to enable you to justify that pretension that
I will advise you to do this and that. They all found my reasoning good, and in a short time I had got together 30,000
followers. Under the name of a Reformation of Islam I thus
introduced what material reforms I could. To my doctrine is
due the telegraph, the reorganization of the administrative
departments, and many another attempted improvement since
gone to ruin. I had, however, no intention at the outset of
founding a religion. The character of saint and prophet was
forced on me by my followers. They gave me the title of
"Holy Ghost," and the Shah that of "Reformer of Islam." I
wrote a book, a bible of my creed, and enthusiasts maintained
that I worked miracles. At last the Shah was alarmed at my
power, which in truth had become superior to his own. He
sought, in spite of our old friendship, to kill me, and my followers sought to kill him. For two months we both lived in
great fear of assassination, and then we came to an explanation. I loved and revered the Shah, and I asked permission to
travel. My followers took leave of me with tears, even the
Mollahs kissing my feet. I went to Constantinople, thinking
to get permission from the Sultan to reside at Bagdad, and
I in fact went there and gained new converts from among
the resident Persian and Bagdad Shiahs. But the Turks deceived me, and I had to leave my work unfinished. My followers in Persia urged me to return, but I was deterred through
several motives; first, I feared to find my death for a religion
in which I did not believe, secondly, my health broke down,
and, thirdly, I had married a wife. I wrote to the Shah, who
replied, offering me any appointment I would, so I would remain abroad; and I accepted the position of Ambassador-Gen-
eral to all the Courts of Europe.' It was strange to hear this
little old man, in European clothes and talking very good French,

recounting a tale so purely Oriental. I walked home with him afterwards (he lived on the other side of Hyde Park), and he detailed to me his ideas about the East and West, both of which he knows, and knows thoroughly. I left him with the impression that he was the most remarkable man I had ever met, and more convinced than ever of the superior intelligence of the Eastern mind. Who is there in Europe that could have made one thus feel like a child?

This chance meeting, at a fine lady's house in Belgravia in the middle of the London season, affected me profoundly, and to a certain extent revolutionized my ideas. I trace to it, and to other talks which I had later with this singular personage, the conviction which rapidly overcame me that in all my thought of freeing and reforming the East I had begun at the wrong end, and that, if I was to effect anything either for the Arabs or for any other of the Moslem peoples subject to the Turks, I must first make myself thoroughly acquainted with their religious ideas. As yet I had passed among them, in spite of my political sympathy, as a stranger to their more serious thought; without religious prejudice myself of the ordinary Christian kind, I had learned to respect Islam, but I did not comprehend it, nor had I ever discussed its teachings with any one learned in its law or conversant with its modern thought. I saw at once the weakness, nay the absurdity of my position, and I resolved before I went any farther to devote the following winter to a study of at least the main features of the Mohammedan doctrines as they affected Mohammedan politics. With this view I made my plans for the winter. My thought was to go to Jeddah at or about the time of the pilgrimage, and there inform myself as I best could, and then take any occasion that might offer for further action. I wished to penetrate once more into Arabia, if possible through Hejaz, or perhaps Yemen to Nejd. I had an idea that among the Wahhabis I might find a teacher who would give me the Arabian as opposed to the Ottoman view of Islam, and that I might devise with him a movement of reform in which I should suggest the political, he the religious elements. It was a sufficiently wild idea, but I entertained it seriously at the time, and the confession of having done so will explain to Egyptian readers how it came about that I took the line I did at Cairo a year later.

I was influenced, too, at that time in London by another learned Oriental, one Sabunji, whose acquaintance I had made in the character of Arabic teacher. He, too, like Malkum Khan, was of Christian origin, a member of one of the Catholic sects of Syria, and he had even taken priest's orders and served the Congregation of the Propaganda at Rome; but he had latterly thrown off the cassock and, like the Ambassador, was much more in sympathy with Islam than with his own faith. As an Arabic scholar he was very remarkable, and he had a wide acquaintance with the questions, half political, half religious, which were being discussed just then among Mohammedans. He had done the main work for the late Dr. Badger in compiling the Arabic-English Dictionary which goes by Dr. Badger's name, and in 1880 was carrying on in London an Arabic newspaper called "El Nakhleh," the Bee, in which religious reform was preached to Mohammedans once a month, on the most advanced lines of modern thought. There was a mystery about the financing of this little journal, and the motives prompting its issue, which I never quite fathomed. His own account of it was that his chief patron was the Sultan of Zanzibar, a very enlightened and liberal-minded ruler. But I was never quite satisfied with this explanation, and I have since had reason to believe that the funds to support it, and the suggestion of its politics came, in part at least, from the ex-Khedive Ismaïl. Ismaïl was at that time very angry with the Sultan for his betrayal of him to Europe, and the "Bee" was violent against Abdul Hamid, and denounced him especially as an usurper of the title of Emir el Mumenin and Caliph. I do not well remember whether it was from this Sabunji or from Malkum Khan that I first came to understand the historical aspect of the caliphal question and its modern aspects, but, opposed as I was to Ottoman rule, it struck me at once as one of high importance to the kind of reform I was beginning now to look for. There is notice in my journal of my having sent in a memorandum to Mr. Gladstone on the subject, and I have a letter from Hamilton, showing that the idea was considered one of importance by members of the Cabinet and generally in Downing Street.

"*July* 3.—A tea party at A.'s, a 'collection of mystics,' old Rolland, Dunraven, and Oliphant. The two latter and I had a conference in a back room which resulted in our agreeing to act in common on the Eastern question, so as to influence public opinion in England. We are to have a preliminary meeting at Dunraven's on Thursday."

"*July* 8.—Called on Percy Wyndham and converted him to my political creed. Also received a visit on the same subject from Mr. Boyce, M. P. Dined with Dunraven, Oliphant, Otway, Percy Wyndham, Harry Brand, and Whittaker, editor of the 'Levant Herald,' at Limmer's Hotel, to arrange a course of action with a view to influencing public opinion in England respecting Asia. Nothing more definite settled than the formation of a committee for receiving news. Later to Bryce's, where I met one Robertson Smith, who has been lately in the Hejaz." (This was the well-known professor.)

"*July* 13.—Went to a party at Mrs. Gladstone's. We arrived early, before other people had come, and I had twenty minutes' conversation with the great man. I detailed to him my ideas about the regeneration of the East, in which he seemed to take an interest, as far as a man can who is totally ignorant of the A B C of a question. His remarks struck me as the reverse of profound, and his questions contrasted unfavourably with those put to me three years ago by Lord Salisbury. A British steamer had been fired on by some Arabs on the Tigris, and he began by remarking that he feared this fact showed a marked antagonism towards England on the part of Arabia. The state of the Ottoman Empire he considered most *critical*. Probably the East had never been in a more *critical* state than now. If the Treaty of San Stefano had been carried out Turkey could hardly have been more *critically* situated than she was. I succeeded however, I think, in grafting him with two ideas, one that the Caliphate was not necessarily vested in the House of Othman, the other that Midhat Pasha was a fool. He has evidently made up his mind about nothing, and will let himself drift on till the smash comes."

"*July* 15.—Attended a meeting of Philo-Asiatics. In the afternoon to Aldermaston, a fine park with a tiresome modern house; Sir Henry Layard doing the honours. I had a great prejudice against him, but find him agreeable and without pretension, considering his position. He talks well, especially of his travels, and he really understands the East, reminding me a little of Skene and Rolland, both fellow travellers of his in old days. . . . Layard's memoirs would be the most interesting of any man's of the present century. His rise from the position of a wandering outcast among the Kurds, almost himself an outlaw, to that of British Ambassador to the Porte, contains all the romance of human life."

"*July* 17.—An interview with Sir Charles Dilke (Under-Secretary of State) at the Foreign Office. I explained to him my idea of going to Nejd this autumn with Abdallah Ibn Saoud, and to my surprise he seemed to acquiesce. Although our conversation was not a long one, it left me with the impression of Dilke being a superior man. His questions were plain and to the point, and, once understood, he wrote the draft of a despatch to Goschen at Constantinople, referring me for further details to Tenterden (the permanent Head of the Foreign Office), and I am now full of the notion of going to Arabia and heading a movement for the restoration of the Arabian Caliphate. People have been called great who have sacrificed themselves for smaller objects, but in this I feel the satisfaction of knowing it to be a really worthy cause."

Sir Charles Dilke, who was destined to play a considerable part in the events of 1882 in Egypt, had in 1880 been only a few months at the Foreign Office. He and Chamberlain, who were great political friends, represented with Bright the Radical element in the new government. Chamberlain got the Local Government Board and a seat in the Cabinet, and Dilke the Foreign Under-Secretaryship, which, with his chief, Lord Granville, in the House of Lords and an idle man besides, was a position of great power Dilke knew how to take advantage of. Neither of the two men belonged to the class from which Ministers in England are usually chosen, but were looked upon as middle-class men, and I remember the disgust with which Dilke's appointment was received at the Foreign Office, where aristocratic pretensions are traditional among the clerks. Dilke, however, soon showed his mettle by the way he took his work in hand, and, what was even more to the purpose with them, by certain Gallicisms in conversation which were also a Foreign Office characteristic, so that in a very few weeks he found himself not only tolerated but popular. The Abdallah Ibn Saoud referred to in my journal was a certain Abdallah Ibn Theneyyàn

Ibn Saoud, of the old princely family of Nejd, who had found his way to Constantinople, and had there applied to the British Embassy for help to gain or regain a political position in his own country. I had heard of him from Currie, and had jumped to the conclusion that this might be the opportunity I sought in Arabia, and so applied to the Foreign Office to put me in communication with him and favour my projected journey. The plan, however, came to nothing, though, as has been seen, not altogether disapproved at the Foreign Office, for when the matter was referred to Lord Tenterden, the permanent Under-Secretary, he demurred, on the ground that the thing if undertaken with the cognizance of the Foreign Office would be liable to be regarded as a "secret mission," and such missions were contrary to the traditions of the Office. And so the plan was abandoned. Just at this time, too, the news of the disgraceful defeat of the British army under Burrows at Candahar by the Afghans reached London, and I fancy made them doubly cautious in Downing Street. The defeat was a final blow to Lytton, and to the policy of adventure beyond the Indian frontier he had made his own, and at no time within recollection did the imperial fortunes of England seem so low. All the world was depressed by it, even I, little of a Jingo as I had become.

"*August* 5.—To Portsmouth by train, having got a telegram to say the Lyttons are expected to-night or to-morrow. Portsmouth is a strange, old-fashioned town, still without a decent inn; and we are at a pot-house called the 'Star and Garter.' In the house opposite there is a bust of Nelson, and from the windows one can see the 'St. Vincent' and the 'Victory.' Little as one may care for one's country—and Heaven knows I am no Chauvin—it is impossible not to be touched by these relics of England's greatness. I never till this moment quite realized the decay of her fortunes since sixty years ago. What a shock it would be for Nelson and his companions if he could read the papers to-day, full of dastardly congratulations at the discovery that not 2,000 but only 1,000 men were lost on the Helmund, and at General Burrows not having positively run away; of fears lest England should embark single-handed on a war with Turkey, and an abject hope that France may think fit to see us through our difficulties in the East—all this, with Lytton's arrival at Portsmouth, Lytton who, if things go wrong with India, will leave a name in history as the first of the unsuccessful Viceroys of the British Empress and the one most responsible for India's loss. All this, I say, gives one a feeling of sorrow impossible to describe. Yet I do not join with those who cry out on Lytton's policy, still less on its execution. His policy was a necessary one, and its execution has been bold and successful. He has been conspicuous in the history of England's decay only because he is himself conspicuous. He could not have stemmed the tide of events. He went with them, guiding as he could but powerless to do more. England's decay rests upon causes far more general than any one man or party of men can be responsible for. We fail because we are no longer honest, no longer just, no longer gentlemen. Our Government is a mob, not a body endowed with sense and supported by the sense of the nation. It was only by immense industry, immense sense, and immense honour that we gained our position in the world, and now that these are gone we find our natural level. For a hundred years we did good in the world; for a hundred we shall have done evil, and then the world will hear of us no more."

"*August 6.*—After several false alarms the 'Himalaya' was signalled; and, having fortunately met the rest of the small party of friends come to greet Lytton, we went out to meet her and were taken on board just opposite Osborne. At the gangway, brown as a berry and very ill dressed in clothes of four years ago and a flap-away Indian hat, stood Lytton with that cigarette in his mouth which cost him his Viceroyalty. On what trifles success depends! If he could have refrained from smoking out of season, and if he could have gone to church with his wife, all his sins, though they had been like scarlet, would have been forgiven him by the Anglo-Indian public. As it was, he had this against him throughout his reign, and it turned the scale when he was politically defeated. But for this he would never have been recalled. He himself, conscious of having done his best and done well, cares nothing for such things, and he is right. I could envy him this feeling almost as much as I envy him the delight of going home to Knebworth. When we had seen them on shore and taken tea with them at the inn, we wished them good-bye. 'Oh, the dear drunken people in the streets!' Lady Lytton exclaimed, 'how I love them!'"

"*September* 7.—Knebworth. In the morning I wrote and

read, but in the afternoon I went down with Lytton to the fishing house and talked over the Eastern question, in which I find his views not very divergent from my own. We are both agreed that the day of England's *empire* is fast ending—for my own part I do not care how soon. Lytton has more patriotism."

"*October* 29.—Crabbet. Spent the day with Lytton . . . he read me his defence for the House of Lords. He has an immensely strong case, and should make one of the most remarkable speeches of the age if he is allowed to bring forward all the documents in his possession. He showed me these, the Russian correspondence taken at Kabul and the draft of a secret treaty between Shere Ali and the Russians. He also told me that when he was going to India Schouvaloff called on him and proposed to him to divide Afghanistan between Russia and England."

This is nearly the last entry in my journal of 1880, which unfortunately I discontinued till two years later. The full explanation Lytton was never allowed to make in Parliament, and his speech, robbed of its strongest points, fell comparatively flat when he made it before the House of Lords. I will, however, add an extract from a letter he wrote me on the 18th of November, which will complete this chapter of my story. It is of value as giving a very accurate epitome of the political situation of the date: "I saw," Lytton writes, "in one of the papers the other day a statement that the new Sherif of Mecca (Abdul Mutalleb), who is completely a tool of the Sultan, is working actively under orders from Constantinople to put the Mohammedans against us in all parts of the world. The cry is now, 'The Caliph in danger.' This was to be expected, and I fear the opportunity has passed for the good which might have been effected a year ago through the Arabs. The only result of Gladstone's action, so far as I can see, has been to destroy our influence at Constantinople and transfer it to Germany, without substituting for it any other means of controlling the Mohammedan world. The Mansion House speech (Gladstone's), expected with so much curiosity, seemed to me a weak confession of utter failure in the policy of the Government. They drop Greece and Armenia, and everything else, with the admission that their fingers are scorched by the burning end of the stick at which they grasped so wildly nine months ago. And in

Ireland they are drifting into great difficulties which may even break up the Cabinet.   The fact is the policy which the Government wants to carry out is everywhere rejected by the Nation; and the policy which the Nation wants carried out the Government naturally shies at, not wishing to stultify its promises and declarations.   So the result is, for the present, no policy at all. As for myself I keep silence, *morne et profond,* till Parliament meets, though my heart burns within me."

The last weeks of my stay in England that autumn were, however, less occupied with politics than with the publication of a volume of poetry, to which I had been persuaded by Lytton, and the proofs of which I left to him to correct.   This was "The Sonnets of Proteus," which had a considerable success and which has since gone through many editions.   It gave me almost at once a certain rank in the literary world which was not altogether without its influence on my subsequent relations with my political friends.

CHAPTER V

THE REFORM LEADERS AT THE AZHAR

I left England that autumn of 1880 on the 3rd of November, in the first place for Egypt, and without any more definite further plan than to go on from thence to Jeddah and educate myself in view of possible future opportunities. My wilder schemes in regard to the Arabs seemed for the moment impracticable, and all that I hoped for was to gain sufficient knowledge of the doctrine and modern tendencies of Islam to put it into my power to act should circumstances become more favourable. On leaving London I had arranged with Hamilton that we should correspond during the winter, and that I would let him know anything of special interest which might occur on my journey and which he might communicate to Mr. Gladstone, who was still, he assured me, though I had not seen him again, interested in my ideas. At the Foreign Office I was looked upon, though in a friendly way, more as a visionary than as anything seriously likely to affect the official view of Eastern policy, even under a Radical Prime Minister.

At Cairo, where I arrived a few days later, I found much change, and all, as it seemed to me, for the better. The old irresponsible tyranny of Ismaïl had given place to the comparatively mild *régime* of the Anglo-French *Condominium*. The finances had been regularized, and order put into most of the Administrations. I visited some of the same villages I had known in such terrible straits five years before, and found that the worst evils affecting their position had been put a stop to, and, though still poor and highly-taxed, there was no longer that feeling of despair among the fellahin which had made them pour out the history of their woes to me when I had first come among them as a sympathetic stranger. I went to the British Agency, and was delighted to find established there as Consul-

General my friend Malet, who gave me a roseate account of the reforms that had been effected or were in project, for as yet little had been actually done except financially. All was going slowly but steadily on the road of improvement, and the only clouds he could see on the horizon were, first, in the Soudan, which was so great a drain upon Egypt's resources, and, secondly, in the Army, where there had been latterly symptoms of discontent. He spoke much in praise of the new Khedive, Tewfik, and took me to see him at the Palace, and I found him, if not very interesting, at least holding the language of a civilized and liberal-minded Prince. An echo of Malet's optimism may be recognized in my letters from Egypt of that date, and I find the draft of one I wrote to Hamilton of which the following is an extract:

"I find a great change here for the better since five years ago, and, whatever may be the shortcomings the late Government may have to answer for elsewhere, their policy in Egypt certainly was a success. The country people now look fat and prosperous, and the few I have talked to, people who in former years complained bitterly of their condition, now praise the Khedive and his administration. They seem, for once, to have gone the right way to work here, making as few changes as possible in the *system* of government and only taking care that the *men* who caused the disorder should be changed. It was a great stroke of policy getting rid of Ismaïl, and I feel little doubt that with proper management the present man will go straight. Egypt is so rich and such a cheap country to govern that its finances *must* come right, if it limits its ambition to its own natural prosperity. But there are one or two rocks ahead, the government of the Soudan for instance, which will always be an expense and will always be an excuse for maintaining an army. I cannot conceive why Egypt should charge itself with governing the Nile beyond the First Cataract, its old boundary. Putting down the slave-trade in Africa is an amusement only rich countries need afford themselves. It will also be a great misfortune if such protection and supervision as the Government gets from England should be withdrawn, at least for some years and until a new generation has grown up used to a better order of things than the old. I should like immensely to see Syria put under another such *régime*. That, too, if there is no attempt to hold the desert, is a fairly rich country and might be made to pay its way. But it would require a very distinct protection fromEurope to relieve it of the cost of an army. For police purposes a very small force would be sufficient, and I am convinced that people in England exaggerate immensely the difficulty of keeping the peace betwen the mixed Mohammedan and Christian populations there. These have all lain groaning together so long under the same tyranny that the edges of their prejudices have got worn down."

With regard to my plan of seeking Mohammedan instruction, I was from the outset singularly fortunate. Rogers Bey, a distinguished Eastern scholar whom I had known some years before as Consul at Damascus, was now an official of the Finance Office at Cairo, and from him I obtained the name of a young Alem connected with the Azhar University, Sheykh Mohammed Khalil, who came to me daily to give me lessons in Arabic, and stayed to talk with me often through the afternoons. It happened, however, that he was far more than a mere professor of the language of the Koran. Mohammed Khalil, of all the Mohammedans I have known, was perhaps the most single-minded and sincere and at the same time the most enthusiastic Moslem of the larger and purer school of thought such as that which was being expounded at that time at Cairo by his great master, Sheykh Mohammed Abdu. I like to think of him as he then was, a young man of about thirty, serious, intelligent, and good, without affectation, pious and proud of his religion, but without the smallest taint of Pharisaism or doctrinal intolerance or of that arrogant reserve which is so common with Mohammedans in dealing with persons not of their own faith. He was all the contrary to this. From almost the first day of our intercourse he made it his duty and his pleasure to teach me all he knew. His school of interpretation was of the very widest kind. He accepted as true creeds all those that professed the unity of God; and Judaism and Christianity were to him only imperfect and corrupted forms of the one true religion of Abraham and Noah. He would hear nothing of intolerance, nothing of bitterness between believers so near akin. The intolerance and the bitterness were the evil legacy of ancient wars, and he believed the world to be progressing towards a state of social perfection where arms would be laid down and a universal brotherhood proclaimed between the nations and the creeds. As he unfolded to me these ideas and based them on texts and traditions, declaring them to be the true teaching of Islam, it may be imagined how astonished and delighted I was—for they were very close to my own—and the more so when he affirmed that they were the views beginning to be held by all the more intelligent of the younger generation of students at his own university, as well as elsewhere in the Mohammedan world. He gave me, too, an account of how this school of enlightened interpretation had sprung up almost within his own recollection at the Azhar.

The true originator of the Liberal religious Reform movement among the Ulema of Cairo was, strangely enough, neither an Arab, nor an Egyptian, nor an Ottoman, but a certain wild man of genius, Sheykh Jemal-ed-din Afghani, whose sole experience of the world before he came to Egypt had been that of Central Asia. An Afghan by birth, he had received his religious education at Bokhara, and in that remote region, and apparently without coming in contact with any teacher from the more civilized centres of Mohammedan thought, he had evolved from his own study and reflection the ideas which are now associated with his name. Hitherto all movements of religious reform in Sunnite Islam had followed the lines not of development, but of retrogression. There had been a vast number of preachers, especially in the last 200 years, who had taught that the decay of Islam as a power in the world was due to its followers having forsaken the ancient ways of simplicity and the severe observance of the law as understood in the early ages of the faith. On the other hand, reformers there had been of a modern type recently, both in Turkey and Egypt, who had Europeanized the administration for political purposes, but these had introduced their changes as it were by violence, through decrees and approvals obtained by force from the unwilling Ulema, and with no serious attempt to reconcile them with the law of the Koran and the traditions. The political reforms had been always imposed from above, not suggested from below, and had generally been condemned by respectable opinion. Jemal-ed-din's originality consisted in this, that he sought to convert the religious intellect of the countries where he preached to the necessity of reconsidering the whole Islamic position, and, instead of clinging to the past, of making an onward intellectual movement in harmony with modern knowledge. His intimate acquaintance with the Koran and the traditions enabled him to show that, if rightly interpreted and checked the one by the other, the law of Islam was capable of the most liberal developments and that hardly any beneficial change was in reality opposed to it.

Having completed his studies in 1870, and being then thirty-two years old, he passed through India to Bombay and joined the pilgrimage to Mecca, and, this duty accomplished, he came on to Cairo and afterwards to Constantinople. He remained on this first visit no more than forty days in Egypt, but he had time to make acquaintance with certain of the Azhar students and to lay the foundations of the teaching he afterwards developed. At Constantinople his great eloquence and learning soon asserted itself, and he was given a position in the *Anjuman el Elm,* where he lectured on all subjects, his knowledge being almost universal. He had great quickness of intellect and an astonishing memory, so that it is said of him that he could read a book straight off on any subject and master the whole contents as inscribed upon his mind forever. Beginning with grammar and science, his lectures went on to philosophy and religion. He taught that Sunnite Islam was capable of adapting itself to all the highest cravings of the human soul and the needs of modern life. As an orthodox Sunni, and with the complete knowledge he had of the *hawadith,* he was listened to with respect and soon got a following among the younger students. He inspired courage by his own boldness, and his critical treatment of the received commentaries, even those of El Hánafi, was accepted by them as it would hardly have been from any other. Their consciences he was at pains to free from the chains in which thought had lain for so many centuries, and to show them that the law of Islam was no dead hand but a system fitted for the changing human needs of every age, and so itself susceptible of change. All this stood in close analogy to what we have seen of the re-awakening of the Christian intellect during the fifteenth and sixteenth centuries in Europe and its adaption of orthodox doctrines to the scientific discoveries of the day. It is strange, however, that in Western Islam the new spirit of criticism should have been initiated as it was, by

One whose education had been made in such unprogressive lands as those of Central Asia, and at a university so far away.

Sheykh Jemal-ed-din's career at Constantinople was a brilliant but a short one. He was essentially a free lance, and, like most Afghans, a disregarder of persons and of those ceremonial observances which regulate among the Ottoman dignitaries the personal intercourse of the great with those who attend their levées. Although protected by certain of the Liberal States-men, and notably by Ali and Fuad Pashas, who saw in his teaching a support to their unorthodox political reforms against the old-fashioned Ulema, Jemal-ed-din had managed to give of-fence to the high religious authorities, and especially by his independent personal attitude to the Sheykh el Islam, and these soon found in his lectures matter for reproof and condemnation. Advantage was taken of certain passages in his lectures to denounce him to the Government as an atheist and a perverter of the law, and when the Afghan reformer had replied by a courageous demand to be confronted with his high accusers and heard in a public discussion the official sense of propriety was shocked and alarmed. The challenge was producing an im-mense excitement among the Softas, the younger of whom were all on Jemal-ed-din's side, and the quarrel seemed likely to lead to serious trouble. Notice was somewhat reluctantly given that he had better leave once more for Egypt and the Holy Places. It was thus under the cloud of religious persecution that he returned to Cairo, but not without having sown the seed of inquiry which was to mature some years later at Con-stantinople in the shape of a general demand among the Softas for constitutional reform. It was the religious part of the movement which was to culminate in the political revolution attempted by Midhat Pasha in 1876.

At the Azhar, when he returned to Cairo in 1871, Jemal-ed-din's reputation had of course preceded him, and, though Egypt was then in the darkest night of its religious unintelligence, for the moral corruption of the Government, especially in Ismaïl's reign, had infected all classes and had extinguished every tradi-tion of courage and independence among the Ulema, consider-able curiosity was felt about him. The few friends he had made on the occasion of his first visit welcomed him, if not openly, in secret, and presently the wonderful fire and zeal of his conversation drew around him, as it had done at Constantinople, a group of young and enthusiastic followers. The most remarkable of these, his earliest disciples at the Azhar, were Sheykh Mohammed Abdu, who was to play so important a part in public affairs later and who is now Grand Mufti of Egypt, and Sheykh Ibrahim el Aghani the well-known publicist. To these he was able to communicate without reserve his stores of varied knowledge, and to inspire them with his critical spirit and something of his courage. Courage indeed was needed in those days for any man at Cairo to speak out. Ismaïl brooked no kind of opposition and wielded power so absolute in the country that independent speech, almost independent whispering, had disappeared from men's mouths. It was only the fellahin of the village, already despoiled of all, that dared complain, or those in the city too poor and insignificant to be of any political count. The highest religious authorities, as well as the highest officials, had long been silent about injustice and had chosen their part of acquiescence, content so long as they could get their share, each one however small, of the general plunder.

On this dark state of intellectual and moral things Jemal-ed-din's courageous teaching broke like an apparition of strange light, and his very courage for awhile secured him a hearing undisturbed by admonition from the Government. Perhaps his quarrel at Constantinople was a passport to Ismaïl's tolerance, perhaps he deemed this Afghan too insignificant a force to call for suppression. Perhaps, like Ali and Fuad Pashas, he thought to turn the new teaching to account in his long war with the European Consuls. Be this as it may, Jemal-ed-din was allowed during the whole of the remaining years of Ismaïl's reign to carry on his lectures, and it was only on Tewfik's accession and the establishment of the Anglo-French condominium that he was arrested on an executive order, sent untried to Alexandria, and summarily exiled. He had, however, already done his work, and at the time of which I am writing his principles of Liberal reform upon a theological basis had so far prevailed at the Azhar that they had already been adopted by all that was intellectual there among the students. The reformer's mantle had fallen upon worthy shoulders, shoulders indeed it may be said, worthier even than his own. My little

Arabic instructor, Mohammed Khalil, was never weary of speaking to me of the virtues and intellectual qualities of him who was now his spiritual master, Sheykh Mohammed Abdu, the acknowledged leader at the Azhar, in Jemal-ed-din's succession, of the Liberal Party of reform.

I find a note among my papers that it was on the 28th of January, 1881, that I was first taken by my enthusiastic Alem to Mohammed Abdu's little house in the Azhar quarter, a day to be marked by me with an especially white stone, for it began for me a friendship which has lasted now for nearly a quarter of a century with one of the best and wisest, and most interesting of men. When I use these words of him it must not be thought that they are light or exaggerated judgment. I base them on a knowledge of his character gained in a variety of circumstances on very difficult and trying occasions, first as a religious teacher, next as leader of a movement of social reform and as the intellectual head of a political revolution; again, as prisoner in the hands of his enemies, as exile in various foreign lands, and for some years under police surveillance at Cairo when his exile had been annulled; lastly, by the strength of his intellect and his moral character reasserting himself as a power in his own country, resuming his lectures at the Azhar, placed in the judicature, named Judge of Appeal, and finally, in these last days, Grand Mufti at Cairo, the highest religious and judicial position attainable in Egypt.

Sheykh Mohammed Abdu when I first saw him in 1881 was a man of about thirty-five, of middle height, dark, active in his gait, of quick intelligence revealed in singularly penetrating eyes, and with a manner frank and cordial and inspiring ready confidence. In dress and appearance purely Oriental, wearing the white turban and dark kaftan of the Azhar Sheykhs and knowing as yet no European language, or, indeed, other language than his own. With him I discussed, with the help of Mohammed Khalil, who knew a little French and helped on my insufficient Arabic, most of those questions I had already debated with his disciple, and between them I obtained before leaving Cairo a knowledge really large of the opinions of their liberal school of Moslem thought, their fears for the present, and their hopes for the future. These I afterwards embodied in a book published at the end of the year under the title of

"The Future of Islam." Sheykh Mohammed Abdu was strong
on the point that what was needed for the Mohammedan body
politic was not merely reforms but a true religious reformation.
On the question of the Caliphate he looked at that time, in
common with most enlightened Moslems, to its reconstitution
on a more spiritual basis. He explained to me how a more
legitimate exercise of its authority might be made to give a
new impulse to intellectual progress, and how little those who
for centuries had held the title had deserved the spiritual head-
ship of believers. The House of Othman for two hundred
years had cared almost nothing for religion, and beyond the
right of the sword had no claim any longer to allegiance. They
were still the most powerful of Mohammedan princes and so
able to do most for the general advantage, but unless they
could be induced to take their position seriously a new Emir el
Mumenin might legitimately be looked for. Certainly a new
political basis was urgently required for the spiritual needs of
Islam. In all this there was a tone of moderation in the expression of his views very convincing of their practical wisdom.

In the course of the winter I made with my wife our intended visit to Jeddah, where I gathered much information
of the kind I sought as to the opinions of the various sects
of Islam. No place accessible to Europeans could have been
better chosen for the purpose, and I made the acquaintance of a
number of interesting Moslems through the help of one Yusuf
Effendi Kudsi, who had a connection with the English Consulate.
Among them the most remarkable were Sheykh Hassan Johar,
a learned and very intelligent Somali, Sheykh Abd-el-Rahman
Mahmud from Hyderabad in India, Sheykh Meshaat of Mecca,
several members of the Bassam family from Aneyzah in Nejd,
and a certain Bedouin Sheykh, a highly educated man, from
Southern Morocco. My stay in Jeddah, however, was but a
short one, as I fell ill of a malarious fever very prevalent there,
and this prevented any idea I may still have had of penetrating
into the interior. The moment, too, I found was a most unfavourable one for any plan of this kind, through the new
hostility of the Meccan authorities to England. Already the
Sultan Abdul Hamid had begun to assert himself, a thing for
many generations unknown to his Ottoman predecessors, as
spiritual Head of Islam, and in Arabia especially he had be-

come jealous of his authority, while his quarrel with our Government made him suspicious, more than of any other, of English influences. Only a few months before my visit to Jeddah he had made a vigorous assertion of his authority at Mecca by the appointment of a new Grand Sherif of strong reactionary and anti-European views. The former Grand Sherif Huseyn Ibn Aoun had been a man of liberal ideas and known for his friendly relations with the English Consulate, and had so incurred his displeasure and met a violent death. Whether this was in reality contrived by the Sultan, or perhaps his Valy, it is not possible precisely to say, but it was certainly believed to have been so when I was at Jeddah.

I learned the particulars of the Sherif Huseyn's death from his agent at Jeddah, Omar Nassif, who most certainly laid it to the Sultan's charge. According to this account, which I have since had confirmed to me from other quarters of authority, Huseyn had just ridden down from Mecca at the close of the pilgrimage, as the custom was, to Jeddah, there to give his blessing to the departing pilgrims. He had travelled down by night and was making his entrance on horseback to the seaport riding in state with an escort, partly Arab, partly Ottoman, intending to alight at Omar Nassif's house, when an Afghan pilgrim poorly dressed, came forward from the crowd as if to ask alms and stabbed him in the belly. The Sherif, though wounded, rode on and died in his agent's house in the course of the day, having, as I heard, been unskilfully treated for his wound which need not have been fatal. There were various circumstances which seemed to differentiate the case from one of fanaticism or common murder. The assassin was no Shiah schismatic, as was first supposed, but an orthodox Sunni, and he used language after his arrest which seemed to show that he considered himself commissioned. "There was an elephant," he said, when asked the reason for his deed, "the greatest beast of the forest, and to him was sent an ant, the least of living creatures, and the ant bit him and he died." Also there was no open trial made of the assassin, who was executed within four days of his arrest, while everything was done to hush up as far as was possible and conceal the affair.

Huseyn's successor who was of the rival house of Zeyd, the Sherif Abdul Mutalleb, belonged to the extremest school of

Mohammedan reaction. He was an aged man, old enough to have been Sherif at the time Mecca was occupied by the Wahhabis, when he had conformed, at least outwardly, to the Wahhabi doctrine. Now, in extreme age, he was reinstated as Prince in order to further the Pan-Islamic views held at Constantinople. Under Huseyn it would have been very possible for an Englishman to have travelled through the Hejaz without molestation, and both Doughty and Professor Robertson Smith had received his aid and protection. Now any such attempt would have been very dangerous, and, in fact, the French traveller Hüber lost his life in venturing in that same year. We consequently returned to Suez, and later by Ismaïlia into Syria.

Passing through Egypt I received the following letters from Hamilton in answer to two of mine. They are principally interesting as showing how the Government's attention to Eastern matters was already being diverted and distracted by their troubles nearer at home in Ireland. It is a curious and melancholy thing to observe how the necessity, as the Whigs in the Cabinet considered it to be, of putting down nationalism and liberty in Ireland reacted upon the fine feelings they had expressed so readily out of office of sympathy with national freedom in the East. Gladstone, whose inclination no doubt would have been for liberty in both directions, had weighed himself in the Cabinet by these Whig Ministers, his colleagues, who were all along bent on leading him in the opposite direction. Ireland throughout the history of the next two years proved the stumbling-block of his policy, and, as I will show in its place, the decision of coercion there was decided on in 1882 at the self-same Cabinet Council with the decision to coerce in Egypt. The connection of misfortune between the two countries was a fatality not a little tragical, both to the countries themselves and doubly so to English honour.

"10, Downing Street, *Decr.* 22, 1880.
". . . I took the liberty of showing your letter to several who I knew would like to read it, including Lord Granville, Rivers Wilson, Pembroke, and Harry Brand. I think it especially pleased Rivers Wilson, who looks with a very tender eye on his work in Egypt, and who was naturally gratified to hear

from an independent source that what he had so prominent a hand in had resulted in so much good. I am afraid he considers that his own contribution to the result has not been fully appreciated.

"Ireland has continued to monopolize all the time and energies of the Government, and I am afraid it is difficult to exaggerate the grave state of affairs in that distracted country. Thank goodness, we are now within hail of the re-assembling of Parliament. Whether or no the Government has erred on the side of over-patience and excessive forbearance remains to be proved, and it is not for me to venture to express an opinion. The present state of things is certainly a disgrace to this country; and the Government are driven reluctantly to hark back on the old stereotyped course of strong coercive measures. I am beginning, most unwillingly, to think that Ireland is not fitted for a Constitutional Government, and that, however much we may try to remove legitimate grievances, she will not be got into hand again without a return to something like a Cromwellian policy. It is heart-breaking work all round, and unless some extraordinary transformation can be effected, we shall probably have to submit in this country to any amount of shipwrecks of governments within the next few years. I feel very gloomy as to the look out. Would that we could apply to Ireland a regeneration such as you have found in Egypt. . . . That wretched Ireland has nearly knocked the Government out of time as regards foreign policy. They will, however, still manage, I hope, to find a corner of room for Greece, and not let that question entirely slide, which would inevitably mean war between Turkey and Greece. Greece could never contend single-handed with Turkey successfully, and Turkey at war would probably be the signal for a general revolt in Eastern Roumelia and Macedonia. I still trust some sort of compromise on the question of adjusting the territory of the kingdom of the Hellenes may be effected by the intervention of the Powers in the direction of a small slice northwards, and perhaps the handing over of Crete. There is no doubt that a means of strengthening and opening out Greece must be found, not only to keep the peace temporarily in the East, but to lay the foundations for some power that may grow into a set-off against the Slavic nationalities. . . ."

"10, Downing Street, *Feby.* 11, 1881.

"Your letter has since its receipt made a little ministerial round. I read parts of it to Mr. Gladstone; and Lord Granville and Mr. Goschen have both had the benefit of perusing it themselves, and of perusing it, as I am told, with interest. Lord Granville, moreover, sent a copy of your postscript, which related to Indian matters, to Lord Hartington. I hope in having turned your information to official account I shall not be considered to have abused your confidence. I have shown it also to Harry Brand. His father, the Speaker, has had difficulties to encounter such as no predecessor in the Chair ever had before; and he has come out of the ordeal magnificently. What with unprecedented continuous sitting of the House for days and nights and wholesale suspensions of obstructive Members, we have been having most exciting Parliamentary times. I trust, however, that the neck of obstruction as of the Irish land-agitation has been fairly well broken; and when once the Coercive, or rather Protective, measures have been passed, and a fair, just and strong and comprehensive Land Bill has become law, we shall not be troubled again immediately with the Irish nightmare.

"Meanwhile of course all public attention has for the last few months been centred on that wretched God-forsaken country, and the public have not troubled their heads much with foreign affairs. However, the Greek question has not been forgotten. Lord Granville has been pulling the strings most diplomatically, and not, I hope, without success. Of course the great stumbling-block of making head with this difficult question has been the very shabby part which France has played, first blowing so hot and then blowing so cold. However, Bismarck has been induced to take the initiative in making a new proposal which may possibly lead to good results. The primary condition of all the Powers is of course to maintain the peace of Europe. If it were not that the outbreak of war between Turkey and Greece would almost inevitably lead to the outbreak of disturbances and fighting in Bulgaria and Eastern Roumelia, and if it were not that Greece's chances single-handed in a combat would be very small, the natural preliminary to Greece raising herself in the European scale would be by an appeal to the sword. The modern Romans would not have had a united kingdom but for fighting for it, and the modern Greeks could hardly complain were they obliged to face similar difficulties and dangers. But apart from the dangers of a stand-up fight, Greece, having been made the special protégé of Europe, has a right not to be thrown overboard now. If the Berlin award cannot be enforced peacefully—and owing to France's action this seems to be admitted—I believe the massacre of the award has been termed in diplomatic phraseology, 'Le Barthélemy de St. Hilaire'—the best alternative seems to be to find some equivalent for Greece—I mean by compensating her elsewhere for what she does not obtain, Thessaly and Epirus, which she would accept and which the Powers would in concert help her to obtain. Such a proposal as this may possibly be the new departure. I am afraid your remedies, though far more effective, are too drastic for acceptance by Europe."

I do not remember what in my letters can have suggested this long digression about Greece, which did not particularly interest me at the time. The phraseology of the letter is so like Mr. Gladstone's own that I half think this and the previous letter must have been more or less dictated by him. For this reason I quote them almost *in extenso,* and because the long account of the difficulties of his Greek policy suggested to me the idea that perhaps he might, if there was a rising on the Greek frontier, also encourage one concurrently with it of the Arabs in Syria.

Our journey from Ismaïlia was an interesting one. Once across the Suez Canal we struck due eastwards, over a long track of sand dunes, to a very little known hill region called the Jebel Hellal. This, on a small scale, has some of the characteristics of Nejd, in vegetation and in the arrangement of its sand drifts, and we made friendly acquaintance there with the Aiaideh, the Teyyaha, and, further north, with the Terrabin tribes, as well as with those very Azazimeh with whom we had been so nearly having an encounter five years before. All these tribes were at that time independent of the Ottoman Government, living as they did in the no man's land which forms the frontier between Syria and Egypt. They had, however, as is always the case in independent Arabia, been at feud with each other and, with debts of blood on either side, the war had gone on and on, causing much disturbance even to the confines of Gaza. The Ottoman Government, to put an end to the trouble, had resorted to one of their common devices. They had invited the chiefs of the two principal tribes to a friendly conference with the Muteserif of Gaza, and had had them treacherously surrounded and captured, and were now holding them as hostages for the peace of the frontier in prison at Jerusalem. At that time the long tradition of English influence in Turkey was still alive among the Arabs, and as we passed through the tribes the relations of the imprisoned sheykhs besought my intervention with the Government to obtain their release. In pity for them I consented to do what I could, and I took with me the acting Sheykh of the Teyyaha, Ali Ibn Atiyeh, and the little son of the Sheykh of the Terrabin, who rode on with us to Jerusalem, making our way over the hills by no road so that we arrived at El Kuds, or rather at Bethlehem, without having entered a single town or village on all our journey. At Jerusalem I called at once upon our Consul, Moore, and obtained through him from the Pasha an order to visit the prisons, and found there the sheykhs I was in search of in an underground dungeon near the Mosque of Omar. They were in a pitiable condition, suffering from disease and long confinement, and I made an application to the governor on their behalf for an amnesty for them on condition that a general peace should be agreed to between the tribes, an agreement which I had got them to sign and seal. The Muteserif, however, declared himself incompetent to order their release, and referred me to his superior, the Valy of Damascus, as being in a position to do so; and to Damascus we therefore went, still accompanied by Ali Ibn Atiyeh and with our camel caravan, by way of the Jordan valley and the Hauran plain, a beautiful and interesting journey, for the whole country, there having been heavy rain, was a garden of Eden with flowers. In the Hauran we found war going on between the Ottoman troops and the Druses, but managed to slip by between the two armies without molestation and so arrived at Damascus, where we alighted at a little house in the Bab Touma quarter which

I had purchased, with an acre of garden behind it, on our visit
of three years before when we were starting for Nejd.

Our house at Damascus was next door to that of the well-
known Englishwoman Lady Ellenborough, or, as she was now
called, Mrs. Digby, who, after many curious adventures in the
East and West, had married in her old age a Bedouin sheykh
of one of the Anazeh tribe, and was living with her husband,
Mijwel, at Damascus, being no longer able to bear the hardships of her former desert life.   From her and from her excellent husband, whom we knew well, we received the advice
that we should put our case for the release of the prisoners
neither before the Consul nor directly before the Valy, but
indirectly throught the intermediary of their distinguished friend
and our acquaintance of 1878, Seyyid Abd-el-Kader, whose
influence at Damascus was more powerful on all things relating to the Arabs than any other with the Government.   Abd-
el-Kader was then a very old man, and was leading a life of
religious retirement and held in great reverence by all in the
city, and amongst the Arabs in Syria especially, he had a large
following, for he had often proved their protector.   Mijwel
assured me that it would be merely a matter of money with
the Valy and that if the Seyyid would undertake the negotiation
with a sufficient sum in hand it could be easily managed.   I consequently called with him and Ali Ibn Antiyeh on Abd-el-Kader,
whom we found with his eldest son Mohammed, a very worthy
man, born to him while he was still in Algeria of an Algerian
mother, and explained our errand, and the Seyyid gladly consented to be our intercessor with the Pasha, and if possible
to arrange for the release of the Teyyaha and Terrabin sheykhs
on the condition prescribed of a general peace between the tribes,
and I left with him a bag containing 400 Napoleons in gold,
which he considered would be a sufficient sum to obtain what
we required.   Bribery was so much a matter of course in
dealing with Ottoman officials in those days that I do not think
either the Seyyid or I or any of us had a scruple about offering
the money.   The sum was a large one, but my sympathy was
strong with the imprisoned Bedouins, and I had it at heart to
be able to send Ali Ibn Atiyeh back to Jerusalem with an order
of release for them.   So I made the sacrifice.   As it turned

out, however, the negotiation failed of the effect intended. A few days later the bag was brought back to me by Mohammed Ibn Abd-el-Kader untouched, with a message from his father that the Valy sent me his compliments and would have been very pleased to be agreeable to me in the matter but it was beyond his competence; it had already been referred to Constantinople, and it was there alone that the thing could be arranged.

The sequel of this little incident is curious, and has a direct bearing on events the following year in Egypt. Finding my local efforts vain, I took the Valy's advice and wrote to Goschen, our Ambassador at Constantinople, and laid the case before him, urging as a reason for his interesting himself in it, that possibly some day our Government might have need of securing the passage of the Suez Canal from possible attack on the eastern side should England happen to be at war with any other power. Goschen, if I remember rightly, took some steps in the matter, and when a few weeks later Lord Dufferin succeeded him at the embassy it was handed on to him, and eventually, after long waiting, what I had asked was granted, and the sheykhs were set free. My suggestion, however, about the tribes was to bear fruit later of a kind I did not at all contemplate or intend, for when in the summer of 1882, the military expedition under Wolseley was decided on, it was remembered by Goschen, or some one else connected with the Government, and, using my name with the Bedouins, a secret agent was sent precisely to the tribes I had befriended south of the Gaza to draw them into alliance with the English forces against the Egyptian Nationalist army. I was therefore, as they say, unworthily "hoist with my own petard." This was the famous Palmer mission, about which I shall have more to say in its place.

Syria and all the Arab frontier was at this time in a great state of political ferment. There were two currents of feeling there among Mohammedans, the one of fanaticism fostered by the Sultan, the other in favour of liberal reform, representing the two sides of the Pan-Islamic movement, and at Damascus it was represented to me that the feeling against the Sultan and the corrupt Ottoman administration was so strong that a general revolt might at any time occur. I spoke to Mohammed Ibn

Abd-el-Kader about it, and found that he and his father were strongly on the liberal side and that, like the rest of the Arabic speaking Ulema, they favoured the idea of an Arabian Caliphate, if such could be made to come about; and the thought occurred to me that no one then living had a better title to be candidate for the Ottoman succession than Abd-el-Kader himself might have. I therefore begged Mohammed to sound the old Seyyid on the subject, and to ask him whether he would be willing, should such a movement come to a head, to be put forward as its leader. Mohammed did so, and brought back a message from his father to the effect that, though too old to take any active part in a movement of the kind himself, his sons would be willing, and he would not refuse to give his name as a candidate for the Caliphate, should such candidature be thrust upon him. There would, however, be no chance of success to the movement unless it should have support from without, the Ottoman Government being militarily too strong, and it was arranged that I should communicate his answer confidentially to our Government and ascertain what attitude England would assume in case of a Syrian rising. This therefore I did, using my usual channel of communication with Mr. Gladstone, his private secretary Hamilton, asking what help the Arabian movement might count on. I suggested, in reference to Hamilton's letter already quoted, that such a movement might be favourably regarded by our Government, especially in connection with their difficulties with the Porte about Greece. Gladstone's interest, however, in the East and in foreign politics had by this time altogether cooled down, and Hamilton's answer was brief and discouraging. "I hope," he wrote, "that there is good prospect that the war between Greece and Turkey will be averted, and therefore I trust there will be no necessity to resort to your scheme in Syria. I can, I am afraid, only say that it is conceived that such a state of things might arise when something of the sort you suggest might be necessary, but that the case is not considered to have arisen. This is confused and enigmatic, but I fear I can say no more." With this I had to be content, and I made no delay in communicating the result to the Seyyid.

The rest of our journey that summer was without political

interest. We again visited our friends the Anezeh Bedouins, whom we found encamped near Palmyra, but our dealings with them were merely about horses. The Anezeh care nothing about politics other than those of the desert and as little for the affairs of religion. They can hardly indeed be counted as even nominally Mohammedans, as they neither fast nor pray nor practice any Moslem observance. Their only connection with Islam is that they have in common with it the old Arabian customary law on which the law of the Sheriat was founded, but they do not, as far as I have ever been able to ascertain, hold any of the Moslem beliefs except vaguely and negatively the unity of God. They are without respect for Prophet or Saint or Koran, and know nothing whatever of a future life. With them we travelled northwards to the border of their wanderings and found ourselves at the beginning of the summer heat at Aleppo, and soon after once more in England.[1]

[1] It is worth recording that while at Aleppo on this occasion we made friends with two English officers afterwards prominently connected with Egypt and the Soudanese war, Colonel Stewart, who shared with Gordon in the defence of Khartoum against the Mahdi, and Colonel Sir Charles Wilson who succeeded to the command of the British army at Metemneh after the battle of Abu Klea. Stewart, at my suggestion, made a tour that summer among the Anazeh and Shammar Bedouins, but failed to get on good terms with them, the truth being that he was quite out of sympathy with Orientals. Wilson, a man of far wider ideals, accompanied us on our homeward journey as far as Smyrna, which we reached in the time of Midhat Pasha's arrest. Both were at that date Consuls in Asia Minor of the perambulating kind provided by the terms of the Cyprus Convention.

CHAPTER VI

BEGINNINGS OF THE REVOLUTION IN EGYPT

The summer of 1881 I spent almost entirely at Crabbet, writing the book which was the fruit of my winter experience: "The Future of Islam." It was composed somewhat in haste and under circumstances unfavourable to deliberate judgment, for in the very act of writing it, events crowded so closely on events, and portents upon portents that a calm forecast of Islam's destiny seemed at times almost impossible. Nevertheless, and in spite of many defects, I look upon the work as still of serious value, if only historically, as showing the condition of the Mohammedan hopes and fears of the day when it was written. In it I committed myself without reserve to the Cause of Islam as essentially the "Cause of Good" over an immense portion of the world, and to be encouraged, not repressed, by all who cared for the welfare of mankind. I gave an historical sketch of its origin, its glories, and its apparent decay, a decay which was very similar to that which had seemed to overtake Christendom four hundred years before, and which might be met as Christendom had met its troubles by a religious reformation and the freeing of its thought from the bondage of a too strict tradition impeding its evolution. I expounded the ideas, as I had learned them from Sheykh Abdu, of the liberal school of teaching, and appealed to all that was best among my own countrymen to sympathize with their hopes as against the party of reaction which, hide-bound in the old and evil ways, had nothing to offer but a recrudescence of fanaticism and a last desperate appeal against its many enemies to the sword. To England especially, as interested so largely in the future of Islam through India, I addressed myself, urging that her policy should be an active one of friend-

ship with the better elements of Eastern thought in its struggle
with the worse, not merely to profit by its decay for the extension of her own material interests. "The main point," I
said, "is that England should fulfil the trust she has accepted
(by her inheritance of the Mogul Empire and her long connection with Ottoman affairs) of developing, not destroying the
existing elements of good in Asia. She cannot destroy Islam
or dissolve her own connection with her. Therefore, in God's
name, let her take Islam by the hand and encourage her boldly in
the path of virtue. This is the only worthy course and the
only wise one, wiser and worthier, I venture to assert, than
a whole century of crusade."

The chapters of this little volume, as they came out in
monthly numbers of the "Fortnightly Review," produced a
considerable effect in England and also among the English-
reading Moslems of India, and found their way, to some extent,
in translation to Egypt. Already, while I was writing them, it
had become clear that great events were imminent in the Mohammedan world and were even now in progress. Early in May
the French Government with hardly a note of warning, and in
pursuance of the secret arrangement made at Berlin three years
before between M. Waddington and our Foreign Office, invaded Tunis and, on the fanciful pretext of protecting the Bey
from a quite unreal danger threatened him by his subjects, occupied the western portion of the Regency and proclaimed a
French Protectorate. This sudden act of aggression on a perfectly inoffensive and harmless neighbour was justified by nothing
in the condition of the province either in the way of ill government or danger to Europeans or even financial embarrassment.
The Bey himself was a mild and respectable personage, and
had in no way forfeited the goodwill of his people. The seizure
of his person by General Bréart, and the usurpation of his authority by the French Republic was an act of cynical illegality
almost without parallel in the history of modern aggression
upon weaker nations, if we except the invasion of Egypt by
Bonaparte in 1799, and was generally condemned in England
where the history of the Berlin betrayal was not as yet suspected. In the Mohammedan world it lit a flame of anger and
dismay which gathered in intensity as the truth became slowly

known.   The western Tunisians, taken wholly by surprise at
first, had hardly fired a shot against the French, and the Bey
had been forced to sign the Treaty presented to him at the
sword's point by Bréart, which surrendered the independence of
the Regency, before the real state of the case came to be understood.   But in the eastern provinces the tribes of the desert
took up arms, and before the middle of summer the revolt had
spread to the Algerian Sahara and a wave of anger against
Christendom was rolling eastwards which, as will be seen, had
begun to affect Egypt dangerously, and remains in truth to this
day responsible for precipitating the action of the liberal reformers there and of the army in demanding self government.

It is worth noting, as showing the complicity of our Government in this scandalous affair, that Lord Granville allowed himself to be content with an assurance given him by the French
Government, that the occupation of the Regency was only for
the restoration of order, though it was patent that order had
not been so much as threatened, and that it would not continue a day longer than might be necessary to secure the safety
of the Bey's Government—a line of falsehood closely imitated
by Lord Granville himself the following year when the positions of France and England were reversed in Egypt.   It is
most noticeable too that, though Parliament was sitting at the
time, Lord Salisbury, the leader of the opposition, maintained
an absolute silence about Tunis, though his followers, who did
not know his secret reasons, were clamorous for explanations.
Bismarck was equally silent at Berlin, and no single Power of
those who had been represented at Berlin dissented, though the
Italian public was deeply aggrieved by the French action.   The
Sultan alone of them recorded his public protest, Tunis having
been always reckoned as part of the Ottoman dominions.   By
the European Governments it was accepted speedily as a *fait
accompli*.

The history of the rise of what in the summer of 1881 began
to be known as the Egyptian National movement needs here
to be told.   It had its origin as a practical idea in the last
desperate efforts made by the Khedive Ismaïl when he had
quarrelled with Wilson to maintain himself in power against the
consular tutelage in which he had, by his folly and his debts,

placed himself. He sought to recover the moral status he had lost and the goodwill of his subjects by making to them a popular appeal for support, and in the spring of 1879 he proclaimed his intention of calling together an assembly of Notables. There is little doubt that his intention was, under the cloak of a national demand, to repudiate at least a portion of the debt, and though no one in Egypt, except perhaps certain European residents, thought him sincere, the idea of a constitutional form of government as a remedy for the ills they were suffering began from that time to be popularized at Cairo. Sheykhs Jemal-ed-din and his school had always maintained that the growing absolutism of Mohammedan princes in modern times was contrary to the spirit of Islam which in its essence was a Republic where every Moslem had the right of free speech in its assemblies, and where the authority of the ruler rested on his conformity to the law and on popular approval. Ismaïl was condemned by the Azhar reformers on the double ground of his being a breaker of the law and a political tyrant. In the spring of 1879 it had been much discussed among them in private how, and by what means, he could be deposed or even, if there were no other way, removed by assassination. It was the consciousness of his double peril, both at home and from Europe, and of the opinions held at the Azhar that determined him to appear as a Constitutionalist. Constitutionalism, it must, moreover, be remembered, was much in the air just then not only in Egypt, but at Constantinople, where an assembly had met convoked by decree of the Sultan only five years before. Little, therefore, as Ismaïl was trusted by the Reformers, his new move was one of which they could not but approve, and it was taken up and expounded by such printed organs of opinion as had furtively begun to be established at Cairo under their direction. Apart from the Azhar, there were not a few of the high officials who at this time were Constitutionalists, notably Sherif Pasha, Ali Pasha Mubarak and Mahmud Bey Sami el Barodi. Nor was this all. The Khedive's heir apparent and eventual successor, Mohammed Tewfik, had come under Jemal-ed-din's potent influence, and through him was in close communication with the Reformers, and had given them repeated pledges that if ever he came to the Khedivial throne he would govern on strictly constitutional lines. Ismaïl's latest Ministry, which lasted three months, included Tewfik and Sherif, Constitutionalists both, and they were actually in charge of the administration when the old Khedive was deposed.

Tewfik's accession was therefore greeted by Jemal-ed-din and the Reformers as a stroke of good fortune, and, though they regretted that it had not been in the power of the Egyptians themselves to depose the tyrant, they looked forward to the new *régime* with the confident expectation of men who had at last obtained a lever to their wishes. The new Khedive, however, like many another heir apparent when he has succeeded to power, was not long in changing his opinion, and a month had hardly elapsed before he had forgotten his promises and betrayed his friends. Tewfik's character was one of extreme weakness. The son of a woman who had been a servant only in his father's house, he had been from his childhood treated as of small account by Ismaïl and brought up by his mother in bodily fear of the unscrupulous Khedive, and in those habits of insincerity and dissimulation which in the East are the traditional safeguards of the unprotected. He had grown up in this way, in the harem more than with men, and had been unable to rid himself of a certain womanish timidity which prompted him always to yield his opinion in the presence of a stronger will than his own, and after yielding, to regain his ground, if possible, by indirect means and covertly as is the habit of women. He had, too, a large share of the womanish quality of jealousy and of the love of small vengeances. Otherwise, in his domestic life he was well-conducted as compared with most of his predecessors, and not unadorned with respectable virtues. As a ruler his was too negative a character not to be a danger to those who had to deal with him. His first impulse was always to conceal the truth and to place upon others the blame of any failure that might have occurred by his fault. His resentments were shown not by open displeasure, but by tale-bearing and false suggestion and the setting of one against another where he desired to prevail or be revenged. It has been said of him that he was never sincere, and that no one ever trusted him who was not betrayed.

When therefore on his accession Tewfik found himself placed

between two forces with opposite ends in view, the force of his
reforming friends urging him to fulfil his constitutional promises,
and the force of the consulates forbidding him to part with
any of his power, a power they intended to exercise in his name
themselves, he consented first to his Minister Sherif's suggestion that he should issue a decree granting a Constitution and
then at the instance of the Consuls refused to sign it. This
led to Sherif's resignation, and the substitution in his place
of a nominee of the Consulates, Riaz Pasha, on whom these
counted to carry out their ideas of financial reform while
leaving him full power, under the Rescript of 1878, to carry on
the internal administration as he would, without check from
any Council or Assembly, in the Khedive's name. The weakness shown by the Khedive in this, the first important decision
of his reign, was the cause of all his future troubles. Had he
remained loyal to his promises to the Reformers and to his
Ministers, and summoned at that time a Council of Notables, he
would have had his subjects enthusiastically with him and would
have been spared the intrigues and counter intrigues which
marked the next two years and prepared the way for the revolution of 1882. As it was, he found himself by his compliance
deprived of all authority, and treated as a mere dummy prince
by Consuls whose will he had obeyed and by his new Minister.

The character of Riaz has been much debated. At the
time of my visit to Egypt in the autumn of 1881, his name was
in execration with the Nationalists as the author of the violent
but abortive measures which had been taken for their repression, but as I now think in part unjustly. Riaz was a man of
the old *régime* and as such a disbeliever in any but the most
absolute forms of government, and he carried on the administration while in power according to the received methods which had
prevailed in Ismaïl's time, by espionage, police rule, arrests, and
deportations. But he was neither unjust nor personally cruel,
and he was certainly animated throughout his public career by
a real sense of patriotism. His idea in taking office under the
joint control of the English and French Consulates, and the
assistance he gave them in opposition to the popular will, was,
as he has since assured me, simply to recover Egypt from its
financial misfortunes and redeem the debt and so get rid as

speedily as possible of the foreign intervention, nor is there any doubt that in the first year of his being in office great progress had been made in relieving the fellahin from their financial burdens. But the process of redemption must in any case have been a very slow one, and there is no probability that he would have succeeded either in freeing Egypt from the tutelage imposed on it or even of seeing the grosser evils of the administration which still weighed upon the people sensibly relieved. The *régime* of the Joint Control which Riaz served looked solely to finance and troubled itself hardly at all about other matters. The fellahin were still governed mainly by the kurbash, the courts of justice were abominably corrupt, the landed classes were universally in debt and were losing their lands to their creditors, and the alien caste of Turks and Circassians still lorded it over the whole country. There was no sign during the period of anything in the shape of moral improvement encouraged by the Government or even of improvement in the administrative system. This was the weak side of the Anglo-French *régime* and the cause of its failure to win popular favour. Nevertheless, it may be questioned whether the crisis would have come as speedily as it did, but for the Khedive's own insincerities and intrigues against his Minister. It was his character, as I have explained, to yield outwardly to pressure but at the same time to seek to regain his end by other means. Thus it happened that he had hardly taken Riaz to his counsels before he began to intrigue against him. He was jealous of his authority and grudged the power that he had given to his too independent Minister. This is the true history of the series of crises through which Egypt passed in 1881, including, to a large extent, the military troubles which ended in Riaz' fall from power.

The intervention of the army during the winter of 1880-81 as a political force in Egypt is so important a matter that it needs careful explanation. As an element of discontent, it may be said to date from the disastrous campaign in Abyssinia which destroyed in it the Khedivial prestige, and at the same time by the financial difficulties it had involved made the pay of the soldiers precarious and irregular. The men who returned from the campaign had no longer any respect for their generals who had shown themselves incompetent, and the subordinate officers for the most part made common cause against them with the men. This came about the more naturally because the higher posts in the army were occupied exclusively by the Turkish-speaking "Circassian" class which at that time monopolized official power, while the common soldiers and the officers to the rank of captain were almost as exclusively drawn from the Arabic-speaking fellahin population. The class feeling became strong when it was precisely these that were mulcted of their pay, while the Circassians continued to enjoy their much larger salaries undiminished. During the last three years, therefore, of Ismaïl's reign the rank and file of the army had fully shared the general discontent of the country, and there had been conspiracies, never made public, among the lower officers which at one moment very nearly came to the point of violent action. A leader in this class feeling in the army was, as early as 1877, Ahmed Bey Arabi, whose rank as lieutenant-colonel, a very unusual one to be held by a fellah, gave him a position of exceptional influence with his Arabic-speaking fellow countrymen. A short biography of this remarkable man will not be here out of place.

Arabi was born in 1840, the son of a small village sheykh, the owner of eight and a half acres of land, at Horiyeh, near Zagazig, where his family had been long established and enjoyed a certain local consideration of a semi-religious kind. Like many other village sheykhs they claimed a strain of Seyyid blood in their otherwise purely fellah lineage, and had a tradition of being, on that account, somewhat superior to their rustic neighbours. How far this claim was a valid one—and it has been disputed—I do not know, but it had at least the effect of giving them a desire for better religious education than is to be found in the Delta villages, and Arabi, like his father, was sent as a youth to Cairo and was a student there for two years at the Azhar. At the age of fourteen he was taken for a soldier, and as he was a tall, well-grown lad and Saïd Pasha, the then Viceroy, had a scheme for training the sons of village sheykhs as officers, he was pushed on through the lower ranks of the army, and at the early age of seventeen became lieutenant, captain at eighteen, major at nineteen, and Caimakam, lieutenant-colonel, at twenty. This rapid and unexampled advancement in the case of a fellah was due in part to the protection of the French general under whom he was serving, Suliman Pasha el Franzawi, but still more to the favour shown by the Viceroy, who affected to be, like the mass of his subjects, an Egyptian, not merely a member of the alien Turkish caste, and wished to have fellah officers about him. Arabi, a presentable young fellow, even so far enjoyed his favour as to be named his A. D. C., and in this capacity he accompanied Saïd to Medina the year before his death. It was during this close intercourse with the Viceroy that he acquired his first political ideas, which were those of equality as between class and class, and of the respect due to the fellah as the preponderating element in Egyptian nationality. It is this particular advocacy of fellah rights which distinguished Arabi from the other reformers of his day. The Azhar movement was one of general Mohammedan reform, without distinction of race. Arabi's was essentially a race movement and as such far more distinctly national and destined to be far more popular.

The unexpected death of his master, Saïd, was a great blow to Arabi's hopes. Under Ismaïl the favour shown to the fellah officers was withdrawn, and all preferment was once more given to the Circassians. Arabi found himself treated with scant courtesy by these, and was given only subordinate duties to perform in the transport service and semi-civilian posts. This threw him into the ranks of the discontented and made him more than ever the advocate of the rights of his own class. He was eloquent and able to expound his views in the sort of language his countrymen understood and appreciated, not very precise language perhaps, but illustrated with tropes and metaphors and texts from the Koran, which his Azhar education supplied. He thus exercised a considerable influence over those with whom he came in contact. During this period he came a good deal into the society of Europeans, especially at Alexandria, where he had been sent on business, not altogether military, connected with the Khedive's Daira. His relations with these were friendly, and throughout his career he remained free from the least taint of fanatical intolerance in regard to Christians. On points of religion, though his practice was strict, he belonged to the largest and most liberal school of Mohammedan interpretation, and he was essentially a humanitarian in his ideas of the frater- nity of nations and creeds. He knew no language, however, but his own, and maintained his integrity free from the European vices which are so easily acquired.

In the Abyssinian war Arabi saw some service, but only on the communication lines between Massawa and the front, and he returned from the campaign like all the rest, incensed at the way in which it had been mismanaged. It was this that turned his attention decidedly to politics and gave a wider scope to his indignation now principally directed against the Khedive. This was intensified when he found himself arrested, with an- other fellah officer, Ali Bey Roubi, on a false charge of having been concerned in the attack on Nubar, a manœuvre of Ismaïl's intended to screen his own part in the affair; and, after his re- lease, he for a moment joined with others in a plan which, how- ever, came to nothing, of deposing the Khedive. It is probable that, if Europe had not intervened when it did, this result would have ultimately happened, either through the action of the army or perhaps by Ismaïl's assassination, for such a solution too was at one time seriously discussed at the Azhar. All the Reform- ing party it is certain, and the soldiers with them, rejoiced at Ismaïl's downfall. It is a mistake also to suppose that Arabi was at the outset hostile to the new *régime*. Neither with Tewfik nor with the European Consuls had he the smallest quarrel. On the contrary, he saw in Tewfik a friendly in- fluence, and in the Consuls protectors for the fellahin from their old oppressors. Moreover, he had obtained the command of a regiment of the guard, and was quartered where he would most have desired to be, in the Abbassiyeh barracks at Cairo. Had moderate prudence been used in dealing with the soldiers' very real grievances, and a War Minister less hostile to the fellah officers been appointed, there is every reason to believe that neither he nor any of his fellow officers would have thought of taking up an attitude hostile to the Government. Action in self defence was forced upon them, and for this the Khedive's jealousy of Riaz was mainly responsible.

The trouble came about in this way: when the new Ministry under Riaz was formed, Osman Rifky, a Turkish pasha of the old school, was made Minister of War. He was an extreme representative of the class which for centuries had looked upon Egypt as their property and the fellahin as their slaves and servants, His attitude, therefore, towards the fellah officers was from the first a hostile one, and in the appointments made by him it was to the Circassian, not the fellah, element in the army that preference was always given. The soldiers too were angry at being made use of for purposes outside their military duty, and subjected to a kind of *corvée* of hard labour such as the digging of canals and agricultural work on the Khedivial estates, to which they had become unaccustomed, and it was for taking their part and refusing to allow the men of his regiment to be ordered away to dig the Towfikiyeh Canal that Arabi first incurred the Minister's displeasure. There were questions too of pay withheld which called for redress, and on the 20th of May, 1880, a first petition was sent in by the fellah officers, of whom Arabi was one, setting forth their grievances.

The address included nothing political, and was made in proper form to the Ministry of War, and led, through the intervention of the French and English Consuls, to an official inquiry which proved the justice of the complaints. In this matter the French Consul, M. de Ring, took the part, as was just, of the officers, and from that time gave them to a certain extent his protection, especially when during the course of the Inquiry he had found himself in personal altercation with Riaz. Arabi in all this, while taking a leading part, was prudent and moderate, and his conduct was approved by the Consuls. Since his return to Cairo, as Colonel of the Fourth Regiment, he had renewed his acquaintance with the reformers of the Azhar and the Constitutional party, and through a mutual friend and Arabi's fellow officer Ali Bey Roubi, was in communication with two of the Ministers, Ali Pasha Mubarak and Mahmud Bey Sami. These, though Constitutionalists and adherents of Sherif Pasha, had retained their places as Ministers of Public Works and Religious Foundations *(Awkaf)* when Sherif had been dismissed. By Mahmud Sami, Arabi and the fellah officers were especially befriended.

It was in this conjuncture of affairs that the Khedive, see-

ing in it the elements of an intrigue against Riaz, put himself
in communication with the officers through the intermediary of
his A. D. C., Ali Bey Fehmi, an officer of fellah origin but attached through his Circassian wife to the Palace, and Colonel
of the 1st regiment of the Guard.   This Ali Fehmi was a very
worthy young officer, and though he had not taken any part
in the petition sent in to the Ministry and was without political
bias, was already on friendly terms with Arabi and the rest,
and had no difficulty in persuading them that the Khedive too
was on their side in the quarrel, and had sent him to warn them
that worse things were being designed against them by Osman
Rifky and Riaz, and that unless they could procure the dismissal
of these they would always be in danger.   Arabi was the easier
persuaded of this because Riaz had already had many of the
Constitutionalists arrested, and some of these had been friends of
his own.   Sheykh Jemal-ed-din had been summarily dealt with,
and a young landowner of the Sherkiyeh, Hassan Mousa el Akkad, a special friend of Arabi, had been deported only a short
time before to the White Nile, for the mere reason that in response to an invitation publicly made by Sir Rivers Wilson he had
petitioned against the Moukabalah confiscation.   It was therefore suggested to the officers that they should be beforehand
with Osman Rifky and should petition for his dismissal, a request which the Khedive would view favourably.

The affair came to a crisis about the end of the year 1880,
when one evening, Arabi being with other officers at the house
of Nejm el Din Pasha, he learned that it had been decided at
the Ministry that he and his fellow Colonel of the Black
Regiment, Abd-el-Aal Bey Helmi, were to be deprived of their
commands and dismissed the service; and almost at the same
time news was brought him that Ali Fehmi was at his own
house and desired to see him.   On returning home, therefore,
he found Ali Fehmi waiting for him, and with him Abd-el-Aal
who confirmed what he had heard, and after taking counsel
it was decided that they should all three together—for Ali
Fehmi expressed himself willing to throw in his lot with theirs
—go to the Prime Minister and insist upon an end being put to
their persecution by the dismissal of Osman Rifky; and this the
next day they did.   Arabi's own account given to me of their

interview with Riaz is interesting and I have no doubt correct: "We went," he says, "with our petition to the Ministry of the Interior and asked to see Riaz. We were shown into an outer room and waited while the Minister read our document in the inner room. Presently he came out. 'Your petition,' he said, 'is *muhlik,* a hanging matter. What is it you want? to change the Ministry? And what would you put in its place? Whom do you propose to carry on the government?' And I answered him, '*Ya saat el Basha,* is Egypt then a woman who has borne but eight sons and then become barren?' By this I meant himself and the seven Ministers under him. He was angry at this, but in the end said he would see into our affair, and so we left him."

At the Council of Ministers which assembled immediately after this incident the Khedive played a treacherous part. In order to involve the Ministry in an open quarrel with the officers, in which he knew the officers would have M. de Ring's protection, he proposed that they should be arrested and placed upon their trial by Court Martial, but to this Osman Rifky objected because he also would thus be put on trial, while Riaz was against making it a case of public scandal at all, and took the officers' part. It was pointed out however to Riaz privately that his opposition would be misinterpreted, and would be looked upon as an act disloyal to the Khedive, and he withdrew his opposition, and a compromise was come to according to which Osman Rifky was to be left to deal with the officers summarily, and according to methods common in Ismaïl's reign. No open action therefore was taken against the officers, and the case was left undecided by the Council.

What followed is well known. Some days later the three Colonels who had signed the petition received an invitation to attend at the Kasr el Nil Palace to arrange with the Minister what part their regiment should take in some festivities which were being organized for the Princess Jamila's wedding. Arrived there, they found a number of their superior officers, Circassians, with Osman Rifky, and were at once arrested, disarmed, and insulted. Arabi has always maintained that it was intended to put them on board a steamer which was lying in the river outside, and have them conveyed up the Nile and drowned; and I see no reason to doubt that this was the case. Osman Rifky's object was to avoid a trial, which would have exposed his own tyrannical proceedings, and it would doubtless have been reported that the officers had been dismissed the service and gone to their homes. Be this however as it may, they were speedily released by the soldiers of Ali Fehmi's regiment, who, under the command of their major, Mohammed Obeyd, a good and loyal man who was afterwards killed at Tel-el-Kebir, marched down on news being brought and forced the Palace doors. The Circassian Generals then beat a retreat as they best could, and Osman Rifky was forced to an undignified flight through a ground-floor window, whereupon the three Colonels marched back at the head of their troops, and with drums beating, to their barracks. Here they drew up a letter telling what had happened, and explaining that their action had been one of self-defence only, and in no way endangered the safety of any one, and addressed it to M. de Ring, begging his intercession with the Khedive, and that another Minister might be appointed in Osman Rifky's place, to which in the course of the day the Khedive readily acceded. It is certain, however, that he and M. de Ring together made a strong effort to get Riaz also dismissed, on the plea that as Prime Minister he was principally responsible for the disorder which had happened. Nevertheless Riaz was too strongly supported by the Financial Controllers and by the German Consul General, and, I think, by Malet, who was at that time, as I have recorded, by no means favourably disposed to the officers, and on the matter being referred to London and Paris the Khedive's wish was disregarded, and shortly after M. de Ring was recalled by his Government in disgrace.

The date of this first military disturbance at the Kasr el Nil was 1st February, 1881. It took place while I was still in Egypt, but after I had left Cairo, and I do not remember to have heard Arabi's name mentioned before it happened. The public part, however, that he played that brought him into immediate notoriety, and at once his name was in all men's mouths as that of a man who had been able successfully to defy the Government and bring about a change of Ministers. His position in a very few weeks became one of power in the country, or at least of imputed power, and, as the custom is in Egypt, petitions of all kinds poured in upon him from persons who had suffered wrong and who sought his aid to get justice. The fact that he had appeared in the affair as champion of fellah wrongs against the Turkish ruling class gave him popularity outside of Cairo, and many of the Notables and country sheykhs put themselves into communication with him. To all he returned what good answers he could and help as far as his limited power extended, and wherever men met him his fine presence, attractive smile, and dignified eloquence in conversation conveyed a favourable impression.

In personal appearance Arabi was at that time singularly well endowed for the part he was called upon to play in Egyptian history as representative of his race. A typical fellah, tall, heavy-limbed, and somewhat slow in his movements, he seemed to symbolize that massive bodily strength which is so characteristic of the laborious peasant of the Lower Nile. He had nothing in him of the alertness of a soldier, and there was a certain deliberation in his gesture which gave him the dignity one so often sees in village sheykhs. His features in repose were dull, and his eyes had an abstracted look like those of a dreamer, and it was only when he smiled and spoke that one saw the kindly and large intelligence within. Then his face became illumined as a dull landscape by the sun. To Turkish and Circassian pashas this type of man seemed wholly negligible, that of the peasant boor they had for generations dominated and held in slavery and forced to labour for them without pay, and it seemed impossible to them he should be used otherwise than as a tool in their astute hands. Riaz from first to last despised him, and even the intellectual Reformers of the Azhar took little count of him as a political force. But with his own peasant class his rusticity was all in his favour. He was one of themselves, they perceived, but with their special qualities intensified and made glorious by the power they credited him with, and by the semi-religious culture he had acquired at the Azhar superior to their own. It must be remembered that in all Egyptian history, for at least three hundred years, no mere fellah had ever risen to a position of any political eminence in Egypt, or had appeared in the light of a reformer, or whispered a word of possible revolt. I doubt, however, whether his qualities alone, which were after all rather negative ones, or his talents, of which he had as yet given no proof, would have sufficed to bring him to the front as a National leader, but for the unwise persecution to which he was subjected by Riaz in the months following the affair of Kasr el Nil, and which, through the intrigues of the Minister's political enemies, he was always able to thwart and circumvent. The most important of these, and the man in the best position to warn him of his dangers was the new Minister of War, Mahmud Bey Sami, who, through M. de Ring's influence, had been given Osman Rifky's succession, and who, as one of the ex-Minister Sherif's party, was a strong Constitutionalist. Though not personally acquainted with Arabi hitherto, he had already been friendly disposed towards him, and with one of the fellah officers, Ali Bey Roubi, he was on terms of intimacy. Having become Minister of War, he was in a position to help them actively, and to give them notice of designs against them such as came to his ears; and he was able to do this the more effectively because he still saw little of Arabi personally, though remaining in touch with him through Ali Roubi. He had made the officers a general promise that if at any time the Khedive joined actively against them they would know it, even if he did not warn them directly, by his retirement from the Ministry.

Mahmud Samiel Barodi's part in the revolution of that year was a determining one in the course it took. Of a Circassian family long established in the country, and so of the traditional ruling class, he was, like Sherif Pasha, a reformer and a patriot. Intellectually, he was far superior to Arabi, and was indeed one of the most cultivated intelligences in Egypt, with a good knowledge of literature, both Arabic and Turkish, and especially of Egyptian history, besides being an elegant and distinguished poet. English writers, following the lead, or mislead, of the Blue Books, talk of him only as an intriguer, but he was something much more than this, and it must be remembered that in intriguing, as he undoubtedly did here against Riaz, he acted against a Minister who was of a different party from his own, and whom he had not elected to serve. At the time Riaz took office in 1879, Mahmud Sami was already in the

Ministry, and there had been an understanding that he and Ali Mubarak, who were Constitutionalists, should remain on ..n independent footing as far as their own departments were concerned. In the spring of 1881 they were both undoubtedly intriguing against Riaz, but it was with the object of restoring their own party chief Sherif Pasha, to power. This puts a different complexion upon Mahmud Sami's action, and I fancy might find many a parallel in the annals of our own English Cabinets. His part, as I see it, throughout the troubles that were coming was a perfectly loyal one, both to the Constitutional and the National cause, and he paid dearer for his constancy, for he was a rich man and so had more to lose, than any other concerned in the rebellion.

The Khedive's part in the next seven months was far less straightforward. He seems throughout to have been torn with irresolutions, jealousies, fears, and ambitions. Riaz' enemies had suggested to him that that masterful Minister was plotting against him to supplant him as Khedive, an altogether absurd suspicion which he nevertheless at times gave ear to. At other times Arabi's growing popularity aroused his jealousy, and he was constantly shifting from one dread to the other, while his ambition was to regain his own or rather his father's lost authority. The Anglo-French control irked him sorely, and he knew that by the bulk of his subjects he was disliked and despised. His Circassian *entourage,* the men of his Court, were all violent against the fellah officers and were constantly urging him to take strong measures against them, while Sherif Pasha and the Constitutionalists were for his making use of them on the lines already attempted to get rid of Riaz and the Consular subjection in which he lay, by another military demonstration. Such was the state of things in the month of August when the general ferment in the Mohammedan world, caused by the French invasion of Tunis, brought matters at Cairo to a definite crisis.

CHAPTER VII

It is difficult to determine the precise part played by the Khedive in the final act of the revolutionary drama, the military demonstration of the 9th September at Abdin Palace. According to Ninet and certain other writers there was a complete pre-arrangement and community of action between Tewfik that day and the military leaders with the object of bringing about the fall of Riaz and with it of the Consular tutelage in which Tewfik found himself enmeshed. But this is only true in a general sense. Arabi himself has always assured me that during the summer of 1881 he had no personal relations with the Khedive beyond those official ones which his service as colonel of one of the guard regiments entailed. He only on three occasions had speech with His Highness, and on these no political subject was touched on between them. At the same time it is quite certain that the idea of a demonstration with the objects named had been suggested from time to time during the summer by Tewfik to the officers through the intermediary of his A. D. C., Ali Fehmi. Ali Fehmi, though he had been concerned with Arabi in the affairs of the Kasr-el-Nil and had been arrested with him, was none the less received back into the Khedive's favour, who thought to make use of him still in the double capacity of spy on the fellah officers and intermediary, if he required it, with them. Ali Fehmi's connection with the Court through his marriage seemed to Tewfik a guarantee of his fidelity, and it was on account of his ultimately siding entirely with Arabi, notwithstanding his Court connection, that Tewfik's resentment was afterwards so bitter against him. Tewfik, however, was a man, as we have seen him, of varying moods, and while he still counted on the help of the army to rid himself of Riaz he was also swayed by occasional fits of jealousy of Arabi's rapidly growing popularity. This popularity was very marked all through the summer months and brought him into communication with innumerable country sheykhs and Notables to whom the idea of fellah emancipation which he preached was naturally congenial. He began to be talked of in the provinces as *"el wahhíd"* the "only one," and in truth he deserved the appellation, for he was the only man of purely fellah origin who had for centuries been able to resist successfully the tyranny of the reigning Turco-Circassian caste.

It cannot be too strongly emphasized that the National movement of 1881 was essentially a fellah movement, having for its object the emancipation of the fellahin, and that it was directed primarily against the iniquitous Turkish Government, which had ruined the country, and only incidentally against the Anglo-French control when this last declared itself openly the ally and supporter of that tyranny. Other interests, however, naturally joined in with the movement; and besides being sought out by the fellah Notables, Arabi soon found himself approached as an ally by the professed Constitutionalists, many of whom were members of the ruling caste, and were at heart as much opposed to fellah liberty as was Riaz himself. The idea of a Constitution in the minds of men of this class was one in which the supreme power, though taken from the Khedive, should remain in the hands of the Turco-Circassian oligarchy, the only ones they considered capable of governing the country. The chief of these Turkish Constitutionalists was Sherif Pasha, and the course of the summer found him in indirect but close correspondence with Arabi as the means of bringing about the Constitution which should be the road for him to a resumption of office. Arabi, always sympathetic to the Constitutional plan, lent himself readily to the idea, and the more so because Sultan Pasha, the most powerful of the fellah Notables, was himself a strong Constitutionalist, and acted as intermediary between him and Sherif. It was arranged between them all that, when a favourable moment should occur, Arabi should add the weight of the army's influence to any pressure that it might be necessary to bring to bear upon the Khedive to obtain his consent to the Constitutional demand,

Nor was the Khedive by any means averse from the thing demanded, as it necessarily included the dismissal of Riaz, an object still to him of prime importance; and, at the time when this feeling predominated in his mind, he, through Ali Fehmi, encouraged Arabi to go forward with his plan and assured him of his approval.

The first message received by Arabi in this sense was one very characteristic of Tewfik's indirect and timid methods of intrigue. Speaking one day with Ali Fehmi about the growing power of the army as a political influence, he said: "You three, Arabi, Abd-ed-Aal, and yourself, are three soldiers—with me you make four." And he bade him deliver this declaration as a message to Arabi. It was followed by hints far more direct, so that it was soon accepted as certain that any demonstration that might be made by the army which should demand Riaz' dismissal would have the Khedive's secret approval if not his open favour. It was necessary, in order to put constraint upon the Consuls, that the Khedive should seem to yield to a physical necessity when consenting to a change of Ministers.

Nevertheless, when the moment for action actually arrived, it was far from certain what line the Khedive would take. The crisis came about in this way. In the month of August Riaz Pasha, who up to then had despised the fellah movement too completely to think it at all dangerous, became for the first time alarmed. The part in it played by the soldiers he had thought to be able to cope with by some of those irregular methods which are the time-honoured tradition of Turkish Government. He had beset Arabi and his fellow colonels with spies and had sought constantly to involve them through the police in some personal quarrel or street disturbance which should put them in his power, but always in vain. The soldiers invariably received warning of any serious design through their friend at the War Office, Mahmud Sami, and were constantly on their guard. It had been arranged, too, between Mahmud Sami and Arabi that if ever the Minister should be forced to retire from the War Office, it would be a sign to the fellah officers that they must expect the worst, even if they should hear nothing of it from himself. When, therefore, in August Riaz, losing patience, quarrelled with the War Minister and it was announced that Mahmud Sami had resigned, the officers saw that the moment for action, as far as they were themselves concerned, could not long be delayed.   Riaz had insisted with Mahmud Sami on the banishment of the two leading colonels with their regiments from Cairo and had got the Khedive, in one of his fits of jealousy at Arabi's popularity, to go with him in ordering it, and when Mahmud Sami demurred, his dismissal had been summarily announced to him.   The Khedive and Riaz were at the time away still for the summer season at Alexandria, and Mahmud Sami, in his disgrace, had been ordered by letter to leave Cairo at once for his village, and so had not had time to communicate with his military friends.   These, nevertheless, knew that trouble was in store for them, and it was the more apparent because Mahmud Sami's successor was no other than a certain Circassian general of the worst reactionary type, Daoud Pasha Yeghen, the Khedive's brother-in-law, whom they knew to be especially their enemy.   In the first days of September the Court returned to Cairo, and the colonels, having taken counsel only with Sultan Pasha and their most intimate civilian allies, prepared for immediate action.   They were resolved that, which way soever the Khedive might now be inclined towards them, they would carry out the projected demonstration and insist on a change of Ministry as a guarantee of their personal security.   They saw plainly enough that if they allowed themselves to be separated from each other and removed from Cairo it would be an easy matter for Riaz to ruin them in detail.   The least they might expect at his hands would be dismissal from the service, and it was far more likely that they would be arrested and tried for mutiny in connection with their doings in February.   It was part, too, of their program to obtain an increase of the army, and they added to it a demand of the Constitution, which seemed to all the only permanent guarantee against arbitrary government.

The crisis came suddenly on the 8th of September.   Daoud Pasha, who like most men of his class held the fellah officers in supreme contempt and who anticipated no resistance from them, issued his order for the departure of the two regiments,

Arabi's to Alexandria and Abd-el-Aal's to Damietta, and on receiving it the colonels decided upon instant action. That they counted upon the Khedive's tolerance, if not his sympathy, is certain, and they knew his weak character too well to doubt that, whatever he might have resolved on in counsel with Riaz the day before, on the day of trial he would be found on the side of the strongest battalions. All they were in any real anxiety about was the attitude of Ali Fehmi, though on him too they counted as almost certainly a friend. Ali Fehmi and his regiment, the first of the guard, had been excepted from the Ministerial order of removal from Cairo, and was still quartered at Abdin barracks, and if the Khedive was really hostile to them, and Ali obedient to orders, the result might be a conflict. Otherwise the demonstration had all the probability of being a pacific one. In order, however, to minimize the risk of a misunderstanding they sent word in writing to the Khedive apprising him of their plans, and as a proof that there was no hostility intended to himself declared that they would not march to his residence in the Ismaïlyeh quarter but to Abdin, the official palace, and begged him there to meet them and hear their complaints.

The rest may be best told in Arabi's own words: "The next morning," he says in his most complete account of the affair, "I wrote a letter stating our demands and sent it to the Khedive at Ismaïlyeh Palace saying that we should march to Abdin Palace at the Asr (mid-afternoon) there to receive his answer. And the reason of our going to Abdin, and not to Ismaïlyeh where he lived, was that Abdin was his public residence, and we did not wish to alarm the ladies of his household. But if he had not come to Abdin we should have marched on to Ismaïlyeh. When, therefore, the Khedive received our message he sent for Riaz Pasha and Khairi Pasha and Stone Pasha (the American), and they went first to Abdin barracks, where both the Khedive and Riaz Pasha spoke to the soldiers, and they gave orders to Ali Fehmi that he should, with his regiment, occupy the palace of Abdin. And Ali Fehmi assented, and he posted his men in the upper rooms out of sight, so that they should be ready to fire at us from the windows. But I do not know whether they were given ball cartridge or not. Then the Khedive, with the Generals, went on to the Kaláa (citadel), and they spoke to the soldiers there in the same sense, calling on Fuda Bey to support the Khedive against us, the Khedive scolding him and threatening 'I shall put you in prison.' But the soldiers surrounded the carriage, and the Khedive was afraid and drove away. And he went on by the advice of Riaz to Abbassiyeh to speak to me. But I had already marched with my regiment by the Hassaniyeh quarter to Abdin. And they stopped to ask about the artillery and were told that it also had gone to Abdin.

"And when the Khedive arrived at Abdin he found us occupying the square, the artillery and cavalry being before the west entrance and I with my troops before the main entrance. And already when I arrived before the Palace I had sent to Ali Fehmi who, I had heard, was there and had spoken with him and he had withdrawn his men from the Pálace, and they and Ali Fehmi stood with us. And the Khedive entered by the back door on the east side, and presently he came out to us with his Generals and aides-de-camp, but I did not see Colvin with him though he may have been there. And the Khedive called on me to dismount and I dismounted. And he called on me to put up my sword, and I put up my sword; but the officers, my friends, approached with me to prevent treachery, about fifty in number, and some of them placed themselves between him and the palace. And, when I had delivered my message and made my three demands to the Khedive, he said 'I am Khedive of the country and I shall do as I please' (in the Egyptian patois) '*ana Khedeywi el beled, wa amal zay ma inni awze.*' I replied, 'We are not slaves and shall never from this day forth be *inherited*' (*nahnu ma abid, wa la nurithu bad el yom*). That is to say, 'We shall never be, as slaves are, subject to being bequeathed by will from one master to another.' He said nothing more, but turned and went back into the palace. And presently they sent out Cookson to me with an interpreter, and he asked why, being a soldier, I made demand of a parliament. And I said that it was to put an end to arbitrary rule, and I pointed to the crowd of citizens supporting us behind the soldiers. Then he threatened me, saying 'But we will bring a British army'; and much discussion took place between us.

And he returned six or seven times to the palace, and came out again six or seven times to me, until finally he informed me that the Khedive had agreed to all. And the Khedive mentioned Haidar Pasha to replace Riaz, but I would not consent. And when it was put to me to say it, I named Sherif Pasha, because he had declared himself in favour of a *Mejliss-el Nawwab,* Council of Notables. I had known Sherif a little in former years when he was serving in the army. And the same evening the Khedive sent for me, and I went to him at the Ismaïlia Palace, and I thanked him for having agreed to our requests, but he said only: 'That is enough, go now and occupy Abdin, but let it be without music in the streets.' "

This seems to me a very straightforward account and agrees with everything else that I have been able to learn about the events of the day from native evidence, and even in a general way with the Blue Books. The Khedive's part in it was, according to its showing, hardly heroic, but it was less a case with him of physical cowardice than the English official account suggests. He knew perfectly well that he ran no danger from the soldiers, nor was there anything they had asked of him that he was not quite willing to grant or at least to promise. He stood, as they say, to win in either event, and was in the secret of much that, to Cookson and Colvin, was altogether a mystery.

These two Englishmen, mentioned by Arabi, were respectively Sir Charles Cookson, the British Consul at Alexandria temporarily in charge of the English Agency in Malet's absence on leave at Cairo, and Sir Auckland Colvin, the English Financial Controller. They were almost the sole representatives of the Foreign official body then in Egypt—for M. de Sinkiewicz, the new French Minister, had not yet arrived, and M. de Blignières, Colvin's French colleague, was also away. They had, therefore, the leading part to play in advising the Khedive and reporting the matter home. Colvin, an Indian official with the traditions of the Anglo-Indian art of government, and being quite unsuspicious of the semi-understanding there was between Tewfik and the officers, was all for violent measures, and recommended that the Khedive should adopt such an attitude towards them as might have been taken successfully by Mohammed Ali sixty years before, but was quite unsuited to the actual circumstances. His advice was that he should without more than a short parley shoot Arabi with a pistol with his own hand. Cookson, who knew Tewfik's timidity better, though he also was ignorant of his partial collusion with the officers, was for compromise, and effected precisely that solution which Tewfik had schemed so long to obtain, namely, the dismissal of Riaz and the recall of Sherif. His account of the affair may be read with profit in the Blue Books, as also Colvin's narrative of it in the "Times," to which he communicated the account published, and in the "Pall Mall Gazette," of which he was the regular correspondent. The publicity thus given to their action gained the thanks of the English Government for both officials, and for Colvin the honour of a knighthood and a political position in Egypt he did not till that time possess. And so the matter ended. Riaz, who with the recollection of Nubar's and Osman Rifky's adventures had taken no part in the discussion with the soldiers but had remained prudently inside the Palace, received that evening his dismissal and retired to Alexandria and thence to Europe to remain there till help should come to him from the protecting Powers; and Sherif Pasha, after some show of reluctance, was installed Prime Minister in his stead. All Egypt woke next morning to learn that not merely a revolt but a revolution had been effected, and that the long reign of arbitrary rule was, as it hoped, for ever at an end. The Khedive had promised to assemble the Notables and grant a Constitution, and henceforth the land of the Pharaohs and the Mamelukes and the Turkish Pashas was to be ruled according to the laws of justice and administered not by aliens but by the representatives of the Egyptian people themselves.

The three months which followed this notable event were the happiest time, politically, that Egypt has ever known. I am glad that I had the privilege of witnessing it with my own eyes and so that I know it not merely by hearsay, or I should doubt its reality, so little like was it to anything that I had hitherto seen or am likely, I fear, ever to see again. All native parties and, for the moment, the whole population of Cairo were united in the realization of a great national idea, the Khedive no less it seemed than the rest. He was delighted, now the crisis was over, in the success of his plot for getting rid of Riaz, and with him the most irksome features of the Dual Control, and he trusted in Sherif to rid him sooner or later of Arabi. Sherif and the Turkish liberal magnates were no less elated at their return to power, and even the reactionary Turks, who were by no means at one with Riaz, shared in what they considered a triumph against Europe. The soldiers were relieved of the incubus of danger which had so long weighed on them, and the civilian reformers rejoiced at the civil liberties they now looked on as assured. Those who had most doubted and held back longest acknowledged that the appeal to force with its bloodless victory had been justified by results. Throughout Egypt a cry of jubilation arose such as for hundreds of years had not been heard upon the Nile, and it is literally true that in the streets of Cairo men stopped each other, though strangers, to embrace and rejoice together at the astonishing new reign of liberty which had suddenly begun for them, like the dawn of day after a long night of fear. The Press, under Sheykh Mohammed Abdu's enlightened censorship, freed more than ever from its old trammels, spread the news rapidly, and men at last could meet and speak fearlessly everywhere in the provinces without the dread of spies or of police interference. All classes were infected with the same happy spirit, Moslems, Christians, Jews, men of all religions and all races, including not a few Europeans of those at all intimately connected with native life. Even the foreign Consuls could not but confess that the new *régime* was better than the old, that Riaz had made mistakes, and that Arabi, if he had not been wholly right, had at least not been wholly wrong.

Arabi's attitude both towards the Khedive and towards the new Ministers was correct and dignified. He had several interviews with Tewfik which, at any rate on Arabi's side, were of a most cordial character, while with the Sherif and Mahmud Sami (restored as Minister of War) he showed himself perfectly willing, now his work was done and the liberty of the country obtained, to stand aside and leave its development to his civilian friends. All his speeches of that time—and some of them are to be read in the Blue Books—are in this reasonable

sense and reveal him as deeply imbued with those lofty and
romantic humanitarian views which were a leading feature of
his political career. There is not a trace in them of anything
but a large-minded sympathy with men of all classes and creeds,
nor is it possible to detect unfriendliness even to the European
financial control whose beneficial influence on Egypt he, on the
contrary, cheerfully acknowledges. The old *régime* of Turkish
absolutism is past and done with—that is the theme of most of
the speeches—and a new era of national freedom, peace, and
goodwill to all men has begun. On the 2nd of October, a fortnight after Sherif's installation at the Ministry, we find Arabi
leaving Cairo with his regiment for Ras-el-Wady amid the
universal enthusiasm of a grateful city.

There was only one cloud at that date visible on the Egyptian
horizon, the possible hostility of the Sultan to the idea of a
Constitution. Abdul Hamid, after playing for a while with
Constitutionalism at Constantinople, had shown himself at last
its implacable enemy, and that very summer had ordered the
mock trial and condemnation of Midhat, its most prominent
advocate. The appearance, therefore, of a Special Commission at Cairo early in October representing the Sultan and
instructed to inquire into what was happening in Egypt
disturbed, to a certain extent, men's minds, and doubtless hastened the departure both of Arabi to Ras-el-Wady and of Abd-
el-Aal to Damietta. The visit, however, of the Commissioners
passed off quietly. The new Ministers were able to explain
that in the political movement which was now avowedly a national one, no disloyalty was intended to the Sultan. On the
contrary, the fate of Tunis had convinced the Egyptians that
their only safety from European aggression lay in strengthening, not loosening, the link which bound them to the Ottoman
Empire, and that in reality the object of the Revolution had
been to prevent further encroachments by the Financial Control
of France and England on Egypt's political independence. All
was for the best, and the country was now content and pacified.
Ali Pasha Nizami, the chief commissioner, was consequently
able to take back with him a favourable report of the situation,
and this was strengthened by the second commissioner, Ahmed

Pasha Ratib, who had an opportunity of personal talk with Arabi on his way to Suez and Mecca.

This interview, which had important consequences later for the growth of the political situation, took place in the train between Zagazig and Tel-el-Kebir, Arabi had assured me on his part an accidental one, he having gone to Zagazig to visit his friends Ahmed Eff. Shemsi and Suliman Pasha Abaza and being on his way home. "As I was returning," he has told me, "by train to Ras-el-Wady it happened that Ahmed Pasha Ratib was on his way to Suez, for he was going on to Mecca on pilgrimage. And I found myself in the same carriage with him, and we exchanged compliments as strangers, and I asked him his name and he asked me my name, and he told me of his pilgrimage and other things. But he did not speak of his mission to the Khedive, nor did I ask. But I told him I was loyal to the Sultan as the head of our religion, and I also related to him all that had occurred, and he said, 'You did well.' And at Ras-el-Wady I left him, and he sent me a Koran from Jeddah, and later, on his return to Stamboul, he wrote to me, saying that he had spoken favourably of me to the Sultan, and finally I received the letter dictated by the Sultan to Sheykh Mohammed Zaffer telling me the things you know of." The Ottoman Commission therefore passed off without leading to any immediate trouble. It was coincident with the arrival at Alexandria of a French and an English gunboat, which had been ordered there by the two Governments at the moment of receiving the news of the demonstration at Abdin; and the gunboats and the commissioners left on the same day in October. Malet by this time had returned to his post, and so had Sinkiewicz, and it was agreed between them that the situation needed no active intervention. Malet indeed wrote at that time in the most favourable terms to his Government both of the new Ministers and of Arabi, whose honesty and patriotism, though he had had no personal communication with him, he was now inclined to believe in.

It was at this junction of affairs in Egypt that early in November I returned to Cairo. I had had no recent news from my Azhar friends, and was ignorant of what had happened there during the summer beyond what all the world knew, and it was not even my intention when leaving London to do more than pass through the Suez Canal on my way back (for such was again my plan for the winter) to Arabia. I had been deeply interested in the crisis which was being witnessed throughout the Mohammedan world, and I still hoped to be able to take some personal part in the great events -I saw impending—I hardly knew what, except that it should be as a helper in the cause of Arabian and Mohammedan liberty. When the revolt took place in Algeria in connection with the French aggression on Tunis, I had written to my friend Seyyid Mohammed Abd-el-Kader at Damascus asking him for an introduction to its leader, Abu Yemama, but this he had not been able to give, and I had also tried in vain to discover Sheykh Jemal-ed-din Afghani's whereabouts in America, where, after wandering two years in India, he was said to be, and now my thoughts were once more turned to Arabia which I had come to look upon as a sacred land, the cradle of Eastern liberty and true religion. Strangely enough, I did not suspect that in the National movement in Egypt the chief interest for me in Islam already lay, as it were, close to my hand, and it was a mere accident that determined my taking any part in what was coming there, even as a spectator.

The reason for my blindness and indifference was that in England the events of September had been represented in the Press as purely military, and even at the Foreign Office there was no knowledge of their true significance. I share with most lovers of liberty a distrust of professional soldiers as the champions of any cause not that of tyranny, and I found it difficult to believe, even as far as Malet did, that Arabi had an honest purpose in what he had done. I knew also that Sheykh Mohammed Abdu and the rest of my Azhar friends were for other methods than those of violence, and that the reforms they had so long been preaching would in their opinion take a lifetime to achieve. It seemed impossible to understand that the events of a single summer should have brought them already to maturity. As to the promised Constitution, the London Press declared that it was mere talk, a pretext of the kind that the ex-Khedive Ismaïl had made use of against Wilson, and Malet was reported to have declared that it would remain a promise only because the Sultan whom he had seen at Constantinople on his way back to Egypt would never allow it.

The Ottoman Commission added to my distrust of the whole movement and the fact that Arabi had demanded an increase of the army to the number of 18,000 men. These were the common views of the day in England and I had no special knowledge in correction of them. I remember shortly before leaving London, that when I called on my cousin Philip Currie at the Foreign Office, he surprised me by expressing an opinion that perhaps there was something more in the National Movement in Egypt than appeared on the surface. "Malet," he said, "is rather inclined now to believe in it. I wonder you do not go there. Perhaps you might find in Arabi just the man you have been looking for." He knew of course my ideas, which he had never taken quite seriously or as more than a romantic fancy, and his words were lightly spoken and we laughed together without discussion. Yet afterwards I recalled them to memory and wondered that I had been so little responsive. My thoughts, however, were fixed elsewhere.

It is worth recording that the night before I started I entertained at dinner at the Travellers' Club three of my then rather intimate friends, John Morley, who had recently become editor of the "Pall Mall Gazette" besides being editor of the "Fortnightly Review," Sir Alfred Lyall, and our Consul at Jeddah, Zohrab. With these I had a long talk about Mohammedan and Eastern affairs, and it was agreed between me and Morley that, if I found the champion of Arabian reform that I was seeking, I should let him know and he would do his best to put his claims prominently before the English public. Morley was not as yet in Parliament, but he already held a position of high influence with the Government through his personal connection with Chamberlain; his paper, the "Pall Mall," was one of the few Mr. Gladstone read, the only one, I believe, in the soundness of whose views he had any confidence. It was a pleasant dinner and we all took rather enthusiastic views as to the possibilities of the future of Islam. On the subject of Egypt, however, Morley was unfortunately already under other influences than mine. His correspondent for the "Pall Mall Gazette" was no other than the Financial Controller, Sir Auckland Colvin, and so it happened that when the crisis came in the spring he was found, contrary to what might have been expected of him, on the English official and financial side, and one of the strongest advocates of violent measures for the suppression of liberty.

On my way to Egypt an incident occurred which I shall have to return to when its full importance comes to be considered. At Charing Cross Station I found Dilke and his private secretary, Austin Lee, on their way, as I was, to Paris, and I made the whole journey in their company. Dilke that day was in the highest possible spirits. His intimate friend Gambetta had just, 15th November, succeeded St. Hilaire as French Prime Minister; and Dilke, who had been for the last six months the English Commissioner at Paris for the negotiation of a renewal of the Commercial Treaty with France without having succeeded in concluding it, was now returning to his work confident that with the change at the Quai d'Orsay he should no longer have any difficulty. Gambetta, on his side, had a plan of his own in which Dilke as Under-Secretary at the Foreign Office could be of the greatest use to him. St. Hilaire had made a terrible mess of the Tunis invasion and had left all North Africa in a blaze for his successor to deal with. Gambetta had come into office determined to use strong measures, and, as they say, to "grasp the nettle" with both hands. He was filled with apprehension of a general Pan-Islamic rising, and saw in the National movement at Cairo only a new and dangerous manifestation of Moslem "fanaticism." He was closely connected, too, through his Jewish origin with the great financial interests involved in Egypt, and had made up his mind to better St. Hilaire's halting aggression on Tunis by forcing our intervention also in Egypt. In this he wanted our Government to go with him and join in an anti-Islamic crusade in the name of civilization, and as a first measure to strengthen the hold of the European Joint Control at Cairo. On both these matters, the Commercial Treaty and Egypt, Dilke was most communicative, though he did not put all the dots upon the i's, treating the former as a special English interest, the latter as specially a French one. It was a point of party honour with the Liberal Government, which was essentially a Free Trade Government, to show the world that their Free Trade declarations did not prevent them from getting reciprocity from other nations, or favorable commercial terms from protectionist governments, and Dilke knew that it would be a feather in his cap if he could obtain a renewal of the French concessions. So eager indeed was he about it that I distinctly remember saying to myself, half aloud, as we parted at the Gare du Nord: "That man means to sell Egypt for his Commercial Treaty." Nor did the event prove it otherwise than exactly a true prophecy. It will be seen a little later that to the trivial advantage of obtaining certain small reductions of the import duties levied on English goods in France, the whole issue of liberty in Egypt, and to a large extent of Mohammedan reform throughout the world, was sacrificed by our Liberal Government. But of all this in its place.

My going at all to Cairo that winter was, as I have explained, somewhat fortuitous, providential I might almost say, if I was not afraid of giving my personal action in Egypt too much importance and too high a meaning. The ship which was to bring me out my servants and camp equipage, after nearly foundering in the Bay of Biscay, ran aground in the Canal and I was obliged to wait at Suez. I left it for Cairo, meaning to be there for a few days only. It had been reported in England that the Azhar Ulema had been won back from their ideas of reform and had adopted the Sultan's reactionary Pan-Islamic views. Half distrustful of the result, I sent a message to my first friend at the University, Sheykh Mohammed Khalil, and then another curious accident occurred. In answer to my note begging him to come and see me at the Hôtel du Nil, where I had alighted, behold, instead of the young Alem whom I knew so well, another Azhar Sheykh of the same name, Sheykh Mohammed Khalil el Hajrasi, a perfect stranger who greeted me with a stranger's welcome. The newcomer had received my message, and, thinking it had come from a European merchant with whom he had dealings in connection with his native village in the Sherkieh, had followed close upon the heels of the messenger. This Mohammed el Hajrasi, though a man of less intrinsic worth than my real friend, was a person of some importance at the Azhar, and proved to be perhaps of even more interest to me at the moment than the other could have been from the fact that he was intimate with the chiefs of what was then called the military party at Cairo and was personally acquainted with Arabi. This my own Mohammed Khalil was not, and, as I presently found, neither he nor his chief Sheykh Mohammed Abdu, would have served me as an intermediary with these, for, as already said, they had disapproved of the immixture of the army in political affairs in September and, though rejoicing at the result, were still to a certain extent holding aloof. Hajrasi, however, when he had recovered from his surprise at finding me an Englishman and not the man he had expected, was nothing loath to talk of Arabi and his doings, and when I went on to explain my views to him of reform upon an Arab basis he at once became confidential and explained to me his own views which were not very different from mine. He was one of the principal Sheykhs, he told me, of the Shafeite rite, and had close relations with the Liberal party of reform at Mecca, who were then in avowed opposition to Abdul Hamid and were looking forward to a new Arabian Caliphate. This was a great point of sympathy between us, and it was not long before we had made a full exchange of our ideas; and I think no better proof could be given of the wonderful liberty of thought and speech which marked those days in Egypt than that this eminent religious Sheykh, who certainly a year before would have locked his secrets jealously in his bosom, even perhaps from a friend, should suddenly have thus unloosened his tongue in eloquent response to my questions and should have unfolded to me, a European and a complete stranger, his most dangerous aspirations in politics. It no doubt, however, was in some part due to the presence with me of my learned Arabic professor, Sabunji, whom I had had the happy inspiration to bring with me from London to help out my poor resources of that language.

It was thus from Hajrasi that I first learned the details of what had been going on at Cairo during the summer and the true position of the soldiers in regard to the National Party, facts which I soon after had confirmed to me from a number of other sources including my original friends, Mohammed Khalil and Mohammed Abdu. Sabunji, moreover, who had a real genius for this kind of work, was presently busy all the city over seeking out news for me, so that in a very few days we knew between us pretty nearly everything that was going on. Nor were we long before we had made acquaintance with some of the fellah officers who had taken part with Arabi in the demonstration, especially with Eïd Diab and Ali Fehmi, with whom I was pleasantly impressed. The matters being principally discussed at the moment were, first, the character of the Khedive—was he to be trusted, or was he not, to fulfil the promises he had given? He had promised a Constitution, but was this to be a real transfer of power to Ministers responsible to a Representative Chamber, or only the summoning of a Chamber of Notables with common consultative powers? Tewfik was mistrusted on this point, and it was generally believed that he was being advised to shuffle in this way out of his engagement by Malet who, as already said, had just come from Constantinople and had declared that the Sultan would never agree to real Constitutional government.

The more advanced section of the Nationalists were bitter against the whole house of Mohammed Ali and especially of the branch of it to which Tewfik belonged, his father Ismaïl and his grandfather Ibrahim, a cruel and treacherous race which had brought untold woes upon the fellahin and had ruined the country morally and financially, and had, by their misconduct, brought about foreign intervention. Secondly, there was the question of reforms. Now that the Press was free, attacks were beginning to be made upon various gross abuses, the injustice of the taxation which, under the foreign Financial Control, favoured Europeans at the expense of the native population; of the unnecessary multiplication of highly paid offices held by foreigners, French and English; of the hold obtained by these over the railway administration and the administration of the domains which had passed into the hands of representatives of the Rothschilds; of the scandal of £9,000 a year subvention being granted still, in spite of the poverty of the land, to the European Opera House at Cairo. A campaign was being carried on, especially by the "Taif" newspaper, edited by a hot-headed young man of genius, Abdallah Nadim, against the brothels and wine-shops and disreputable cafés chantants which under protection of the "Capitulations" had invaded Cairo to the grief and anger of pious Moslems. There was an echo, too, of the bitterness felt by all Mohammedans just then on account of the French raid in Tunis where it was affirmed that mosques had been profaned and Moslem women outraged. Nevertheless the feeling at Cairo between native Christian and native Mohammedan was altogether friendly. The Copts were as a rule wholly with the revolution, and their Patriarch was on the best of terms with the Ministry of which Butros Pasha was a prominent and respected member. Even the native Jews with their Chief Rabbi were all for the Constitutional reform. With the officers the point of principal concern was naturally that of the promised increase of the army, which they affirmed was necessary in view of what had taken place in Tunis, where the Bey had been found quite unprepared with a military force sufficient to defend his country. The legal maximum allowed by the Sultan's Firman in Egypt was 18,000 men and the army must be raised to that point.

My earliest intervention in the affairs of the Nationalists of any active kind came about in this way. About the end of November my friend Sheykh Mohammed el Hajrasi informed me of an agitation which was going on among the students of the Azhar, especially those of the Shafeite and Malekite rites, to depose the actual Sheykh el Islam, or as he is more generally called, Shevkh el Jama, the head of the Hanefite rite, Mohammed el Abbasi. The reason given me for this was that, as a nominee of the Khedive, he could not be relied on to give an honest *fetwa* (legal opinion) as to the legality of constitutional government, and that it was believed that he would be made use of to refuse a *fetwa* in its favour and so give the Khedive an excuse for withdrawing from his full promise. The Hanefite rite has always been the Court rite in Egypt, the Turkish Viceroys, even since the time of Sultan Selim, having usurped the privilege of Court appointment, and the Government has always named a Hanefite to the supreme religious office. At the same time by far the larger number of the students, who amount in all to some 15,000, have been and are of the other two rites, and an attempt was now to be made in accordance with the revolutionary ideas of the day to revert to the more ancient form of nomination, namely by general election. He had come, el Hajrasi said, to consult me about this because the idea was prevalent that Malet was behind the Khedive in the support he was giving to el Abbasi and in the plan of evading his constitutional promise. The difficulty he thought I might be able to remove, if I went to Malet and used my influence with him in their favour. To this I very readily assented, and with the result that I found Malet entirely ignorant of the whole matter and quite ready to say that the religious disputes of the Ulema were outside his province, and that he should interfere on neither side. On the 5th of December, therefore, el Abbasi was by vote of the students deposed from his office and a Sheykh of the Shafeite rite, el Embabeh, named in his place. El Embabeh had not been the most popular candidate, for the majority of the students had been for the Malekite el Aleysh, a man of high courage and religious authority, who afterwards played a leading part during the war and died in the first months of the English occupation in prison, it is generally believed poisoned from his outspoken evidence at the time of Arabi's trial. Embabeh, a man altogether his inferior, obtained the vote only as the result of a compromise, the Khedive having refused el Aleysh. Four thousand students voted at this election and there were only twenty-five dissentients. The little service thus rendered them gave my friends among the Nationalists confidence in my will and power to serve them, and they asked me to delay my departure and stay on at least some weeks to see them through their farther difficulties. To this I readily agreed, seeing in the development of a movement so congenial to my ideas work of the very kind that I was seeking and one in which I could be of real use, as interpreter of their perfectly legitimate ambitions, both with Malet at the Agency and at home with Gladstone.

In the following few weeks I saw Malet almost daily, and acquired considerable influence over him. Though not unsympathetic towards the Nationalists, I found him very ill informed as to their views and objects. He knew none of their leaders personally except Sherif Pasha, and depended in regard to the general drift of affairs on what Sherif and the Khedive thought fit to tell him. For what was passing in the street he had nobody on whom he could rely except his Greek dragoman Aranghi who picked up his news at the cafés of the European quarter. Thus he had little means of understanding the situation, nor was Sinkiewicz, his new French colleague, much better informed.   Malet was also in terrible perplexity as to the real wishes of his own Government.   Lord Granville had just written him the well-known despatch of November 4th, in which he had stated in vague terms the sympathy of Her Majesty's Government for reforms in Egypt.   But this might mean almost anything, and was no guide as to the attitude he should observe if any new conflict should arise between the Khedive and the Nationalists, or between these united and the Financial Controllers.   Above all he was in doubt as to Mr. Gladstone's mind in the affair of the Constitution.   It was, therefore, a real relief to him to find in me some one who had a definite policy to suggest, and mine was very clearly that he should support the Nationalists.

I was able, too, to assure him about Gladstone that he need not doubt that when the Prime Minister came to know the facts he *must* be on the Constitutional side.   I received support, too, with Malet on this point from certain English friends of mine whom I found at Cairo, winter visitors, whom I was able to influence to my views.   Among these the most prominent were two ex-Members of the House of Commons, Lord Houghton, who in early life had been an enthusiastic advocate of freedom in the East, and Sir William Gregory, an old follower of Gladstone's and a well-known Liberal.   By the middle of December I had succeeded in bringing round nearly all the English element at Cairo to my view of the case.   Even Sir Auckland Colvin, the English Financial Controller, who had three months before given the Khedive the heroic advice to shoot Arabi, professed himself converted and half inclined to come to terms with the revolution.

CHAPTER VIII

On the 6th of December Arabi, who up to this time had been in retirement at Ras-el-Wady, a military post close to Tel-el-Kebir, arrived at Cairo and on the 12th for the first time I saw him. He had hired a house close to his friend Ali Fehmi's, who was now wholly with him, and not far from the Abdin Barracks. It was in company, if I remember rightly, with Eïd Diab, and taking Sabunji with me, that I went to him, it having been arranged beforehand that I should do so by some of our mutual friends. Arabi was at that time at the height of his popularity, being talked of through the length and breadth of Egypt as "El Wahíd," the "only one," and people were flocking from all sides to Cairo to lay their grievances before him. His outer room was full of suppliants, as was indeed the entrance from the street, and this was every day the case. He had already heard of me as a sympathizer and friend of the fellah cause, and received me with all possible cordiality, especially, he told me, on account of what he had also heard, my family connection with Byron, whom, though he knew nothing of his poetry, he held in high esteem for his work for liberty in Greece. The point is worth noting, as it is very characteristic of Arabi's attitude towards humanity at large without distinction of race or creed. There was nothing in him of the fanatic, if fanaticism means religious hatred, and he was always ready to join hands in the cause of liberty with Jew, Christian, or infidel, notwithstanding his own, by no means lukewarm, piety.

I talked to him long and without reserve on all the questions of the day, and found him equally frank and plain spoken. Towards the Khedive he expressed his perfect loyalty "so long as he kept to his promises and made no attempt to baulk the Egyptians of their promised freedom." But it was clear that he did not wholly trust him, and considered it his duty to keep a strict eye over him lest he should swerve from the path. In a letter that I wrote soon after, 20th December, to Mr. Gladstone, when I had had several other conversations with him, I said of him: "The ideas he expresses are not merely a repetition of the phrases of modern Europe, but are based on a knowledge of history and on the liberal tradition of Arabian thought, inherited from the days when Mohammedanism was liberal. He understands that broader Islam which existed before Mohammed, and the bond of a common worship of the one true God which unites his own faith with that of Judaism and Christianity. He disclaims, I believe, all personal ambition, and there is no kind of doubt that the army and country are devoted to him. . . . Of his own position he speaks with modesty. 'I am,' he says, 'the representative of the army because circumstances have made the army trust me; but the army itself is but the representative of the people, its guardian till such time as the people shall no longer need it. At present we are the sole national force standing between Egypt and its Turkish rulers, who would renew at any moment, were they permitted, the iniquities of Ismaïl Pasha. The European Control only partially provides against this, and makes no provision whatever by national education in self-government for the day when it shall abandon its financial trust. This we have to see to. We have won for the people their right to speak in an Assembly of Notables, and we keep the ground to prevent their being cajoled or frightened out of it. In this we work not for ourselves but for our children and for those that trust us. . . . We soldiers are for the moment in the position of those Arabs who answered the Caliph Omar when, in old age, he asked the people whether they were satisfied with his rule, and whether he had walked straightly in the path of justice. "O son of El Khattab," said they, "thou has indeed walked straightly and we love thee. But thou knewest that we were at hand and ready, if thou hadst walked crookedly, to straighten thee with our swords." I trust that no such violence will be needed. As Egyptians we do not love blood, and hope to shed none; and when our Parliament has learned to speak, our duty will be over. But until such time we are resolved to maintain the rights of the people at any cost and we do not fear, with God's help, to justify our guardianship if need be against all who would silence them.' "

This kind of language, so different from that usually used by Eastern politicians in their conversations with Europeans, impressed me very deeply, and I made a strong mental contrast between Arabi and that other champion of liberty whom I had met and talked with at Damascus, Midhat Pasha, altogether in Arabi's favour. Here was no nonsense about railroads and canals and tramways as nostrums that could redeem the East, but words that went to the root of things and fixed the responsibility of good government on the shoulders which alone could bear it. I felt that even in the incredulous and trifling atmosphere of the House of Commons words like these would be listened to—if only they could be heard there!

With regard to the Sultan and the connection of Egypt with Turkey, Arabi was equally explicit. He had no love, he told me, for the Turks who had mis-governed Egypt for centuries, and he would not hear of interference from Constantinople in the internal affairs of the country. But he made a distinction between the Ottoman Government and the religious authority of the Sultan, whom, as Emir el Mumenin, he was bound, as long as he ruled justly, to obey and honour. Also the example of Tunis, which the French had first detached from the Empire, and then taken possession of, showed how necessary it was to preserve the connection of Egypt with the Head of the Moslem world. "We are all," he said, "children of the Sultan, and live together like a family in one house. But, just as in families, we have, each of us provinces of the Empire, our separate room which is our own to arrange as we will and where even the Sovereign must not wantonly intrude. Egypt has gained this independent position through the Firmans granted, and we will take care that she preserves it. To ask for more than this would be to run a foolish risk, and perhaps lose our liberty altogether." [1] I asked him rather bluntly whether he had been, as was then currently asserted, in personal communication with Constantinople, and I noticed that he was reserved in answering and did so evasively. Doubtless the recollection of his conversation with Ahmed Ratib, of which I then

[1] Sir William Gregory, who saw Arabi about the same date as I did, has recorded in the "Times" very similar language as used by him.

knew nothing, crossed his mind and caused his hesitation, but he did not allude to it.

Finally we talked of the relations of Egypt with the Dual Government of France and England. As to this he admitted the good that had been done by freeing the country of Ismaïl and regularizing the finances, but they must not, he said, stand in the way of the National regeneration by supporting the Khedive's absolute rule or the old Circassian Pashas against them. He looked to England rather than to France for sympathy in their struggle for freedom, and especially to Mr. Gladstone, who had shown himself the friend of liberty everywhere—this in response to what I had explained to him of Gladstone's views—but like everybody else just then at Cairo he distrusted Malet. I did what I could to ease his mind on this point, and so we parted. This first interview gave me so favourable an opinion of the fellah Colonel that I went immediately to my friend, Sheykh Mohammed Abdu, to tell him how he had impressed me, and suggested that a program, in the sense of what Arabi had told me, ought to be drawn up which I might send to Mr. Gladstone, as I felt certain that if he knew the truth as to the National aspirations, in an authoritative way, he could not fail to be impressed by it in a sense favourable to them. I spoke, too, to Malet on the same subject, and he agreed that it might do good, and I consequently, in conjunction with Sheykh Mohammed Abdu and others of the civilian leaders, drew up, Sabunji being our scribe, a manifesto embodying succinctly the views of the National party. This Mohammed Abdu took to Mahmud Pasha Sami, who was once again Minister of War, and gained his adhesion to it, and it was also shown to and approved by Arabi. This done I forwarded it, with Malet's knowledge and approval, to Gladstone, explaining to him the whole situation and inviting his sympathy for a movement so very much in accordance with his avowed principles. "I cannot understand," I said, in concluding my letter to Gladstone, "that these are sentiments to be deplored or actions to be crushed by an English Liberal Government. Both may be easily guided. And I think the lovers of Western progress should rather congratulate themselves on this strange and unlooked for sign of political life in a land which has hitherto been reproached by them as the least thinking portion of the stagnant East. You, sir, I think, once expressed to me your belief that the nations of the East could only regenerate themselves by a spontaneous resumption of their lost national *Will,* and behold in Egypt that *Will* has arisen and is now struggling to find words which may persuade Europe of its existence."

While sending this "Program of the National Party" to Gladstone, I also at the same time, by Sir William Gregory's advice, sent it to the "Times." Of this course Malet disapproved as he thought it might complicate matters at Constantinople, an idea strongly fixed in his cautious diplomatic mind. But Gregory insisted that it ought to be published, as otherwise it might be pigeon-holed at Downing Street and overlooked; and I think he was right. Gregory was a personal friend of the then excellent editor of the "Times," Chenery, whose services to the National cause in Egypt at this date were very great. Chenery was a man of a large mind on Eastern affairs, being a considerable Arabic scholar, and had published a most admirable English translation of the "Assemblies of Hariri"; and he was able thus to take a wider view of the Egyptian question than the common journalistic one that it was a question primarily concerning the London Stock Exchange—this although he was himself an Egyptian Bondholder. He consequently gave every prominence to the letters Gregory and I wrote to him during the next few months in support of the National movement, and to the last, even when the war came, continued that favour. In the present instance, indeed, Chenery somewhat overdid his welcome to our program, stating that it had been received from Arabi himself, an inaccuracy which enabled Malet, who knew the facts, to disown it through Reuter's Agency as an authentic document.

It will perhaps be as well to explain here the way in which the London Press and especially Reuter's News Agency was at this time manipulated officially at Cairo and made subservient to the intrigues of diplomacy. Very few London newspapers had any regular correspondent in Egypt, the "Times" and the "Pall Mall Gazette" being, as far as I know, the only two that were thus provided. Both, as far as politics were concerned, were practically in the hands of Sir Auckland Colvin, the English Financial Controller, an astute Indian official, with the traditions of Indian diplomacy strongly developed in his political practice. He had some experience of journalism, having been connected with the "Pioneer" in India, an Anglo-Indian journal of pronounced imperialistic type with which he was still in correspondence. He was also Morley's regular correspondent in the "Pall Mall Gazette," and had through him the ear of the Government. The importance of this unavowed connection will be seen later when he made it his business to bring about English intervention. Lastly, on all important diplomatic matters he inspired the "Times," whose regular correspondent, Scott, depended on him for his information. With regard to Reuter and Havas, the Telegraphic Agencies, both were heavily subventioned by the Anglo-French Financial Control, receiving £1,000 a year each, charged on the thin resources of the Egyptian Budget. Reuter especially was the servant and mouthpiece of the English Agency, and the telegrams despatched to London were under Malet's censorship. This sort of manipulation of the organs of public news in the interests of our diplomacy exists in nearly all the capitals where our agents reside, and is a potent instrument for misleading the home public. The influence is not as a rule exercised by any direct payment, but by favour given in regard to secret and valuable information, and also largely by social amenities. In Egypt it has always within my knowledge been supreme, except at moments of extreme crisis when the body of special Press correspondents at Cairo or Alexandria has been too numerous to be kept under official control. In ordinary times our officials have had complete authority both as to what news should be sent to London, and what news, received from London, should be published in Egypt. It is very necessary that this, the true condition of things, should be steadily borne in mind by historians when they consult the newspaper files of these years in search of information.

Down, however, to near the end of the year 1881, except for this small difference of opinion, my relations with Malet remained perfectly and intimately friendly. He made me the confidant of his doubts and troubles, his anxiety to follow out the exact wishes of the Foreign Office, and his fears lest in so difficult a situation he should do anything which should not gain an official approval. He professed himself, and I think he was, in full sympathy with my view of the National case, and he leaned on me as on one able, at any rate, to act as buffer between him and any new violent trouble while waiting a decision in Downing Street as to clear policy. Thus I find a note that on the 19th December I was asked by him and Sir Auckland Colvin, whose acquaintance I had now made and who affected views hardly less favourable than Malet's to the Nationalists, to help them in a difficulty they were in about the Army Estimates.

It was the time of year when the new Budget was being drafted, and the Nationalist Minister of War, Mahmud Sami, had demanded £600,000 as the amount of the year's estimates for his department. It was an increase of I forget how many thousand pounds over the estimate of 1881, and was necessitated, Mahmud Sami said, by the Khedive's promise of raising the army to the full number of men allowed by the Firman, 18,000. The Minister had explained his insistence on the plea that a refusal would or might cause a new military demonstration, the bug-bear of those days; and I was asked to find out what sum the army would really be satisfied with for their estimates. Colvin authorized me to go as far as £522,000, and to tell Arabi and the officers that it was financially impossible to give more. He had no objection, he said, to the army's being increased so long as the estimates were not exceeded. He thought, however, the sum proposed would suffice for an increase up to 15,000 men. I consequently went to Arabi and argued the matter with him and others of the officers; and persuaded them, on my assurance that Colvin's word could be trusted, to withdraw all further objection. They said they would accept the increased sum of £522,000 as sufficient, and make it go as far in the increase of soldiers as it could. They meant to economize, they said, in other ways, and hoped to get their full complement of men out of the balance. They promised me, too, on this occasion to have patience and make no further armed demonstrations, a promise which to the end they faithfully fulfilled. Arabi's last words to me on this occasion were *"men sabber dhaffer,"* "he who has patience conquers." I sent a note the same day to Colvin informing him of the result, and I was also thanked by Malet for having helped them both out of a considerable difficulty.

Nevertheless Malet, about a week later, surprised me one afternoon, 28th December, when I had been playing lawn tennis with him, as I often did at the Agency, by showing me the draft of a despatch he had just sent to the Foreign Office mentioning my visit to Egypt and the encouragement I had given to the Nationalists, and without mentioning what I had done to help him, complaining only of my having sent the Program against his wishes to the "Times." As we had up to that moment been acting in perfect cordiality together, and nothing whatever had occurred beyond the publication of the manifesto, I took him pretty roundly to task for his ill faith in concealing my other services rendered to his diplomacy, and insisted that he should cancel this misleading despatch, and with such energy that he wrote in my presence a cancelling telegram, and also a second despatch repairing in some measure the injustice he had done me. I have never quite understood what Malet's motive was in this curious manœuvre. I took it at the time to be a passing fit of jealousy, a dislike to the idea that it should be known at the Foreign Office that he owed anything to me in the comparatively good relations he had succeeded in establishing with the Nationalists; but on reflection I have come to the conclusion, as one more in accordance with his cautious character, that he was merely guarding himself officially against public responsibility of any kind being fixed on him for my Nationalist views, should these be condemned in Downing Street. It is the more likely explanation because his private conscience evidently pricked him about it to the extent of avowing to me what he had officially done. The insincerity, however, though repented of, was a warning to me which I did not forget, and while I continued for some weeks more to go to the Agency it was always with a feeling of possible betrayal at Malet's hands. I was ready, nevertheless, to help him, and it was not long before he was again obliged, by the extreme circumstances of his political isolation at Cairo, to resort to my good offices, and, finding himself in flood water altogether beyond his depth, to send me once more as his messenger of peace to Arabi and the other Nationalist leaders.

All had gone well so far, as far as any of us knew, in the political situation at Cairo down to the end of the year, and during the first week of the new year, 1882. There was a good understanding now between all parties in Egypt, the army was quiescent, the Press was moderate under Mohammed Abdu's popular censorship, and the Nationalist Ministers, undisturbed by menace from any quarter, were preparing the draft of the Organic Law which was to give the country its civil liberties. On the 26th of December, the Chamber of Delegates summoned to discuss the articles of the promised Constitution had met at Cairo, and had been opened formally with a reassuring speech by the Khedive in person, whose attitude was so changed for the better towards the popular movement that Malet was able, on the 2nd of January, to write home to Lord Granville: "I found His Highness, for the first time since my return in September, cheerful in mood and taking a hopeful view of the situation. The change was very noticeable. His Highness appears to have frankly accepted the situation." Arabi had ceased to busy himself personally with the redress of grievances, and it had been arranged with the approval of the French and English agents that Arabi should, as they expressed it, "regularize" his position and accept the responsibility of his acknowledged political influence by taking office as Under-Secretary at the War Office. This it had been thought would be putting the dangerous free lance in uniform and securing him to the cause of order.

The only doubtful point was now the attitude of the Deputies in regard to the details of the Constitution they had been assembled to discuss; and the majority of them, as were my reforming friends at the Azhar, seemed disposed to moderation. "We have waited," said Sheykh Mohammed Abdu, "so many hundred years for our freedom that we can well afford now to wait some months." Certainly at that date Malet and Colvin, and I think also Sinkiewicz, were favourably disposed to the claim of the Nationalists to have a true Parliament. They had begun to see that it was the universal national desire, and would act as a safety-valve for ideas more dangerous. A frank public declaration of goodwill at that moment on the part of the English and French Governments towards the popular hopes would have secured a workable arrangement between the Nationalist Government and the Dual Control, which would have safeguarded the bondholders' interests no less than it would have secured to Egypt its liberty. Nor did we think that this would be long delayed.

On the first day of the New Year the National Program I had sent to Mr. Gladstone was published in the "Times," with a leading article and approving comments, and in spite of Malet's prognostication of evil had been well received in Europe, and even at Constantinople where it had drawn down no kind of thunderbolt. Its tone was so studiously moderate, and its reasoning so frank and logical that it seemed impossible the position in Egypt should any longer be misunderstood. Especially in England, with an immense Liberal majority in the House of Commons, and Mr. Gladstone at the head of affairs, it was almost inconceivable that it should not be met in a friendly spirit—quite inconceivable to us who were waiting anxiously for Gladstone's answer at Cairo, that at that very moment the English Foreign Office should be proceeding to acts of menace and the language of armed intervention. Unfortunately, however, though none of us, not even Malet, at the time knew it, the decision, adverse to the Egyptian hopes, had already been half taken. The program reached Mr. Gladstone, as nearly as I can calculate it, a fortnight too late. We were all expecting a message of peace, when, like thunder in a clear sky, the ill-omened Joint Note of January 6th, 1882, was launched upon us. It upset all our hopes and calculations and threw back Egypt once more into a sea of troubles.

It is right that the genesis of this most mischievous document, to which is directly due the whole of the misfortunes during the year, with the loss to Egypt of her liberty, to Mr. Gladstone of his honour, and to France of her secular position of influence on the Nile, should be truly told. Something regarding it may be learned from the published documents, both French and English, but only indirectly, and not all; and I am perhaps the only person not officially concerned in its drafting who am in a position to put all the dots with any precision on the i's. In Egypt it has not unnaturally been supposed that, because in the event it turned to the advantage of English aggression, it was therefore an instrument forged for its own purposes at our Foreign Office, but in reality the reverse is true and the note was drafted not in Downing Street but at the Quai d'Orsay, and in the interests, so far as these were political—for they were also financial—of French ambition.

I have told already how I travelled with Sir Charles Dilke from London to Paris, and of our conversation on the way and of the impression left on me by it that he would "sell Egypt for his Commercial Treaty"; and this is precisely what in fact had happened. The dates as far as I can fix them were these: On the 15th of November St. Hilaire had gone out of office, and had been succeeded by Gambetta, who found himself faced with a general Mohammedan revolt against the French Governmen in Tunis and Algeria. He was alarmed at the Pan-Islamic character it was taking, and attributed it largely to the Sultan Abdul Hamid's propaganda, and he thought he saw the same influence at work in the National movement in Egypt, as well as the intrigues of Ismaïl, Halim, and others. France had been traditionally hostile to the sovereign claims of the Porte in North Africa, and Gambetta came into office determined to thwart and deal with them by vigorous measures. He was besides, through his Jewish origin, closely connected with the *haute finance* of the Paris Bourse, and was intimate with the Rothschilds and other capitalists, who had their millions invested in Egyptian Bonds. Nubar Pasha and Rivers Wilson were then both living at Paris, and his close friends and advisers in regard to Egyptian matters, and it was from them that he took his view of the situation.

He had, therefore, not been more than a few days in office before he entered into communication with our Foreign Office, with the object of getting England to join him in vigorous action against the National movement, as a crusade of civilization and a support to the established order at Cairo of Financial things. In London at the same time there was a strong desire to get the Commercial Treaty, which was about to expire, renewed with France as speedily as possible, and advantage was taken at the Foreign Office of Sir Charles Dilke's personal intimacy with the new French Premier to get the negotiation for it finished. A commission for this purpose, of which Dilke and Wilson were the two English members, had been sitting at Paris since the month of May, and so far without result. Dilke's visit to Paris was in connection with both matters, and was resolved on within a week of Gambetta's accession to power.

Reference to newspapers of that date, November 1881, will show that the negotiations between the two Governments about the Commercial Treaty were just then in a highly critical state, and it was even reported that they had been broken off.   Dilke's presence, however, gave them new life, or at least prevented their demise.   Between the 22nd of November and the 15th of December he passed to and fro between the two capitals; and at the latter date we find Gambetta (Blue Book Egypt 5, 1882, page 21) approaching Lord Lyons, our Ambassador at Paris, with a proposal to take common action in Egypt.   He considers it to be "extremely important to strengthen the authority of Tewfik Pasha; every endeavour should be made to inspire him with confidence in the support of France and England, and to infuse into him firmness and energy.   The adherents of Ismaïl and Halim and the Egyptians generally should be made to understand that France and England would not acquiesce in his being deposed. . . . It would be advisable to cut short the intrigues of Constantinople," etc.   This language is communicated by Lord Lyons to the Foreign Office, and on the 19th Lord Granville "agrees in thinking that the time has come when the two Governments should consider what course had better be adopted," etc.   Thus encouraged, Gambetta on the 24th proposes to take occasion of the meeting of the Egyptian Notables to make "a distinct manifestation of union between France and England so as to strengthen the position of Tewfik Pasha and discourage the promoters of disorder."   The Egyptian Chamber meets on the 26th, and on the 28th Dilke, who has returned the day before to Paris, has a long conversation with Gambetta about the Treaty of Commerce ("Times)," while on precisely the same day Lord Granville agrees to give "assurance to Tewfik Pasha of the sympathy and support of France and England, and to encourage His Highness to maintain and assert his proper authority."

This identity of date alone suffices to fix the connection between the two negotiations, and shows the precise moment at which the fatal agreement was come to, and that my communication of the National Program to Gladstone, which was posted on the 20th, must have been just too late to prevent the disaster.   Letters then took a week to reach London, and Gladstone was away for the Christmas holidays, and cannot have had time, however much he may have been inclined to do so, to forward it on to the Foreign Office. Our Government thus committed to Gambetta's policy, Gambetta on the 31st (Blue Book Egypt 5, 1882) presents to Lyons the draft, drawn up with his own hand, of the Joint Note to be despatched to Cairo in the sense of his previous communication of the 24th— and, be it noted, on the same day negotiations for a renewal of the Commercial Treaty are announced as formally renewed. On the 1st of January the Paris correspondent of the "Times" sends a précis of the Joint Note to London, explaining that he only now forwards it, having been instructed by M. Gambetta only to divulge it "at the proper moment." This is understood to mean the final success of Dilke's commercial mission, and the following day, 2nd January, he returns to London. I trace, nevertheless, the influence of my appeal to Gladstone in the delay of five days, still made by Granville before he unwillingly signs the Note, and the reservation he stipulates for on the part of Her Majesty's Government that "Her Majesty's Government must not be considered as committing themselves thereby to any particular mode of action," a postscript typical of Granville's character, and, as I think too, of a conflict in ideas, afterwards very noticeable, between the Foreign Office, pushed on by Dilke, and Gladstone as Prime Minister.

Such is the evidence which, intelligently read, can be gathered from the published documents of the day. I have, however, a letter from Sir Rivers Wilson dated a few days later, 13th January, in answer to one of mine, which explains in a few words the whole situation. "I am above all pleased," he writes, "at the interest you are taking in Egyptian politics. You confirm what I believe to be the case in two particulars at least, viz., that the soldiers express the feeling of the population, and that Tewfik has been working with the Sultan. As regards the latter circumstance I must say there is nothing surprising in it. Six weeks ago Gambetta said to me, 'Le Khedive est aux genoux du Sultan.' But the reason is plain. Tewfik is weak and cowardly. His army is against him. The Harems hate him. He found no support there where he naturally might have looked for it, viz., at the hands of the English and French Governments, and so he turned to the only quarter where sympathy and perhaps material assistance were forthcoming. It

was to remedy this state of things that the idea of the Joint
Declaration was conceived, whatever gloss or subsequent explanation may be now put forward, and I shall be disappointed
if it does not produce the desired effect and cause the officers,
Ulemas, and Notables to understand that renewed disturbance
means armed intervention in Europe. Our Government may
not like it, but they are bound now by formal engagement to
France and cannot withdraw."

This letter, coming from Wilson at Paris, holding the official
position there he did, and being, as he was, on intimate terms
both with Dilke and Gambetta, is a document of the highest
historical importance, and fixes beyond the possibility of doubt
on the French Government the initiative in the designed intervention, though the Yellow Books also are not altogether silent.
These, though most defective in their information, do not hide
Gambetta's initial responsibility. I heard at the time, and I
believe that the form of joint intervention he designed for
Egypt was that England should demonstrate with a fleet at
Alexandria while France should land troops. Had that come
to pass we cannot doubt that French influence would now be
supreme in Egypt. It was only frustrateed that winter by the
accident of Gambetta's unlooked-for fall from power by an
adverse vote on some domestic matter in the Chamber at the
end of the month, for Gladstone at that time was far too
averse from violent measures to have sent an English fleet
with a French army, and the landing of troops would have been
certainly needed.

There is more than one moral to be drawn from this historic
episode, and the most instructive is, perhaps, the fact that
neither of the two Ministers, with all their cleverness and in
spite of their apparent success each in his own scheme, really
effected his purpose. Gambetta and Granville in the first
weeks of January doubtless plumed themselves on having gained
an important object and strengthened the friendly link between
their two Governments by a common agreement. Gambetta
had got his note, Granville his treaty. But neither rogue was
really able to bring home his booty. Gambetta, though he
exerted all his influence with the Chamber to get the Commercial Treaty with England renewed, failed to obtain a majority and the treaty lapsed, and with it the Liberal argument that

Free Trade was not isolating England. On the other hand, though he had got Granville unwillingly to sign the Note, which he intended to use for the glory of France, Gambetta found that he had forged a weapon which he could not himself wield and which within six months passed into his rival's hand, while the friendly arrangement proved almost as soon as it was come to, to be the destruction of all cordial feeling between the two nations for close on a generation. Personally, in the disappointment of the two intriguers and the rival interest of the two nations, I am able to hold a detached attitude. What seems to me tragic in the matter is that for the sake of their paltry ambitions and paltrier greeds a great national hope was wrecked, and the cause of reform for a great religion postponed for many years. The opportunity of good thrown away by the two statesmen between them can hardly recur again in another half century.

The effect of Gambetta's menace to the National Party was disastrous at Cairo to the cause of peace. I was with Malet soon after the note arrived, and he gave it me to read and asked me what I thought of it. I said: "They will take it as a declaration of war." He answered: "It is not meant in a hostile sense," and explained to me how it might be interpreted in a way favourable to the National hopes. He asked me to go to the Kasr el Nil and persuade Arabi, who had just been made Under-Secretary of War, to accept it thus, authorizing me to say, "that the meaning of the Note as understood by the British Government was that the English Government would not permit any interference of the Sultan with Egypt, and would also not allow the Khedive to go back from his promises or molest the Parliament." He also told me, though he did not authorize me to repeat this on his authority, that he hoped to get leave to add to the Note a written explanation in the sense just given. I know that he telegraphed repeatedly for some such permission, and that he wrote strongly condemning the note as impolitic and dangerous. Not a word, however, of these important protests and requests is to be found in the Blue Books, though the Blue Books show that Lord Granville must have paid attention to them to the extent of expressing himself willing to give some such explanation of the Note but being prevented from doing so by Gambetta. Sinkiewicz seems also to have asked his Government to be allowed to explain the Note, but was forbidden. Sir Auckland Colvin, too, condemned the Note in conversation with me quite as strongly as Malet had done.

I went accordingly to the Kasr el Nil about noon on the 9th (the text of the Note had reached us on the 8th) and found Arabi alone in his official room. For the first and only time I have seen him so, he was angry. His face was like a thundercloud, and there was a peculiar gleam in his eye. He had seen the text of the Note though it had not been published—indeed, it had only as yet been telegraphed—and I asked him how he understood it. "Tell me, rather," he said, "how you understand it." I then delivered my message. He said: "Sir Edward Malet must really think us children who do not know the meaning of words." "In the first place," he said, "it is the language of menace. There is no clerk in this office who would use such words with such a meaning." He alluded to the reference to the Notables made in the first paragraph of the Note. "That," he said, "is a menace to our liberties." Next, the declaration that French and English policy were one meant that, as France had invaded Tunis, so England would invade Egypt. "Let them come," he said, "every man and child in Egypt will fight them. It is contrary to our principles to strike the first blow, but we shall know how to return it." Lastly, as to the guarantee of Tewfik Pasha's throne. "The throne," he said, "if there is one, is the Sultan's. The Khedive needs no foreign guarantees. You may tell me what you will, but I know the meaning of words better than Mr. Malet does." In truth, Malet's explanation was nonsense, and I felt a fool before Arabi and ashamed of having made myself the bearer of such rubbish. But I assured him I had delivered the message as Sir Edward had given it me. "He asks you to believe it," I said, "and I ask you to believe him." At leaving he softened, took me by the arm to lead me down and invited me still to come as before to his house. I said: "I shall only come back when I have better news for you," by which I intended to hint at a possible explanation of the Note such as Malet had telegraphed for permission to give. None however came. Nor did I see Arabi again till more than three weeks later, when a letter from Mr. Gladstone reached me which I interpreted in a more hopeful sense and which caused us great rejoicing.

On returning to the Residency, Malet asked me how I had fared. "They are irreconcilable now," I answered. "The Note has thrown them into the arms of the Sultan." Such indeed was the effect, and not with the soldiers alone, but as soon as the Note was published with all sections of the National Party, even with the Khedive. Gambetta, if he had expected to strengthen Tewfik's hands, had missed his mark entirely. The timid Khedive was only frightened, and the Nationalists, instead of being frightened, were enraged. The Egyptians for the first time found themselves quite united. Sheykh Mohammed Abdu and the cautious Azhar reformers from that point threw in their lot wholly with the advanced party. All, even the Circassians, resented the threat of foreign intervention, and on the other hand the most anti-Turkish of the Nationalists, such as my friend Hajrasi, saw that Arabi had been right in secretly leaning upon the Sultan. Arabi thus gained immensely in popularity and respect, and for many days after this I hardly heard anything from my Egyptian friends but the language of Pan-Islamism. It was a Roustan [1] policy over again, they said.

I did my best to smooth down matters with them till the explanation should arrive which Malet had promised us; but I found my efforts useless. It was an alarming three weeks for us all, from the delivery of the Note till Gambetta's fall. News come that a French force was being assembled for embarkation at Toulon, and that was the form of intervention generally expected. Indeed, I think it is not too much to say that Gambetta's resignation on 31st January alone saved Egypt from the misfortune, even greater perhaps than what afterwards befell her, of a French invasion avowedly anti-Mohammedan and in purely European interests.

[1] Roustan was the French diplomatist at Tunis who had engineered the French designs on the Regency.

CHAPTER IX

FALL OF SHERIF PASHA

The political crisis at Cairo, by the middle of January, was evidently approaching fast. Indeed it had become inevitable. The publication of the Joint Note happened to coincide with the drafting of the new *Leyha* or Organic Law, which was to define the power of the Representative Chamber in the promised Parliament. In regard to this, the Financial Controllers had been insisting with the Ministry that the power they had been exercising for the last two years of drawing up the yearly Budget, according to their own view of the economic requirements of the country, should remain intact, that is to say, that it should not be subject to discussion or a vote in the Chamber; and to this Sherif Pasha had agreed, and had already drafted his project of law without assigning to the Chamber any right in money matters. The majority of the delegates, however, were not unnaturally dissatisfied at this, arguing that the Foreign Financial Control, having its sole status in the country as guardian of the foreign obligations, and as the interest on the debt amounted only to one-half of the revenue, the remaining half ought to be at the disposal of the nation.

Nevertheless, there is no reason to suppose that the point would not have been conceded by them, especially as Sultan Pasha, who had been named their President, was with Sherif in considering it prudent to yield, had things remained during the month as they were at the beginning. It has been seen how readily the War Office had come to terms with the Controllers in the matter of the Army Estimates. Now, however, under the menace of the Note, the Notables were no longer in a mood of conciliation, and met Sherif's draft with a counterdraft of their own, adding a number of new articles to the Leyha, largely extending the Parliamentary powers, and subjecting the half of the Budget not affected to the interest of the debt to vote by the Chamber. This brought the Controllers into active conflict with them, M. de Blignières taking the lead in it and bringing Colvin into line with him. The Controllers declared it absolutely necessary that the Budget should remain whole and undivided in their hands, and denounced the counter-draft as being a project, not of a Parliament, but of a "Convention." The phrase, founded on memories of the French Revolution, was doubtless de Blignières', but it was adopted by Colvin, and pressed by him on Malet. The dispute was a serious one, and might lead to just such mischief as Malet feared, and give excuse to the French Government for the intervention it was seeking. Sherif having already committed himself to the Controllers' view, was being persuaded by them to stand firm, and the Khedive's attitude was doubtful. A quarrel between the Khedive and his Parliament on a financial question involving European bondholding interests was just such a case as the French Government—for Gambetta was still in office—might be expected to take advantage of for harm.

In this emergency Malet—and Colvin, who though he wished to get his way as Financial Controller had no mind for French intervention—joined in asking me yet once again to help them, and to make a last effort to induce the extreme party among the Notables to yield something of their pretensions, and after consultation with Sheykh Mohammed Abdu, who as usual was for prudence and conciliation, it was arranged that I should have a private conference at his house with a deputation from them, and argue the case with them, and show them the probable consequences of their resistance—namely, armed intervention. Accordingly, I got up the case of the Controllers with Colvin, and drew up with Malet the different points of the argument I was to use. These I have by me in a paper headed, "Notes of what I have to say to the Members of the Egyptian Parliament, 17th January, 1882."

According to this my instructions were to represent to the Members of the Deputation that the existing procedure respecting the Budget was an international affair, which neither Sherif nor the Parliament had any right to touch without gaining the consent of the two controlling Governments. I was to recite the history of the Control's establishment, and show them a private Note which had been appended by Malet and Monge (the French Consul-General), 15th November, 1879, to the Decree instituting it.   I was to invite the members to consider whether an alteration in the form of determining the Budget was not an international matter, and, as such, outside the sphere of their action.   They had admitted that international matters must be left untouched by them.   The control of the Budget was an international matter.   Therefore it should be left untouched by them.   I was, however, authorized by Colvin to say that personally he had no objection to a slight modification of the present arrangement, such as should give the Parliament a consultative voice which might later become a right of voting.   Should they accept such a compromise, Malet would represent the matter favourably to his Government, though he had no authority to promise its acceptance by France or England.   All other differences with Sherif they must settle with him themselves, etc., etc.

On this basis, with Sabunji's help and Mohammed Abdu's, I argued the case thoroughly with them, and convinced myself that there was no possibility of their yielding.   They agreed, indeed, to modify three or four of the articles which the Controllers had principally objected to as giving the Chamber powers of a "Convention," and the amendments I proposed in these were in fact incorporated later in the published Leyha.   But on the Article of the Budget they were quite obdurate, notwithstanding the support Sheykh Mohammed Abdu gave me.   They would not yield a line of it, and I returned crestfallen to report my failure, nor did I again undertake any mission of mediation between Malet and the Nationalists.   I had done my best to help him to a peaceful solution of his difficulties, but our points of view from this time forth became too divergent for me any longer to be able to work with him.   Although I had done my very best to persuade the Notables to give way—for I was then firmly convinced that they were menaced with intervention—I could not help in my inner mind agreeing with them in their claim of controlling the free half of the Budget as a sound one, if Parliamentary Government was to be a reality for them, not a sham.   Malet's despatches of the time show that they were all of one mind on this point, and even Sultan Pasha, who was a timid man and easily frightened, declared roundly that Sherif's draft was "like a drum; it made a great sound but was hollow inside." As between Sherif and the Notables in the quarrel which followed, my anti-Turkish sympathies put me on their side rather than on his. At Malet's suggestion I had a little before called on Sherif and had discussed the matter with him, and had been unfavourably impressed.

Sherif was a Europeanized Turk of good breeding and excellent manners, but with all that arrogant contempt of the fellahin which distinguished his class in Egypt. Malet had a high opinion of him because he was a good French scholar and so was easy to deal with in the ordinary diplomatic way, but to me he showed himself for this very reason in disagreeable contrast with the sincere and high-minded men who were the real backbone of the National movement, and for whom he expressed nothing but the superior scorn of a fine French gentleman. He was cheerfully convinced of his own fitness to govern them and of their incapacity. "The Egyptians," he told me, "are children and must be treated like children. I have offered them a Constitution which is good enough for them, and if they are not content with it they must do without one. It was I who created the National Party, and they will find that they cannot get on without me. These peasants want guidance." When, therefore, a fortnight later the quarrel became an open one between him and them I had no difficulty in deciding which way my sympathies lay.

I was no longer at Cairo when the news of Sherif's resignation on the 2nd of February reached me. The failure of my negotiation, just described, with the Notables, had depressed my spirits. I felt that by undertaking it I had risked much of my popularity with my European friends, and that they perhaps distrusted me for the pains I had taken to convince them against a course on which their hearts were set; and I had retired to a distance from the conflict which I could no longer control or help in to any good purpose. While living at the Hôtel du Nil during the winter I had all the time had a camp with tents and camels and attendant Arabs, pitched outside the city, to which I had occasionally gone, and now I retired to it altogether. The camp was pitched on the desert land between Koubba Palace and Matarieh, then a wholly desert region at a point now called Zeitoun, where there were the insignificant ruins of what had

once been a *shaduf,* the sole sign of human habitation. Here
we were completely alone, except that at the distance of a mile
there was another camp, that of Prince Ahmed, outside Materieh.   There was no communication then by any form of public
conveyance with Cairo, and when at rare intervals we went in,
we rode our camels to a point between Abbassiyeh and Faggalah
where donkeys were to be hired.   There was not a single house
on the sands beyond Abbassiyeh to the north-east.   For a moment thus I was able to forget politics and to enjoy what I have
always loved best, life in the open air.   I had, however, rendered a last service to my friends by writing a warm defence of
the Egyptian National policy in the "Times."   To this I was
urged by my friend, Sir William Gregory, who had himself sent
more than one powerful letter in the same sense to what was
then emphatically the leading journal of Europe.

It is hardly possible to exaggerate the importance a letter on
any subject had in those days when published by the "Times,"
and the certainty there was, if it was on any political question, of
its being read by the statesmen concerned and treated with full
attention.   Nor is it, perhaps, too much to say that Gregory's
letters and mine, especially his, were largely the means of obtaining a respite for Egypt from the dangers that threatened
her.   As they came back to Cairo and were reproduced in Arabic by the native Press, our Egyptian friends were reassured
about us and their confidence in me revived.   It was at the expense, however, of Malet's goodwill.   Like all diplomatists he
hated publicity, and he was angry with us both because we, who
had both been in the Government service, had appealed as it
were over the head of the Foreign Office and his own to the
Press.   With the regular Press correspondents he knew how to
deal, but he could not deal with us who were independent writers, or exercise the smallest censorship on our opinions.   There
was an end therefore to the close intimacy I had, up to that
point, in spite of small disagreements, had with the Agency.
This was unfortunate, as it threw Malet, who always needed
to lean on some one stronger than himself, into other and less
conciliatory hands.

On the 31st of January, the very day of the change of
Ministry at Paris, I find a note to the effect that I went in to
Cairo and saw Colvin and had a remarkable conversation with

him. This has become of great historical importance through subsequent events, for it marks the date within a few days of the change of the temper of the English Financial Control, and with it of our diplomacy towards Egyptian Nationalism, and also fixes upon Colvin, what is indeed his due, the chief responsibility of the rupture which afterwards through his contriving came about. I have already said something of Sir Auckland Colvin's character. He was a typical Anglo-Indian official, strong, self-reliant, hard, with the tradition of methods long practised in India, but which were still new to our European diplomacy, endowed with just enough sympathy with Oriental character to make use of it, without loving it, for English purposes; but cold in manner and unattractive. I had at an earlier stage of affairs taken Sheykh Mohammed Abdu to call on him, thinking to bring about a *rapprochement,* and I had also tried to do the same with the officers. But his manner had repelled the Sheykh, and the officers had been too shy to come with me. He was sometimes astonishingly frank in speech. I remember his telling me, on one occasion, when we were talking of Eastern duplicity, that it was a mistake to suppose that in this Orientals were our masters. An Englishman who knew the game, he said, could always beat them at their own weapons, and they were mere children in deceit when it came to a contest with us.

In the present instance he was more than usually outspoken. The quarrel between the Notables and Sherif was at its acutest stage; and I asked him what he thought of the situation. He said he considered it most grave. It was evident that the Nationalists were resolved upon the fall of Sherif, and, if they succeeded, he (Colvin) would have no more to do with them. He told me he had completely changed his mind about them. He had thought them amenable to reason, but he found them quite impracticable, and he would do his best to ruin them if ever they came into office. I asked him how he proposed to do this, or stop a movement which he had so lately approved, but which had gone quite beyond his or anybody's control—how, except by that very intervention we had all along been trying to avoid. He said he had changed his mind about intervention too; that he believed it now to be necessary and inevitable, and that he would spare no pains to bring it about. I expostulated with him,

urging that intervention meant only war and war meant only annexation. He said he quite understood it in that sense. The
same thing had been seen over and over again in India. England
would never give up the footing she had got in Egypt, and it was
useless to talk about the abstract rights and wrongs of the Egyptians. These would not be considered. He repeated what he
had said about ruining the National Party, and added that he
had made no secret of his view. He should work for intervention and, if it must be so, for annexation. I am quite sure I am
not mis-quoting this conversation in any essential feature. It
was not merely half a dozen words spoken in haste, but an argument which lasted half an hour; and it affected me so strongly
that I decided to warn my Egyptian friends, to whom I had
pledged my word for Colvin's good feeling towards them, that
they must now expect the worst of him. They answered that
they knew it, as they had received information already in the
same sense about him.

This conversation opened my eyes to a new danger. Only the
day before I had received two letters, written the one from the
Liberal, the other from the Tory camp in England, and both
conveying the same warning. John Morley, in answer to a letter I had written asking his sympathy with the National cause,
wrote: "Whether your schemes will come to much I am at this
moment inclined to doubt. Egypt, unluckily for its people, is
the battlefield of European rivalries; and an honest settlement in
the interests of its population will be prevented to suit the convenience of France. I don't see my way out of it. It is that
curse of the world, *la haute politique,* which will spoil everything." Lytton also had written: "That small portion of the
British public which thinks at all of foreign affairs is much pre-
occupied and disturbed in mind by the false position into which
we are drifting in Egypt, and almost too frightened to speak
loudly on the subject. It seems to me, however, that their ideas
are very hazy. In my own mind there is no doubt that this is
only the firstfruits of a radically wrong policy which has lost
us the co-operation of Germany and Austria, and placed us practically at the mercy of France, a power with which we can never
have any sound or safe alliance." Both letters had been written
before the fall of Gambetta, and here I seemed to hear an echo
of their words, especially Morley's words, la haute politique,"

from the man who had it most in his power to spoil an honest settlement, and that to suit the convenience, not of France merely,
but of England.   I was very much alarmed.   I have often regretted my last words to Colvin on this occasion.   "I defy you,"
I said, "to bring about English intervention or annexation."   I
regret it because I think it added a personal as well as a political stimulus to his subsequent action.   It had become a trial of
strength between us.

Two days later, 2nd February, Sherif Pasha, finding he could
not bend the National Delegates to his will, and under the influence, I make little doubt, of Colvin's threat of intervention,
resigned office, and was succeeded, at the choice of the Delegates,
by Mahmud Pasha Sami as Prime Minister, with Arabi as Minister of War, a thoroughgoing Nationalist combination at which
all Egypt rejoiced.[1]   I heard the news at my retreat in the
desert with mixed feelings of jubilation and anxiety, an anxiety
which was only relieved when on the 27th I received an answer
from Mr. Gladstone to my letter of six weeks before enclosing
to him the National program.   The long delay in replying
was doubtless due to the embarrassment and perplexity as to a
policy which Lord Granville's deal with Gambetta had involved
him in.   Gambetta's providential fall, however, had now to a
large extent freed our Government's hands, and a passage was
being inserted in the Queen's speech at the opening of Parliament which conveyed something like an expression of sympathy
with the National Egyptian hopes.   This, Mr. Gladstone sent
me later, and his letter concluded with the following reassuring
words: "I feel quite sure," he said, "that unless there be a sad
failure of good sense on one or both, or as I should say, on all

[1] There were one or two weak points in the formation of the new Ministry, the
most important being in the choice made of their Minister of Foreign Affairs.
Neither Mahmud Sami nor Arabi, nor any other of the fellah leaders, knew any
European language, and, as a knowledge of French was essential in dealing
with the Consulates, a man not of their own party or way of thinking was taken
in from the outside.   This was Mustafa Pasha Fehmi, a man of fairly liberal
notions, but a member of the old ruling class, and a follower of Sherif's—the
same who had been Ismaïl's A. D. C. in 1878 and had taken an unwilling part in
the death of the Mufettish.   It was his horror at this crime that had converted
him to constitutional ideas.   But like Sherif he despised his fellah colleagues.   He,
when the pinch came two months later, did these much ill-service by his weak
or hostile presentment of their case in the official correspondence.   This, as they
could not read his notes and despatches, they were unaware of till it was too
late to remedy.

sides, we shall be able to bring this question to a favourable issue.   My own opinions about Egypt were set forth in the 'Nineteenth Century' a short time before we took office, and I am not
aware as yet of having seen any reason to change them." [1]

The reference thus made to his article "Aggression on Egypt,"
was of the very highest importance, for, as already mentioned,
the article was a scathing denunciation of just that forward policy
of intervention and annexation which Colvin had propounded to
me.   Armed with this proof of Gladstone's goodwill I went back
joyfully to Cairo, and was able to tell Arabi that I had not assured him of my sympathy in vain.   I found him at the War
Office surrounded by his friends, and in converse with the Coptic
Patriarch, and with a tribe of idle sycophants as well, Levantines
and Europeans, come to salute the rising sun.   Among these the
new Minister moved with a certain dignified superiority which
became him well.   He was no longer the mere colonel of a regiment, but a man sobered by the sense of public responsibility, a
fellah still, and still a patriot, but also with the manner of a
statesman.   He took me aside, and I showed him Gladstone's
letter, and we rejoiced over it together as a message of good
omen.

The first fruits of Colvin's hostility, nevertheless, we had not
long to wait for.   Who precisely was the originator of the lie I
do not know, it was probably the Khedive, whose malicious jeal-
cusy was already at work against his Ministers, but a false report was telegraphed by Reuter to Europe that the action taken
by the Notables against Sherif was due to military intimidation.
A story was related and was repeated at some length in the
"Times" to the effect that Sultan Pasha, the president of the
Chamber, had only yielded to personal menace, and that Arabi
had drawn his sword in his presence, and had threatened to
make the old man's children fatherless.   It was a foolish tale,
for Sultan happened to be without offspring, and at Cairo it
was laughed at by all who knew the truth, and how close an intimacy there was between the two, but it was sufficient as a
weapon to "ruin the Nationalists," and easily passed the censorship of the Agency, being reproduced even in Malet's despatches
of the day, as was a similar tale, which had also been telegraphed,

[1] For full text of this letter *see* Appendix.

that the Khedive's acceptance of Sherif's resignation had been extorted under a like pressure.

Absurd, however, as the tale was, Sultan was offended by it, and, as I was now generally known to the Deputies as their friend, he begged me to call on him and convey to Malet his emphatic denial of the whole story. I consequently went to Sultan's house, where he had assembled a large party of Deputies and other high personages, among whom were the Grand Mufti el Abbasi, Abd el Salaam Bey Mouelhy, Ahmed Bey Siouffi, Ahmed Effendi, Mahmud, Rahman Effendi, Hamadi, and El Shedid Butros, a leading Coptic deputy. All these, with Sultan, absolutely denied and repudiated the idea that they had acted under any kind of pressure, and Sultan spoke with indignation of the absurdity of the tale as regarded himself. "Ahmed Arabi," he said, "is as a son to me, and knows what is due to me and due to himself. His place is at the War Office, mine with the Parliament. It is of me that he would ask advice rather than venture to give me any on my own concerns, and as to his drawing his sword in my presence he could only do so if I were attacked by enemies. These are stories which no one who knows us both could for an instant believe, and they are absolutely false. You may take it for certain that the least of the members present who represent the people are better judges of their wants than the greatest of the soldiers. We respect Ahmed Arabi because we know him to be a patriot and a man of political intelligence, not because he is a soldier." These words of Sultan Pasha's are quoted from a memorandum I made of them at the time. The old man also spoke bitterly of Malet for encouraging the newsmongers, and begged me to tell him the facts, and also to telegraph them to Mr. Gladstone, and make them known in the London press. This I did to the best of my ability. I sent a full account of it to the "Times," though, if I remember rightly, it was, for some reason, never printed, and I telegraphed in the same sense to Mr. Gladstone, and also wrote him a long letter giving my view of the general situation.

To Malet I went straight from Sultan's house and expostulated with him warmly. But he insisted on the truth of his tale, which he had got, he told me first, from Sultan himself, and then not from Sultan but at second hand from "some one on whom he could depend," and, when I pressed him further as to who this was, lost temper and said I had no right to cross-question him.   This was my last talk with him on any political matter.   Malet's new attitude proved to me that he, like Colvin, had gone over to the enemy's camp, and was now no longer to be trusted.   I saw that the situation was a very dangerous one, for between them they had the Press and the Foreign Office wholly in their hands, and though I possessed at home the Prime Minister's ear and a certain publicity for my views in the "Times," I felt that I was fighting against them at an extreme disadvantage.   I consequently decided to delay no longer my return to England, where I could do more for the Egyptian interests than I could at Cairo, by word of mouth and by a personal appeal to Gladstone.   Before going, however, I had numerous conversations with the leading Deputies and with my friends at the Azhur, to whom I communicated my design, of which they all approved; and I arranged with Sir William Gregory that after my departure he should continue to defend the National cause, in which he was as enthusiastic as I was, in the "Times" and by letter with his friends in England.   My thought was to return to Egypt, perhaps, in a few weeks' time, and take part in any further developments that might arise.

I paid a last visit to Arabi the morning of the day I left for England, 27th February.   I had been little more than three months in Egypt, and it seemed to me like a lifetime, so absorbing had been the interests they had brought me.   I looked upon Egypt already like a second *patria,* and intended to throw in my lot with the Egyptians as if they were my own countrymen. I was estranged from those of my countrymen in blood, except Gregory, who formed the then little English colony at Cairo. Following Colvin's lead they had all gone over like sheep to ideas of intervention, for be it noted that it was now no longer French intervention that was talked of, but English, and at once in English eyes the immorality of aggression had been transformed into a duty.   What had been abominable when threatened by Gambetta now appealed to them as just and desirable and patriotic when proposed by Granville.   Similarly the new Prime Minister at Paris, M. de Freycinet, having reversed his predecessor's policy of intervention, the French colony were for peace with the Nationalists, all except de Blignières and those who had official posts they feared might be suppressed in the new reign of National economy.

Colvin and de Blignières were industrious in spreading trepidation among the holders of sinecure offices, and it was amusing to note how suddenly and completely the poet Lord Houghton abandoned his first attitude of romantic sympathy with Egyptian liberty when his son-in-law, Fitzgerald, who had one of these sinecures, represented to him that his daily bread was thereby threatened. It was well known, as part of the Nationalist program, that it was intended to reduce the expenditure on unnecessary salaries and to suppress the duplicated posts. This was ascribed by Colvin not to its true cause, a very legitimate economy, but to "fanaticism," a convenient word which began now to be freely used in describing the National movement. What, however, I think more than anything else was condemned just then by the little group of English officials was the "monstrous" determination which the Egyptian Chamber was said to have come to, if it could secure the right of voting the Budget, to cut down the subvention of £1,000 a year paid to Reuter's Agency. Without this it was felt that it would be impossible any longer to know at Cairo the odds on the Oxford and Cambridge boat race or even on the Derby or Grand Prix. There was a dark hint, too, thrown out that the charge of £9,000 a year then figuring in the Budget as a grant in aid to the European Opera House might be reduced, and on this astounding proof of "fanaticism," Fitzgerald, as a patron of the ballet, was especially insistent. These things, with others almost as trifling, were made a serious crime to the Notables and to the new Ministry, who were countenancing the reductions. I used to hear the tale of their complaints from Gregory, who was now in much closer touch with them than I any longer was. It was in answer to their threats of intervention, which were beginning to have an effect on the Stock Exchange in the lowered price of Egyptian Bonds and of property generally in Egypt, that I at this time resolved to give proof of my confidence in the national fortunes by buying a small estate for my future residence in the neighbourhood of Cairo, and the result was my purchase of Eheykh Obeyd Garden, a property of some forty acres, between Merj and Materieh.

It will be interesting to Egyptian readers to know what the

prices of land in that neighbourhood then were. There was, as I have said, at that time not a single house built on the desert strip between Abbassiyeh and Kafr el Jamus, and the Government was willing to sell it to anybody who would buy it at the rate of a few piastres an acre. I thought at one moment of establishing myself on the land where my camp of the moment stood, and I made inquiry of my friend Rogers Bey, who was in the Land Department of the Ministry of Finance, and I find among my papers the draft of an application I sent in for a hundred acres, where now the suburb of Zeitoun stands, for which, at his suggestion, I offered fifteen piastres (three shillings) an acre. The same land is worth to-day, 1904, at least two hundred pounds an acre, ground value. But while I was in negotiation for it I chanced to hear that Sheykh Obeyd Garden was in the market, and I purchased it, so to say, "over the counter" from the Domains' Commission for £1,500. It was then the best fruit garden in Egypt, enclosed in a wall with a bountiful supply of water, and contained, on estimation, 70,000 fruit trees, all in splendid order.

The history of the garden is worth recording. It was a piece of good land standing on the desert edge, belonging in the early part of the nineteenth century to the Imam of Ibrahim Pasha's army during the campaign of Arabia but the Imam falling into indigent circumstances, the Pasha bought it of him, enclosed thirty-three acres with a wall, dug the sakiehs, and laid it out as it now is some time in the early thirties. The fruit trees with which it was planted were brought in part from Taif in the Hejaz, in part from Syria. Ibrahim had a passion to make it the best of its kind, and in his time and the time of his nephew, Mustafa, to whom it descended, the fruit from it brought in a yearly revenue of £800, the labour being all done by *corvée* of the fellahin of the neighbouring villages. The pomegranates of the garden were so large that it was a tradition with the gardeners there that thirty went to a camel load, and that they were sent yearly to Constantinople as a present to the Sultan. What is certain is that in the time of Ibrahim's grandson, Tewfik, when in his father's reign he was living in retirement at Koubba, the ladies of his household used to be carried there every Friday during the spring season to spend the day.

In the ruin of Ismaïl's fortunes it came, in 1879, to the Domains Commissioners, and was one of the smaller properties scheduled by them for sale, and so it chanced into the market. On our way to Syria the year before we had camped one night outside its walls and had wondered at its beauty with the apricot trees in full flower. No sooner did I hear of it as a possible acquisition than I abandoned all other schemes of purchase; and in one of its shady walks I am writing my memoirs to-day.

But to return to my farewell visit to Arabi. On this occasion we talked all the questions over which were being debated at the moment by the Nationalists with their plans of reforms and their hopes and fears at home and abroad. The few weeks that Arabi had been in high office had matured him and strengthened him, and he discussed things with me with all possible sobriety of thought and language. He assured me emphatically that he and his fellow Ministers were most anxious to come to a friendly understanding with the English Government on all matters in dispute between them and the Agency at Cairo; and he begged me to convey to Mr. Gladstone a formal message to that effect. He complained, however, strongly of Malet and Colvin, whose recent action and the part they were taking in the campaign of misrepresentation being organized in the English Press proved their hostility. "There will never be peace at Cairo," he said, "as long as we have only these to deal with, for we know that they are working mischief against us in secret, if not openly. We shall stand aloof from both of them. But we do not on that account wish to quarrel with England. Let Mr. Gladstone send us whom he will to treat with us, and we will receive him with open arms." He also talked at great length of the practical reforms Mahmud Sami and the other Ministers were contemplating, most of which have since been included in the list of benefits conferred on the country under British occupation, and which Lord Cromer has adopted as his own. Such were the abolition of the *corvées* which the rich Turkish pashas levied on the villagers, their monopoly of the water at the time of the high Nile, the protection of the fellahin from the Greek usurers, who had them in their clutches through the iniquitous abuses of the International Tribunals,

and even that latest remedy for agriculture distress on which
Lord Cromer specially prides himself, an agricultural Bank
under Government direction.

Other questions discussed were the reform of Justice, then
fearfully corrupt, the education of men and also of women, the
mode of election to be adopted for the new Parliament, and the
question of slavery.   On this point he dwelt at some length,
because the European officials of the department concerned in
its suppression were beginning, like the other foreign officials,
to fear that in the new National scheme of economy their salaries would be reduced, and were pretending that the Mohammedan revival would mean a revival of the slave trade.   Arabi
showed me how little ground there was for this pretence, that
the only persons in Egypt who still had slaves or wished to
have slaves were just the Khedivial princes and rich pashas,
against whose tyranny the fellah movement was directed, that
according to the principles of the Liberal reform all men were
to be henceforth equal, without distinction of race, or colour,
or religion.   The last thing compatible with these was the revival of slavery.   Lastly, as to the necessity of military preparation for a possible war, which as a soldier and war minister
he had uppermost in his mind, he spoke plainly and with energy.
The National Government would not disarm or relax its precautions until the true Constitutional *régime* was firmly established and acknowledged by Europe.   He hoped not to exceed
the War Estimates agreed on with Colvin, or to be obliged to
increase the number of men recruited beyond the 18,000 allowed by the Firmans.   If, however, the menace of armed intervention were long continued they would adopt the Prussian
system of short service, and so gradually bring a larger force
as a reserve under arms.   He asked my opinion of the chances
of a conflict, and I told him plainly that from what Colvin had
boasted to me of his intention to bring it about, and from the
means of Press agitation he had already adopted with that end,
I considered the danger a real one, and that it was to neutralize,
as far as I could, the campaign of lies which had begun that I
was going to England.   My business there would be to preach
the cause of peace and goodwill.   At the same time I could not
advise him to do otherwise than stand firmly to his ground.
The best chance of peace was to be prepared for defence.   The

great enemies of Egypt were not so much the European governments as the European financiers, and these would think twice about urging an armed attack if they knew that they could not do so without the risk of ruining their own interests in Egypt by a long and costly war. An armed nation resolute and ready to defend its rights was seldom molested. I remember quoting to him Byron's lines, "Trust not for freedom to the Franks," of which he greatly approved; and these, I think, were our last words. I promised him that if it came to the worst I would return and throw in my lot with theirs in a campaign for independence.

CHAPTER X

MY PLEADING IN DOWNING STREET

Such is the history faithfully and fully told of the part I played that winter in Egypt. In telling it I have relied for the accuracy of my memory of the main incidents on such letters and short notes as I have been able to find among my papers, and especially on an account of it drawn up by me while the war of 1882 was in progress, and published in the September number of the "Nineteenth Century Review" of that year. Of this, my present memoir is little more than an amplification. What follows will be comparatively new matter, for though most of it has long been written in a disjointed way, I have never found a moment suited to its completion. For dates and incidents, however, I am supplied with ample materials of a contemporary value, first in a brief diary which from the time of my arrival in England I now once more regularly kept, and next in the many published and unpublished letters still in my possession, which passed between me and various public personages with whom I had found myself in correspondence during the four months which elapsed between my arrival in England and the bombardment of Alexandria; and again after Tel-el-Kebir with those who on my behalf were conducting Arabi's trial. These form a body of evidence which I shall quote where needful, either in the text of my narrative or in an appendix to it. Taken together, with the necessary thread of explanation, they of themselves form an almost complete history of the causes of the war.

The political situation which I found on my arrival, 6th March, in London, was a wonderful contrast to that which I had left behind me a week before at Cairo. Gladstone had been now nearly two years in office, and the enthusiasm for Eastern nationalities and Eastern liberty, which at the elections

of 1880 had carried him into power, had cooled down everywhere, and in official circles had given place to ideas of imperial
coercion, especially in the case of the Nationalists of Ireland,
which were by no means of good augury in regard to Egypt.
The Cabinet was divided into two sections of opinion. The
great Whig leaders who controlled the chief departments of
the Administration, Hartington, Northbrook, Childers, and the
rest were all for strong measures, Gladstone, with Harcourt and
Bright, almost alone for conciliation, and the general feeling of
the country was violent against all "lawlessness" everywhere.
The Habeas Corpus Act had been suspended in Ireland, and
Parnell and a score more of the Nationalist members of Parliament were actually shut up, untried, in Kilmainham Gaol.
Business in the House of Commons was being obstructed by the
remainder of the Irish members, and the very name of Nationalism to the Liberal Party had become a byword and reproach.
The atmosphere of Westminister and the public offices was therefore not at all favourable to my propaganda of nationalism on
the Nile. The only persons really interested in Egypt were
those few who held Egyptian bonds, and these had been persuaded by Colvin's manipulation of the Press that Arabi and
the National Party were a set of fanatical incendiaries who
would burn down the Stock Exchange if they could get the
chance, and who had already succeeded in lowering the value
of securities and making dividends precarious.

At the Foreign Office the position about Egypt was this.
Granville, old and deaf and very idle, finding himself relieved
from the incubus of Gambetta's forward policy, was following
his instinct of doing nothing and letting things settle themselves
as placidly as circumstances would allow him. He did not want
to intervene or to take action hostile to the Nationalists or,
indeed, action of any kind. He did not even give himself the
trouble to read the despatches, and he left the work of learning
what was going on to his private secretaries, and more especially
to the Under-Secretary of State, Sir Charles Dilke, who was
able to sift the news for him and set before him such facts as
he selected, and such views as suited him. Dilke, who had been
with Gambetta the responsible author of the Joint Note of 6th
January, was, now that Gambetta had disappeared from the
direction of affairs in France, become a prime mover on his own

account in the policy of intervention, and was working with Colvin and the financiers to bring things to such a pass that his unwilling chief, in spite of himself, should be obliged to intervene. Though not himself a Cabinet Minister, Dilke in this had behind him the powerful support in the Cabinet of Chamberlain, a personal friend and ally, whom on foreign matters, which Chamberlain did not affect to understand, he could securely count on. The two together had the reputation of being the most advanced Radicals in the Ministry, and so carried great weight with just that section of the Liberal Party which was least inclined on principle to foreign adventures. The mass of the Radicals in the House of Commons knew nothing and cared nothing for questions in dispute so far away.

Nevertheless I found that personally I could command considerable attention. My letters to the "Times" had been widely read, and there was a certain curiosity to hear what I had to say. Gregory and I had managed to invest Arabi with that halo of romance which as champion of the fellah wrongs was certainly his due, and on that ground, if no other, I could always obtain a hearing. Rumours of all kinds were afloat about him, ludicrous tales which portrayed him as a Frenchman or a Spaniard in Egyptian guise, as the paid agent, in turn of the ex-Khedive Ismaïl, of the pretender Halim, and of the Sultan—as everything in fact but what he really was. I, who had seen him, could explain. It was a matter not of serious interest with anybody, but, as I have said, of considerable curiosity. And so I was listened to.

My first visit on arrival was to 10, Downing Street. Here, though I did not see Mr. Gladstone himself, I found my friend Hamilton, his private secretary, and had with him an altogether satisfactory talk. I was a little doubtful, seeing that I had quarrelled with Malet, how I might be received. But he hastened to assure me that my "interference" with Malet's diplomacy was in no way resented by his chief. On the contrary, Mr. Gladstone was very much obliged to me for my letters, and for the line I had taken in Egypt. It was a busy time for him, however, just then, the busiest of the official year, the weeks before Easter, and the thoughts of ministers were elsewhere than in Egypt. The Irish question was priming everything in Mr. Gladstone's mind. I might, however, make my own mind comfortable about the dangers which seemed to threaten at Cairo. They could not lead to serious trouble. Whatever might be the ideas "over the way" (meaning the Foreign Office), Mr. Gladstone would see that they were not put in practice. Armed intervention with Mr. Gladstone in power was an "impossibility." The mere thought of it was ridiculous. We would talk of it again and I should see Mr. Gladstone later. In the meanwhile Hamilton would let Lord Granville know that I was come. I left him entirely reassured.

Another visit I paid the same morning was to my cousin, Algernon Bourke (then generally known as "Button" to his friends). His rôle in Egyptian affairs that year was destined to be an important one, and his name, or rather his pseudo-name, constantly recurs in my diary. His position in life was that of a young man of fashion, closely connected with the official world, for he was a younger son of the Lord Mayo who had been Viceroy of India, and was nephew to the Rt. Hon. Robert Bourke (afterwards Lord Connemara), who had been Under-Secretary for Foreign Affairs, and was now, in 1882, leader of the Tory opposition in the House of Commons on all questions of foreign politics. Button had also a position on the staff of the "Times," not as a writer, but as an intermediary for Chenery, the editor, with political personages. As a peer's son he had the *entrée* to the galleries of both Houses of Parliament, knew everybody and everything that was going on there, was intimate with people about the Court, with the high world of finance, and generally with the wire-pullers in the various departments of the State. Our friendship was a close one, and throughout the trying months that followed he was my chief confidant and adviser, having more worldly wisdom than I then could boast, and a fertility of resource in action altogether admirable. To him I owed three parts of the publicity I obtained for my views in the Press, and of the help given me in parliament. On arrival I narrated to him all that had happened during the past winter in Egypt as well as my plans for the future. His view of the position was a very different one from Hamilton's, for his intimacy with the Rothschilds made him aware of the financial strings that were being pulled in the City to bring about intervention, and he had a low opinion of Gladstone's ability to understand foreign questions or deal with a case where the money interests of all the Stock Exchanges of Europe were so largely concerned. Still he advised me to maintain the footing I had acquired in Downing Street, and use my influence there to the best of my ability, holding in reserve, if Gladstone should fail me, his own friends of the Opposition, whose assistance, in case of need, he promised me. For the moment the best I could do would be to talk to everybody I knew who was in Parliament on both sides of the House, and to go on writing letters to the "Times." This sound advice I accordingly proceeded without delay to follow.

I find in my diary that on the 9th of March I went to see George Howard and his wife (now Lord and Lady Carlisle), and succeeded in enlisting their sympathies, especially hers, to my plans. She was then, as now, a strong politician, and was an absolute believer in Gladstone, and she advised me to put my whole trust in him and he would certainly prevent any mischief being done to liberty. Her husband was less sanguine, but he readily agreed to take me to the House of Commons, of which he was a member, that afternoon, and introduce me to his friends there of the Liberal Party, such as he thought could help me best. And so together we went, and I made the acquaintance of Dilwyn, Bryce, and other influential members who had been specially interested in the affairs of Bulgaria and Armenia at the time of the Berlin Congress. These all promised me their assistance, as did that excellent man Mr. Chesson, with whom, and with Howard's brother-in-law, Lyulph Stanley, we had a long talk in the tea-room. Chesson, though not a Member of Parliament, was a person of considerable political power, as he made it his business, as secretary of the Aborigines Protection Society, to organize agitations on all questions where aggression on non-European peoples was threatened, and he proved throughout of the greatest assistance to me, as he was in daily communication with the best of the Radical members. Howard, however, advised me not to put my case into the hands of the "professional non-interventionists," but rather to work my propaganda on an independent basis. I was at that time quite new and inexperienced in English politics, so new that though I was forty-one years of age this was the first time I had ever been inside the lobbies of the House of Commons. I was, however, from that date a frequent visitor there, across to the inner lobby being at that time almost free.

The same day I had a talk with Philip Currie at the Foreign Office, and a long discussion about Egypt. I found him at first rather put out with me at what I had been doing at Cairo, the effect of Malet's complaints of me, and affecting to believe that I had been playing a "large practical joke at the expense of the Foreign Office." But this did not last, and I was able to convince him of the seriousness of the matter, and of my own earnestness, if not that I was right in my views, and he arranged that I should see Dilke the next day, and also Granville.

I find also at this date that I had a talk with Lord Miltown, an Irish peer, which shows the curious connection between Egypt and Ireland in the political ideas of the day. "His, Miltown's, account of Ireland is singularly like that of Egypt by the European officials. He thinks the difficulty in Ireland got up by agitators; that the Irish fellahin are not really with the National Party, and that armed intervention would set things right."

On the 10th I saw Dilke at the Foreign Office, having first gone to his house in Sloane Street. He was in a hostile mood, and instead of listening to what I had to say, poured out a string of complaints against the new Egyptian ministry, telling me "that Arabi's government had spent half a million sterling on the army since they came into office," and other absurdities. I knew this story could not be true, as the Nationalists had only been in power six weeks, and went to Sanderson, who was then Lord Granville's private secretary (now Sir Thomas Sanderson and head of the Foreign Office), and made him look up the question of the fabulous half million, when, on referring to the despatch about it, we found that the sum had been spent, not as Dilke had told me in the last *six weeks,* but in the last *year.* This extraordinary misstatement of Dilke's, which he had made to me as a matter beyond dispute, may of course have been only a gross blunder, but it was repeated in the newspapers of the day, several of which were under Dilke's inspiration, and is a good example of the way in which news, however absurd, prejudicial to the Egyptian Nationalists, was then being circulated by him. Morley was one of the channels he principally used, and all through the spring and early summer of 1882, the "Pall Mall Gazette" (the only paper Gladstone read attentively) was, through Dilke's influence, and Colvin's, made a channel of preposterous lies and the most uncompromising advocate of intervention.   Morley, I am willing to believe, persuaded himself that the things they told him were true, and acted in good faith, but it is nevertheless certain that on him more than on any other journalists of the time lies the responsibility of having persuaded Gladstone to the act of violence in Egypt which was the chief sin of Gladstone's public career. Morley's position, however, was then not an independent one, and he was hardly the master of his own published thoughts. He was not yet in Parliament, but waiting for a seat, and all his hope of a political career lay in the patronage of his political friends, Dilke and Chamberlain, so that he had practically no choice, if he was not to sacrifice his ambition, but to follow the lead Dilke gave him about Egyptian affairs.   He was afterwards sorry for the evil he had done, and has never, I think, liked to recall to memory the part he then played.   But without doubt his responsibility for bringing on the war was great. The whole of the Egyptian episode in Morley's "Life of Gladstone," it may be noticed, has been slurred over in a few pages But history is history, and his mistake needs to be recorded.

This matter settled with Sanderson, Currie took me in to see Lord Granville, whom I did not as yet know, and another conversation followed.   Lord Granville was a man of singularly urbane manners, and began by inquiries after my stud of Arab horses, paying me a number of polite compliments about them. Then, turning to the subject of Egypt, he "informed me plump that he had certain knowledge that Arabi had been bought by Ismail, and that the whole thing in Egypt was an intrigue to restore the ex-Khedive!"   This was another of the preposterous stories that were being foisted on the Foreign Office and the public to prejudice opinion against the Egyptian cause.   It had reached the Foreign Office, as far as I have been able to ascertain, in a despatch or private letter from Sir. Augustus Paget, then British Ambassador at Rome, to whom the ex-Khedive appears to have boasted at Naples that he had "ce gaillard là," meaning Arabi, in his pocket.

It is hardly necessary to inquire what motive of the moment Ismail may have had for making this assertion, for his word was never of any value, while the whole tenor of Arabi's career proves it to have been the absolute reverse of fact. Arabi's attitude at the date in question was more than ever one of hostility to the Circassian pashas, Ismail's adherents, who were actively intriguing with Tewfik against him. Ismail, however, had purposes of his own to serve in making it appear that the trouble in Egypt had come about on his account. He always clung to the idea that the day would come when the Powers of Europe would repent of having deposed him, and would return to him as the only possible ruler of a country distracted because he was no longer there to control it. At the moment I did not know the quarter from which the story was derived, nor could I do more to refute it than by telling Lord Granville how utterly opposed to the ex-Khedive the National fellah leader had always been.[1] This I did, and I delivered also the message Arabi had entrusted me with for Mr. Gladstone. His only answer was "Will they give up the claim of the Chamber to vote the Budget?" I told him that I feared it was hopeless to expect this, as the Deputies were all of one mind. "Then," he said, "I look upon their case as hopeless. It must end by their being put down by force." I told him I could not believe the English Government could really intervene, on such a plea, to put down liberty. But he maintained his ground, and I left him much dissatisfied, resolving that I would waste no more time upon trying to persuade the Foreign Office, but would put what pressure I could on them from the outside. "I must see Gladstone."

I also, the same day, saw Morley at his newspaper office, to try to neutralize the effect of the falsehoods with which he was being flooded, but I feared without success. He believed implicitly in Colvin, who was his regular correspondent at Cairo, and there were other influences besides, as we have seen, at work upon him and which were too strong for me to combat in his mind.

[1] Since the above was in print I have lit on the following entry in my diary of 1884, which at the same time confirms and corrects what is said of Paget's connection with this colony: "Vienna, Sept. 20. Dined at the Embassy. Sir A. Paget very amiable, talked about Egypt. He remembers Nubar Abba's dragoman. He asked my opinion of Arabi, and I asked him in turn whether it was true that Ismaïl had told him that Arabi was in his pay. He said he had never talked to Ismail about Arabi, but he remembers having heard that Ismaïl said, 'ce gaillard là m'a conté les yeux de la tête.'"

On the 11th I dined with Button, who had invited a party specially to meet me. These were Sir Francis Knollys, the Prince of Wales's secretary, Reginald Brett (now Lord Esher), who was then Lord Hartington's secretary, Clifford, a leader writer of the "Times," and General Sir John Adye, who was a friend of Wolseley's and served under him that year in the Egyptian Campaign, remaining, nevertheless, a warm sympathizer with the Egyptians throughout, and, as will be seen, rendering good service to the cause of humanity after Tel-el-Kebir. We had a pleasant evening, and all showed themselves interested in my Egyptian views, and I remained talking with some of them till one in the morning. Knollys I know was impressed by what I told him, but Brett, who was a friend of the Rothschilds and other financiers who were clamouring for intervention, proved afterwards one of our bitterest enemies. He was working at the time for Morley in the "Pall Mall Gazette," and inspired, if he did not write, some of the articles which so influenced Gladstone.

On the 13th I saw Goschen, having been sent to him by Hamilton, on Mr. Gladstone's suggestion, as a man who, though not a member of the Government, was much trusted by them and advised them, especially on Egyptian affairs. With him I went more thoroughly than with either Dilke or Granville into the details of the National case. He affected much sympathy with me, more probably than he felt, and was particularly anxious to impress on me the notion that he was not taking a financial view of the situation. This was, doubtless, because his past connection with Egypt had been as representative of Ismaïl's creditors. I found him agreeable in manner, with much charm of voice, and I was with him quite two hours. His last words to me were: "You may be sure at least of one thing, and that is, that whatever the Government may do in Egypt they will do on general grounds of policy, not in the interests of the Bondholders." This was satisfactory and seemed to be in harmony with the situation of the moment, for that very morning the news had been published of de Blignières' resignation of his post at Cairo of French Financial Controller. The event had been interpreted in London as signifying a quarrel between the French Government and the Nationalist Ministry, but I knew that this was not the case. De Blignières had been even more and earlier than Colvin a worker for intervention, and I read his resignation for what it really was, a sign that his Government had thrown him over. If Colvin at the same time had been made to resign—and things, I believe, were very near it—all the subsequent trouble might have been avoided. Colvin, however was too strongly backed up by Dilke just then to be displaced.

I went on from Goschen's to lunch with Button, and found him with Lord De la Warr, a very worthy Tory peer and country neighbour of my own in Sussex, who had been the year before in Tunis, and had there imbibed, during the French invasion, a certain sympathy with the Arabs. Later we worked a good deal together on the Egyptian question, and he proved of considerable assistance when things came, in July, to a crisis. I was at that time urging that a Commission of Inquiry should be sent to Cairo, and it seemed that he, perhaps, might fill the post.

The same afternoon I saw Hamilton in Downing Street. A violent article, headed "Smouldering Fires in Egypt," had just appeared in the "Pall Mall," which was little better from beginning to end than a tissue of the old malicious stories, with some new ones prejudicial to the Nationalists. To these Hamilton pointed as a convincing proof, seeing they were in the "Pall Mall," that I must be wrong, "Or why," he said, "should Morley, who is so good a Liberal, take such a very illiberal line?" I explained to him Colvin's position in regard to Morley, which I had not yet done, and urged him again to let me speak with his chief. Up to this point, from a feeling of loyalty to men who had been my friends, and with whom I had acted during the earlier stages, I had refrained from making complaints against them, though Malet had not scrupled to complain of me. But now I saw that further silence on my part would be only mischievous, and I was resolved to tell Gladstone all the truth about them. Morley had the day before warned me of the impending article as one to which I would not assent, and had invited an answer to it. But I was too angry to reply, except with a short private note, which I followed next day by a visit to Northumberland Street, where I reproached him with printing the malicious nonsense. The evil, however, had been done, for the publication had immediately preceded a motion in the House of Commons brought forward by Sir George Campbell in regard to Egypt where the defamatory tales had been made use of. I was present at the debate on the motion, in which the principal speaker for the Government was Goschen, who adopted a conciliatory attitude, but less than a quite friendly one to Egyptian Nationalism. My conversation with him in the morning may have saved us from a worse pronouncement. Still there was no definite declaration made favourable to liberty.

My diary for 14th March notes a talk with Sir Henry Rawlinson, the former Minister to Persia, a distinguished Oriental historian, his views being of the strongest Anglo-Indian official type. The Egyptians had always, he said, been slaves, and slaves they would remain. Their country would be absorbed with the rest of Asia by England or Russia. He knew Asiatics too well to believe they had any taste for self-government. Also another talk with Walter, the proprietor of the "Times," whom Button had suggested I should see. He conversed in platitudes for half an hour, and in the end, promised he would send a special correspondent to Cairo for independent news. (This, however, was not done, Macdonald, the manager, objecting on the score of needless expense.)

On the 15th I went to see Sir Garnet Wolseley at the Horse Guards, and had with him a conversation which needs special mention. "After a little talk about Cyprus, we got upon Egypt and the chance of resistance on the part of the Nationalists in the case of intervention, and he asked me my opinion. I said, of course, they would fight, and not only the soldiers but the people also, and afterwards, perhaps, use other methods. He refused to believe that the army would fight at all. But I maintained the contrary, and told him if they sent him out to conquer Egypt in its present mood, he must be prepared to take with him at least 60,000 men." In this I no doubt exaggerated the case, for my object was to represent it as a very difficult one, which the Government should think twice about before attempting. "He volunteered the information that he had been consulted two or three times during the winter with a view to immediate occupation. He assured me, however, that nobody wanted to intervene, that the occupation of Egypt would be most unpopular with the army, and that he himself should be very sorry to have to go there.　He would far rather the Egyptians should disband their army and trust to European protection.　But I told him I could not advise them to do that, and that people were not often attacked who really meant fighting.　He said, 'Well, of course there is no such thing as honour in war, and if there were really any question of fightinb, they ought not to trust us more than other people.' "　He then talked about the various military routes to Cairo, Bonaparte's, by the left bank of the Nile, and especially the desert way between the Suez Canal and the Delta, so that I felt pretty sure that if troops were landed it would be on that side.　But I was careful to give him no information which could be of the least use to him, and I only laughed when he half seriously asked me whether I would go with him and show him the way if it came to a campaign.　My impression of Wolseley was of "a good smart soldier, an Irishman, with a rough touch of brogue, good humoured, and I should fancy enterprising.　But he does not impress me as a man of genius—what Napoleon used to call a *'général à dixmille hommes.'*"　It is worth noting that in writing to Sheykh Mohammed Abdu, through my secretary, Sabunji, soon after this conversation, I alluded to the danger there might be, in case of intervention, of their being attacked from the Ismaïlia side, and I believe it was in consequence of this hint that the lines of Tel-el Kebir were begun to be traced by Arabi's order.

The same day I saw Lyall, whom I found just starting for India, where he had been namel Lieutenant-Governor of the North-West Provinces.　I found him much less sceptical about the National Party in Egypt than was the case then with most Anglo-Indians.　In the evening I dined with Hamilton and Godley, Gladstone's two private secretaries, and showed them the draft of a letter I had written to Lord Granville, in which I had formally delivered Arabi's message of goodwill to the English Government, and also his complaint against Colvin and Malet, which I had not mentioned to him, for the reason already given, when I saw him at the Foreign Office.　Of this draft the two secretaries highly approved, and especially Godley, who was the senior of the two, and he made me strike out a phrase I had introduced of apology for my interference in this important public matter.　He said emphatically, "Your interference needs no excuse." Godley was a singularly high-minded man, representing the better and more enthusiastic side of Gladstone's public character, the large sympathy with what was good in the world and the scorn of what was base. Except that he had great practical ability for his official work, he was absolutely unlike the men usually found in our public offices, and throughout the Egyptian crisis he gave me his warmest support and sympathy. Hamilton, though also sympathetic, was more so because he was my personal friend than from any natural enthusiasm for the kind of cause I was defending. My letter ended with a suggestion that something in the nature of an official inquiry should be sent to Cairo to examine into the facts in a spirit friendly to the Egyptians. They both urged me to send in the letter, and I consequently did so four days later, under the date 20th March. Its importance justifies my giving it here *in extenso:*

"London, *March 20th,* 1882.

"The kindness with which your Lordship was good enough to listen to me on certain points of the political situation in Egypt, encourages me to offer you the following suggestions for your further consideration:

"If I rightly understood your Lordship, Her Majesty's Government are not desirous of precipitating matters in that direction, but would be willing to accept a peaceable solution, could such be found, of the question in dispute between the Control and the Egyptian Government, and would only resort in the last instance to force were the political interests of England to be seriously impaired, or international engagements actually broken by the National Party now in power.

"Now, I am sufficiently well acquainted with the views of that party, or, at least, of their most prominent leaders, to be able to speak positively to the fact that there is nothing nearer to their wishes than a good understanding with Her Majesty's Government. Indeed, I have the authority of Arabi Bey to assure your Lordship that, if addressed in a friendly manner, he will use his utmost influence with his party, and it is very great, to allay the bitter feelings which have arisen between the Egyptians and the English and other officials employed in the country, and that he would meet half-way any negotiations which may be entered into with a view to a peaceable arrangement. He has begged me, however, to lay before you the difficulties of the position in which he is placed by the attitude of personal hostility displayed towards him by the English Controller-General, and to a certain extent also by Her Majesty's Minister.

"Sir Auckland Colvin, as your Lordship is well aware, has taken a prominent political part in the various ministerial changes, and in what it is perhaps necessary to call the revolution, which the last six months have witnessed in Egypt. On the 9th of September it was he who advised the Khedive to arrest and shoot this very Arabi Bey, now Minister of War; and he has taken no pains to conceal the fact, having himself, as I understand, communicated the details of what then happened to the English newspapers. It is also well known to the Egyptians that he has been and still is in communication with the press in a sense hostile to the National Party, and especially to the army, and that on the occasion of Sherif Pasha's resignation he unreservedly stated his intention to 'use every means in his power to ruin the National Party and bring about intervention.' If these things were known only to Arabi, he might, he assures me, overlook them; but, unfortunately, they are matters of public notoriety, a fact which makes it impossible for him to show himself on terms of intimacy with their author.

"Of Sir Edward Malet he has expressed himself less decidedly, but still partly in the same sense. It has been a misfortune of Sir Edward's position with the Egyptians that his visit to Constantinople closely coincided with the strong advocacy of Turkish intervention which the English press displayed last autumn, and I am myself convinced that the French Government are responsible for the belief, which is ineradicable in all minds at Cairo, that he has at various times suggested military action. I know, myself, that this is untrue, and that Sir Edward has, on the contrary, deprecated any such solution of his difficulties; but certain facts remain, which lend a colour to the idea. Thus to the very date of the assembling of the Egyptian Chamber he refused to recognize the National demand for Constitutional Government as a serious matter; again, he joined Sir Auckland Colvin in displaying a marked partisanship for Sherif in his quarrel with the deputies; and he has since given offence by expressing his belief in a story, wholly unfounded and peculiarly irritating to those deputies, namely, that their President, Sultan Pasha, a man universally respected, had been personally insulted by Arabi.

"Be this as it may, it is certain both Sir Edward Malet and Sir Auckland Colvin, instead of being in a position to advise and restrain are practically 'in Coventry' with the Egyptian Government. They are shut out from all true sources of information regarding their plans, and are compelled to leave the field open to intriguers of other nationalities who have no interest in advising moderation or desire to avert a rupture.

"If your Lordship should find that there is any reason in my argument thus stated, I may perhaps be permitted to make the following suggestion.

"The National Ministers are now engaged in preparing a series of grave complaints against the working of the system established by England and France and sanctioned by the Control, some of which complaints are certainly well founded. They are willing to approach the inquiry in a moderate and friendly spirit, but they will certainly approach it in a hostile one if the Control and diplomacy continue hostile. The matters in dispute are largely matters of fact which, if justice is to be observed and an undoubted moral standing ground acquired by Her Majesty's Government, should be examined in an absolutely impartial mood and on the evidence no less of the Egyptians than of the Europeans. That evidence, I submit, it is out of the reach of Her Majesty's representatives, diplomatic and financial, to procure, and that impartiality will certainly be suspected in their case by the Egyptians. Would it not then be advisable, during the six months which must elapse before the Egyptian Parliament reassembles and the conflict be engaged, to send something in the nature of a commission of inquiry to examine into the facts complained of in a friendly spirit, the only spirit which can possibly avert disaster."

To continue from my diary I find that on the 16th I wrote, with Sabunji's help as scribe, a long letter to Arabi, telling him that I was asking for a Commission to be appointed and that I was in good hopes, but entreating him to be cautious; and also to Gregory, who was still at Cairo. The situation in

Egypt then was that the Chamber of Delegates, having insisted upon the right they had claimed to vote that half of the Budget which was not affected to the payment of the interest on the debt, a new *Leyha,* or organic law, granting a Constitution on European models had been signed, as we have seen, by the Khedive and published. The Ministers had also presented to the Chamber of Deputies a list of practical reforms, all of which were much needed and most of which have since, after many years, been carried out. Which done, the Chamber had been adjourned till the autumn. Absolute tranquillity had meanwhile prevailed throughout the country, and the sole cause of quarrel with Europe was the financial one of the vote, a dispute which could not become acute for at least six months, when the next new budget would be framed. There is not the smallest doubt that if Colvin had been induced to join his French colleague, de Blignières, in retiring from Egypt, and my suggestion of the Commission had been adopted, things in Egypt would have quieted down and all cause for armed intervention would have disappeared. The Egyptian Ministry desired nothing more than to live at peace with the whole world and to come to an understanding with the Dual Governments on all disputed questions.

On 20th March I lunched at Button's to meet his uncle, Robert Bourke, who was to bring forward the Egyptian question next week formally in Parliament. With him was another Tory member, Montague Guest, who had interested himself in the cause of Tunis. These were among the second strings to my bow, if Gladstone should fail me. Then I attended a meeting of the Asiatic Society, to which I had just been elected, and in the evening dined with Rivers Wilson. With Wilson I "quarrelled fearfully about Egypt." He told me he had helped to draw up a new Note, at the Foreign Office, which was now being despatched to Malet, "insisting on the fulfilment of all International engagements," a Note intended to be a new menace to the National Party, but which I think was never sent, or perhaps cancelled, as it does not appear in the Blue Book. My letter to Granville may have been the cause of its suppression. Wilson insisted that the whole National movement was an invention of Ismaïl's, and that "if the ex-Khedive were to land to-morrow at Alexandria, every Egyptian would come to him on his hands and knees." From this dinner I went on to a party at Lady Kenmare's, where I met Lady Salisbury, who took me aside, and cross-questioned me with much appearance of sympathy about the Egyptian cause, and I laid it before her to the best of my ability, knowing that what I said would be repeated to her husband. Of course there could be no real sympathy in any of the Tories, especially in Lord Salisbury, for my views on Egyptian liberty, but it suited the Opposition to take me up to just the extent that would help them to bring the Government into discredit, Salisbury himself was throughout a thoroughgoing advocate of intervention. I walked home that evening with Hamilton, whom I had found at the party, and told him of Wilson's boast about the new Note, and entreated him to get me immediate audience of his chief, and he urged me to send in my letter at once to Granville, and also a copy of it to Gladstone. This I did the following morning, entrusting both to Hamilton for delivery. He had already, 21st March, arranged an interview for me with his chief for the next day. A dinner in the evening at Robert Bourke's, General Taylor, the Opposition Whip, Lady Ely, and a number more Tories.

March 22.—This was a most important day. I had now been a full fortnight in England, and, though I had certainly not let any grass grow under my feet, I had neverthless failed as yet to get speech of the Prime Minister. To-day, however, made me ample amends. I went a little before the hour appointed to Downing Street, so as to have time for a few words with Hamilton, who told me his chief had read my letter; and at twenty minutes past eleven I was received by him. Mr. Gladstone I found looking far better and younger than when I had seen him last, nearly two years before. Then he had seemed on his decline, but now he seemed vigorous and singularly alert in mind and body. He received me very kindly. My letter to Lord Granville was before him on the table, and he was evidently prepared and eager for what I had to say. He told me to tell him all, and, without talking much himself, listened. His manner was so encouraging and sympathetic that I spoke easily and with an eloquence I had never had before, and I could see that every word I said interested and touched him. He let me speak on for perhaps a quarter of an hour, only from time to time interjecting some such words as "you need not tell me this, for I know it," as when I would prove the reality of the National feeling in Egypt. His sympathy was obviously and strongly with the movement.

Then he asked me a question about the position of the army and the reason of the prominent part taken by it in public affairs. Of this he was suspicious. I explained the history to him and assured him that the interference of the soldiers had been greatly exaggerated, and the stories of their intimidation of the Deputies were quite untrue; that the sole reason for the present military preparations was the dread of foreign intervention. I explained the feeling of the Party towards the Sultan and the Viceregal family—towards Tewfik, the ex-Khedive, and Halim. He asked me whether I had told all this to Lord Granville. I said: "He stopped me at the outset by telling me that Arabi had been bought by Ismaïl! What could I say?" Just at that moment somebody looked in and told Mr. Gladstone that Lord Granville was in the house and had sent up his name, and I was terribly afraid Mr. Gladstone was going to let him in, which would have prevented me from telling my full story. But with a look of annoyance he went out for an instant, and sent Lord Granville away, and then came back with a sort of skip across the room and rubbing his hands as one might do on having got rid of a bore. The gesture was an extraordinary encouragement to me, and he at once made me go on.

I delivered all Arabi's messages about the Slave Trade and the other projects of reform, and then went on to explain Colvin's position and Malet's. He said, almost pathetically, "What can we do? They are esteemed public servants and have received *honours* for their work in Egypt." He insisted upon the word *honours*. He then asked me to tell him something about the civilian leaders of the National Party, and I explained the position of some of them, Mohammed Abdu, Ahmed Mahmud, Saadallah Hallabi, Hassan Shereï, and others of the Deputies, and, lastly, Abdallah Nadim, journalist and orator. This designation at once excited Mr. Gladstone, and the account of his eloquence, and he took down his name upon a slip of paper. Thus time slipped away till it was twelve o'clock, and he had another appointment. I had been with him forty minutes—a very fast forty minutes too. As I was going out I turned and asked him, with a sudden thought, whether I might

not send Arabi some message from him in answer to his messages. He thought an instant and said, "I think not." And
very slowly and deliberately: "But you are at liberty to state
your own impression of my sentiments," and then in a sort of
House of Commons voice, which was in strange contrast with
the extremely personal and human tone in which he had been
conversing: "If they wish to judge of these, let them read what
we say in Parliament, especially what I say, for I never speak
lightly in Parliament. In our public despatches we are much
hampered by the opinion of Europe, which we are bound to consider, and this is not favourable to Liberal institutions in Egypt.
But they should read our speeches." He had turned to the
table, for we were half-way across the room, and took up a
paper which was on it, a despatch already signed, and which I
felt sure was that which Wilson had told me he had helped to
draft, and seemed on the point of showing it to me—and then
refrained and put it down again. Once more his manner became natural and intimate. He thanked me again for my
letters and all that I had told him, and begged me to let him
hear if any new combination arose. His extreme kindness as
he shook hands with me moved me greatly and I was near shedding tears, and went away feeling that he was a good as well
as a great man, and wondering only how any one with so good
a heart could have arrived at being Prime Minister. *"El
hamdu l'Illah. El hamdu l'Illah,"* I kept repeating to myself,
"El nasr min Alah, wa fathon karibon."

Such was the Gladstone I saw unveiled for a moment that
day—a man of infinite private sympathy with good, and of
whom one would affirm it impossible he should swerve a hair's
breadth from the path of right. But, alas, there was another
Gladstone, the opportunist statesman, who was very different
from the first, and whom I was presently to see playing in public
"such fantastic tricks before high Heaven as make the angels
weep." I will attempt a character, drawn from my observation
of him, which was a close one, during the next ten years, of
this very remarkable personality.

Gladstone, as I have said, was two personages. His human
side was very charming. He had an immense power of sympathy, and what I may call a lavish expenditure of enthusiasm
for such things as attracted him, and he had also a certain hu-

mility of attitude, often towards persons far inferior to himself, which compelled their affectionate regard, as did certain little human weaknesses which have found no place in any memorial of him that has yet been published. All this made him beloved, especially by the young, by the women who knew him well, both those who were good and those who were less good. This was the happy, the consistent part of him. His public life was to large extent a fraud—as indeed the public life of every great Parliamentarian must be. The insincerities of debate were ingrained in him. He had begun them at school and college before he entered the House of Commons, and by the time he was thirty he had learnt to look upon the "Vote of the House" as the supreme criterion of right and wrong in public things. In deference to this he had had constantly to put aside his private predilections of policy, until towards the end of his life his own personal impulses of good had assumed the character of tastes rather than of principles. They were like his taste for music, his taste for china, his taste for *bric-à-brac,* feelings he would like to indulge, but was restrained from by a higher duty, that of securing a Parliamentary majority. This was his ultimate reason of all action, his true conscience, to which his nobler aspirations had constantly to be sacrificed. His long habit, too, of publicity, had bred in him, as it does in actors, a tendency to self-deception. From constantly acting parts not really his own, he had acquired the power of putting on a character at will, even, I believe, to his inmost thoughts. If he had a new distasteful policy to pursue, his first object was to persuade himself into a belief that it was really congenial to him, and at this he worked until he had made himself his own convert, by the invention of a phrase or an argument which might win his approbation. Thus he was always saved the too close consciousness of his insincerities, for like the tragedian in Dickens, when he had to act Othello, he began by painting himself black all over. I believe this is not an unfair estimate of Gladstone's public character. Certainly it is the light in which his actions showed him to me in his betrayal that year of the Egytian cause.

As yet, however, I had no misgiving, and in the next few days wrote letters to my friends at Cairo detailing the good news. With Gladstone on our side, what more was there to fear? Only I prayed them to be patient till the Commission I had asked for should arrive. That some attempt was made by Lord Granville to carry out my suggestion is clear from the Blue Books. But Granville's heart was also as clearly not in it, or he was thwarted by Dilke or others in the Foreign Office. He wrote me a note on the 24th asking me to luncheon, when I should have an opportunity of discussing the question of the Commission, but by an accident, which was probably not an accident, the note did not reach me till too late, a manœuvre which was repeated with the same result a week later. The Blue Books record a little abortive negotiation with France for a special inquiry, but it was soon dropped, and Lord Granville's favourite method of dawdling things out is responsible for the rest. Before many weeks had passed, the intriguers at Cairo had effected their purpose of a new disturbance, and the difficulties of conciliation had become enormously increased.

The rest of the short session before Easter in London may be briefly told. I went down for a few days to Crabbet to see after my private affairs, but that did not prevent me from writing to my friends in Egypt, Arabi and Mohammed Abdu and Nadim, telling them of my success with Gladstone and imploring their prudence. On the 26th I received a letter from Button, enclosing a note from a person in a very responsible position, which I find still among my papers. It is so short and instructive that I give it as it stands:

"*22nd.* I am very anxious that Mr. Wilfrid Blunt should meet and see Natty Rothschild, whose Egyptian interests require no explanation. He goes to Lord Granville and the Foreign Office so constantly, and in this matter, like St. Paul, 'dies daily.' To bring them to an intelligent understanding on this vexed question would be a real service. I am desired to ask if you could bring W. Blunt to luncheon at New Court on Friday next at 1 P. M. *Do* if you possibly can. It will be *useful* in many ways."

Here, of course, was the real crux of the situation, the nine millions of the Rothschild loan supposed to be in danger in Egypt, half of which, Button told me, was still held by the Rothschilds themselves. I consequently went up to London on the morning of the 27th, the day named, and under Button's wing to the City, but by misfortune only to find that "Natty" had been called that morning abroad on account of the illness or death of a near relation, I forget which. We consequently did not see him, but he had left a message instead, begging me to write him my views. I regret the accident which prevented the meeting, for it would have been interesting, though I do not suppose it would have effected any good. I have often wondered since what would have been the nature of the "intelligent understanding" so much desired; and I have sometimes suspected that the common financial argument might have been tried with me in the shape of shares to bring about an arrangement with Arabi for the betrayal of his political trust. Some such, it seems, was tried upon Arabi two months later through another channel. Nothing, however, came of the visit, except that I wrote my memorandum, too long a one here to quote, the object of it being to recommend, as a matter of policy, that financiers who had interests in Egypt should accept the revolution that had occurred and make the best of it, and predicted that bondholders would lose more by a war than by conciliation. I have since been told that Rothschild, who, after great tribulation and anguish of mind at the time of the bombardment of Alexandria and nearly in despair thinking he had lost his millions eventually recovered the value of all, resented my prediction of evil as that of a false prophet. But that does not greatly concern me. My memorandum was drawn up not in his interest as creditor but in that of his Egyptian debtors.

Another curious entry, 28th March, gives a hint of the ideas current in Printing House Square. This was the first time I had been to the "Times" office, and Button was again my *cicerone.* We saw there Macdonald, the manager, with the object of trying to get him to send out a new correspondent to Cairo, who should give the "Times" independent news, and Mackenzie Wallace had been thought of for the purpose. But Macdonald, with Scotch caution, would not go to the expense. He was quite satisfied from a business point of view, he said, with the kind of news Scott, their correspondent at Alexandria, was sending them. English people, he said, had only two interests in Egypt, the Suez Canal and their bonds, if they held any, and Scott's views on these two matters were what they wanted. Beyond this they did not care in any special way about the truth. He complimented me all the same on my own letters, which as I was not paid for them they were obliged to me for, and they would always be glad to print whatever more I had to say. But a special correspondent just then was not needed.

I was in correspondence about this time with Allen, the Secretary of the Anti-Slave-Trade Society, a very worthy man but of extremely narrow views. Sir William Muir had taken me to task in the "Times" for having asserted in one of my letters that it was part of the National program in Egypt to suppress what remained of slavery in Egypt, and he had been at the pains to prove by chapter and verse from the Koran, that slavery was and must always be an institution of a religious character with Mohammedans. Allen, too, I found indignant at the idea of Arabi's being actively in favour of its suppression, which he, Allen, seemed to consider was the sole business of the Society's anti-slavery agents at Cairo. His anger was very much what a master of foxhounds might express at the unauthorized destruction of foxes by a farmer. Mohammedans, he considered, had no business to put down slavery on their own account, or what would become of the Society. This at least was the impression his argument left on me.

Lastly, I find a note of having been asked, 1st April, to meet the Prince of Wales, who wanted to see me, at dinner, *en partie carrée*. My host on this occasion was Howard Vincent, who was at that time on intimate terms with H. R. H. I was stupid enough not to go to the dinner, which would have been interesting. But I unfortunately had a previous engagement for the same day to meet Princess Louise of Lorne at the Howards, and did not like to break my engagement, which was also an important one. I went, however, in the evening to Vincent's and had some talk with the Prince of Wales about Egypt, though not on the subjects connected with it that most interested me.

Here the first Act of my English campaign may be said to end. Up to this point all, in spite of huge difficulties, had gone well with my propaganda. My preaching of the National Egyptian cause had been almost everywhere well received, and the talk of intervention had subsided. At one moment my hopes were very high, for Button had ascertained that the Commission I had asked for was to be sent, and he named to me even the person said to have been chosen. But, alas, it proved a vain rumour. Then everybody went out of London for the Easter recess, and before they returned the news of the Circassian plot was upon us. It was the beginning of the pitiful end.

CHAPTER XI

How fair the prospects in Egypt still were in the first week of April, notwithstanding the many rumours of disturbance there which were being spread through Europe, may be judged from the following two letters written to me at that time by Arabi, and still more by a third which I received at the same time from Sheykh Mohammed Abdu. Sheykh Mohammed Abdu's high character throughout his life for the strictest veracity and the exalted position he now holds as Grand Mufti of Egypt, give to his testimony a historical value which can hardly be exaggerated, and may well be placed in accepted contradiction of the multiform falsehoods of the Blue Books. His functions that spring as Director of the Official Journal and Censor of the Press at Cairo put him, moreover, in a position of knowledge as to what was passing in the counsels of the National Ministry, which neither Malet nor Colvin nor any European in Egypt could at all pretend to. I draw the special attention, therefore, of historians to these convincing documents:

"Cairo, *April 1st*, 1882.
"To our respected, sincere, and free-minded friend, Mr. Wilfrid Blunt, may God prosper his best projects.

"After offering praise to God, the conqueror of the strong and the upholder of truth, I beg to say that your letter dated March 10th has reached me, and caused me an immense pleasure. Without doubt it will please every free man to see men free like you, and truthful in their sayings and doings, and determined to carry out their high projects for the benefit of mankind generally, and the advantage of their own country in particular.

"The contents of your letter prove that you are enamoured

of the freedom of mankind, and that you are trying your best
to serve the interests of your English nation, being aware that
those interests in the East, and especially in Egypt, can only be
made secure forever by helping the Egyptians to be free and
thus gaining their affection. Free Englishmen should surely
help those who are striving for the independence of their country, for its reform, and for the establishment of an equitable
Government. Your praiseworthy endeavours will, we do not
doubt, secure for you an honourable name with your countrymen,
when they shall come to discover in what way you have laboured
to remove the veil of untruth which interested men have spread
before their eyes.

"As to ourselves, we thank you for your good services as
they concern both Egypt and England, which country we hope
will be the most powerful friend to assist us in establishing good
order on a basis of freedom, and an imitation of civilized and
free nations. Please God, we shall soon see the success of your
endeavours, and we therefore consider your safe arrival home
a good omen of success.

"With regard to the advice you kindly gave us we have to
thank you for it, and beg to say that we are trying our best to
keep things quietly and in order, because we consider it one of
our most important duties to do so, and we are endeavouring to
succeed. We can assure you that all is now tranquil. Peace
reigns over the country; and we and all our patriotic brethren
are with our best will defending the rights of those who dwell
in our land, no matter of what nation they may be. All treaties
and international obligations are fully respected; and we shall
allow no one to touch them as long as the Powers of Europe
keep their engagements and friendly relations with us.

"As to the menaces of the great bankers and financial people
in Europe, we shall bear them with wisdom and firmness. In
our opinion, their threats will only hurt themselves and injure
those Powers who are misled by them.

"Our only aim is to deliver the country from slavery, injustice and ignorance, and to raise our people to such a position as
shall enable them to prevent any return of the despotism which
in time past desolated Egypt.

"These words which I write to you are the thoughts of
every thoughtful Egyptian and free-minded lover of his country.

"Please remember me kindly to your good lady, and oblige your sincere friend,

"AHMED ARABI."

"Cairo, *April 6th,* 1882.
"To our true friend, Mr Wilfrid Blunt.

"After returning thanks to God for the freedom and reforms with which He has been pleased to bless us, I beg to say that I received your second letter after having sent you the reply to your former letter. I avail myself of this fortunate occasion to repeat my sincere thanks for your good endeavours. I consider it to be my duty, and the duty of every pure conscience, even the duty of all men, to thank you for your good services. In acknowledging benefits the ties of friendship are strengthened, and so between nations. We are extremely anxious to come to an understanding about the friendship and mutual interests of ourselves and the Powers with whom we are under engagements, for it is only through friendship that those who have the rights in our country can enjoy the fruit of treaties and contracts, which we consider it our duty to respect and defend. If any rupture should take place, it would affect not us only or principally, but all other Powers, and principally Great Britain. No large-minded Statesman can fail to foresee the advantage which must result to England from befriending us, and helping us in our struggle.

"As to the Control, you may rest assured it will not be hindered in the discharge of its duty, according to the rights guaranteed it by international treaties. It has never been our intention, or the intention of any in this country to touch the rights of the Controllers, or to trespass on any international treaty.

"Should the representatives of the Powers in this country be faithful to their duty, and to the interests of their own countries, they cannot do better than help us in our truly National enterprise, and prove in acts what they promise us in words.

"We have made up our mind to do all we can to give our nation a position among civilized nations by spreading knowledge through the country, maintaining union and good order, and administering justice to every one. Nothing will make us go back an inch from this determination; threats or menaces will not deter us from it; we yield only to friendly feelings, and these we appreciate immensely.

"As to the tranquillity of the country, it is not disturbed. We are endeavouring to efface the bad traces left behind by former Governments.

"As to the questions which you put to us, we have already sent their replies through Sheykh Mohammed Abdu by telegraph. Truly all the rumors spread in Europe about the excessive military expenditure are void of foundation. The military budget has neither increased a para, nor decreased a dirhem. It stands just as it was fixed on 21st December, 1881, in the time of Sherif Pasha. Hence you may rest assured that the rumours you took the trouble to mention are spread only by unscrupulous persons. We regret to see falsehood thus finding continually its way into the newspapers of civilized Europe.

"Let us pray God that He may guide the thoughtful statesmen of Europe to find out the truth, and better learn the condition of our country. So they will render service to their own countries as well as ours by strengthening the ties of good feeling. May God grant us all to enjoy the blessing of peace and a friendly understanding.

"AHMED ARABI."

These letters, written in answer to mine conveying my "impression" of the Prime Minister's friendly sentiments, and which I forwarded at once on receiving them, in translation, to Mr. Gladstone, would, I feel sure, have received his attention had not he been just then away from London and occupied with what was to him a far more absorbing and important affair— for it was threating the existence of his Government—the condition, almost one of revolution, in Ireland. Nor had I any opportunity of seeing either him or Hamilton till the Easter recess was over at the end of the month. In the meanwhile events in Egypt had again become most critical through what is historically known as the Circassian plot, the news of which reached London in the third week of April. I did not pay it much attention at the time, looking upon it as only one of the many false rumours being printed. But it soon turned out to be serious enough, not only in itself, but especially as giving our diplomacy the opportunity it had been waiting for of setting the

Khedive in open quarrel with his Ministers. Malet was by this time completely subjugated by Colvin, and was henceforth guided in his action to the end by Colvin's Anglo-Indian suggestions.

The author of the conspiracy was without question the ex-Khedive Ismaïl. I know this, among other sources of information, from his then secretary, Ibrahim Bey Mouelhi. The ex-Khedive from his retreat at Naples was still pulling the strings of his party at Cairo, and giving advice through them to his son. His chief agent was one Ratib Pasha, whom I remember hearing of in the previous autumn as among the worst enemies of the Nationalists, and it was through him that the plot was worked. The idea was to get up among the Circassian officers of the army a reactionary movement against the fellahin. Arabi and the chief fellah officers were to be assassinated, and a counter-revolution brought about, which Ismaïl hoped might in the whirligig of things lead to his own restoration. I am convinced that there was never at any time the least chance of this, but it will be remembered that Rivers Wilson believed in it as possible, and had, perhaps, even come round to thinking it financially desirable as an alternative to the utter weakness of Tewfik and his inability to support the Control. Tewfik, as usual, was halting between two courses, that of going on with the Constitutional·Ministry and Arabi, of whom he was now profoundly jealous, and that of joining the Turkish reaction at the risk of bringing back his father. Sherif and Malet were working together, and Sherif's house had become a centre of the diplomatic intrigue against the Ministry inspired by Colvin. I do not say that either Colvin or Malet, or even, perhaps Sherif, were cognizant of the intended blow, but it was well known that they would favour any party which should succeed in overthrowing the Ministry, and that gave confidence to the conspirators. The plot, however, was betrayed to Arabi before it had time to come to a head, though not until an unsuccessful attempt had been made on Abd-el-Aal Bey, and the conspirators were promptly arrested and imprisoned. The details of the plot will be found, with other interesting matter, in the following letter I received at the time from Sheykh Mohammed Abdu, dated April 25th:

"As to the promotions of the officers, of which European news-papers are making so much talk, allow me to explain the facts. In the first place, the promotions were not made by Arabi Pasha's sole will and pleasure, nor were they a bribe to gain the officers' affections towards Arabi. They were made in con-sequence of the new military law, which prescribes that offi-cers, after a certain age, or sick, or infirm, or disabled, should retire from active service with a pension. In Sherif Pasha's time this military law began to take effect, and accordingly 558 officers were put on the retired list. Next 96 officers were sent a year ago to the frontier of Abyssinia, Zaila, and else-where, while 100 officers left the army and took civil employ. The total number thus retired is 754. It was thus natural that promotions should be made to fill up vacancies. There are still fifty vacancies reserved for the cadets of the Military School.

"Arabi's title of Pasha was not forced on him by the Sultan, but by the Khedive, who insisted that all his Ministers should hold that rank.

"Let me now dispel from all minds, once for all, the false idea that Arabi, or the Military party, or the National party, are tools of the Turks. Every Egyptian, whether he be a learned man (of the Ulema) or a fellah, an artisan or a merchant, a soldier or a civilian, a politician or not a politi-cian, hates the Turks and detests their infamous memory. No Egyptian can look forward to the idea of a Turk landing in his country without feeling an impulse to rush to his sword to drive out the intruder.

"The Turks are tyrants who have left calamities behind them in Egypt which still make our hearts sore. We cannot wish them back, or wish to have anything more to do with them. The Turks have footing enough with their firmans in Egypt. They must stop there, and try nothing further. But if any at-tempt of this kind comes to our knowledge, we shall hail it as a not altogether unwelcome accident. We have had already some presentiment about this, and it has been the cause of our preparations. We shall make use of the event, if it happens, to recover our full independence. Our clearest minded states-men are now watching every movement of Turkish policy in this country to check it the moment it oversteps its limits. I do not deny that there are Turks and Circassians in Egypt who advocate the cause of the Porte, but they are few—nothing to those who love their country.

"With regard to the Circassian conspiracy against Arabi Pasha's life, it is not really a serious danger.

"The ex-Khedive Ismaïl, the greatest enemy Egypt ever had, and one still envious of her happiness, has long been mining us with plots to destroy (blow up) our present Government, thinking in so doing to prepare the way for his return. But God Almighty has scattered to the wind his hopes, since every Egyptian knows that Ismaïl's return means the ruin of Egypt. The tyrant (*Faraoun*), however, hoping against hope, sent to Egypt one of his followers, Ratib Pasha, who had been banished; and he, by underhand means in Sherif Pasha's time, received admission to Egyptian soil, where he joined his brother, Mahmud Effendi Talaat Beg-bashi, and later secured to his service Yusuf Bey Najati, Mahmud Bey Fouad, Kosrow Pasha's nephew and Otheman Pasha Rifki (all these are Circassians). These worked to make converts to their plan, which was to destroy the actual Ministers, and kill the superior officers of the army, beginning with Arabi Pashi. Through their efforts, about forty of the inferior officers joined their plan, swearing alliance, but at first put off its execution for want of a pretext. This was found in the discontent of nine Circassian officers, who objected to being ordered for service to the Soudan. Ratib's party became aware of what was going on among them, and took advantage of it to suggest to the nine Circassians that they should refuse to go except with promotion.

"The Ministry has long had a suspicion of the mischief which was impending. As long ago as when Ratib first returned to the country, Mahmud Sami, the present Prime Minister when Minister of War, requested Sherif Pasha, in the Khedive's presence, to expel Ratib. He suspected something wrong in the fact that Ratib had left the ex-Khedive so suddently at Naples. But Sherif refused, although Mahmud Sami warned him that he would be held responsible for all that might one day happen. This because Ratib was Sherif's son-in-law, and, as is thought, also perhaps his accomplice in the design of restoring Ismaïl.

"It happened, however, that Ratib's party invited a certain Circassian officer, Rashid Effendi Anwar, to join them, and that this officer refused to have anything to do with their plan, and, leaving the conspirators where they were, came straight to Arabi and disclosed the plot. Thus they were arrested, and brought to trial by court-martial.

"The event has caused little excitement among the common people. Every one knows that Arabi's life is exposed as other men's, to dangers daily. Nor is it possible for a man, however great he be, that all should wish him well. But we should only laugh if it were stated publicly that Engand was on the verge of anarchy because a madman, sodier or civilian, had tried to shoot your Queen.

"The Circassians in the army number in all eighty-one persons, and no one in his senses need be alarmed at the chance of so small a number of men succeeding against the Government.

"Now, as to the Slave Trade. The present Ministry is trying hard to suppress domestic slavery. The Mohammedan religion offers no obstacle at all to this; nay, according to Mohammedan dogma Moslems are not allowed to have slaves except taken from infidels at war with them. In fact, they are captives or prisoners taken in legal warfare, or who belonged to infidel peoples not in friendly alliance with Mohammedan princes, nor protected by treaties or covenants. But no Moslem is allowed to be taken as a slave. Moreover, if a person is an infidel, but belongs to a nation in peaceful treaty with a Mohammedan prince, he cannot be taken as a slave. Hence the Mohammedan religion not only does not oppose abolishing slavery as it is in modern time, but radically condemns its continuance. Those learned gentlemen in England and elsewhere who hold a contrary opinion should come here and teach us, the Sheykhs of the Azhar, the dogmas of our faith. This would be an astonishing spectacle. The whole Mohammedan world would be struck dumb when it learned that a Christian had taken upon him the task, in the greatest Mohammedan University in the world, of teaching its Ulema, professors, and theologians the dogmas of their religion, and how to comment on their Koran.

"A Fewta will in a few days be issued by the Sheykh el Islam to prove that the abolition of slavery is according to the spirit of the Koran, to Mohammedan tradition, and to Mohammedan dogma.

"The Egyptian Government will endeavour to remove every obstacle in the way, and will not rest till slavery is extirpated from Egyptian territory.

"MOHAMMED ABDU."

The plot thus on the 25th of April seemed to be frustrated, nor would it have led to any more serious complications but for the action taken by Malet in regard to it. Instead of supporting the Ministry against whom it had been directed, his official sympathies were given wholly to the conspirators. These had been tried by court-martial and condemned to the not overwhelming punishment of being banished to the White Nile, a penalty constantly enforced in Egypt even in the time of the Dual Control. Malet, however, wrote home that the sentence was a monstrous one, equivalent to death, while the "Times" correspondent was allowed to publish the story, an altogether false one, that Arabi had privately visited the prison and there had had the conspirators tortured under his eyes. That there was no truth in this tale it is hardly necessary to affirm. Yet Malet gave it a certain countenance in his despatches to the extent of mentioning it as a report prevalent, and that cries had been heard issuing at night from the prison. What is certain is that it was made a pretext with him for encouraging the Khedive to quarrel with his Ministers by taking the case out of their hands into his own, and commuting their sentence into one of simple exile, an act which according to the new Constitution was beyond his right.

To go back to my journal in London, I find that on 28th April I went to Downing Street "rather wroth" about nothing having been done for Egypt, but Hamilton bade me be patient and said that my idea of a Commission had been taken up. Also, the next day, Button congratulated me on my success. "He tells me there has been a fearful crisis about Egypt; that the Sultan was for sending troops there, deposing Tewfik, setting up Halim, and hanging Arabi. The English and French Governments, however, have prevented this, and Arabi is to be supported and a Commission sent." On Tuesday there was to be a declaration of their Egyptian policy in the House of Lords by the Government. This news of the Sultan's intervention seems, in fact, to have been a crisis of the moment brought on by the Rothschilds with the support of Bismarck. The relations between Constantinople and the National Party in Egypt had become strained in the last few weeks through various circumstances which it is time now to explain, as well as the peculiar communications which passed in the month of February between the Sultan and Arabi, communications which are of the greatest possible importance in estimating Arabi's growing position of political power in Egypt superior to that of his fellow Ministers.

It will be remembered that when the Sultan's Commissioners visited Egypt in the autumn of 1881 Ahmed Pasha Ratib (not to be confounded with Ratib Pasha, the ex-Khedive's agent), who was one of them and the Sultan's A. D. C., met Arabi in the train on his way to Suez and Mecca, and that they had interchanged ideas and made friends, and that the Pasha had promised to represent him favourably to his master as a good Mohammedan and one loyal to the Caliphate. This had led to correspondence between them, of which I have in my possession the originals of the following two important documents. They came into my hands, with a mass of other papers, at the time of Arabi's trial. The two letters were written within three weeks after the Government of Mahmud Sami was formed, in February, 1882, in which Government Arabi was Minister of War. The first is from Ahmed Ratib, the second from Sheykh Mohammed Zafir, one of the great religious sheykhs of Constantinople, who at that time was charged with the Sultan's secret correspondence; and both were written at the Sultan's personal command.

"To the Egyptian Minister of War, Ahmed Arabi Bey

"I related to His Majesty the Sultan the conversation we had on the railway between the stations of Zagazig and Mahda on my return to Constantinople, and it caused great pleasure to His Majesty, and he ordered me to communicate to you his Imperial compliments. I related to His Majesty all the kind treatment I received at your hands and the courtesy my eyes witnessed while I was at Cairo, and His Majesty was extremely gratified thereat, so that the satisfaction he felt in your devotion and fidelity was increased manyfold. People had made him think that you were acting, I know not how, contrary to right, and had succeeded in perverting His Majesty's idea about you, but now as I have exposed the true state of the case to him, I swear to you that His Majesty deeply regrets ever having paid any attention to these false and lying statements about you; and as a good proof of this His Majesty has commanded me to write this letter, and to express to you the sentiments which follow:

"It matters nothing who is the Khedive of Egypt. The thoughts of the ruler of Egypt, his intentions and his conduct must be governed with the greatest care, and all his actions must tend to secure the future of Egypt and to uphold intact the sovereignty of the Caliph, while he must show the most perfect faith in upholding the faith and the country's rights. This will be required of him of the persons who have been on the Khedivial Throne. Ismaïl Pasha and his predecessors gave bribes to Ali Pasha, Fuad Pasha, Midhat Pasha and their representatives of the Sublime Porte, traitors; and, after shutting the eyes of the officials, dared to overtask and oppress the Egyptians. And, in addition to this, they made heavy debts and brought the Egyptians under a grievous yoke. And to-day, in the eyes of the world, their state has specially appealed to our pity, but the whole position is an extremely delicate one which calls for the necessity of finding a speedy and sure remedy. Therefore it behooves you above all things to prevent anything that might lead to foreign intervention, and never to stray from the just and true path nor to listen to any treacherous falsehoods, but in every way with watchful care to hinder the seditious projects of foreigners. This is the great hope of the Sultan.

"And, since we two shall correspond in the future, you must take necessary precautions to prevent our letters from falling into strange hands. For this the easiest way at present, and there is no safer channel you can find, is to submit your correspondence to the true and trusty man who carries this letter and that of Sheykh Mohammed Zafir.

"I would also add that it is indispensable that you should send secretly some officer who knows well what is going on in

Egypt, and who is a trusted friend of yours, to present at the footstool of His Majesty the reports on the state of the country in true detail.

"I beg you to send the answer by the man who brings this letter.

AHMED RATIB, Aide-de-Camp of the Sultan.
"4th Rebi ul Akhar. 22nd Feb., 1882."

"To His Excellency the Egyptian Minister of War.

"I have presented your two faithful letters to His Majesty the Sultan, and from their contents he has learnt all your sentiments of patriotism and watchfulness, and especially have the promises you make of your efforts to guard faithfully and truly His Majesty's interests been a cause of lively satisfaction to His Majesty, so much so that His Majesty ordered me to express his pleasure and his favour to you, and further bade me write to you as follows, viz.:—As the maintenance of the integrity of the Caliphate is a duty which touches the honour of every one of us it is incumbent on every Egyptian to strive earnestly after the consolidation of my power, to prevent Egypt from passing out of our hands into the rapacious grasp of foreigners as the Vilayet of Tunis has passed, and I repose all my confidence in you, my son, to exert all your influence and to put forth every effort to prevent such a thing happening. And you are to beware never for one moment to lose sight of this important point, and to omit none of the precautionary measures which are called for by the age in which we live, keeping all ways before you, as a perpetual goal, the defence of your faith and of your country; and especially you are to persist in maintaining your confidence and the ties which bind you.

"That country (Egypt) is of the highest importance to England and France, and most of all to England, and certain seditious intrigues in Constantinople, following in the path of these Governments, have, for some time past, been busy with their treacherous and accursed projects, and, since they have found it to their profit zealously to promote these intrigues and seditions in Egypt, it is the especial desire of His Majesty that you should keep a very careful eye on these persons (or things?). And, according to the telegrams and news sent by the Khedive, Tewfik Pasha, one of this party, we see that he is weak and capricious; and also it is to be re-marked that one of his telegrams does not corroborate another, but they are all in contradiction (wound each other). In ad-dition to this I may tell you that Ali Nizami Pasha and Ali Fuad Bey have spoken to His Majesty most highly in your favour, and Ahmed Ratib Pasha also has repeated to His Ma-jesty the substance of the conversation he had with you in the railway carriage between the stations of Zagazig and Mahda, and as His Majesty places the greatest confidence in Ahmed Pasha, His Majesty desires me again for this to express his trust in you, and to say that as he considers you a man of the highest integrity and trustworthiness he requires of you, above all things, to prevent Egypt from passing into the hands of strangers, and to be careful to allow them no pretext for inter-vention there.

"The orders which Ahmed Pasha Ratib will receive on this head will be separately communicated to you. Both my letter and that of Ahmed Pasha Ratib, by order of His Majesty, have been written by one of His Majesty's own private secre-taries, and after we have affixed our seals to the letters; we also put an extra seal on the envelopes.

"And, in a special and secret manner, I tell you that the Sultan has no confidence in Ismaïl, Halim, or Tewfik. But the man who thinks of the future of Egypt and consolidates the ties which bind her to the Caliphate; who pays due respect to His Majesty and gives free course to his firmans; who assures his independent authority in Constantinople and elsewhere; who does not give bribes to a swarm of treacherous sub-officials; who does not deviate one hair's-breadth from his line of duty; who is versed in the intrigues and machinations of our Euro-pean enemies; who will watch against them and ever preserve his country and his faith intact—a man who does this will be pleasing and grateful, and accepted by our great lord the Sul-tan.

"If I have not entered into any further details in this letter of mine, I beg you to excuse me because Ahmed Ratib Pasha only arrived three days ago, and yet in that time, owing to his declarations of your fidelity and true intentions, His Majesty has expressed his full confidence in you. I only received the message I have just given you yesterday. I hope to be able to send you by next week's post a more detailed letter. In every case be careful not to let any letter you send fall into strange hands but try to get a special messenger, and, as for this time, it would be better if you would send your answer by the hand of the man who brings this letter.

"Your Servant, MOHAMMED ZAFIR.

"4th Rebi ul Akhar, 22nd Feb., 1882."

These two letters are records of such high historical importance that if ever my memoirs come to be printed they should be annexed to them in facsimile. They explain much of what happened later in June at the time of the Dervish Mission, and they prove that if Arabi took upon himself then and during the months of the war the position in some degree of dictator in Egypt, it was not without ample justification from a Mohammedan point of view, in the commands of the Caliph as head of his religion to protect the province against Christendom. They show, too, why it was that in the month of August Abdul Hamid was so loath to proclaim him a rebel, and how absurd was the charge of rebellion brought against him at his trial.

Nevertheless, it must not be assumed from this that Arabi had made himself the Sultan's tool in anything that concerned the administrative independence of his country. His position on this point was a firm one.. He hated the Turks, and would certainly have resisted in arms any attempt from Constantinople at military intervention. Of this Sheykh Mohammed Abdu's letter is ample proof, and it is in harmony with all that Arabi has himself told me. His position, therefore, at the Caliphal Court was a changing and precarious one. He had strong friends there in Ahmed Ratib and Mohammed Zafir, but he also had strong enemies. Sabit Pasha, the Khedive's Turkish secretary, was especially one of them, and reported to Yildiz everything he could find against him. Thus, when the arrest of the Circassian conspirators occurred, among whom were Osman Pasha Rifki, and other important Turks, it is quite possible there was a wave of anger against Arabi in the Sultan's mind. But it does not seem to have lasted, and from the moment when it became once more a question of resisting Europe, Arabi again had the Sultan's approval. As between Tewfik, the puppet of the Anglo-French Control, and Arabi the defender

against the two Christian Powers of the independence of a
Moslem state, there could be no hesitation in the Caliph's sympathies.

I think it is to be regretted that the Sultan's wish to depose
Tewfik and set up Halim was not carried out. Though Arabi
did not belong to the party of Halim in Egypt, he would certainly not have opposed it after Tewfik had gone over to the
English against him, and it would have been accepted by a considerable number of respectable men in Egypt who knew Halim to be both more intelligent and more liberal in his views
than the other. The Sultan's intervention, therefore, would
have been a peaceable one if he had refrained from sending an
army to enforce it. On the whole it was probably the best solution. The French Government, however, were strongly opposed
to the immixture of the Sultan in Egyptian affairs, and our diplomacy at Cairo was pledging itself more and more every day
to Tewfik. All that came of the idea of Turkish intervention
and of the commission I had asked for, and which had been almost promised, was an absurd compromise of the two things,
in the shape of a proposal made, but not insisted on, by Lyons
to Freycinet at Paris, that a French, an English, and a Turkish
general should be sent to Egypt to "restore discipline in the
Egyptian army." Lord Lyons, be it remarked, had a special
reason for taking Malet's view of the situation in Egypt in
the fact that Malet had been for years his private secretary
and devoted servant in the profession.

Nothing, therefore, was really done of what I had been told
at Downing Street to expect, not even those few words of goodwill in Parliament which Gladstone had begged Arabi to wait
for. By a synchronism, tragic for Egypt, the crisis at Cairo,
so long worked up to, coincided exactly with that other crisis
which had also been impending in Ireland. There a *régime* of
threats and coercion under Forster, the Chief Secretary, had
been tried all through the winter. Members of Parliament
had been imprisoned without trial, and the arts of police despotism had been put into more rigorous practice than for many
years, and without any result of pacification. Gladstone had
persuaded his Cabinet to try conciliatory measures. According
to a secret arrangement made with Parnell, the Irish leader,
while he was in gaol at Kilmainham, and known as the Kilmain-

ham treaty, Parnell and his political friend, Dillon, had b'een released; and, as a consequence, Forster on the 2nd of May resigned his office and attacked the Government for their pusillanimity in the House of Commons. The very same day, 2nd May, had been fixed for a Ministerial statement about Egypt, on a motion made by Lord De la Warr in the House of Lords, and I find the following entry in my journal:

"*May* 2.—Met Lord De la Warr at the House of Lords. He took me in, and I expected to hear the promised statement about Egypt, but heard instead Lord Granville's announcement of Mr. Forster's resignation in Ireland. A good deal of excitement. Lord Granville seemed rather shy and badgered. Lord Salisbury interrupted once or twice. . . . I heard Rosebery say a few words in a very impressive and dignified manner, etc., etc. Egyptian affairs are put off as of no importance." Ireland for the next few weeks drove out all English interest in Egypt, so much so that when on the 6th I took Mohammed Abdu's important letter, explaining the Circassian plot, to Morley, he refused to publish it on the ground of its length, and that "nobody cared about Egypt."

This, however, was but the first act of the coming tragedy. On the 7th Lord Frederick Cavendish, a brother of Lord Hartington and an intimate friend of Gladstone's, who had been appointed Chief Secretary in Forster's place to carry out the new policy of conciliation, was assassinated at Dublin with Mr. Burke, the chief permanent official, by members of an Irish secret society, known as the "Invincibles." These were in reality quite unconnected with Parnell's Parliamentary party, but the public did not discriminate between the two, and the result was a universal cry for strong measures against all forms of rebellion. For a moment Gladstone battled against this, and it was proposed to Dilke, who, as an advanced Radical, was with Chamberlain at that time friendly to the Parnellites, that he should take the post of danger at Dublin and continue, as Cavendish's successor, the task of conciliating Ireland. But Dilke did not like the look of things, and refused the post. It was found difficult to get any one to accept it. What, however, decided the abandonment of the policy of conciliation was the attitude of Hartington. He took the matter of his brother's death, which he felt deeply, as a personal wrong to

be avenged, and from that moment became the most determined enemy of Irish Nationalism. Gladstone had to choose
between resignation and the abandonment of his policy, and, seeing a majority of his Cabinet against him, he chose the latter.
Trevelyan was sent to Dublin and new coercive measures were
resolved on. And so, too, as to Egypt. Up to this point, in
spite of the unconciliatory views of the Foreign Office, Gladstone,
supreme in the Cabinet, had been able to put a veto on any active form of armed intervention. But now he found himself
out-voted, and Egypt, too, was thrown to the wolves. "Look,"
his colleagues seem to have said to him, "where your policy of
conciliation has led us in Ireland." If I have been rightly
informed, a policy of coercion in Ireland and of intervention in
Egypt was decided on at one and the same Cabinet in the second
week of May. I quote some extracts from my Diary in illustration of the double situation.*

"*May* 8.—In consequence of the ugly look of things in Egypt
I have written an ultimatum to Gladstone begging him to re-
lieve me of the dilemma I am in, caused by the Government's
silence. I have said that I must speak the whole truth if Lord
Granville won't. All the world, however, is agog about Ire-
land. Yesterday came the astounding news of Lord Frederick
Cavendish's and Mr. Burke's murder at Dublin. At first it
seemed as if the Government would have to resign, but to-day
Parnell has written to disown all connection with the crime, and
I think Gladstone will be the stronger for it. On Friday when
I was in the lobby of the House of Commons Artie Brand (the
Speaker's son), who was there, pointed me out 'the three Irish
conspirators' talking together. Parnell is a tall, good-looking
man of about 32, with nothing of the murderer about him.
Dillon is tall and very pale and dark, and would do for Guy
Fawkes in a cloak and dagger. They looked very much like
gentlemen among the cads of the lobby.

"*May* 11.—There is bad news from Egypt. The Khedive
having refused to sign the Circassian sentences, Arabi has convoked the Chamber and they talk of deposing Tewfik. I went
at once to Downing Street and saw Godley, on whom I urged the
necessity of Gladstone giving me an immediate answer. Gladstone is away at Lord Frederick's funeral, and I have agreed to
wait till to-morrow for an answer; but Godley saw I was in earn-

---

* See Lord Eversley's letter quoted in the Preface.

est and promised it should be given. It is, of course, an unfortunate moment." I have a vivid recollection of Godley's sympathy on this occasion. I was myself deeply moved. It seemed to me so tragic a thing that the whole fate of a nation and of the best hopes of reform for a religion, both historic in the world, should depend on the possibility of securing the attention of one old man for half an hour, for I felt sure I could again persuade him. I did not, of course, know the exact position of the Cabinet, but Godley must have known, and he seemed almost as much to feel it, as myself. I know he all along disapproved the Foreign Office policy in Egypt, and I think he felt deeply the disgrace of Mr. Gladstone's share in it when, in spite of his Midlothian speeches, he came forward as the apologist of a war against Oriental freedom in the interests of finance. Very shortly after his chief's change of policy he left his service for a permanent post elsewhere, and I have always fancied it was more or less in protest.

"*May* 12.—Freycinet has declared he will not let the Turks intervene, so I feel easier. . . . Rode to George Howard's who approved my plan (of publishing the whole truth). I have all ready now . . . and the 'Times' will publish. It appears that Rothschild has been working hard with Freycinet to get the French Government to set up Halim instead of Tewfik. . . . In the meanwhile all that has actually been done is to order a fleet to be ready in a fortnight at Plymouth. . . . Saw Eddy Hamilton. He promises the answer to-night. The Howards are very angry with Dilke because he has refused the Chief Secretaryship for Ireland. 'He will lose caste by this.' They looked upon it as the shirking of a post of danger, but it is quite possible that Dilke was better pleased to remain where he was, at the Foreign Office, pulling the strings for Granville in Europe. It would have been well for Egypt if he had accepted.

"*May* 13.—Gladstone's answer has come; he cannot tell me any details, but Lord Granville will speak on Monday, and he begs me to wait till then. He only promises that the Liberal policy shall be in accordance with Liberal doctrines. So I am satisfied. I have written (to Gladstone) to offer to go out as mediator between Arabi and the Khedive. I have sent the following telegram to Arabi: 'I entreat you have patience. Do nothing rashly or without Parliament sanction. Delay action against the Khedive. I am working hard for you, but must have time. There is real danger.' At five o'clock I received an answer from Gladstone to say that he supposed my last letter was written before the arrival of recent news. I cannot understand what he means by that, as there is nothing in the evening papers. . . . Late at night an answer from Arabi: 'Mai 13. Je vous remercie de vos conseils. Différend déféré aux délégués. Tranquillité complète. Certainement aucune crainte pour Européens. Ahmed Arabi.' "

The true history of the crisis which had taken place that first fortnight of May at Cairo, as I afterwards learned it, was this. On the second, the Khedive finding himself pressed by Arabi, his Minister of War, to sign the sentences of exile on the Circassian officers, some of whom were His Highness's personal friends, called Malet to his counsels and received from him the advice, fortified by a promise of English support, that he should refuse his signature; and this must be considered the moment at which Tewfik first resolved to throw himself especially upon English protection in his quarrel with his Ministers. Malet thereupon wrote an important despatch which is published in the Blue Books, extolling in high terms the character of the Khedive, as one deserving the full confidence of Her Majesty's Government. The Khedive, therefore, refused to sign, though constitutionally his signature to the decision of the court-martial could not be withheld.

The refusal, aggravated by the fact, which at once became known, that it had been suggested by a foreign Consul, angered the Nationalist Ministry, and letters were addressed by the Prime Minister, Mahmud Sami, to the members of the National Parliament requesting their attendance at Cairo. This was no doubt an irregular proceeding, inasmuch as the Parliament could only be legally summoned by the Khedive, and it gave umbrage to some of the members who were also annoyed at being called again to Cairo from their country homes at an inconvenient season of the year. Nevertheless, a large proportion of them came in answer to Mahmud Sami's letters, and though they had no formal sitting, decided at a meeting held in Sultan Pasha's house to support the Ministers, and it was resolved by forty-five to thirty, that, if Tewfik persisted in intriguing with the English and French Consuls against them, there was no other way than to impeach and depose him. Malet, however, having by this time received a telegram of approbation from the Foreign Office, and finding the Khedive wavering, informed him that the English and French fleets had been ordered to Alexandria on a plea of protecting European subjects. Upon this the Khedive sent for Sultan Pasha, the President of the Chamber, and exposed the situation to him, and so worked upon his fears, and upon a certain personal jealousy which he knew to have grown up in the Sultan's mind toward Arabi, that he persuaded him to take part with him, and trust to European support rather than run the risk of war. Sultan then, at a new informal meeting of the Deputies, declared himself on the Khedive's side against the Ministers, and obtained the adhesion of six other Deputies to his view, though the large majority of them remained faithful to the Ministry. It was at this juncture that my telegram to Arabi was received at Cairo, and it seems to have had some effect with Sultan, to whom it was doubtless shown. But the English papers of the thirteenth asserted that the Chamber had joined the Khedive against Arabi, and on the fifteenth that Mahmud Sami had resigned. The following is from my journal.

"*May* 14.—Sunday, at Crabbet. I see in the 'Observer' that Sultan Pasha went yesterday to the Khedive to make terms between him and Arabi; so I conclude my telegram came just in time. The papers all say that he and the Chamber have sided against Arabi with the Khedive, but I will not believe that till I hear further. What is likely is that Sultan Pasha has been put out at the Chamber being invoked without a legal summons, and at an inconvenient time of the year. The army has had too much influence in the Ministry not to have made itself enemies. There is probably jealousy, but I do not believe in more. The whole thing has doubtless been fostered by Colvin and Malet. and the Circassians have been encouraged by the idea of Turkish intervention. They have ordered ships to Alexandria, which, if I am not mistaken, will have the effect of uniting all once more against the Europeans.

"In the afternoon a perplexing telegram from Abdu, 'Il n'y a pas discorde entre Sultan Pasha et le Parlement. Le loup (meaning the ex-Khedive Ismaïl) dont participation dans le complot Circassian est supposé dans ma lettre a Sabunji, est en effet complice. Différend principal est deféré aux délégués. Tranquillité publique n'est pas menacée.' "

Van Benningsen, the distinguished Dutch judge, author, under the title of "Un Juge Mixte," of one of the most valuable works about Egypt under the Dual Control, was staying with me at Crabbet at the time, and I found him an ardent sympathizer with the Nationalists.

The next day, 15th May, was that of the long promised explanation by the Government of their Egyptian policy, and I went up to London in high hopes of something good, being fortified by the telegram I had received. I was doomed, however, to a new disappointment. Though the matter of Egypt was discussed in the House of Lords, Granville had nothing better to promise the Egyptians than a repetition of the old menace of Gambetta's Joint Note, and the statement, which I felt certain was untrue, that the Deputies at Cairo and the whole country were supporting the Khedive in his quarrel with his Ministers. This, then, was the famous "Liberal policy" Hamilton had promised me. I felt myself absolved from all obligation of reticence towards Gladstone, who seemed to have played with and deceived me. I left the House of Lords as soon as I had heard the speech, in great anger, and resolved henceforth to act without further reference to prudence on my part or the Government's convenience. After thinking the matter over during the night in much perplexity, I decided upon a bold step. I was resolved to defeat the intrigue I knew was going on. As soon as the telegraph offices were open in the morning, 16th May, I sent the following message to Cairo:

"To Arabi Pasha, Minister of War. Lord Granville states in Parliament that Sultan Pasha and the Deputies have joined the Khedive against you. If untrue, let Sultan Pasha telegraph me contradiction. United you have nothing to fear. Could you not form a Ministry with Sultan Pasha as Prime Minister? But stand firm."

"To Sultan Pasha, President of the Chamber of Deputies. I trust that all who love Egypt will stand together. Do not quarrel with Arabi. The danger is too great."

Also to each of the following Deputies: "Butros Pasha, Abu Yusuf, and Mahmud Pasha Falaki. Parti national, est il actuellement content d' Arabi? Le Gouvernement Anglais prétend le contraire. Si vous vous laissez désunir de l'année, l'Europe vous annexera."

And I sent the same last telegram to Mohammed Abdu, to Sheykh el Hajrasi, and to Abdallah Nadim, the orator. All the eight telegrams were signed with my name, and I knew that in thus sending them I was sure to incur the anger of the Foreign Office, if not of Mr. Gladstone, for it could hardly be unknown to the Agency at Cairo, as messages sent by the Eastern Telegraph Company were at that time pretty well common property there. I was resolved, however, to run the risk of this, my only doubt being how to express succinctly the nature of the danger against which I warned the Deputies. The words, "Europe will annex you," seemed to me to do this best, for though, perhaps, our Government had no immediate thought of annexation nor yet the French Government, the ultimate end seemed certain, and Colvin's words rang in my ears; nor do I think that the event so far has otherwise than justified me. Then, having fired my shot, I went back to the country repose of Crabbet to wait for what should happen. The answer came sooner than I at all expected, and that very evening, as I was sitting down to dinner, I received the following from Sultan Pasha:

"Le différend qui existait entre le Khedive et les Ministres complètement disparu. Nous sommes tous d'accord à maintenir le repos et la tranquillité et à appuyer le Ministère actuel. Sultan."

In delight I telegraphed it at once to Gladstone, and to the "Times" for publication.

"*May* 17.—To London again in the highest spirits, and on my way received new answers."

From the Sheykh el Islam, el Embabeh:

"Le différend entre le Khedive et le Ministère est applani. Le Parti National est content d'Arabi. Le nation et l'armée sont unies."

Another unsigned, but no doubt from one of the Deputies:

"Tout le pays avec Arabi and le Ministère Sami. Fellahs, Bedouins, Ulemas, tous sont unis. Il n'y a qu'un seul_d'entre nous qui soit contre la liberté Egyptienne et qui tache de fausser l'opinion publique."

And a third of like character from Mohammed Abdu.

Moreover, in confirmation of the glorious news, the morning papers announced that in the afternoon of yesterday the Khedive, through Sultan Pasha's mediation, had forgiven the Ministry. It was clear that I had won a first diplomatic victory. With such powerful proofs in my hand, I went with a light heart to Downing Street and showed my telegrams, and found Hamilton and Godley, who congratulated me on my success. I told them the telegrams I had sent had cost me £20, and Hamilton said they ought to be repaid me out of the Secret Service Fund. Though this was, of course, said jokingly, it proves that, at least on Mr. Gladstone's side of Downing Street the result I had gained against the Foreign Office was cordially approved. Moreover, as I had not seen Gladstone himself, Hamilton and Godley advised me to write him another formal letter and press home my point against the Foreign Office, on the ground of their false information, and I agreed to do so, and spent the night at this work, having first arranged with Button that, if need should be, the letter should be published in the "Times," and in the meanwhile I sent Sultan a telegram begging him to congratulate the Khedive.

The morning, nevertheless, was to bring me a sharp reverse, if not yet a defeat. At a very early hour, having slept in London at my then town house, 10, James Street, Buckingham Gate, I sent for the morning papers, and found in all of them a Reuter's telegram from Cairo giving the text of my telegram to the Deputies, the one ending "Europe will annex you," as having been addressed by me to the Sheykh el Islam, and stating that the Sheykh el Islam had since recanted the telegram he had sent me in reply. Also in the "Standard" there was a telegram from its correspondent at Cairo saying that he was authorized by Sultan Pasha to contradict the telegram from him which had been published in the "Times" of yesterday, the same having been written under military intimidation. I consequently at once wrote a second letter to Gladstone, and sent him the two by the same messenger before noon, with a note to Hamilton saying, that I considered it necessary both should be published. I had found Button at home, and had shown him the letters, which he promised should appear in the morrow's "Times." He was delighted with them, and assured me they would make a sensation. [1]

Nevertheless, though they had already been put in type, for I had left copies of them with Button, the two letters were not published. The reason for this is given in my diary. At six o'clock I found a note from Eddy Hamilton saying he would be at home all the afternoon, so I went to him. He said he thought the telegram to the Sheykh el Islam an unfortunate one, and advised me strongly not to publish. "I asked him what assurance he could give me that nothing violent was intended at Alexandria. He said he understood that the fleet going there only meant the securing of the lives of British subjects. He did not think it at all likely there would be any demand made for the disbanding of the Egyptian army or any disembarkation of troops. Also he assured me that a Commission, such as I had proposed, would be sent to Egypt. I am quite satisfied with this, and have sent David (my servant) to the 'Times' office to stop the publication of the letters.'"

I do not doubt that the assurances given me in Downing Street on this occasion were given in good faith, but they were soon belied by the Foreign Office, and my silence as to the telegrams did me, from that time forth, an injury with the public. The "St. James's Gazette" spoke of me that very evening as an "incendiary," and other journals, seeing I did not reply, followed suit. Their language re-acted on the Government, and doubtless also on Gladstone, though he knew the truth, which the public as yet did not. I continued, it is true, my communications and visits to Downing Street, but they became inevitably on a less and less intimate footing. For this reason I regret that I allowed myself to be persuaded, and that the letters did not appear, as had been arranged that night, in the "Times." Had they done so I cannot help thinking that the fatal ultimatum of 25th May would not have been issued.

---

[1] These two letters are practically embodied in my letter subsequently published on June 20. See Chapter XIV.

CHAPTER XII

INTRIGUES AND COUNTER INTRIGUES

The history of the next six weeks in Egypt, from the arrival of the English and French fleets at Alexandria to the bombardment of the city is that of a desperate attempt by our diplomacy one way or another to regain its lost footing of influence, and failing that to bring about a conflict; and of a no less desperate and unscrupulous attempt by the Foreign Office at home to force Gladstone's hand to an act of violence. In all this there was far less of statemanship, or even financial intrigue, than of personal pique. The tone neither in the Chancelleries of Europe nor of the Stock Exchange was so urgent as to make a peaceful treatment of the case impossible. France, under Freycinet, had withdrawn entirely from Gambetta's aggressive designs, and would readily have made the best at any moment of a political situation by no means hopeless at Cairo, while Germany and Austria, representing the financial interests, especially of the Rothschilds, were for a repetition of the remedy found efficacious in 1879, the Sultan's intervention in the form of a new firman, substituting Halim for Tewfik. This would have been an easy solution of the quarrel which had arisen between Tewfik and his Ministers, and though not the ideal to which the Nationalist leaders looked, would have been accepted by all parties as an ending of the crisis. The other countries of Europe were for the most part in sympathy with the National movement, Switzerland and Belgium strongly so, while Italy was so enthusiastic that at one time, in spite of the Government, which supported English policy, a corps of volunteers was being enrolled under Menotti Garibaldi to help Arabi. It was only in England that public opinion, worked upon systematically through the Press primed by our diplomacy, was at all excited or called for vigorous action.

The personal element in the struggle is easy to understand. Malet and Colvin had committed themselves at the time of the change of Ministry in February to an attitude of uncompromising hostility to the Nationalists, and any solution of the crisis which should leave these in power at Cairo they knew would mean their own disgrace. Colvin would certainly have had to follow his French colleague, de Blignières, into retirement, and Malet would have been removed to some minor post in the service where his blundering would have been of less grave consequence. The Foreign Office, too, had its own *amour propre* to save. Dilke was an ambitious man, and did not mean to fail, and even old Granville, fond as he was of his ease, had his public phrases to make good. Thus from the middle of May to the 11th of July, the date of the bombardment, we have the spectacle of a series of diplomatic manœuvres wholly indefensible by any valid plea of necessity, absolutely at variance with all the avowed principles of Mr. Gladstone's Midlothian policy, and so cynically unscrupulous that I doubt if in the annals of our Foreign Office anything comparable to them exists.

On the other hand, in native Egypt, we see the National Party just at the moment when it had secured for the country the right of self-government and an existence of personal and civil freedom which it had never before in all its history enjoyed, when its Parliament had met, and after a first happy session had adjourned, when its mind was busy with projects of reform and when the general desire was to rest and be thankful, at peace with all the world, hurried from its attitude of calm into a sea of apprehension from without, and of treachery, backed by foreign intrigue, from within. Three letters written to me at the beginning of the crisis, the first two from Arabi himself, the third from that gallant old Swiss gentleman, John Ninet, who alone of the European sympathizers with the National fellah cause remained on in Egypt and took part with the army during the war, will show what the earlier feeling in native Cairo was.

"Cairo, *May* 15, 1882.
"To my dear and sincere friend Mr. Blunt.
"Praise be to God, your letter of the 20th April duly reached

me. We have read it with great pleasure. Let us hope that the fruit of your endeavour will soon be gathered. Indeed, every sound-minded lover of freedom bears witness to your philanthropic efforts. My pleasure was increased by learning from you that my two letters reached you in a favourable hour. May God in his mercy give peace to our minds, and better the condition of affairs, and lead us to what he thinks for the good of our country.

"As to the publication of my two letters I only wished to refute the attacks made upon me by my enemies, those who accused me of being a man extravagant in his ideas and seeking after despotic power. These are mere calumnies, as you know full well. I like better to remind you that as a member of the Egyptian Government I am responsible as Minister of War for the acts of my office, as we all are responsible for our departments. I have but one voice in the Cabinet, and I act according to the policy imposed upon me by the Prime Minister, as shown in the letter he presented to the Khedive when he first formed the Ministry. You may reply upon my truthful word that we are all of us in anxious watch over our country, and trying to rule it according to just principles, and we have made up our minds, by God's help, to overcome all difficulties. If any among the European nations, who love mankind and love civilization, will take us by the hand and help us in our struggle, we shall be infinitely grateful to them. If not we have to thank God only, who has been our support from the beginning.

"As to the state of the country, it is in perfect peace. Our only perplexity is caused by the lies published by unscrupulous men in the European press. This is a gratuitous hostility, but we hope that soon the veil of prejudice will fall from their eyes.

"AHMED ARABI."

"Cairo, *May* 21, 1882.

"After offering to you our best salutations and compliments, we tender you our thanks for your endeavours, and for the interest you take in the welfare of our country, and for your constant inquiries, either by telegrams or by letters, after the events which have been taking place, and we have already replied, as the rest of us did, explaining the true state of things. We now add these few further explanations.

"All the people in the country are grieved at the despatch of the French and English ships, and they look on this as a sign of evil intentions on the part of the two Powers towards the Egyptians, and as an intrusion into our affairs, without necessity and without reason; and truly the Egyptians have made up their minds not to give in to any Power which wishes to interfere with our internal administration. They are also determined to keep their privileges confirmed to them by the treaties of the Powers. And they will never allow a tittle of these to be taken from them as long as they have life. And they will also try their best to watch over European interests and the lives of European subjects, their property and honour, as long as these keep within the limits prescribed to them by law.

"We all endeavour to do our duty, and we trust in God in defending our rights, and through His help we hope to obtain our purpose. This is the welfare of our country and the peace of those who live in it. We also trust in the justice of Europe that the Powers shall not begin the attack upon us, but on the contrary that they may behave wisely with us. Because this will really be better for the success of their own wishes, and their interests in our country.

"It will be better for Great Britain if she does not rely on her representatives in this country, because they are persons who have private motives, which they wish to serve. And we think that even if they succeed it will be for the disadvantage of their Government.

"This is enough now of the present state of things, and the future will tell the rest.

"Herewith I send you a letter addressed to Sir William Gregory, and beg you to be kind enough to hand it to him.

"Please present my compliments to Mr. Sabunji and Lady Anne Blunt, and may God preserve you all.

"AHMED ARABI."

Ninet's letter is of especial value from its date, 19th May, the last day of Egypt's peaceful enjoyment of self-government. It says:

"My heart of an old Swiss patriot bleeds now at the most unjust of all international interventions. The country is entirely united in favour of its honest leader, sprung, like the

fellahin, from the *limon du Nil* (the black mud of the Nile).
The Egyptian people has loyally accepted its debt contracted
for it by an unscrupulous despot, one who in sixteen years
squandered more than three hundred millions sterling to fill
his own pockets, the pockets of the diplomacy, high and low, and
of the Semitic and Nazarene usurers. . . . A peaceful revolution has been accompanied by and with the will of the nation.
Not a single act unbecoming a scrupulous government has taken
place during the great change effected. But Europe, interested
more in the dealers in stocks and shares than in the aspirations
of a people, sends her fleets. Why? Because the Chamber
of Representatives found it proper to claim the right of discussing the Budget! Where is the crime? . . . Suppose a
Minister of your Queen, having a disagreement with her, were
to receive news that a powerful combined fleet of the Catholic
Powers would go to Ireland and pacify it? Even so the analogy is not complete. Egypt is quiet. Not a European or
Christian can complain. Would not the position be intoler-
able? . . . Arabi is wise and tranquil, awaiting the future
like a sage of ancient times. The army, the country, the towns
are with him. The French Consul-General has been a silent
member. Sir E. Malet has been *cassant, parti pris inconciliant*,
sowing fear in Cairo, instead of reassuring the people. You
have no idea, my dear sir, of the abominable lies every day telegraphed to the 'Times,' 'Standard,' 'Daily News,' by the telegraphic agencies. . . . Well, never a word, not an insult from
the population—we have been and are as quiet here as an English congregation on a Sunday in Regent's Park. The fleets
are expected to-morrow."

Other letters of a later date will show it in its later stages.
The supreme injustice of the attack being made on them by
England, the country above all others which had been associated
in their minds with a traditional love of liberty and of those
humanitarian doctrines of which she had been the apostle, re-
volted men's minds and roused in them feelings of anger foreign
to their natural attitude. Under constant threat of violence,
now from England, now at English instigation from the Sultan,
and knowing not whom to trust and fearing everywhere betrayal, it is not surprising that wild ideas prevailed even among

those who had been soberest hitherto in their expression. At the same time it is not a little remarkable what few mistakes were made in action by the leaders under circumstances of such extreme and constantly changing difficulty, and the closer one examines these the more they redound to their credit. Nothing but the desperate shifts of our agents, when one after another their treacherous expedients had failed them and they found themselves faced with a disgraceful diplomatic defeat, to bring about a violent solution through the guns of the fleet, forced the Egyptians at last from their calm attitude and enabled our Foreign Office to claim a victory.

This may be affirmed without attributing either to Arabi or to any other of the leaders qualities of a first-class kind. They were neither diplomatists nor administrators nor soldiers at all to be compared with their opponents, and they were most of them quite inexperienced in the arts of government and the subtleties of international usage. Arabi's best quality, I think, was a certain dogged determination not to be driven from the position he had originally announced, namely, that, while ready to be friends with all the world, it was his duty to defend his country against all hostile comers. In this he rendered in those weeks an incalculable service to his fellow countrymen, which it is right they should be reminded of. Nothing is more certain than that, if Arabi had been less obstinate than he was in refusing either for threat or bribe to leave Egypt, and if thereby the Egyptians had not fought, the fellahin would still be the double slaves they were in 1880, slaves to their Turkish masters as well as slaves to Europe. What does any patriot suppose would have resulted from Arabi's compliance? Liberty in any form? A continuance of self-government? Foreign rule less strenuous than now? Certainly, none of these things. What would have come to pass is very clearly shown by the *régime* established at Cairo immediately after the war. It would have been one of police despotism, espionage, and secret punishments, unmitigated by any further interest taken in Egyptian nationality by the moral sense of Europe. It is possible that as a matter of form a Chamber of Notables might have been allowed to remain in existence for a few sessions as what is called a consultative body, but it would have been one wholly powerless and wholly discredited of patriotism. The

Turco-Circassian rule would have been ruthlessly re-established, and the Financial Control, reinforced with new political powers and exercised entirely in financial and European interests, would have had neither the will nor the power to enfranchise the fellahin from their Turkish masters, themselves the slaves of Europe. The whole legend of fellah nationality would have vanished in a disgraceful smoke, for a nation which has never dared fight for its existence is justly despised. The native press would have been reduced to the condition we find it in in Tunis. There would have been neither civil nor personal liberty, nor any regard paid to native rights. It would be still, in fact, what Egypt was in 1883, a land where no man could speak above his breath or count on his next door neighbour not to betray him. Arabi at least saved his countrymen from this, and, if when it came to the point of actual warfare he was found incapable as a soldier, they still owe him as a patriot much. He prevented them from incurring the supreme disgrace of not having fought at all on the only occasion in all their history when the chance was theirs to stand up for their freedom.

Having said this much, I will return to my story. The true history of the telegrams, as I afterwards learned it, at Cairo was this. They had arrived at a most critical moment when the attitude of the Deputies and of some among the weaker-kneed of the other civilian leaders was exceedingly doubtful. Malet had persuaded the Khedive to take heart and quarrel with his Ministers, and the Khedive had persuaded Sultan Pasha to join him partly by working on his jealousy of Arabi, for he was disappointed at not having been included by Mahmud Sami in the Ministry of February, partly by informing him that the English and French fleets were on their way to Alexandria. And Sultan, in his turn, had persuaded thirty, as against forty-five, of the Deputies. So that Malet had been able to telegraph to the Foreign Office that the Chamber was supporting the Khedive. My telegrams, however, had given new heart to waverers and had put such pressure upon Sultan that he had gone at once to the Khedive (who was engaged in drawing up a new list of Ministers under the Presidency of Mustafa Pasha Fehmi, the colourless Minister of Foreign Affairs) and effected a reconciliation between him and Mahmud Sami. The ministerial crisis was considered by everybody at an end. Hardly, however, was the arrangement made than it was undone. Malet, having got wind of the telegrams, sent for Sultan Pasha, and partly by threats about the fleet, partly by promises, once more persuaded him to take sides with the European Control.

Sultan Pasha, who afterwards deeply regretted his defection from the National cause at this critical moment, always affirmed that Malet, to win his support, gave him his word of honour that day that the rights of the Egyptian Parliament would be respected; and I have been told by his friends that Sultan died reproaching himself that he had been fool enough to believe him. Nevertheless, with the exception of Sultan, nobody of any importance among the Deputies allowed himself again to be detached from the National cause. All who had received my telegrams believed me rather than Malet, and Arabi's hands had been immeasurably strengthened when ten days later the next great crisis came. Malet's coup with the fleet had been discounted, and it ended in a complete fiasco. The sending of the fleet had been intended by Lord Granville as a *brutum fulmen,* which was to effect its purpose without real violence, a method in which he greatly believed and of which his success the year before at Dulcigno in the matter of the Greek frontier had specially enamoured him—indeed, it was one of his maxims that "a threat is as good as a blow." Malet also, who knew Lord Granville's mind, counted at that time on a bloodless victory. He throughout miscalculated the power of the National sentiment; and it was only when he saw that he had failed diplomatically that, following Colvin's lead, he prepared for force. The dates are: May 17th, Malet finally secures Sultan Pasha. It demands the resignation of the Ministry and Arabi's Alexandria. May 25th, Malet and Sinkiewicz issue their ultimatum, stating that it has been suggested to them by Sultan Pasha. It demands the resignation of the ministry and Arabi's retirement from Egypt. May 27th, the Mahmud Sami Ministry resigns. May 28th, Cairo rises and insists upon Arabi's reinstatement as Minister, and Arabi is reappointed Minister of War with something like dictatorial powers.

In England during all this crisis the outlook for me was a black one, made darker by the unfortunate defection, just at the moment when his support was most needed, of my fellow champion of the Egyptian cause in London, Sir William

Gregory. Gregory had committed himself quite as deeply to the National Party in its earlier stages as I had, and had written a number of powerful letters in support of Arabi in the "Times," and his influence stood far higher than mine in official quarters and with Chenery, the "Times" editor.   The prospect, however, of possible hostilities in connection with the arrival of the fleets alarmed him, and he had latterly begun in his letters to doubt and qualify his published opinions.   Since leaving Egypt in April he had been travelling on the Continent and I had been hoping daily for his arrival in London to reinforce my pleadings with the Government.   Instead of this, I found to my dismay that, if not exactly against us, he was doing us little service.   We were to have gone together to an anti-aggression meeting but now he refused to go.   I find in my journal :

"*May* 19.—Gregory has failed us.   He dined last night with Chenery who has frightened him, and he refuses now to go to the meeting.   I went to the meeting and made my speech and answered a number of questions put to me, giving the true history of the telegrams, and I got Dilwyn, the chairman, to vote my conduct patriotic.

"*May* 20.—I hear Lord Granville is furious with me about the telegrams."

On Sunday, 21st May, the very next day, after this entry, I had an embarrassing meeting with Granville.   I had been asked with my wife some time before by her cousin, the present Lord Portsmouth, to spend that Saturday to Monday at Hurstbourne, and the Granvilles had also been asked and several other persons more or less political.   I fancy Granville had wished to meet me, as it is called "accidentally" in diplomatic parlance.   But in the interval grave events had taken place, and I was not a little disturbed when I found him staying there, for I had not myself been told of it.   The moment was an unfortunate one, for that morning we had brought down with us the "Observer" newspaper which contained an account of the first rebuff given to the fleet at Alexandria.   "We arrived with Lowell, the American Minister, and found the house empty, every one gone to morning church.   On their return I perceived to my horror, for I was not expecting it, Lord Granville and Lady Granville walking back with the rest of the party. Things however went off well, for I had the sympathy of most of the party with me, especially as we had brought news down with us that the arrival of the fleets at Alexandria had been resolutely answered by Arabi by a call to arms, and that 4,000 of the Redifs (reserve men) had responded to it. His Lordship looks worried, so I argue well for the Nationalists. I had a deal of conversation with him on every subject in the world except Egypt. Lord Granville is very pleasant company, a *raconteur* of the old-fashioned type, each story being neatly and concisely got up, not always apposite to the moment but almost always good. With the rest of the party Egypt was gaily and sympathetically discussed. Henry Cowper was charming— Lowell and Stuart Rendall most sympathetic—the last, that is, when Lord Granville was out of hearing. . . . It was a lovely day and we sauntered about the park and gardens, Henry Cowper telling good stories, amongst others one, *à propos* of the Eastern Question, of Disraeli. He had heard him say 'Tancred is a book to which I often refer, not for amusement but for instruction.' " Lowell, as already said, was the whole of that summer a strong believer in the National Party, and always gave me support in conversation about it when we met.

It is worth noticing in connection with this visit to Hurstbourne that Lord Granville two days later, 23rd May, sent the fatal telegram authorizing Malet to "act as he thought fit," with the result that the Ultimatum was issued on the 25th. The view of the case in Egypt as printed at that date by John Morley in the "Pall Mall Gazette," runs thus: "Affairs still remain in a very critical condition at Cairo. Ourabi [1] persists in maintaining an attitude of defiance. He is playing his last card. The reserves are being brought up from the villages—in chains —troops are being hurried to the coast to resist a landing and artillerymen are being sent to the ports at Alexandria, the guns of which, such as they are, surround our ironclads. All this, probably, is only a game of brag, intended to extort better terms for himself." "The experiment," says Morley, "of vigorous

[1] This French spelling of Arabi's name used by the P. M. G. was due originally, I believe, to Colvin's French colleague, de Blignières, and was adopted by him and by Baron Mallortie who, with Colvin, was Morley's principal correspondent that year at Cairo.

representations emphasized by ironclads at Alexandria has been fairly tried, and there seems to be no doubt that it has completely failed."

"*May* 22.—To London.   Harry Brand, whom I met at the Club, tells me Dilke tells him 'it must end in intervention,'

"Old Houghton sent to say he wished to consult me about Egypt, and I had a long talk with him in the Lobby of the House of Lords. . . . I advised him, if he was pushing the Government to land troops in Egypt, to send at once for his daughter home.

"*May* 23.—Lord Granville in the Lords has made a jocular answer to demands for information about Egypt.

"*May* 26.—Gladstone has spoken about Egypt, a long rigmarole of which the only thing remarkable is that he expresses his confidence in a peaceful solution. . . . The Consuls have delivered an Ultimatum stating that their object is to restore the Khedive's personal authority and demanding the exile of Arabi.

"*May* 27.—Sultan Pasha denies having suggested the terms of the Ultimatum. . . . The Ultimatum is refused . . . Saw Gregory.   We think the Egyptians will have to fight now, and I feel I ought to go out and join them. . . . Telegram in the evening papers that Arabi's Ministry has resigned.

"*May* 28.—Sunday at Crabbet.   Things all seem gone to ruin in Egypt.   I suppose the Khedive's personal authority under the Control will now be revived.   If Arabi leaves the country and the army is disbanded, or reorganized under Circassian officers, Egypt may bid good-bye to liberty.   She will share the fate of Tunis.   Vicisti O Colvine!

"*May* 29.—I could not sleep but began roaming about soon after 3.   It tormented me to think I did not go to Egypt immediately on hearing Lord Granville's speech.   I might have saved matters. . . . Now all is bright again.   By an extraordinary transition the papers announce that Cairo has risen and has demanded Arabi's recall as Minister of War, the Khedive acquiescing.   The news seems too good to be true, but it cannot be doubted from the anger of the newspapers.   This shifts things back into more than their old place, and now there is nothing to fear except from the Porte.   I have made up my mind to go at once to Egypt.   Went up to London, saw

Gregory, lunched with the Howards, and wrote a letter to Eddy Hamilton announcing my intention. Mrs. Howard advises me to trust all to Gladstone, and in my letter to Hamilton I have done so implicitly. Only it is a wrench to leave England in June and face the turmoil and the heat of Cairo. I am happier though, feeling that at least I am doing all I can do and doing my duty. Anne will go with me."

My letter to Hamilton, written under the influence of the Gladstonian atmosphere of Palace Green, runs thus:

"May 29th, 1882.

"DEAR EDDY,

"Though Mr. G. is, I fear, displeased with me for the telegrams I sent to Egypt a fortnight ago, I do not wish to take any important step without his knowledge. I am convinced that some day he will forgive me for what I have done, and approve what I intend to do; and I have perfect confidence in him that he will act towards Egypt on the Liberal grounds you spoke of, as soon as he is certain of the truth. I believe, also, that I may still be of use to England as well as to Egypt in circumstances which may occur; and with that idea, I am going, unless anything unforeseen occurs, next Friday to Cairo.

"I will tell you exactly what I shall advise the National leaders. I shall urge them, first of all, to sink all petty differences in the presence of a great danger. I shall urge them, as I have always done, not to quarrel with the Khedive; and if I have an opportunity I shall urge the Khedive not to allow himself to be persuaded by the Consuls to quarrel with the people. I shall fortify Arabi in his determination to retain the full direction of the army in his hands by remaining Minister of War, but shall advise him to leave all other offices of State to civilians, and especially to members of the Chamber. I shall urge the Egyptians to keep on the best terms they can with the Sultan, short of admitting his soldiers into their country, and on the best terms with the European Powers short of yielding their constitutional rights. At the same time, I shall advise them strongly, as I advised them last January, to yield something to the Controllers of their present claim regarding the Budget—that is to say, to postpone their rights at least for this next year. I shall explain to them the position, as far as

I understand it, of the English Government, anxious not to destroy their independence, yet bound by ties contracted by their predecessors; of the French Government, traditionally inclined to push its powers in the Mediterranean, and forced on by the financiers; of the German Government, willing to divert the French from home affairs and dissolve the English alliance; and, lastly, of the Sultan, with his Caliphal dreams, a matter which they probably understand at least as well as I do.

"I do not propose myself to take any part in military operations, should such occur, except in the last necessity, against the Turks, for I know nothing of military matters, and have a horror of war. But I shall urge the Egyptians to resist invasion, from whatever quarter, and, if vanquished, to pursue a persistent policy of refusing taxation not sanctioned by their laws—whereas, if unmolested, I would have them pay their debt to the last farthing. I shall have no need to repress fanaticism, for they are not fanatics; but I shall join my voice to Arabi's in favour of the humanest interpretation of the laws of war. I also wish to be at hand in case of need, to protect European residents at the first outbreak of hostilities.

"I do not think I am acting unadvisedly in telling you this. My idea of a policy for the Egyptians is, that they should act by a rule diametrically opposite to the common Oriental ones. I would have them tell the truth, even to their enemies—be more humane than European soldiers, more honest than their European creditors. So only can they effect that moral reformation their religious leaders have in view for them.

"I am, yours affectionately, W. S. B."

The "Pall Mall" utterances of this date are again worth quoting, as they show the absurdly unreal view of the situation in Egypt put forward at that time by the Foreign Office, Colvin, Dilke, and the rest. Malet's despatches had led the Foreign Office to believe that Arabi had behind him no popular following outside the army, that the Khedive was in reality beloved by his subjects, and it was thought that it only needed now a little additional show of outside help from Constantinople being at hand to bring about a manifestation in Tewfik's favour which, if it did not force the army to submission, would lead to civil war demanding intervention.

The "Pall Mall Gazette," 26th May, says: "The Ultimatum which England and France have addressed to the Egyptian Ministry is to be accepted or rejected in twenty-four hours. This afternoon, therefore, the crisis ought to be over and the order despatched to Constantinople for the Ottoman *gens d'armes* who are to restore the authority of the Khedive under the control of England and France." Again, on 27th May: "A few hours may decide whether the crisis in Egypt is to be solved peacefully, or whether the country is to be the scene of civil war and foreign occupation. The Ministry has resigned, and so far the terms of the Anglo-French Ultimatum have been complied with. . . . On the other hand it is at least likely that Ourabi . . . may throw off the mask and declare boldly against his head." The kind of civil war expected is explained next day, 28th May: "Last night the Khedive slept at the Ismaïlia palace surrounded by twelve thousand loyal Bedouins. The presence of these children of the desert in the Capital of Egypt constitutes a material safeguard against a new *pronuncia mento*. No doubt it is a fearful prospect, that of a civil war in the streets of Cairo between the Bedouins and the regular army; but its possibility is a security for a pacific solution of the crisis. . . . Ourabi's position is no longer what it was. Even the power of the sword is no longer exclusively in his hands. If the Khedive with the swords of the Bedouins, the ironclads of England and France, and the support of the Chamber of Notables cannot reduce Ourabi to submission, the position must be more hopelessly complicated than any one has hitherto ventured to affirm."

What a fantastic account! Twelve thousand loyal Bedouins camped round the palace of Ismaïlia! The Chamber of Deputies devoted to the Khedive! Arabi standing alone intimidating them all! Yet it was with these lies, of which honest John Morley was made the popular mouthpiece, that Gladstone was being persuaded to apply the astonishing remedy for unruly Egyptian Nationalism of bringing in on it the "unspeakable Turk," the "Bashi-bazouk," fresh from his "Bulgarian atrocities," and the "man of sin" himself, Sultan Abdul Hamid. The illusion of the Khedive's popularity only lasted forty-eight hours. Then we read in the "Pall Mall Gazette" of 30th May: "The time has at last come for immediate action in Egypt. The Khedive is a prisoner in his palace. The twelve thousand

Bedouins who were reported to be encamped around their sovereign have vanished into thin air," etc., etc.

Meanwhile I was awaiting an answer from Downing Street, and making my preparations for an immediate start for Egypt. Mr. Gladstone was out of town, staying with Lord Rosebery at the Durdans, in my eyes an ominous circumstance. I knew Rosebery's view of the Egyptian question, for a few weeks before I had found him at Downing Street with Hamilton, and had walked with them both by the little garden exit through St. James's Park. On the way I had asked him his views about Egypt, and he had answered very briefly, "I have no views at all but those of a bondholder." He was, in fact, through his wife, a Rothschild, largely interested in the financial aspect of the case; and I looked upon Gladstone's visit to him just then as an evil symptom. Rosebery was not as yet in office, but had influence with Gladstone, and I knew through Button that he was being pushed forward by the Rothschilds to do their political work for them. This continued for some years, and his mission to Berlin in 1885 was suggested and made successful by the Rothschilds, and later at the Foreign Office he worked consistently in their interests on Egyptian questions, though I have heard that before taking office he got rid of his Egyptian stock.

"*May* 30.—No answer from Eddy. I see Mr. G. is out of town at the Durdans. All however is going on well in Egypt, Arabi the acknowledged master of the situation. . . . I found a note yesterday from Houghton asking again to see me, and I went to him at his house in Mayfair, and told him of my plan of going to Egypt. By his manner I am convinced that he has been commissioned by Lord Granville to sound me. . . . I have told Glyns (my bankers, Messrs, Glyn, Mills, and Currie) to get me £1,000 in French gold, the sinews of war. I feel very loath to go, but happy, being sure that I am doing what is right. . . . Sabunji will go too. . . .

"*May* 31.—To London early and found another note from Houghton saying 'surely I won't go.' I am certain this is an unofficial hint." Houghton's note was characteristic: "My dear Blunt, assuredly you had better not go to Egypt just now. Whatever you say or do there will be exaggerated and probably misinterpreted. The alliance between the Military Party and the Porte seems complete, and that won't suit your views. You could let me know if you hear anything precise. My daughter is still at Alexandria, but I am anxious for Fitzgerald, who must be obnoxious to the army from his military economies. I am yours very truly, Houghton. Bring your friend (Arabi) back with you if you do go, and come and dine here with him.''

"Also a telegram from Eddy. 'Your letter received. I implore you to do nothing till after seeing me. Shall be back this evening.' He is at Salisbury. . . . At half past five found Eddy in Downing Street. He implored me not to go, as my position in Egypt, and my known connection with Gladstone would be misunderstood, and make a terrible row. He promised me there would be no landing of troops or intervention at all. On this assurance I consented not to go. I told him, however, that I hoped they would not consider me responsible for accidents which might occur, and which it was my main object in going to prevent. He said they would not.

"A large card has come from Lady Granville inviting us to the Foreign Office on the 3rd to celebrate the Queen's birthday. I shall keep this as an answer to Harry Brand's charge of treason. . . . Now I am quite contented. Sabunji is to go instead of me, and will do just as well. He has telegraphed by my orders to Arabi in answer to a letter I have received from him: 'Letter received. Do not fear the ships. No intervention. Issue public notices in every town for the safety of Europeans.' This in accordance with a suggestion of Eddy's.

"*June* 1.—Everything seems going on beautifully. Arabi acknowledged master of the situation in Egypt. The Sultan supposed to be so at Constantinople. Button thinks the 'Times' will pay for my telegrams Sabunji may send them. If so, so much the better. I have agreed to give Sabunji £30 a month and his expenses. . . . Went to the House of Commons with Nigel Kingscote (the Prince of Wales's equerry), who got me into the Speaker's Gallery. Gladstone was giving his announcement of a conference at Constantinople as the upshot of it all. No troops are to be mobilized in India, and no troops to be landed in Egypt. He considers such a course would endanger European lives. McCoan, an M. P., formerly editor of the 'Levant Herald,' asked whether it was true I was 'about to proceed to Egypt to put myself at the head of the insurrection.' Dilke answered that he believed I had 'relinquished my intention.' Gladstone then made the astounding statement that Arabi had 'thrown off the mask,' and had threatened to depose the Khedive and put Halim on the throne of Egypt. This is too absurd, but it is playing into my hands, because the statement must be at once disproved, and the fact of its having been made will show how ignorant the Foreign Office are. Gladstone will now probably be angry with Malet for having led him into such a blunder. Frank Lascelles, however, who walked home with me from the House, tells me he has seen Malet's telegram respecting this, and all it says is that the Khedive told him this, and he does not vouch for its truth. So are things done!"

Malet's telegram, as it stands in the Blue Book (Egypt, No. 11, 1882), says even less than this. It runs thus: "The Khedive sent for M. Sinkiewicz and me this morning and informed us that it had come to his knowledge that the military intended this afternoon to depose him and proclaim Halim Pasha as Khedive of Egypt. . . . The Khedive said he hardly believed the truth of this information." Yet on such a slender rumour Gladstone, who had declared to me that he never spoke lightly in Parliament and had bidden me wait for his spoken word in the House of Commons as a message of goodwill to the Egyptians, fires off, to give point to his speech, this quite untrue announcement, his first definite utterance since I had seen him on Egypt. It is a curious comment on the ways of Ministers and the processes of the Gladstonian mind. The immediate effect on me of the Prime Minister's speech was a complete and lasting disillusion. Never after this did I place the smallest trust in him, or find reason, even when he came forward as champion of self-government in Ireland and when I gave him my freest support, to look upon him as other than the mere Parliamentarian he in truth was. I do not say that on that wonderful 22nd of March he was not for the moment in earnest when he spoke to me so humanly, but it was clear that his sympathies with the cause of right, however unfeigned, were not the law of his public action, which was dictated, like that of all the rest of them, by motives of expediency. The discovery destroyed for me an illusion about him which I have never regained.

"*June* 2.—Lord De la Warr, Gregory, Brand, and Button met at my house, and all but Brand seemed highly pleased at the situation. Harry still calls me a traitor, and declares that Arabi has made a gigantic fortune, and that he must and will be suppressed out of Egypt. Button then drew up with Sabunji a code of signals for him to telegraph us news; and I gave him £100 for his expenses, for which he will have to account. The telegrams are to be sent to me and I am to communicate them to Button for the 'Times.' I have given Sabunji my instructions, of which the two most important are that Arabi is to make peace with Tewfik and on no pretence to go to Constantinople. Now we have packed him off, anxious only lest he should be stopped at Alexandria. Button tells me that if I had persisted in going, orders would have been given to Sir Beauchamp Seymour to prevent my landing. . . . My mind is at rest."

If I had heard Gladstone's speech before agreeing with Hamilton to renounce my journey to Egypt I probably should have persisted in my intention, but, as things turned out, I doubt if it would have resulted in any good. Even if I had not been prevented from landing I could hardly have used more influence personally with Arabi and the other leaders than I succeeded in exercising through Sabunji. Sabunji was an admirable agent in a mission of this kind, and it is impossible I could have been better served. His position as ex-editor of the "Nahleh," a paper which, whether subsidized or not by Ismaïl, had always advocated the most enlightened views of humanitarian progress and Mohammedan reform, gave him a position with the Azhar reformers of considerable influence, and he was, besides, heart and soul with them in the National movement. As my representative he was everywhere received by the Nationalists with open arms, and they gave him their completest confidence. Nor was he unworthy of their trust or mine. The letters I sent him for them he communicated faithfully, and he faithfully reported to me all that they told him. These letters remain a valuable testimony, the only one probably extant, of the inner ideas of the time, and a *précis* of them will be found at the end of this volume. Sabunji landed at Alexandria on the 7th of June and remained till the day before the bombardment.[1]

[1] Sabunji remained in my employment till the end of 1883. Then he left me and visited India, where he had relations, and after many vicissitudes of fortune drifted to that common haven of Oriental revolutionists, Yildiz Kiosk, where he obtained the confidential post with Sultan Abdul Hamid of translator for the Sultan's private eye of the European Press, a post which I believe he still holds, 1907.

CHAPTER XIII

DERVISH'S MISSION

I have now come to a point in the history of this wonderful intrigue where, if I had not semi-official published matter in large measure to support me, I should find it hopeless to convince historians that I was not romancing. It seems so wholly incredible that a Liberal English Government, owning that great and good man Mr. Gladstone as its head, should, for any reason in the world financial, political, or of private necessity, have embarked on a plan so cynically immoral as that which I have now to relate. John Morley in his published life of Gladstone slurs over the whole of his astonishing Egyptian adventure that year in a single short chapter of fifteen pages, out of the fifteen hundred pages of which his panegyric consists, and with reason from his point of view, for he could have hardly told it in any terms of excuse. It is necessary all the same that historians less bound to secrecy should have the details plainly put before them, for no history of the British Occupation will ever be worth the paper it is written on that does not record them.

By the 1st of June it was generally acknowledged that the policy of intimidation by mere threat, even though backed by the presence of the fleets, had ignominiously failed. Mahmud Sami's Ministry indeed had resigned, but the initial success had been immediately followed only by a more complete discomfiture. The Ultimatum had expressly demanded that Arabi should leave Egypt, and not only had Arabi not obeyed, but the Khedive had been obliged by the popular voice to reinstate him as Minister of War, with even larger responsibilities than before, and in even more conspicuous honour. Our Foreign Office, therefore, found itself in the position of having either to eat its empty words in a very public manner, or to make them good against one who was now very generally recognized in Europe as a National hero. Its colleague in the matter, France, had long shown a desire to be out of the sordid adventure, and Mr. Gladstone's Government was left practically to act alone, if it insisted on going on, according to its own methods. The method resolved on was certainly one of the most extraordinary ever used by a civilized government in modern times, and the very last which could have been expected of one owning Mr. Gladstone as its chief. It was to beg assistance from the Sultan and persuade him to intervene to "get rid of Arabi," not by a mere exercise of his sovereign command nor yet by openly bringing in against him those Ottoman *gens d'armes* which had been talked of, but by one of those old-fashioned Turkish acts of treachery which were traditional with the Porte in its dealings with its Christian and other subjects in too successful rebellion against it.

A first hint of some such possible plan may be found in the "Pall Mall Gazette," in one of its little inspired articles, as far back as the 15th May, in which John Morley, explaining with satisfaction the Government policy of "bottle holding" the Khedive, adds that "Ourabi may before long be quietly got rid of." The full plan is of course not divulged in the Blue Books, but it is naïvely disclosed a little later in the "Pall Mall," where, without the slightest apparent sense of its impropriety, the dots are put plainly on the i's. The idea as I learned it at the time was that the Sultan should send a military Commissioner to Egypt, a soldier of the old energetic unscrupulous type, who, by the mere terror of his presence, should frighten the Egyptians out of their attitude of resistance to England, and that as to Arabi, if he could not be lured on ship-board and sent to Constantinople, the Commissioner should invite him to a friendly conference, and there shoot him, if necessary, with his own hand. The suggestion was so like the advice Colvin had given to the Khedive, and had boasted that he gave, nine months before, that there is nothing improbable in its having been again entertained. A Commissioner was consequently asked for at Constantinople, and one Dervish Pasha was chosen, a man of character and antecedents exactly corresponding to those required for such a job, and despatched to Cairo.

The excellent Morley, in an enthusiastic paragraph describing the arrival of this new Ottoman *deus ex machina,* grows almost lyrical in his praise.

"The Egyptian crisis," he says, "has reached its culminating point, and at last it seems that there is a man at Cairo capable of controlling events.   There is something very impressive in the calm immovable dignity of Dervish Pasha, who is emphatically the man of the situation.   After all the shiftings and twistings of diplomatists and the pitiful exhibition of weakness on the part of the leading actors in this Egyptian drama, it is an immense relief to find one 'still strong man' who, by the mere force of his personal presence, can make every one bow to his will.   Nothing can be more striking than his assertion of authority, and nothing more skilful than his casual reference to the massacre of the Mamelukes.   Dervish is a man of iron, and Arabi may well quail before his eye.   One saucy word, and his head would roll upon the carpet.   Dervish is quite capable of 'manipulating' Arabi, not in the Western but in the Eastern sense of that word.   In this strong resolute Ottoman it seems probable that the revolution in Egypt has found its master."

And again, 15th June: "The past career of Dervish Pasha is filled with incidents which sustain the impression of vigour he has laid down at Cairo.   He is at once the most vigorous and unscrupulous of all the Generals of the Ottoman army.   Although he is now seventy years old, his age has not weakened his energy or impaired his faculties.   His will is still as iron as it was of old, and he is quite as capable of ordering a massacre of the Mamelukes as was Mehemet Ali himself. . . . His early military experience was acquired fighting the Montenegrins, who always regarded him as the most dangerous Commander whom they had had to meet.   In one of the last acute fits of hostility (about 1856) between the Porte and Montenegro, Dervish penetrated to Grakovo, the northernmost canton of the Vladikate, as it then was; and the Voivode of the district, cut off from retreat to the South, took refuge in a cave, the habitual hiding-place of the people against sudden raids, it being so situated that the usual expedient of attack, smoking out by fires kindled at the mouth, was inapplicable.   The attempts of the Turks to force a passage were easily repulsed, and Dervish entered into negotiations, the result of which was a surrender on condition of the lives, liberty and property of the besieged being respected.   The

Turkish engagements were kept by the extermination of the entire family of the Voivode. The prisoners were marched off to Trebinji and thrown into the dungeon of the fortress, tied back to back, one of each couplet being killed and the survivor not released for a moment from the burden of his dead comrade. . . . Dervish's *modus operandi* during the late Albanian campaign is not generally understood. He went into Albania to enforce the conscription in which he utterly failed, though he had very slight military opposition, most of the battles he reported being purely mythical. But he was very successful in another plan of operation, which consisted in quartering himself on the Estates of the principal Beys, and extorting from them the last pound which could be squeezed out, when he moved on to the next one. He sent quantities of coin to Constantinople, but no recruits. If any prediction of the latest result of Dervish's mission may be based upon the history of those in which he was formerly engaged, we should say he would succeed with Arabi as he succeeded with the Lazis and Albani ans. . . . Egyptians are less warlike than Albanians and Lazis, but even in Egypt the Gordian knot may have to be severed with the sword."

These are pretty sayings which, if he remembers them, should, I think, sometimes make John Morley a little ashamed of the part he was persuaded by his Foreign Office friends to play that summer as apologist of their iniquities. No wonder he has dismissed the whole Egyptian episode from his history in a few pages. Pretty doings, too, for Gladstone to explain to his non-professional or even his professional conscience! The shade of Disraeli may well have smiled!

The Sultan's new mission, nevertheless, was not, as arranged by Abdul Hamid, quite so simple a piece of villainy as our Foreign Office imagined. The Emir el Mumenin had no real idea of lending himself as the mere cat's paw of the Western Powers to do their evil work for them. He was pleased to intervene, but not blindly, and he was much in the dark as to the real situation in Egypt, and desired to be prepared for all contingencies. Arabi still had friends at Court who represented him as championing the faith at Cairo, and in Tewfik, Abdul Hamid had never had any kind of confidence. He still desired to replace him with Halim. Following, therefore, the method usual with him of checking one agent by another agent, he added to his appointment of Dervish as chief commissioner a second commissioner more favourable to Arabi, Sheykh Ahmed Assad, the religious Sheykh of one of the confraternities (*tarikat*) at Medina, whom he had at Constantinople with him, and was in the habit of employing in his secret dealings with his Arabic speaking subjects, consulting him on all matters connected with his Pan-Islamic propaganda. Thus it happened that on its arrival at Alexandria the Ottoman mission in reality bore a double character, the one of menace in the person of Dervish, the other of conciliation in that of Assad. This Sheykh had it for his special present business to inform the Sultan of the tone of Arab feeling in Egypt, and especially of the Ulema of the Azhar, and he was provided with a private cipher, unknown to Dervish, with which to correspond with his imperial master. Arabi and his intimates gained knowledge of this and were consequently prepared beforehand to receive the mission as one not wholly unfavourable to them, and the spectacle was witnessed of both parties in the state showing pleasure at its arrival—the Turks and Circassians at the appearance of Dervish, and the Egyptians at that of the Medina Sheykh.

Both the Khedive as head of the State, and Arabi as head of the Government, sent their delegates to Alexandria to receive the mission, Zulfikar Pasha on the part of the Khedive, Yakub Pasha Sami, the Under-Secretary for War, on that of the Minister, and both were well received. Arabi, too, had commissioned Nadim the Orator to go down some days before to prepare public opinion to give the envoys a flattering reception, and at the same time to protest aloud against the Ultimatum delivered by Malet and his French colleague. Consequently, when the procession was formed to drive through the streets to the railway station, the two envoys in their respective carriages, having with them each a delegate, there was general acclamation on the part of the crowd. *"Allah yensor el Sultan,"* was shouted, "God give victory to the Sultan"; and at the same time *"El leyha, marfudha, marfudha,"* "The Ultimatum, reject it, reject it!" "Send away the fleet!" These cries had their effect at once upon the Chief Commissioner, and made Dervish cautious. Both at Alexandria and at Cairo deputations waited on him at his levees from the Notables, merchants, and

officials. To all alike Dervish gave a general answer. The
Sultan will do justice. He, Dervish, was come to restore order
and the Sultan's authority. Only to the Turks he announced
Arabi's speedy departure for Constantinople, to the Egyptians
the as speedy departure of the fleets. Sheykh Assad meanwhile in private reassured Arabi, declaring to him that the
Sultan meant him no evil.

As to the fire-eating attitude attributed by our Foreign Office
to Dervish, and alluded to by Morley with so much praise in
the passage already quoted, it was not in reality of a very determined kind. Dervish was old and was far more intent on
filling his pockets than on engaging in a personal struggle
with the fellah champion. Tewfik had managed to get together
£50,000 for Dervish as a *backshish,* and that with £25,000
more in jewels secured him to the Khedive's side, but he made
no serious attempt at any *coup de main* against Arabi. A single
unsuccessful attempt at brow-beating the Nationalists showed
him that the task would be a dangerous one. On the Friday
after his arrival at Cairo he made a round of the mosques and
expressed his annoyance at the boldness of certain of the
Ulema, who, on his leaving the Azhar, presented him with
a petition, and still more clearly in the afternoon when the main
body of the religious Sheykhs called and stated their views to
him with a freedom he was unaccustomed to. All these, with
the exception of the ex-Sheykh el Islam, el Abbasi, of the Sheykhs
Bahrami and Abyari and the Sheykh el Saadat, who had espoused the Khedive's cause, declared themselves strongly in
favour of Arabi and urged him to reject the Ultimatum, and
especially that part of it which demanded Arabi's exile. Dervish upon this told them to hold their tongues, saying that he
had come to give orders, not to listen to advice, and dismissed
them, at the same time decorating with the "Osmanieh" the
Sheykh el Islam and the other dissentients.

Popular feeling, however, immediately manifested itself in
a way he could not mistake. The Sheykhs returned from their
audience in great anger, and informed every one of the turn
things were taking, and the very same evening messengers were
despatched by the Nationalist leaders by the evening trains to
the provinces to organize remonstrance. Private meetings of
a strong character were held during the night at Cairo, de-

nouncing the Commissioner, and the next morning, Saturday, a monster meeting of the students was held in the Azhar mosque to protest against the insult offered the Sheykhs. There Nadim was invited to address the meeting from the pulpit, and he did so with the eloquence habitual to him and with its usual effect. The report of this shook Dervish's self-confidence, and within a few hours of its reaching him he sent for Arabi, whom he had hitherto refused to see, and Mahmud Sami, and addressed them both through an interpreter in terms of conciliation, Sheykh Assad being with him and supporting him in Arabic. At this meeting, though no coffee or cigarettes were offered (an omission remarked by them) Dervish adopted towards them a tone of friendliness. He made the Nationalist Chiefs sit beside him and expounded the situation with apparent frankness. "We are all here," he said, "as brothers, sons of the Sultan. And I with my white beard can be as a father to you. We have the same object in view, to oppose the Ghiaour, and to obtain the departure of the fleet, which is a disgrace to the Sultan and a menace to Egypt. We are all bound to act together to this end, and show our zeal for our master. This can best be done," addressing Arabi, "by your resigning your military power into my hands—at least in appearance—and by your going to Constantinople to please the Sultan." To this Arabi replied that he was ready to resign his command. But that, as the situation was very strained, and as he had assumed the great responsibility of keeping order he would not consent to any half measure; if he resigned, he would resign in fact as well as name, but he would do neither without a written discharge in full. Moreover, he would not be held responsible for things laid already to his charge of which he was innocent. He had been falsely accused of tyrannical acts, of malversation and other matters, and he would not leave office without a full discharge in writing from all complaints. Also he would defer his voyage to Constantinople till a time when things should be more settled, and then go as a private Moslem to pay his respects to the Caliph. Dervish was not prepared for this answer and he did not like it. His countenance changed. But he said, "Let us consider the matter as settled." Then, alluding to the excitement there was at Alexandria, he added, "You will telegraph at once to Omar Pasha Lutfi [the Governor of Alexandria] and the commander of the garrison at Alexandria to say you have resigned your charge on me, and that you are acting as my agent, and on Monday there will be a meeting of the Consuls and the Khedive, and we will give you your discharge." Arabi, however, refused to do this, declaring that until he had received his written discharge he should retain his post and his responsibility. And so, without a definite understanding having been come to between them, he and Mahmud Sami withdrew.

Such is the account, I believe a true one, told by Ninet and confirmed by others who should know of this important interview. It took place about noon on Saturday, the 10th of June, and is of importance in many ways and especially for its bearing on what followed the next day, as is notorious, a riot, originating in a quarrel between an Egyptian donkey boy and a Maltese, broke out there about one o'clock in the forenoon and continued till five, with the result that over two hundred persons lost their lives, including a petty officer of H. M. S. "Superb," and some two hundred more Europeans. Also Cookson, the English Consul, was seriously hurt, and the Italian and Greek Consuls received minor injuries, the disturbance being only quelled by the arrival of the regular troops. It was the first act of popular violence which, during the whole history of the year's revolution in Egypt, had been committed, and the news of it, spread throughout Europe by telegraph, produced, especially in England, a great sensation.

As the responsibility for this affair, so unfortunate for the National cause in Egypt, was afterwards laid upon the person it had most injured, Arabi, and as the incident was made use of by our Foreign Office and Admiralty, with other excuses not less unjust, to bring about the bombardment of Alexandria and the war that followed, the plea being that Egypt was in a "proved state of anarchy," it will be well here, before we go any further, to place upon the right shoulders what criminality there was in the whole incident. When I heard of it in London my first instinct was that, if not the accident the papers said it was, it was part of the plot I knew to have been designed through Dervish Pasha at the Foreign Office to entrap and betray Arabi, but it was not till after the war that I came into possession of the full particulars concerning it, or had it in my power to refute the false accusations made a little later against the Nationalists of having themselves devised and brought it about. The very contrary to this was then shown to be truth. As we now all know, who are in the secrets of that time, the riot, though perhaps accidental in its immediate origin, had for some weeks previously been in the designs of the Court party as a means at the proper moment to discredit Arabi as one capable of preserving order in the country.

The position of things at Alexandria was this: Alexandria, more than any other town in Egypt, was in large part a European city, inhabited, besides the Moslem population, by Greek, Italian and Maltese colonists, all engaged in trade and many of them money-lenders. At no time had there been much love between the two classes and the arrival of the fleets, avowedly with the intention of protecting European interests, greatly increased the ill-feeling. It needed much loyalty, firmness, and tact on the part of the Governor of the town to preserve order, and great discretion on the part of the fleet. Unfortunately the Governor, Omar Pasha Lutfi, was a man entirely opposed to the Nationalist Ministry. He was a Circassian, a member of the Court party, and a partisan of the ex-Khedive Ismaïl's, and at the time of the Circassian plot had done service to Tewfik by entering into communication with the Western Bedouins to gain them to the Khedive's side. He had, therefore, rather encouraged than repressed the element of disorder in the Mohammedan population. The Greeks, on the other hand, had proceeded to arm themselves, with the assistance of the head of their community, Ambroise Sinadino, a rich banker, who was also agent of the Rothschilds in Egypt; and the Maltese, a numerous community, did likewise through the connivance of Cookson, the English Consul. Things, therefore, were all it may be said, prepared for a riot as early as the last week of May, in expectation of that "civil war" which, it will be remembered, the "Pall Mall Gazette" foresaw as an approved alternative, should the Nationalist Ministry refuse to resign and Arabi to accept suppression.

There is no doubt that disturbance, as a proof of anarchy, was a thing looked forward to by our diplomacy at Cairo as probable, and even not undesirable in the interests of their "bottle-holding" policy. That Omar Lutfi had a personal interest in the suppression of Arabi is also easily proved. In the telegrams of the day, when the Ultimatum was about to be launched, a list is given of the purely Circassian and Khedivial Ministry which it was intended should succeed that of Mahmud Sami, and Omar Lutfi is named in it as the probable successor of Arabi at the War Office. Nor was this announcement unfounded, for a few days later we know that Omar Lutfi was, in fact, sent for by the Khedive to the Ismaïlia Palace and offered the post.[1] The Ultimatum was delivered on the 1st of June, and the Ministers resigned on the 2nd, having waited a day because the Khedive had told them he would first telegraph for advice to Constantinople, though on the following morning, when they again came to him, he informed them that his mind was made up to accept the Ultimatum notwithstanding that he had received no answer. When, therefore, on the 3rd the Khedive had been obliged, through the popular demonstration in Arabi's favour, backed by the German and Austrian Consuls, who saw in Arabi the man best capable in Egypt of maintaining order, to rename Arabi Minister of War, the disappointment to Omar Lutfi is easily understood, and the temptation he was under of creating practical proof that the German Consuls were wrong. We have, besides this, evidence that on the 5th of June the Khedive, who, no less than Omar Lutfi, had received a great rebuff, sent him a telegram in the following words: "Arabi has guaranteed public order, and published it in the newspapers, and has made himself responsible to the Consuls; and if he succeeds in his guarantee the Powers will trust him, and our consideration will be lost. Also the fleets of the Powers are in Alexandrian waters, and men's minds are excited, and quarrels are not far off between Europeans and others. Now, therefore, choose for yourself whether you will serve Arabi in his guarantee or whether you will serve us." On this hint Omar Lutfi immediately took his measures. As civil governor he was in command of the Mustafezzin, the semi-military police of Alexandria, and through them directed that quarter-taves, (*nabuts*) should be collected at the police stations

[1] The "Pall Mall" of 28th May, has the following: "Cairo, 27th May, Omar Pasha Lutfi, Sherif Pasha, Ragheb Pasha, and Sultan Pasha, President of the Chamber of Notables, assembled at noon to-day at the Ismaïlia Palace. . . . The Presidency of the Council will probably be held by Sherif Pasha or Omar Pasha Lutfi. . . . Omar Pasha Lutfi will be Minister of War."

to be served out at the proper moment, and other preparations
made for an intended disturbance. Ample proof may be found
in the evidence printed in the Blue Books of the complicity of
the police in the affair, though a confusion is constantly made
by those who give the evidence between these and the regular
soldiers by speaking of the police, as is often loosely done in
Egypt, as *soldiers*. The regulars were not under the civil, but
the military governors, and took no part in the affair until
called in at a late hour by Omar Lutfi when he found the riot
had assumed proportions he could not otherwise control. It
is to be noted that the chief of the Mustafezzin, Seyd Kandil,
a timid adherent of Arabi's, refused to take part in the day's
proceedings, excusing himself to Omar Lutfi on the ground
of illness.

The disturbance was therefore prepared already for execution
when Dervish and his fellow Commissioner landed on the 8th
at Alexandria. It was probably intended to synchronize with
the plot of Arabi's arrest, and to prove to the Sultan's Commissioner, more than to any one else, that Arabi had not the power
to keep order in the country that he claimed. I am not, however, at all convinced that Dervish was in ignorance of what
was intended, and I think there is a very great probability that
he had learned it before his interview with Arabi, and that if
he had succeeded in getting Arabi to resign his responsibility
the riot would have been countermanded. As it is, there is
some evidence that the outbreak took place earlier than was
intended. It is almost certain that the immediate occasion of
it, the quarrel between the donkey boy and the Maltese, was
accidental, but probably the police had received no counter-
orders, and so the thing was allowed to go on according to the
program. What is certain is that the Khedive and Omar
Lutfi, the one at Cairo, the other at Alexandria, monopolized
telegraphic communication between the two cities, that Omar
Lutfi put off on one and another pretext, from hour to hour,
calling in the military, who could not act without his orders as
civil governor in a case of riot, and that the occurrence was regarded at the Palace as a subject of rejoicing and by Arabi and
the Nationalists as one to be regretted and minimized. Also,
and this is a very important matter, the committee named to
inquire into the causes of the affair by the Khedive was com-

posed almost entirely of his own partisans, while he secured its being of no effective value as throwing light on the true authors, by appointing Omar Lutfi himself to be its president. The connection of Omar Lutfi and the Khedive, moreover, is demonstrated in the fact that, while given leave of absence when suspicion was too strong against him among the Consuls, he nevertheless reappeared after the bombardment and, joining the Khedive, obtained the post he coveted of Minister of War, a post which he held until May, 1883, when Lord Randolph Churchill having brought the case against him and the Khedive forward in Parliament, he at the end of the year retired into private life. Fuller proof of their complicity will be found in the Appendix.

One point only in this sinister affair is still a matter for me of much perplexity, and that is to determine the exact amount of responsibility assignable in it to our agent at Cairo and Alexandria. There are passages in Malet's despatches which seem to show that he was looking forward, about the time when the disturbance was first contemplated, to some violent solution of his diplomatic difficulties, and there is no doubt that it had been for some time past part of his argument against the Nationalist Government that it was producing anarchy. Also it is certain that Cookson had connived at the arming of the Maltese British subjects at Alexandria. Still, from that to complicity in a design to create a special riot there is a wide difference, and everything that I know of Malet's character and subsequent conduct in regard to the riot convinces me that he did not know this one at Alexandria was intended. Malet honestly believed in Tewfik as a trustworthy and amiable prince, and accepted whatever tales he told, and his undeception about him after the war I know to have been painfully complete. With regard to Colvin much the same may be said. He was probably as ignorant of the exact plan as he had been of the Khedive's true action the year before at Abdin, though it is difficult to understand that either he or Malet should not have soon afterwards guessed the truth. They had both allied themselves to the party of disorder, and when disorder came they accepted the Khedive's story without any close inquiry because it suited them to accept it, and they made use of it as an argument for what they wanted, the ruin of Nationalist Egypt

and armed intervention.   That is all the connection with the
crime I personally lay at their doors.

What followed may be briefly sketched here before I return
to my journal.   The immediate effect of the riot was not exactly
that which the Khedive and his friends intended.   It had been
allowed to go much farther than was in their plan, so much
farther that the regular army had been obliged to be called
in, and intead of discrediting Arabi it so seriously frightened
the Levantine population of Alexandria, who were a chicken-
hearted community, that they began to look to him as their
only protector.   Even the Foreign Consuls, all but the English, came round to this view of the case, and the perfect order
which the army from this time on succeeded in maintaining,
both there and at Cairo, largely increased his prestige.   I believe that then, late though it was in the day, Arabi, if he had
been really a strong ruler, which unfortunately he was not,
and if he had been a better judge of men and judge of opportunity—in a word, if he had been a man of action and not what
he was, a dreamer, he might have won the diplomatic game
against his unscrupulous opponents.   For this, however, it was
necessary that he should denounce and punish the true authors
of the riot; and that he should have proved with a strong arm
that in Egypt he was really master, and that any one who dared
disturb the peace should feel the weight of it.   Then he would
have appealed to Europe and to the Sultan in the words of a
strong man and they would not have been disregarded; nor
would our Government in England, who, after all, were no pal-
adins, have stood out against the rest.   Unfortunately for
liberty Arabi was no such strong man, only, as I have said, a
humanitarian dreamer, and with little more than a certain basis
of obstinacy for the achievement of his ideals.   He was absolutely ignorant of Europe, or of the common arts and crafts of
its diplomacy.   Thus he missed the opportune moment, and
presently the Europeans, frightened by Malet and Colvin, who
were playing a double game with him, getting him to preserve
order while they were preparing the bombardment, lost confidence in him and his chance was over.   From that moment
there was no longer any hope of a peaceful solution.   A wolf
and a lamb quarrel was picked with him by Sir Beauchamp Seymour, who had sworn to be revenged on the Alexandrians for

the death of his body-servant, a man of the name of Strackett, who had been killed in the riot; and the bombardment followed. A greater man than Arabi might, I say, have possibly pulled it through. But Arabi was only a kind of superior fellah, inspired with a few fine ideas, and he failed. He does not however, for that deserve the blame he has received at the hands of his countrymen. Not one of them even attempted to do better. [1]

Now to return to London and my journal:

"*June 3.*—To Lady Granville's party at the Foreign Office. All the political people there. Everybody connected with the Foreign Office ostentatiously cordial. Talked about the situation to Wolseley, Rawlinson, the American Minister (Lowell) and others. Also had a long talk with Sir Alexander and Lady Malet, who were very kind in spite of my political quarrel with their son. People seem relieved at the crisis in Egypt being postponed. But Wolseley tells me the Sultan has refused the Conference. The Khedive's cousin, the fat Osman Pasha, was there, and the Princes of Wales and Edinburgh and Prince Leopold and the Duke of Cambridge and other bigwigs. I was surprised to find Henry Stanley, too, quite cordial. He said he had a great admiration for Arabi as champion of the Faith, and that they would promote him, and both he and Tewfik remain at Cairo. So, as he represents Constantinople views, I conclude there is no danger from that quarter. The game seems won now, barring new accidents."

This last reference, which is to Lord Stanley of Alderley, is of importance. He was a very old and close friend of mine, but we had hitherto differed about Egypt, and on this ground. He had been many years before, in the time of Lord Stratford de Redcliffe, Attaché to our Embassy at Constantinople, and had imbibed there the extreme philo-Turkish views then in fashion with Englishmen. In 1860, while travelling in the

[1] Arabi was probably deterred from taking open action against Omar Lutfi, in part by the strong solidarity there is among Moslems in all quarrels with non-Moslems, in part by his suspicion of the Khedive's complicity, which at first was a suspicion only. He was extremely loath to quarrel with Tewfik at that moment, as he had just been reconciled to him, and only a few days before had sworn to protect his life as he would his own. He preferred therefore, in his language at the time, to attribute the chief blame to Cookson and Sinadino, who truly on their side were not without blame. This will be seen in Sabunji's letters and other documents concerning the riot printed in the Appendix.

East Indies, he had become a Mohammedan, and I had first
made his acquaintance in a rather singular way. I was on my
way in the autumn of that year from Athens and Constantinople to England, and was travelling up the Danube when there
came on board our steamer at one of the Roumanian ports the
family of an ex-hospodar, and with them an Englishman of no
very distinguished appearance, and of rather plain, brusque
manners, whom I took to be their tutor or secretary. As our
journey lasted several days, I made friends with my fellow
traveller, and found him interesting from his great knowledge
of the East, but he did not tell me his name. On our arrival,
however, at Vienna, he proposed to go with me to the Embassy,
and I then discovered who he was, and we travelled on together to Munich, where his younger brother, Lyulph Stanley,
a Balliol undergraduate, was learning German, and in this way
I became acquainted little by little with all his family. I came
to know him very well, and I take this opportunity of saying
that, though he was undoubtedly eccentric in his ideas, he remained through life one of the sincerest and least selfish men I
have known. As a Moslem he was entirely in earnest, and
in many ways he sympathized with my views, but he would not
hear of my preference of the Arabs to the Turks, whom he
considered the natural leaders of Islam. In London he was
always in close relations with the Ottoman Embassy, and his
view of the position as between the Sultan and Arabi—the
Dervish mission was already in the air—has on this account
considerable historical value.

"*June* 4.—Sunday at Crabbet. The first day for weeks I
have not thought about Egypt. I consider the whole matter
settled now, and have played tennis all the afternoon with a
light heart. The Wentworths, Noels, Frank Lascelles, Henry
Cowper, Molony, and others came down from London.
Lovely weather.

"*June* 5.—To London again. . . . Lady Gregory tells me
they are displeased now with Colvin—consider him not suited
to his place in Egypt—this from Lord Northbrook. Lord
Granville has sent to consult him (Sir William Gregory)."
Lady Gregory, be it noted, had remained more staunch than
had her husband to the National cause; and later they both
rendered once more important services to Arabi, especially at
the time of his trial. The London newspapers at this time

were beginnning to take a more intelligent interest in Egyptian affairs, most of them having sent special correspondents to Cairo or Alexandria, among them the "Daily Telegraph," whose correspondent became a strong Arabist.

"*June* 6.—The 'Daily News' is already preparing itself for a renewal of the *status quo ante ultimatum,* and the other papers seem likely to follow suit,—all but the 'Times' and 'Pall Mall," just the two papers which had the truth preached to them and which rejected it. English opinion, however, is hardly now a straw in the balance. . . . I had another long talk with Lascelles, and hope that I have more or less converted him. In the evening I rode with Bertram Currie, who offers to wager Arabi will have been extinguished in a fortnight." (*N. B.*—Bertram was the elder brother of Philip Currie, a banker, and strong practical supporter of Gladstone, with whom he was personally intimate. His opinion, no doubt, reflects that of Downing Street at the moment.)

"*June* 7.—Lady Gregory came in and gave me news. She tells me that Lord Granville told her husband that all their hopes now rested on Dervish's mission from Constantinople. 'Dervish,' Lord Granville said, 'is quite unscrupulous, and he will get rid of Arabi one way or other.' I suppose this means by bribing; [1] indeed, Lord Granville seems to have said as much, but it may also mean by 'coffee.' I do not, however, fear the latter. The Sultan's object will be to get Arabi to Constantinople, not to kill, but to keep him as a hostage. I am anxious all the same Sabunji should arrive. I cannot help fancying they may try and prevent his landing, knowing his connection with me. A note has come from him written in the train, with additions to our code of signals which are rather amusing. . . . Later saw Gregory, who confirms all his wife told me of his interview with Granville. He thinks Colvin and Malet must be recalled. . . . Pembroke writes to John Pollen that the Foreign Office is unbounded in its anger against me. Never mind. . . . I met Austin Lee, Dilke's secretary, at the Club, and he asked me the latest news from Egypt. I said, 'I hear you are sending a barrel of salt to put on Arabi's

[1] My diary of 1888 records: "Dec. 22, Cairo. To breakfast with Zebehr Pasha. . . . He spoke highly of Arabi, and said that he had been present at a conversation between him and Dervish Pasha, in which Dervish had offered Arabi E£250 a month if he would go to Constantinople. But Arabi had said that, even if he were willing, there were 10,000 men would stand between him and the sea."

tail.' 'No,' he answered with some readiness, 'the salt is to pickle him.' . . . Rode in the evening with Cyril Flower (who had married a Rothschild) advised him to sell his Egyptian Bonds. . . . Dined with Bertram, whom I found much more humane. He believes in Gladstone, and the eventual independence of Ireland. 'Only,' he says, 'Gladstone has the misfortune of being a generation before his age. We shall all believe in attending to our own affairs in another twenty years.'

"Frederic Harrison has written to protest in the 'Pall Mall' against intervention in Egypt." This was a powerful article headed "Money, Sir, Money," which was followed by other letters. I have always regretted that I had not earlier become acquainted with the writer, the soundest and most courageous man on foreign policy then in the Liberal Party, and by far their most vigorous pamphleteer. Had we met a month or two before, I feel sure that he might have prevented the war, for though not in Parliament, he wielded great influence. The misfortune of the public position that Spring was that there was not a single man of great intellectual weight in the party, Harrison excepted, free from official bondage. . . .

"Party at Lady Salisbury's. Talked with Miltown, who was rather angry, I thought, at my handiwork in Egypt, and not quite polite about my telegrams. Also with old Strathnairn, who would like 'to go out with 10,000 men and hang Arabi.' Also with Osman and Kiamil Pashas, the Khedive's cousins, though not about politics. . . . The Sultan's Commission has arrived in Egypt.

"*June* 8.—A telegram from Sabunji at Alexandria announcing his arrival. Now I feel relieved from anxiety. He says the Turkish Commission has gone to Cairo. . . . Harry Brand refuses to come to my lawn-tennis party at Crabbet till he sees how things go at Cairo. I fear he has much of his money in Egypt and will lose it.

"*June* 9.—There is another letter from Frederic Harrison in the 'Pall Mall.' Wrote to propose to show him my correspondence with Gladstone. Saw the Gregorys. The Commission is hailed with a great flourish of trumpets at Cairo, but we fancy this is only to herald a compromise. Sabunji telegraphs that Arabi has declared publicly he will resist the landing of Turkish troops. He is still at Alexandria, which disquiets me. He ought to be in Cairo. Dined at Wentworth House to meet Sir Bartle Frere, a soft-spoken, intelligent man.

"*June* 10.—Luncheon with Mr. and Mrs. Green, very superior and sympathetic about Egypt." (*N. B.*—This was Green the historian. He was already in failing health. I have a clear recollection of his emotional sympathy with me and with the cause I was pleading. His loss to an honest understanding of statesmanship was a great one.) "I am anxious about things there for the first time for a fortnight. The evening papers announced that Dervish has won—bought over—a part of the army and has proclaimed himself Commander-in-Chief, summoning Arabi to submit. Unless he stands firm now all is lost. After much consideration I have sent the following telegram to Sabunji: '7 p. m. Arrest Commission. Fear not but God.' This partly in cipher. My trouble is lest Sabunji should not have gone to Cairo. Or why does he not telegraph? Can he have come to grief? . . . Dinner at Lyulph Stanley's where, besides others, we met Bright. I found him most humane about Egypt, and spoke a few words with him, I hope, in season. I spoke my mind pretty freely. It is now a question of boldness on the part of the National Party. I fancy Dervish's orders have been to test this, and, if he finds them determined, to support them. He will crush them, if he can, through the Circassians. But I trust they may crush him, or at any rate frighten him. The Sultan dares not put them down by force.

"*June* 11, Sunday.—By early train to Crabbet. I was very nervous looking into the papers lest some *coupe de main* should have been made. But the 'Observer' shows that nothing has yet happened. There are the same stories of Dervish's swagger to the Ulema and the officers. But that is nothing. . . . At 2 o'clock the Princes Osman and Kiamil and their cousin —— and their alem Aarif Bey and an English bear-leader, one Lemprière, came down to see our horses. While we were showing them these a telegram came in cipher from Sabunji as follows: 'Cairo, 12 p. m., June 10. I have just had an interview with Arabi. He is supported by the Parliament, the University, and the Army, all except Sultan Pasha and the Sheykh el Islam. The nation is decided to depose the Khedive. The Porte dislikes the proposals of Europe. Arabi insists there will be no peace while Malet and Colvin are here. Arabi will resist a Turkish invasion. He will not go to Constantinople. Sheykh Aleysh has been made head of the Azhar. The Porte has decided to depose the Khedive. Malet has urged the proposals of Europe on the Commission. Abdallah Nadim at a public meeting of 10,000 spoke against these proposals and against the Khedive.' If the Khedive's cousins whom we were entertaining could have read it, it would have spoiled their appetites. We have talked the matter over and are going to telegraph them to proclaim a republic in case they depose Tewfik. I am relieved of all anxiety now that I know Sabunji is with them.

In what I here say of Princes Osman and Kiamil I do them less than justice. They had no love for Tewfik, their father Mustafa having been driven out of Egypt and despoiled of much of his possessions by Ismaïl, and they also had a considerable amount of patriotism. At least they gave proof of it during the war when they were among Arabi's strongest adherents. Their sister, Nazli Hanum, did much to help us at the time of the trial. Aarif Bey was a young man of great ability, a Kurd by birth but with Arab blood, well educated and of high distinction. He afterwards became Secretary to Mukhtar Pasha at Cairo, and edited a literary newspaper, but lost himself in intrigues of all kinds and has disappeared. The fourth person on this occasion was a Europeanized Turk and member of the Sultan's household, but his name in my diary is not recorded. We talked Eastern politics, though not Egyptian, freely at dinner, politics of a Pan-Islamic kind which included the hope that France as well as England would sooner or later be driven out of North Africa.

I may here insert a letter I wrote to Sabunji on the 9th, and one I received from him of the same date as his telegram just given.

"10, James Street, *June* 9, 1882.

"Your telegram announcing your landing in Egypt relieved me of much anxiety. I hope by this time you are at Cairo and in communication with our friends. I think they cannot do better just now than keep on the best possible terms with the Commissioners. Only I would have them beware of trust-

ing them. I know that great hopes are placed by the enemies
of Egypt on Dervish as a man quite unscrupulous in his mode
of dealing with rebels. Every effort will be made to get Arabi
to go to Constantinople. But this he must not do. They will
try to bribe him and persuade him that his going will be for
the good of the country. He must not be deluded. It is possible even they may try to arrest or poison him, though I do
not think that likely. When, however, they see he stands firm
and has got the country with him, they will not quarrel with
him. My strong advice to him is that he should make his submission at once to Mohammed Tewfik as the Sultan's viceroy,
on condition of retaining his place as Minister of War. If he
does this the English and French Governments will have no
just cause of quarrel with him; and the European Conference,
if it assembles, will not sanction their further intervention. I
am sure that our Government will not insist on their Ultimatum as regards Arabi leaving the country. But they and the
French are bound to support Tewfik as nominal sovereign of
Egypt. It would be very dangerous at the present moment
for Arabi to quarrel either with Tewfik or the Sultan. Only
let him hold his ground as practical ruler of the country. . . .
People are very angry here with me, but I do not care, so long
as Egypt gets her liberty."

I give a letter, somewhat condensed, which was written to
me by Sabunji from Cairo on the day of the Alexandrian riot,
but before news of it had reached him.

"Cairo, *June* 11, 1882.
"On my arrival I called on Arabi Pasha, Mahmud Sami and
others who are of the party. They received me with enthusiasm and inquired after you. Mohammed Abdu informed me
that he had been told you had been advised by some influential
people not to come to Cairo. Arabi overwhelmed me with
joy when he saw me. A week before my arrival he addressed
a large audience and read them a letter I had written, in which
I dwelt upon the necessity of perfect union among themselves. . . .
"The situation at present stands thus: In my telegram I
told you how we had talked of all that had happened from

the discovery of the Circassian plot down to the present date. Now Sheykh Aleysh, the great holy man of the Azhar, has issued a *fetwa* in which he states that the present Khedive, having attempted to sell his country to the foreigners by following the advice of the European Consuls, is no more worthy of ruling over the Moslems of Egypt. He must therefore be deposed. All the Sheykhs of the Azhar, who consider Sheykh Aleysh as their spiritual head, have accepted the *fetwa*. . . . Sheykh Mohammed Khodeyr of the Azhar went with twenty-two Notables to meet Dervish Pasha, and presented him a petition signed by 10,000 persons in which they requested him to reject the proposals of the Powers and depose the Khedive. There are fourteen moudiriehs in Egypt. Only three mudirs are personally opposed to Arabi. The Copt and Arab element of the fellahin unanimously supports him. . . . Embabeh (Sheykh el Islam), being afraid of both the Khedive and the National Party, keeps aloof, and avoids politics under plea of ill-health. Arabi told me 'he will never yield either to Europe or Turkey. Let them send European, Turkish, or Indian troops, as long as I breathe I will defend my country; and when we are all dead they will possess a ruined country, and we shall have the glory of having died for our native land. Nor is this all. A religious war will succeed the political one, and the responsibility of this will fall on those who provoke it.' He is determined to resist and will not go to Constantinople; Arabi is now supported by the majority of the nation. Nine only of the Deputies are against him. Sultan Pasha has deserted him and joined the Khedive, being frightened by Malet and the arrival of the fleet. He and the Khedive are now looked upon by all the Arab element as traitors. . . . Deputations from all the provinces came to Dervish requesting the deposition of the Khedive, a fact which it is impossible to explain on the supposition that Arabi compelled them. . . . Ninety thousand persons have signed petitions to Dervish to reject the proposals of Europe and keep Arabi in office.

"All the Azhar Sheykhs except Embabeh, el Abbasi, and the Sheykh el Saadat are supporting Arabi, also Abd-el-rahman Bahrawi. Nadim held a large meeting of about 10,000 persons in Alexandria, and spoke against the proposals of Europe, and proved the unfitness of the Khedive to reign. He brought proofs from the Koran, the Hadith, and modern history to prove his case and persuade his hearers. Arabi also in an animated speech denounced all the misdeeds of the reigning dynasty from Mohammed Ali down to Tewfik. I have spoken to Abdu, Nadim, and others about soliciting letters and signatures from Notables, Ulema, fellahin, merchants, and others, to be sent to you to prove the reality of the National movement. They agree to get the documents in ten days and I shall send them to you.

I have found out that we formed an erroneous idea of Mahmud Pasha Sami. I have had many conversations with him and have got information about him even from his opponents. I find he is one of those who first planned the National movement as long ago as in Ismaïl's time. He suffered a great deal for his liberalism yet stuck to his principles. Several of the leaders of the party, Nadim, Abdu, and even Arabi, confess that they owe their power to his help and constancy. He was tempted by Ismaïl to give up the party, but he refused all money. He spends all his income in doing good to the party, and his house is like a caravanserai. His private life is that of a philosopher, spending little on himself and satisfied with his lot and all that comes. He is not an ignorant man. He is well versed in Arabic literature, better than Arabi, and if he is hated by the Turks it is a proof of his patriotism. He is going to write a letter to Lord Granville to prove the existence of a real National Party in Egypt, and to avow their friendship to England, which they look upon as the champion of liberty, and as a nation which has always taken by the hand people who were struggling for their freedom. I suggested that similar letters from Arabi and Embabeh to Lord Granville and Mr. Gladstone would be of use, and I promised to translate the letters and send them to their destination.

When it was rumoured that the Sultan intended sending Dervish to urge Arabi to accept the Powers' Ultimatum, Nadim went to Alexandria and held a meeting of about 10,000 persons and spoke for two hours against the Note and suggested that every one in the Assembly should protest against it. Nadim, the new Oracle of Delphi, was cordially obeyed. When the men returned home they taught their wives and children to join them in protesting against the Note. In fact, when Dervish landed, the children were heard shouting in the streets *'el leyha, el leyha,'* 'the note, the note,' and from the windows the women called out, *'marfudha, marfudha,'* 'reject it, reject it.' Dervish took a lesson from this and changed his colours. . . .

"Embabeh, who for a few days showed himself hostile to the National Party for having openly sanctioned the deposition of the Khedive, yesterday made peace with them. But Sultan Pasha has disappointed every one. He has joined the Khedive blindly, frightened by the thought of an European intervention, and being assured by Malet that Arabi would not be suffered to remain in office. Thus the poor old fellow fell into the same snare with Sherif. He is no longer popular, and has got nothing for his change of policy.

"Another curious event took place yesterday. When Dervish summoned the Ulema to consult about the best measures to be taken for an honourable peace, two of the Ulema only took the Khedive's part. All the rest pleaded the National cause. Dervish was vexed and dissolved the Assembly, decorating the two dissenting Sheykhs, Bahrawi and Abyari. When the result was published in the papers it created a revolutionary movement in the Azhar. I was present at several of the meetings of the Ulema and other persons, and there was general indignation. The Koran and the Hadith were freely quoted, showing the unfitness of Tewfik to rule over a Mussulman community. They were not satisfied, however, with private meetings, but in my presence insisted upon holding a public meeting in the Azhar to protest against the insult inflicted on them. Accordingly the meeting was held in the Azhar Mosque, in the very place where the prayers are made; and Nadim was ordered by the Ulema to address the Assembly, which exceeded four thousand persons. The effect produced by Nadim's oration I have no time to describe. You have seen Nadim and know how eagerly people hear him and how excited they get by his eloquence."

CHAPTER XIV

A LAST APPEAL TO GLADSTONE

Such was the state of feeling in the inner circle of the Nationalists at Cairo when the Alexandrian riot occurred. The next day I went up to London in high spirits, carrying with me Sabunji's telegram of the 10th to show to Hamilton. The news of the riot met me at the station.

"*June* 12.—. . . Another scare. Riots at Alexandria, Cookson hurt, an officer of the Superb killed, and fifty or sixty Europeans. This has caused great excitement. I am not sure whether it will be for Arabi's advantage or not. It will show he is master of the situation; unless, indeed, it be a trap laid for him by Dervish to get him to go to Alexandria where he might arrest him. . . . I went to Eddy Hamilton and told him I was now in possession of indisputable knowledge that Arabi commanded the country, also that Tewfik was in great danger of being deposed by the feeling of the country, and that, if they did not want a violent solution of the difficulty, they had better come speedily to terms with him. He promised to repeat all I said to Gladstone. It is evident to me now that they would catch at any compromise which should leave Tewfik on the throne.

"Went down to the House of Commons. Harry Brand asked his father, the Speaker, for a ticket of entrance for the 'rebel Blunt,' and he said, 'he does not deserve one,' but gave it. Dilke answered various questions about Egypt, assuming that Dervish and the Khedive were having it all their own way. This has rather frightened me, for there is a report that Arabi has gone down with Dervish to Alexandria (this proved untrue), and I fear treachery. Sabunji, too, has sent a new telegram as follows: 'I have just seen Arabi. Your message delivered. All quiet. Abdallah Nadim addressed four thousand persons at the Azhar, attacking the Turkish Commission and the Khedive. The Commission has withdrawn the proposals of Europe, and I hope for peace. The Circassians are intriguing. The Sheykh el Islam has rejoined, Sultan Pasha has not. The riot is nothing.' To this we composed an answer coming down in the train, and sent it from Three Bridges: 'Dervish means mischief, bribery, perhaps murder. Call a public meeting under Nadim and Abdu and the Azhar University, a hundred thousand persons. Let them insist on Dervish's departure. If this is refused let him be arrested by the police and sent away. Make terms with the Khedive. Be careful the Consuls are not molested. Let Nadim be the mover in action. Arabi and the army must stand aloof.' I am far from easy in my mind.

"Had a long conversation before leaving London with Frederic Harrison, who has written again on Egypt to the 'Pall Mall.' I have shown him my letters to Gladstone. He will be of valuable assistance. . . . Just as we were leaving James Street Lady Malet rushed in wildly, demanding of me the truth of what I had been doing in Egypt. I told her pretty nearly. She said my honour was at stake in clearing myself of the charge of intriguing against my country. She besought me, too, to calm down things there; and I promised to send a message to Arabi not to touch a hair of her son's head. I shall write by to-morrow's mail, and in the meanwhile my telegram will suffice. I do not think he runs the slightest danger. Poor Lady Malet! I am very sorry for her. She told me people said I had been in a conspiracy with Gladstone against her son's policy in Egypt. I assured her that Gladstone was guiltless of my telegrams, and that I accepted the full responsibility of all I had done. She made me promise to come and see her; but—such are the miseries of political life—she looks upon me as Edward's murderer.

"*June* 13.—I was very nervous all night, expecting to hear that Arabi had been arrested or murdered. But the papers show him to be quite master of the situation. The Khedive is forming a new Ministry, in which Arabi is to be Minister of War as ever. I trust, therefore, he has followed my advice about making terms with Tewfik. Now they have only to get Dervish away, and all will go smoothly."

So thought the majority of the London papers, the "Pall

Mall" almost alone dissenting from this view of a peaceful solution having been arrived at, and its comments, prompted by the Foreign Office, show the animus of our officials and their determination there should not be peace on any terms which should leave the Nationalists in power. Morley thus writes: "It would be difficult to make a greater mistake than that into which the 'Times' has fallen this morning, when it mistakes the temporary and provisional arrangement, entered into by the Khedive, the Consuls-General, Dervish, and Arabi for the preservation of order, for the final settlement of the Egyptian difficulty. The excitement in Egypt is so great that Europeans are in danger of their lives. The only restraining force in the country that can hold the mob in awe is the army, and the army is in the hands of Arabi. For the moment, then, Arabi must be made use of to prevent massacre. But because Dervish holds Arabi responsible with his head for the preservation of order, it no more follows that he has abandoned the intention to re-establish the *status quo* than that England and France have come to terms with Arabi because they insisted he should use his troops to suppress the rioting in Alexandria." We were, however, taken in in England, just as Arabi was taken in at Cairo, by the treacherous truce Malet and Colvin had agreed to, and did not suspect its hollowness. Arabi on that occasion gave his word of honour to Tewfik that, come what might, he would defend his life like his own, and this promise the Khedive, who had nothing but treachery towards him in his heart, accepted and abused to the end.

To continue my journal of that day I find: "Button told me yesterday that Rothschild had offered Arabi £4,000 (one hundred thousand francs) a year for life if he would leave Egypt. [1]

[1] Arabi, in answer to a question of mine as to this matter, told me many years afterwards that he had never heard of any offer of a pension *as made him by the Rothschilds*. He said, however, that soon after the ultimatum of 26th May, he received a visit from the French Consul, who, having asked what was the amount of his then pay, had offered him the double—that is to say, E£500 a month—from the French Government, if he would consent to leave Egypt and go to Paris to be treated there as Abd-el-Kader had been treated. He refused, however, to have anything to do with it, telling him that it was his business if necessary to fight and die for his country, not to abandon it. I have a note of this conversation but without date. Compare also the "Pall Mall" of 18th May: "Ourabi is said to be thinking of visiting Europe to recruit his health—a commendable intention, and no harm would be done if he were alotted a handsome travelling allowance on condition that he did not return."

. . . As we went up to London they gave us the following telegram: 'Cairo, June 12th, 11 a. m. I have just seen Arabi, he sends you his salaams. He thinks the European proposals have disappeared and peace is concluded. Arabi master of the situation. Dervish gone. Khedive went to Alexandria. Arabi led him by the arm to the station. National Party triumphant. I worked hard but have triumphed.' . . . I have been between laughing and crying ever since. I went at once to Downing Street, and told Eddy Hamilton and Horace Seymour what had happened. They seemed to think that now, even at the eleventh hour, Gladstone might acknowledge his errors, or rather Malet's errors, and make peace with Arabi. Button thinks this possible too. But the Foreign Office will harden its heart. . . . Dined at home and went to a party at the Admiralty. Found the Gregorys and Sir Frederick Goldsmid there, and had some conversation on Egypt with Lord Northbrook. I spoke my mind to him pretty freely. I said, 'It depends entirely upon you now whether there is bloodshed in Egypt or not.'

"*June* 14.—I am quite worn out. Mrs. Howard, whom I met in the Park, said I looked altered. And in fact I have not had Egypt, sleeping or waking, out of my head since the crisis began. . . . I spent the morning and breakfasted with Goldsmid, who is going this evening on a special mission to Constantinople, and primed him well with my views, showing him all my Gladstone correspondence." (*N. B.*—This General Goldsmid was afterwards employed as chief of the Intelligence Department by Wolseley in his campaign. He was a soft-spoken man, whom I had known the year before at Cairo.) . . . "Had luncheon with Lascelles, who seems to agree with my views about Egypt." (There was some thought, I believe, at that time at the Foreign Office of his being sent out to Cairo to replace Malet, as he already knew Egypt; and on a mission of conciliation he would have done well. Only, unfortunately, none such was decided on.) . . . "There is confirmation of Sabunji's news in to-day's 'Daily Telegraph.' The other papers look upon the Khedive's and Dervish's flight as caused by their desire to restore order at Alexandria. They say Dervish will put himself at the head of 12,000 men who have been massed there and march against Arabi, who is now alone at Cairo (!).

I have telegraphed to Arabi: 'Praise God for victory and peace.'"

This was the last point at which it seemed to me possible that the long game I had been playing against Colvin could be won and war averted. Henceforth it was a losing battle, though I fought it out to the end. The determining cause with Gladstone, in whom alone salvation lay, was, I believe, about this date when certain industrial towns of the North of England protested against the dilatory character of the Government treatment of the Egyptian case, on the ground that the long continuance of the crisis there was injuring trade. This was used upon him as a means of coercion by Chamberlain, egged on by Dilke, in the Cabinet.

"*June* 15.—I am anxious about the state of things at Alexandria, but suppose Arabi can depend upon his men. There is a general stampede there and at Cairo. Malet, I am thankful to say, has left Cairo. Dervish still hangs on at Alexandria. He and the Khedive have gone to Ras-el-Tin Palace, where they are under the guns of the fleet. . . . Another telegram from Sabunji as follows: 'The Khedive's departure has aroused suspicion. Agitation. Activity in army preparations. Nadim, Abdu and the army openly defy the Porte. Arabi is moderate and vigilant. A plot to murder Nadim. There is danger of serious disturbance on European side. Dervish declines retiring till the fleet is withdrawn. Recall Malet for God's sake. All curse and will murder him if he continues.' I went at once to Eddy Hamilton and implored him to get Malet ordered on board ship" (this was done) "and afterwards sent him (Hamilton) a letter warning the Government not to count on Turkish troops. We then sent an answer to Sabunji: 'Turkish Commissioner demands troops from Constantinople. They are not likely to be sent. But prepare. Keep order at all costs. Another riot would be fatal. Malet leaves soon. Patience.' . . . Dined at Lord De la Warr's. . . . On coming home found the telegraph to Cairo interrupted, by the flight, I suppose, of the Eastern Telegraph clerks. This alarms me a little.

"*June* 16.—Went to see Button, who is very hopeful. But I am losing my faith in Gladstone and think the English Government means mischief. I gave my Gladstone correspondence yesterday to Kegan Paul to put in print, so as to have it ready in case of the worst. . . . My telegram has gone after all. . . . In low spirits. Another telegram from Sabunji: 'New Commissioner with unknown instructions arrived. Nation and army in counsel daily to devise defensive plans. They distrust the double Commission. Inform me of Gladstone's policy and of Lord Granville's. Arabi is firm. All the journals closed except the "Wattan" and the "Official Journal." Panic among foreigners. The Khedive has thanked Arabi for keeping order. All is quiet. Nadim has been stopped from calling public meetings.'

"Yesterday when I saw Eddy he told me I had better not return to Downing Street as my visits there were remarked on, but to write him any news I might receive. Now I have written him yet another letter to try and find out what Gladstone's policy really is. Eddy's answer, however, is very unsatisfactory. There is a sensational announcement in the 'St. James's Gazette' of British troops ordered to Egypt. Home to Crabbet in a very nervous state. I see that a hurried meeting of the Cabinet was called yesterday in Mr. Gladstone's private room. Can this ordering of troops have been the consequence? I cannot help thinking they mean to push on an intervention. The French, however, have apparently made their peace with Arabi."

Not the French only, but the other European Powers, especially Germany and Austria, were at that moment in a mood to come to terms with him and to sacrifice Tewfik, for the preservation of order's sake. The "Pall Mall Gazette" of 16th June says: "The German Powers are supposed to advocate an arrangement with Arabi on the basis of Tewfik's abdication in favour of his son with a regency. . . . There are many points in its favour, though 'the solemn obligations of England and France' may make it impossible for them to do otherwise than stand by the man who has implicitly followed their counsels— especially those of the English Representative—it is perfectly conceivable that the practical failure of Tewfik, personal as well as political, may have impressed the other Powers with the expediency of by and by finding some more capable substitute." Compare, too, Malet's despatch of June 14: "The Agents of Austria and Germany have telegraphed to their Governments that the effect of any armed intervention, not excepting Turk-

ish, will place the lives of their countrymen in danger. They
consider the political question as a secondary matter compared
with the security of their fellow subjects. With this object they
are in favour of leaving the matter entirely in the hands of the
Porte, and they believe that the only means of avoiding the
most serious calamities is the departure from Alexandria of the
fleet and myself." Poor Malet at this date, I have heard,
spoke to his friends of his professional career as ruined. All
depended for him and Colvin on bringing on hostilities.

"*June* 17.—Very troubled night. But there is no confirmation of the news about the troops in to-day's papers; and the day
is so fine, I feel again light-hearted. The Sultan dares not interfere. That is proved. The French have made their terms
with Arabi, and it is hinted that Germany and Austria are doing
likewise. So England does not matter.

"The following is our party at Crabbet: Ebrington, Lyming-
ton, Granny Farquhar, Eddy Hamilton, Dallas (of the Foreign
Office), Nigel Kingscote (junior), Button Bourke, and Walter
Seymour. News of despatch of troops contradicted. All
seems going well. We have agreed to talk nothing about
Egypt. But we cannot help it.

"*June* 18.—Sunday, Waterloo day, and never did England
look more foolish. I got a telegram at breakfast announcing
a new Ministry under Ragheb and Arabi, evidently consented
to by the German Powers and Turkey. We are consequently
singing Hallelujahs."

Here I may as well insert three more of Sabunji's letters,
which he wrote in these last days. They throw a valuable light
on what was passing in the Nationalist mind at Cairo:

"Cairo, *June* 14, 1882.

"I called to-day on Arabi Pasha just a few minutes after he
received your telegram. We talked for about an hour and a
half. I asked him why this panic in the country if he and the
Khedive had already come to terms. He said: 'As far as I am
concerned I believe the Khedive would be sincere in his dealing
with me, if left alone and far from Sir E. Malet's advice. He
has by this time become convinced that there is nobody in his
Government who could control the country and preserve peace
except the man whom European statesmen despise, Ahmed

Arabi.   The Khedive has now made peace with me, and in the presence of the Representatives of the six European Powers and of Dervish Pasha, has asked me to take on myself the responsibility of public safety.   I have accepted his order, and pledged my word and sworn to defend his life and the lives of all who inhabit Egypt, of every creed and nation; and, as long as I live and my jurisdiction is not interfered with, I will keep my word.   But, if this peace is looked upon by others as a fictitious and fraudulent peace, that is the Khedive's lookout.   For myself, I am sincere in my dealing with all who deal honestly and sincerely with me; but with those who deal dishonestly I pay them with their own coin, and with the fraudulent I am doubly fraudulent.   Time and Ismaïl, in spite of us, have trained us to Turkish deceit.   As we make use of the arms, guns and ammunition they left us, so we make use of their deceit, *when the Turks force us to do so.*   We will not be the aggressors, but we will resist all who attempt to attack us.   We are a sincere nation, and grateful to those who take us by the hand and help us to reform our country.   We wish for nothing except reforms' (he uttered that with emphasis).   'But those who would cheat us will find us the very roots of fraud, *sudar el ghish.*   Europe, and especially England, looks upon us as barbarians.   They can crush us, they say, in twenty-four hours. Well, if they are willing, let them try it, but they will lose their 80 millions of public debt and the 20 millions the fellahin privately owe to the bankers.   The first shot fired will release us from these engagements; and the nation on this account wishes nothing more than war.'

"I hear much the same language from every one.   Great preparations are going on.   Vast stores of rifles and ammunition have been found, laid up by Ismaïl when he intended to make himself independent of the Porte.   These they will make good use of.   But I tell them I hope there will be no occasion. They say they can resist for years, for God has blessed them with a crop this summer twice as great as in ordinary fertile years.

"I sounded Arabi about Halim.   I found him to prefer Halim to Tewfik, but he says that if Tewfik will only free himself from Malet's influence all will go well.   Malet, he says, has been misled by Colvin, and has done immense harm to his own country, as well as Egypt, by their misrepresentation of facts.

"*June* 17.—Last night I went to Sheréï Pasha's, where Arabi, Mahmud Sami, Abd-el-Aal, Ali Fehmi, Nadim, Hajrasi and many others were being entertained at dinner. After they had dined and we were smoking and talking politics, an officer came in with a letter from an English lady asking protection, as she had been advised to leave Cairo. I was begged to write her an answer at once to assure her there was no danger, and that if there should be trouble Arabi would protect her life as his own. Arabi has become a hero with many of the European ladies, whom I have heard praising him for the protection he has given. When he drives through the town all rush to the windows and balconies. I make converts to the National Party, all I can, among the Europeans I meet.

"*June* 18.—Yesterday at noon, on Ragheb being telegraphed as Prime Minister, I went to see Arabi, who read me a telegram just received from the Khedive requesting him to co-operate with Ragheb as Minister of War. After coffee had been served he wrote a telegram of thanks to the Khedive and handed it to me. It was very politely worded. A few minutes afterwards he said: 'Let us go for a drive through the town to inspire confidence in the minds of the people.' He and Ali Fehmi drove in one carriage, and I and Nadim in the other. We went through Faggala, preceded by heralds. We alighted at Embabeh's house (the Sheykh el Islam's), and Arabi said, 'Come in, I will introduce you to our Pope.' On entering the reception room Arabi took off his boots, and turning to me said, 'We consider this place as the holy abode of our Sheykh.' Accordingly I did the same. On entering, the Sheykh, who was sitting on a low divan, rose and advanced a few paces towards Arabi, who saluted him and kissed his hands. I only shook hands with him, and he invited us to take seats. There were several of the Azhar Sheykhs with him, among them the son of Arusi. At first they talked about the situation and the new Ministry. Then the conversation turned on Embabeh's dealings with the Khedive during the late events. From all I saw I conclude that the report of a coolness having taken place between Embabeh and Arabi was not true. While Embabeh was concluding his narrative coffee was served, and Arabi introduced me formally to him, and explained that I was a friend of Mr. Blunt.   Embabeh then explained to me all about the telegram. He had written the answer, he said, with his own hand, thinking the telegram addressed to him; but he had never apologized to the Khedive about it.   He believes Sir E. Malet heard of it originally through Sultan Pasha, or some of the Khedive's adherents.

"Next Arabi showed Embabeh a proclamation he had made guaranteeing the lives and properties of all the inhabitants of Egypt, whatever their creed or nation, and Arabi begged him to write a similar one, showing, as Sheykh el Islam, that the Mohammedan religion, far from allowing, forbids Moslems to hurt Christians, Jews, or others, and commands the faithful to protect them.   Embabeh agreed to this, and, in my presence and that of the other four Sheykhs, prayed God to help him to succeed in reforming the country.   He also promised to help him in fostering peace between Mohammedans and others, inasmuch as all were brothers notwithstanding the diversity of creeds.

"We then went on to Artin Bey's, where also we were entertained with great honour, and afterwards drove through the Clot Bey Road, the Mouski, and other parts of the town, while the people stood on both sides saying, 'May God exalt you.'

"At the end of the drive Arabi told me he was invited to dine with Seyd Hassan Akkad, and took me with him, with all the pashas, officers, sheykhs, and Ulemas.   Our host's large house was crowded; Arabi, Mahmud Sami, Ahmed Pasha, Abdu, Nadim, and I were in the principal sitting-room, where we recited poetry, making or composing elegies and satires, and amusing ourselves at Ragheb's expense.   Arabi composed a satire, Abdu two, Nadim made four, and Sami two.   At dinner I sat by Arabi.   The courses were about thirty different Arab dishes, besides the European and Eastern cakes, sweetmeats and fruit.

"After dinner we talked freely about politics, and about different plans and forms of government.   The republican form was preferred; and Mahmud Sami, who displayed great knowledge and ingenuity, endeavoured to show the advantage of a republican government for Egypt.   He said: 'From the beginning of our movement we aimed at turning Egypt into a small republic like Switzerland—and then Syria would have joined—

and then Hejaz would have followed us. But we found some
of the Ulema were not quite prepared for it and were behind
our time. Nevertheless we shall endeavour to make Egypt a
republic before we die. We all hope to see the "Saturnia
regna" once more.'

"*June* 19.—Abdu, Nadim, Sami, and I were talking the night
before last about the peaceful means to be taken to tide over the
Egyptian difficulty. Abdu said that he has made up his mind
to get together all the documents he has in his possession, with
others concerning Egyptian affairs, and go to England and depose them himself before Mr. Gladstone and the English Parliament. He would take also with him a worthy person as representative of the leading merchants of the land; and another
who would represent the liberal fellahin. Mahmud Sami approved the idea, and said he also wished he could go to Europe
on such a mission, and Abdu is already preparing for the journey. So is Nadim and Seyyid Hassan Moussa el Akkad, the
leading Arab merchant of Cairo, a man of considerable wealth,
influence, and patriotism.

"Ragheb is made Prime Minister, but his policy being
Turkish nobody is pleased with him except the Circassians.
People suspect some Ottoman intrigue in the matter and are
very uneasy. I am trying to calm their minds and tell them to
keep quiet.

"The last events have increased the hatred in the Arab heart
against the Turks, Circassians, and the Sultan himself. I heard
Sami and Abdu and Nadim curse the Sultans and all the Turkish
generation from Genjis Khan to Holagu and down to Abdul
Hamid. They are preparing the nation for a republican form
of government. A large party is already formed and disposed;
crescit eundo. They will seize upon the first occasion which
presents itself. They expect the armed intervention of Turkish troops with pleasure in this last crisis. It would have been
the signal for a complete independence from the Porte. But
the cunning Turk saw the danger and abstained. Nadim told
me yesterday, while we were coming from Shubra, that he must,
before he dies, crush down the Sultan's throne. —— said:
'This is my aim too—may God help us to succeed.'

"I must tell you that I have been received here with such
honour, respect, and politeness as I never could dream of. All

the pashas, colonels, sheykhs, merchants receive me with open arms, and lavish upon me their kindness and hearty thanks. We have arranged with Nadim to give a dinner party to all the leaders of the National Party in your honour, and to thank you for the help given them in their struggle."

"Cairo, *June* 22.

"Last night I went to Mahmud Sami's house, where I met all our friends and the Pashas and many other of the leaders. We talked politics all night, and I communicated to them the contents of your letters received to-day by Brindisi. I also gave them a summary of the English newspapers you and Lady Anne had sent me. Afterwards I presented to Mahmud Sami, in the presence of Nadim, a petition on the part of the National Party, in which they ask Mr. Gladstone to send to Egypt a Consul who understands the affairs of their country. Sami approved the petition and said they will have it signed when Arabi Pasha comes back to Cairo and present it to Mr. Gladstone through you. At the end of the *soirée* I was informed that Sir E. Malet has for the fourth time urged Tewfik to arrest Abdu, Nadim, Mahmud Sami, and myself.

"*June* 23.—Ah soon as Ragheb Pasha was confirmed by the Khedive as Prime Minister, his first act and order was to call me to Alexandria with Nadim. On Monday night the Under-Secretary sent his carriage to my hotel with his man, who informed me that Hassan Pasha Daramalli wished to see me, and had sent his carriage. I went with Nadim, not trusting myself to go alone. When we got there we were received courteously, and afterwards he informed me that Ragheb Pasha had charged him with a message that he wished me to go and meet him at Alexandria at the Divan of the Administration. I replied 'very well,' and Nadim said he, too, would go with me. And so we left the house with the firm intention of having nothing to do with Ragheb.

"Thus at the very time I was telegraphing to you, 'for God's sake save Malet or he will be murdered by fanatics,' he was urging the Khedive to arrest me. Often, when hot-headed young Egyptians were discussing Malet and Colvin's death, I endeavoured to convince them of their folly, and that no possible good result could come of it to the National cause.

"*June* 24.—Mahmud Pasha Fellaki, who had deserted the

National cause on account of his not having received a place in Mahmud Sami's Ministry, has now been reconciled and has received from Arabi the post of Minister of Public Works."

*   *   *   *   *   *

(Sabunji then describes the crisis preceding Mahmud Sami's resignation, Arabi's appeal to the Sultan, Dervish's mission and Osman Bey's mission, and how they flattered Abdul Hamid with professions of zeal for the Caliphate.)   "As to their real convictions, however, they care for Abdul Hamid as much as they would care for a man in the moon.   They would make use of him as long as he can be useful to them and until they are strong enough to declare themselves an independent republic.   This has been the basis of their program from the beginning.   But they have prudently chosen to proceed by degrees.   Mahmud Pasha Sami assured me in Nadim and Abdu's presence that before they die they must declare themselves independent of the Porte, and Egypt a republic.   Nadim's efforts are employed to instill this idea in the minds of the young generation.   Since I came here I and Nadim have been together night and day. We sit talking and devising plans till one or two every morning. We mix in every society.   Sheykhs, Ulemas, Notables, merchants, and officers receive us with open arms, and we talk to them of your endeavours and of the service which you have rendered to the National cause.   They all long to see you and present you with their hearty thanks.   Indeed, people so good and sincerely kind deserve every attention and help."

I am not able to fix an exact date to the moment when Gladstone finally hardened his heart against the Egyptians and resolved on military operations—he persuaded himself that it would not be war—but it must have been some time between the 20th June and the end of the month.   The considerations that seem to have decided him were, first, of course, parliamentary ones.   His Whig followers were on the point of a revolt, and Chamberlain was pressing him with tales of the impatience of the provinces.   The diplomatic defeat of the Foreign Office was becoming too plain to be concealed.   Granville, with his little maxims of procrastination and using a threat as if it were a blow, had "dawdled it out" in Egypt till England had become the laughing-stock of Europe.   On the Stock Exchange things were looking badly and trade was suffering from the long crisis.

What were called the "resources of civilization," that is to say, lying, treachery and fraud, had been tried by the Foreign Office to more than their extreme limit, and one and all had proved absolutely of no use against the Nationalist obstinacy.   Arabi had been ordered by all the majesty of England to leave Egypt, and he had not gone.   On the contrary he had gained an immense reputation throughout the Mohammedan East at England's expense.   It seemed to many that there would be a Pan-Islamic revolt in India.   England, as I had said on Waterloo day, had never looked so foolish.   Serious officials were alarmed at this, and all the jingoism of the Empire, asleep since Disraeli's parliamentary defeat in 1880, was suddenly awake and crying for blood.   Mr. Gladstone hardened his heart and let his conscience go, not, I think, by any deliberate decision saying that this or that should be done, but simply by leaving it to the "departments," and to the "men on the spot," that is to say, the Admiralty, Sir Beauchamp Seymour, and Colvin (for Malet had been withdrawn) to work out a solution their own way.   We had won our diplomatic game against the Foreign Office too thoroughly.   It was to be the turn now of England's fighting forces.

"*June* 19.—A Stock Exchange scare of Bright and Chamberlain having resigned" (a scare which showed the ignorance of the public as to Chamberlain's position, classing him still with Bright).

"*June* 20.—A more reasonable article in the 'Daily News.' Frederic Harrison strongly advises me to write Gladstone a public letter and have it printed.   He is prepared to answer for its effect in the provinces.   I have accordingly begun one.

"*June* 21.—Finished my letter and took it to the Howards for approval.   He (George Howard) made me modify some sentences, so as not to compromise Gladstone personally.   She warmly approved.   Frank Lascelles was there.   I then arranged with Button to publish it tomorrow, or Friday at latest, and sent it in to Gladstone.

"*June* 22.—To Button early.   We think they mean mischief after all.   Harry Brand writes that if the French hold out on the Note the Government mean to act in Egypt, notwithstanding Germany.   I doubt, however, if France is prepared for this. I shall follow up my letter (to Gladstone) with other letters, if necessary. I am certain that if England lands troops anywhere in Egypt, the Sultan will proclaim a Jehad and that the Mussulmans will rise in India. Things are in a pretty pass."

My letter to Gladstone appeared in the "Times" on the following day, 23rd June, the very day the Conference met at Constantinople. It created a great sensation. It stands thus:

"SIR,   *"June 21st, 1882.*

"The gravity of the present situation in Egypt, and the interests of honour and advantage to the English nation which are there engaged, impel me to address you publicly on the subject of the diplomatic steps which have led to this imbroglio, and to put on record certain facts which, in the case of any new departure taken by the Powers at the approaching Conference, should not be lost sight of.

"You are aware, sir, that during the past winter I was engaged as mediator in a variety of unofficial but important negotiations carried on between Sir Edward Malet and Sir Auckland Colvin on the one hand, and the chiefs of the National Egyptian party on the other, negotiations in which I engaged my personal honour to the loyalty of Her Majesty's agents; also that I have been in close communication with those chiefs since my return to England, and that I am consequently in a position to speak with certainty and authority as to the character and intentions of the popular movement in Egypt. You know, moreover, that I have from time to time warned Her Majesty's Government of the danger they were running from a false appreciation of facts, and that I have repeatedly urged the necessity of their coming to a rapid understanding with those in whose hands the guidance of the movement lay. Finally, you know that in the interests of right and justice, and in accordance with a promise made by me to the Egyptians, I have counselled them to the best of my ability in the recent crisis, and spared no pains to urge them to come to that settlement of their difficulties with the Khedive, Mohammed Tewfik, at which they have now happily arrived. In this I took upon myself a great responsibility, but one which, I think, the event has already justified.

"The main points in the past which I would state are these:

"1. In the month of December last I assisted the National

Party to publish a program of their views, which was just and liberal, and to which they have since rigidly adhered. At this time, and down to the publication of the Dual Note of the 8th of January, the Egyptians had no quarrel whatever with England or the English. Neither had they any real quarrel with the Khedive or the Control, trusting in these to permit the development of political liberty in their country in the direction of Parliamentary and constitutional self-government. Their aim was, and is, the resumption by Egypt of her position as a nation, the redemption of her debt, and the reform of justice. They trusted then, as now, to the army, which was and is their servant, to secure them these rights, and to their Parliament to secure them these ends; and they were prepared to advance gradually, and with moderation, in the path they had traced.

"2. The Dual Note, drawn up by M. Gambetta with the view of making England a partner of his anti-Mussulman policy and understood by the Egyptians as the first step in a policy analogous to that recently pursued in Tunis, changed this confidence into a sentiment of profound distrust. Instead of awing them, it precipitated their action. It caused them to insist upon the resignation of Sherif Pasha, whom they suspected of the design to betray them, and to assist with the Khedive in summoning a Nationalist Ministry to office. This insistence, though represented by the English journals as the work of the army, was, in fact, the work of the nation through their representatives the Notables. Of this I can furnish ample evidence.

"3. The unexpected fall of M. Gambetta prevented the execution of the threat of armed intervention implied by the Dual Note. Nevertheless, a plan of indirect intervention was persisted in. The English and French Controllers-General protested against the Constitution granted by the Khedive on the 6th of February, and the English and French Governments carefully withheld their assent to it, signifying only that the Article, giving to the Egyptian Parliament the right of voting that half of the Budget which was not affected to the payment of the Debt, was an infringement of international engagements. Their argument for this, based on certain firmans of the Porte, and certain decrees of the Khedive, has been constantly denied by the Egyptians.

"4. Acting, it must be presumed, in accordance with their

instructions, the English agents at Cairo have for the past three months set themselves steadily to work to bring about a revolution counter to the will of the people and the liberties granted to them by the Viceroy. The English Controller-General, though a paid agent of the Egyptian Government, has not scrupled to take part in this; and the English Resident Minister has spared no pains to create a quarrel between the Khedive and his Ministers. The Controller-General, sitting in council with the Ministers as their official adviser, has withheld his advice, counting, it would seem, on the mistakes likely to be made by men new to office, and noting these in silence. The English press correspondents, hitherto held in check by the Resident, have been permitted full license in the dissemination of news injurious to the Ministry, and known to be false. I will venture to recall to you some of the scares reported at this time and disseminated through Europe—the scare of banditti in the Delta; the scare of the Bedouin rising; the scare of revolt in the Soudan; the scare of an Abyssinian war; the scare of huge military expenditure; the scare of a general refusal to pay taxes, of the resignation of the provincial governors, of the neglect of the irrigation works, of danger to the Suez Canal; the scare of Arabi Pasha having become the bribed agent, in turn, of Ismaïl, of Halim, and of the Sultan.

"For some of these a very slight foundation may have existed in fact; for most there was no foundation whatsoever.

"On the 20th of March I addressed Lord Granville, by Arabi Pasha's request, on this subject, and pointed out to him the danger caused to peace in Egypt through the attitude of the English agents urging that a Commission should be sent to Cairo to examine into Egyptian grievances.

"In the month of April advantage was taken by the English and French Consuls-General of the discovery of a plot to assassinate the National Ministry, and traced by these to an agent of Ismaïl Pasha's, to induce the Khedive to put himself in open opposition to his Ministers. Those implicated in the plot and condemned to banishment were men of position, Turks and Circassians, and as such of the same race and society with the Khedive and he was unwilling to ratify their sentence, and suffered himself to be persuaded to refuse his signature. This led to the rupture which the previous diplomatic action of the

Consuls-General had prepared.   A summons was then sent by
Mahmud Sami Pasha to the Deputies to come to Cairo and
decide between the Ministers and the Khedive, and the Deputies came.   Sultan Pasha, however, through jealousy, refused
to preside at any formal sitting; and advantage was again taken
of the circumstance by the Consuls-General to encourage all who
were in opposition to the National Party to rally round the
Khedive.   A section of the rich Egyptians, fearing disturbance,
sided with the Circassians, and the Consuls-General, deceived by
appearances, ventured a *coup de main.*   An *ultimatum,* dictated
by them, was sent in to the Ministers, insisting on the resignation of the Ministry and Arabi Pasha's departure from the country.   The step for an instant seemed to have succeeded, for
the Ministry resigned.   It became, however, immediately apparent that the feeling of the country had been miscalculated by
our diplomacy, and Arabi, by the manifest will of the nation,
returned next day to power.

"I cannot understand that the action of our Consul-General
in this matter was justified by any principle of Liberal policy;
it has certainly not been justified by success.

"6.   When the Fleet was ordered to Alexandria, I endeavoured to convey a warning, as my private opinion, based upon
all I had witnessed last winter of the temper of the Egyptian
people, that the presence of English men-of-war at that moment
in the port of Alexandria, especially if their crews should be
allowed on any pretence to land, would be exceedingly likely to
provoke a serious disturbance and it was my intention to go
myself to Egypt to do what I could towards mitigating what I
feared would be the results.

"7.   About the same time the English Government consented
to the despatch of a Turkish Commissioner to Cairo.   It was
supposed that the authority of the Sultan was so great in Egypt
that obedience would be shown to whatever orders his representative might bring, or that, at any rate, little opposition
would be offered.   In any case, the Porte was authorized to
act in its own way.   Dervish Pasha was sent; and it is lamentable to record that the English Foreign Office at that time seems
to have counted mainly on the fact that he was a man notoriously
unscrupulous in his method of dealing with rebels.   I have
reason to know that what was expected of him was, that he

should summon Arabi Pasha to Constantinople; that, failing this, he should have recourse to bribery; and that in the extreme resort, he should arrest or shoot the Minister of War as a mutineer with his own hand. Whether these were really Dervish Pasha's instructions or intentions I will not argue. The Porte seems to have been as little prepared as Her Majesty's Government were for the strength of the National feeling in Egypt; and only the union and courage shown by the people would seem to have convinced the Sultan that methods such as those formerly used by Dervish against the Albanians would here be out of place. Humaner counsels have in any case prevailed, and peace has been recommended between the Khedive and his people.

'Such, sir, is shortly the history of England's diplomatic action in Egypt during the past six months. It is one of the most deplorable our Foreign Office has to record. The future, however, in some measure remains to us, though, when the Conference assembles, England's will be only one of many voices raised in the settlement. It is not for me to suggest the words which should there be spoken; but I will venture to express my conviction that if Her Majesty's representative then comes forward with an honest confession of the mistakes made. and a declaration of England's sympathy with Egyptian freedom, England will regain her lost ground. In spite of the just anger of the Egyptians at the unworthy tricks which have been played upon them by our Foreign Office, they believe that a more generous feeling exists in the body of the English nation, which would not suffer so vast a public wrong to be committed as the subjugation of their country for a misunderstood interest in Egyptian finance and in the Suez Canal. They have, over and over again, assured me, and I know that they speak truly, that their only aim is peace, independence, and economy; and that the Suez Canal cannot be better protected for England, as for the rest of the world, than by the admission of the Egyptian people into the comity of nations. Only let the hand of friendship be held out to them freely, and at once, and we shall still earn their gratitude.

"I am, Sir, your obedient Servant,
"WILFRID SCAWEN BLUNT."

CHAPTER XV

THE BOMBARDMENT OF ALEXANDRIA

We now come to the bombardment of Alexandria, a quarrel deliberately picked by Admiral Seymour and Colvin acting in concert, for the removal of Malet only put the diplomatic power more entirely into Colvin's hands. Malet was replaced, not as I had hoped by Lascelles, whose independence of character and knowledge of Egypt might have enabled him to take a line of his own, but by a simple Foreign Office clerk named Cartwright, who, ignorant and helpless, was a mere passive tool directed by the Controller. I have not much to add to the public records of those last three weeks at Cairo and Alexandria, but my diary will give an idea of what was going on in London. My public letter to Gladstone called down a storm of abuse upon my head from Malet's and Colvin's friends, and generally from the Jingo and financial elements in the Press and Parliament.

"*June* 24.—There is an angry letter from Henry Malet (Edward Malet's elder brother) in to-day's 'Times.' . . . Lord Lamington, too, has given notice of a question as to my 'unofficial negotiations' in the House of Lords for Monday. The more talk the better. . . . A party of people (at Crabbet) for Sunday, Lascelles among them.

"*June* 25.—Wrote an answer to Henry Malet and sent it to the 'Times.' A soft answer turneth away wrath." (I was loath to quarrel in this way with old friends, and I was resolved not to hit back except on compulsion.)

"*June* 26.—A long letter has come from Sabunji (that already given in the last chapter). They are giving a public dinner in my honour at Cairo. . . . Met Lords De la Warr and Lamington (they were brothers-in-law) at the House of Lords, and got the former to ask for Malet's despatch of

December 26th (that which Malet had said he had cancelled).
Lord Lamington was going to have based his speech on Henry
Malet's letter, but I showed him what nonsense this was.   All
the same he made a very strong speech in an indignant tone
about me.   Lord Granville looked white and uncomfortable,
but admitted the fact of my having acted on one occasion to
pacify the army, a point gained.   (This had been denied by
Henry Malet.)   He could not remember about the despatch
of the 26th, but would look for it."   (The reason of the
great embarrassment of the Government on being questioned
about my "unofficial negotiations" was that they had got into
similar difficulties in their Irish policy by making use of Mr.
Errington the year before as a means of communicating unoffi-
cially with the Pope about the attitude of the Irish clergy.)
"Dined with Henry Middleton at his club early, and went
with him to a meeting of the Anti-Aggression League in Far-
ringdon Street.   Sir Wilfrid Lawson, in the chair was excellent.   He is the pleasantest speaker I have listened to.   Also
Sir Arthur Hobhouse was good.   Frederic Harrison read a
lecture in which he stated the Egyptian case fairly."   *N. B.*—
Henry Middleton had been much in Egypt and was intimate
there with the Coptic community.   A letter written to him during the war by the Coptic Patriarch has been published.   It is
interesting as showing how entirely the Copts were with Arabi
at that time.

"*June* 27.—Dinner at Pembroke's.   All the Wilton Club
there, some forty people.   I sat next to Harry Brand and had
a grand row with him about Egypt.   After dinner healths were
drunk, my own among the number, and I had to make a
speech.   I felt myself in rather an unfriendly atmosphere
politically, as most of those present were Jingoes, but I was
specially complimented for my public services by Eddy Hamilton, who proposed my health.   I said in reply that some served
their country in one way and some in another, but that as long
as one served it and did one's duty, it did not much matter
what one did."   (These speeches, of course, were not serious,
as the Wilton Club was only a convivial gathering of Lord
Pembroke's personal friends who came together at his house
two or three times a year to dine and make merry.)

"*June* 28.—Rode to George Howard's, and showed him Sabunji's letter and my Gladstone correspondence. Sabunji states that the National leaders are thinking of going to England to lay their case before Mr. Gladstone, and I have asked Howard to get me, if he can, an interview with Mr. Bright. Bright is more amenable, I fancy to reason than the rest, and perhaps it might do good to see him. There is no doubt that war preparations are being made, for whatever purpose it may be. I don't believe, all the same, that they are intended as anything more than strengthening Dufferin's hands at the Conference. I have sent a telegram to Sabunji saying that nothing is yet decided about sending troops, and begging patience.

"*June* 29.—Called on Bright at his house in Picadilly. He talked in a friendly tone, but less sympathetically than Gladstone and less intelligently. The upshot, however, is very satisfactory. He assures me that no active steps have yet been taken for hostilities, and he does not believe they will be taken. He considers the Suez Canal to be of little strategical value to us, preferring, with Gladstone, the Cape route for military communication with India. I explained to him my idea of a Mohammedan reformation and how little the movement in Egypt had in common with the Sultan's fanatical ideas. I think my visit may do good by strengthening the peace party in the Cabinet." (*N. B.*—Bright scouted more strongly than this entry would suggest the idea of hostilities at Alexandria. He bade me make my mind quite easy about them. And I am sure he was speaking truly according to his knowledge. But the poor man, whose principles were absolutely opposed to warfare, was kept in complete darkness as to what was going on at the Admiralty and the War Office, and, as he himself afterwards told me, was persuaded that, even when the threat of bombardment was decided on in the Cabinet, it would remain like all the other threats, a *brutum fulmen*. The theory laid before the Cabinet by the Foreign Office was that the mass of the Egyptians were with the Khedive, not with Arabi, and that on the first shot being fired by the British fleet the populace of Alexandria would rise and bring Arabi, who was alone in his intention of resistance, a prisoner to their sovereign's feet. Bright, when he found how he had been cajoled into consent-ing to the bombardment which had led to the burning of Alexandria and the necessity of a regular war, was very angry and resigned his place in the Cabinet, nor did he ever forgive Gladstone for his share in the deception practised on him or the abandonment of their common principles.)

"Called on Lady Gregory, who has written a paper on the Control of Egypt, which is amusing. Dinner at the Howards. She (Mrs. H.) is enthusiastic about my plans.

"*June* 30.—Colvin contradicts flatly through the 'Times' correspondent that either he or Malet have ever made use of my services as mediator or intermediary on any occasion. This puts him in my hands after Lord Granville's admission of the fact on Monday." (*N. B.*—This denial in plain terms by Colvin of things it is impossible he should have forgotten need not be characterized by me. The matter was not made better by a private letter he wrote me, 6th July, in which he repudiated in part his responsibility for the "Times" telegram. I accepted his explanation at the time as genuine, but when a little later I asked him to repudiate the telegram publicly, he declined to do so, and in terms which were merely a repetition and aggravation of the untruth.)

"Breakfasted with De la Warr to meet Broadley, the 'Times' corespondent at Tunis." (*N. B.*—This is the same Broadley whom, at Lord De la Warr's recommendation I afterwards entrusted with the defence of Arabi. He had been practising as lawyer in the Consular Courts at Tunis, and latterly as "Times" correspondent there. He was a man of great ability and had made himself serviceable to De la Warr in many ways, giving him the information about Eastern affairs which were De la Warr's hobby, and preparing, when in England, his speeches for him on such subjects in the House of Lords. At the time of the invasion of Tunis by the French he took a strong part in the "Times" in favour of the Mohammedan rising and published a useful book about it afterwards called "The Last Punic War.") 'He says all are waiting in Tripoli and Tunis for the Sultan to come forward. Otherwise el Senoussi will read the Mohammedan revival. . . . Wrote a letter to the 'Times' in answer to Colvin which ought to smash him. Luncheon at the Gregorys.

"Eddy writes a friendly letter saying that Mr. Gladstone will not go back from his expressions of sympathy with Egyptian independence, if what I have told him proves true. This must be owing to Bright." The letter here referred to is an important one as bearing on the settlement afterwards made in Egypt, and the promise of independence and liberal institutions made at Gladstone's suggestion by Lord Dufferin in his celebrated despatch. But for the hold I had acquired over Gladstone on this point, I have no manner of doubt that after Tel-el-Kebir Egypt would have been annexed to the British Empire. The Whigs in the Cabinet all intended it.

"*July* 2.—At Brocket. This, after Wilton, is the most charming country place I have seen. All in it is exactly as it was fifty and sixty years ago in the days of Caroline Lamb and Lord Melbourne. Lord Palmerston died here. Henry Cowper, whose it is now, is to me very sympathetic. Our party consists of Henry Brand and his wife, the American Minister, Lord Houghton, Lymington, and Frederick Leveson Gower, Lord Granville's brother and secretary. Great wrangling about Egypt but all friendly enough, even Leveson. And the American is on my side. . . . I had a little talk with Leveson after we had played lawn tennis. He spoke very despondingly of the British Empire, but thought England might last without revolution at home. At Brocket such talk is melancholy. . . . There is another fierce attack on me in the 'Observer.'

"*July* 3.—At Brocket. I fancy if there is to be any intervention at all it is to be Italian—at least, if intervention is ordered by the Conference. This I should greatly dislike, for at present the Italians seem sympathetic, but if launched on conquest they would be brutal in their methods. Besides, the Italians are not assailable at home, as we and the French are." (*N. B.*—The Italian Government was being asked at this date to join us in armed intervention in Egypt, but they wisely declined. It would have been very unpopular with the Liberals in Italy where Menotti Garibaldi was organizing a force to help Arabi.) "Drove over to Knebworth to luncheon. Lytton has been building and making a new drive into the Park, certainly a great improvement; we talked about the British Empire, on which subject he is as despondent as I am. He thinks my policy in Egypt might have succeeded, or any policy but that of trusting to chance. Now he foresees a Mohammedan rebellion in India, go things how they may. . . . In the evening to Temple Dinsley where the Brands are.

"*July* 4.—To London; found a telegram saying that Arabi certainly would not go to Constantinople, also a letter from Sabunji, which has made me uneasy. It has evidently been opened in the post, and the contents may have compromised the National leaders at Constantinople. There are telegrams, too, in the papers about a renewed quarrel as to the fortifications at Alexandria; and Lady Gregory, who came to James Street, has heard from Sir Erskine May that Beauchamp Seymour has orders to bombard Alexandria to-morrow." (Sir Erskine May, was I believe, the Chief Permanent Official of the Admiralty. The earliest correspondence referring to a bombardment in the Blue Books occurs on 26th June, when the Admiralty telegraphs to Sir Beauchamp Seymour: "If Egyptian troops are making preparations to attack, communicate with French Admiral and bring ships into position." This telegram shows the wolf and the lamb argument that was being used to excuse our own intended attack. We know from Palmer's journal, to which reference will be made later, that Seymour had resolved to bombard at least as early as 4th July. Among the determining causes with Gladstone and the Cabinet at this time was, I believe, the bogus report of a massacre at Benha, a wholly fabulous incident which was largely made use of to infuriate English opinion against Arabi.) "She [Lady Gregory] has also heard that Colvin has resigned and his resignation been accepted." I don't know whether there was any foundation for this report, but it is too late already for his recall to have made any difference in the result. It was probably altogether a false report.

"*July* 5.—I am very uneasy in my mind now about these threats of bombardment. At twelve I went to the House of Commons and heard Dilke announce that the fleet had orders 'under certain circumstances to act in a certain way.' Had luncheon with Sir Wilfrid Lawson, who is a really charming man, and read him Sabunji's letter describing his dinners and conversations with the National Chiefs. He and others with him will do what they can. But there is nothing now to do. My letters to Gladstone are printed, but I dare not publish them until I see what line the Porte takes. . . . Dined at Lady Rosamund Christie's. Knowles was there and says that the bombardment is to begin to-morrow morning. Fawcett takes my side. My fear is lest the Nationalists should stake all on an artillery duel with the fleet, in which they cannot help being beaten, and so be discouraged. They ought, I think, to abandon Alexandria, and make an entrenched camp out of reach of the guns of the fleet. But I dare not advise." (About this time Button informed me that the Admiralty plan was to effect a landing during the bombardment with the idea of cutting off Arabi's retreat. This news, if I remember rightly, influenced my telegram next day and my letter of the seventh.)

"*July* 6.—Admiral Seymour has sent in an ultimatum, and I have telegraphed to Sabunji as follows: 'Avoid meddling with the fleet. Send Abdu with a message to Gladstone. Patience.' I am not sure whether I am doing right, but prudence is certainly on the right side. Besides, Arabi will judge independently of my opinion, and he has never yet been wrong. I have sent copies of my correspondence with Downing Street to Cardinal Manning and Knowles (and also to Lord Dufferin). After luncheon went to see Hill, the editor of the 'Daily News.' He is now all on our side, it being too late to do any good. He promises, however, to write what he can. . . . In the evening a telegram from Sabunji saying that all is quiet, so I suppose the difficulty is staved off. . . . I wrote to-day to Eddy proposing to show him Sabunji's letters (those already given). It is a desperate remedy, but the circumstances are desperate.

"*July* 7.—Went to see Stanley of Alderley and urged him to see Musurus, so as to prevent any split between Arabi and the Sultan. I told him pretty nearly the facts of the case, but made him understand this was not a moment for Mohammedans to dispute, and that the Turks and Egyptians could settle their domestic differences later. He seems quite to agree with me. . . . Then wrote a letter to Sabunji recommending them not to quarrel with the fleet, but to make an entrenched camp out of reach of the guns. I still think that no English expedition will be landed in Egypt, but that they will have to fight the Turks or possibly the Italians. . . . The papers announce a pacific settlement of the difference between Arabi and the fleet, which is satisfactory so far.

"*July* 8.—At Crabbet. The second post has brought a letter from Eddy Hamilton which seems to imply that Gladstone is still open to conviction. This is more than I expected"—(and more, too, than the letter implied. What Hamilton wrote was, "I hope it goes without saying that it has been the desire of the Government all along to get at the truth, but that, apparently, has not been so easy.") "I have accordingly been preparing a précis of Sabunji's letters. In the Evening Lascelles and others arrived.

"*July* 9.—Sunday. I have consulted Lascelles about sending Sabunji's letters to Gladstone, but he thinks it is too late. Hartington has told him that they intend occupying Egypt and probably annexing it, on the principle *j'y suis, j'y reste*. Chamberlain has said: 'We have got the Grand Old Man into a corner now, and he *must* fight.' I shall, therefore, wait events. The 'Observer' announces a new threat or Ultimatum. This time I shall leave Providence to decide." (What I record here as having been told me by Lascelles is of historical importance. He was in a position to know what was going on more than any of my friends. As a former *Chargé d'Affaires* in Egypt he was consulted at the Foreign Office, and as Lord Hartington's first cousin he had his confidences about what was going on in the Whig section of the Cabinet.)

"*July* 10.—A new Ultimatum is announced, this time in terms which Arabi cannot accept. They want him to surrender the forts. The French, however, refuse to take any part in this act of piracy. M. P., who knows naval people, assures me that Beauchamp Seymour is in a terrible fright; that the 'Invincible' is the only ship with really sound armour plates, and that the fleet is in a most critical position." (There was some truth, I believe, in this. The ships, as they were moored in the harbour, lay directly under the fire of the forts at short range. If the Nationalists had been as unscrupulous as our people were, they might have taken the ships at a disadvantage and perhaps sunk them. But Arabi was not the man for a *coup* of this kind, and he was, besides, a stickler for the common Mohammedan rule of not firing the first shot in war. The quarrel, too, was none of his seeking, and all he was bent on was to avoid all excuse for a collision. He consequently allowed Seymour to move his ships away and choose his own distance.) "Arabi may then be in the right in accepting the duel. At any rate, it is forced on him in such a way that he cannot refuse. Strangely enough, I am in high spirits. My idea is that this bombardment and bloodshed, however it terminates, will produce a revulsion in public feeling here and stop further proceedings. Nobody really wants war or annexation, except the financiers. And these would soon go to the wall if the public spoke. The Powers, too, will probably be angry at this act of violence in the middle of the Conference. For England the outlook seems very bad. It will probably lead to a war with France and the loss of India. . . . To London and saw Lady Gregory, who wants me to send a copy of my Gladstone letters to Gibson, as Gibson is the coming man of the Conservatives, and the Conservatives will soon be in power. Gladstone was beaten on Friday on an important vote. . . . Harrison has written Gladstone a scathing letter, telling him his action in Egypt will ruin his moral character forever in history. This is certain, and I will take care it does so. . . . Lunched with George Currie, who, as a bondholder, is now pleased at the firmness of the Government. They were afraid, he says, at one time that Gladstone would have thrown them over.

"To the House of Commons, where I saw Lawson. He asked me what could be done. I said, 'Nothing.' Dilke made a statement confirming the Ultimatum. . . . Lord De la Warr called at six to ask whether I would not telegraph to advise an arrangement. But I told him I could not do this any longer, for the Egyptians could not give up their forts honourably. Home to Crabbet.

"*July* 11.—At Crabbet. I settled this morning in my mind that if the weather was fine things would go well in Egypt— and behold it is raining! . . . I shall stay here now till all is over, except on Thursday, when I have been asked to Marlborough House, to have the honour of meeting Her Majesty. . . . We shall know all in a few hours. . . . It rained heavily till 2, then cleared. I remained indoors in a nervous state, unable to do anything. . . . At half-past four David brought a 'Globe,' with news showing that the bombardment began at 7 and was still going on at half-past 11. At 5, Anne came from

London with the 'Pall Mall' and 'St. James's,' showing it was not all over at 1.40.   It is evident that the Egyptians fought like men, so I fear nothing.   They may be driven out of the forts and out of Alexandria.   But Egypt will not be conquered. The French fleet has gone to Port Saïd, and it is impossible there should not be an European war.   I have sent my Gladstone correspondence to the Prince of Wales.

"*July* 12.—The forts are silenced, but the Egyptians show no sign of yielding, and the newspapers announce another bombardment for to-day.   This is a monstrous thing.   The Sultan, I am glad to see, stands firm; and a religious war is inevitable, succeeding, as Arabi said it would the political one. The prophecy about Gladstone will thus come true.   His conscience must be a curious study just now, the conscience of a Eugene Aram, and I believe him capable of any treachery and any crime.   I can do no more, and shall stay here.   Went fishing in the forest, a bright warm day, with a slight threatening of thunder about noon.   The evening papers talk of a flag of truce and a heavy swell which has prevented the ships from firing.

"*July* 13.—Saw Button, who tells me an occupation is inevitable.   Old Edward Blount was in the train.   He tells me the French are in no condition to fight.   Their navy is so illfound he doubts their having the ammunition.   He thinks there will be a revolution in a few months. . . .   Found Sir Wilfrid Lawson at home in Grosvenor Crescent and had much discourse with him, but he agrees it is hopeless doing anything with the Government. . . .   Had luncheon with the Howards. She is staunch, he doubtful. . . .   Coming back by underground railway I read the news of Alexandria being in flames, of the evacuation of the town, and of a new massacre by roughs. This is nothing but what must have been.   I am glad of one thing only, and that is the army has got safe out of that mousetrap.   I have had it on my mind ever since Arabi went to Alexandria that he would be caught there in some way by his enemies.   Now he seems to have done just what I recommended, retired to a fortified position out of reach of the guns of the fleet.   People, or rather the newspapers, are very angry because he retired under flag of truce, but I am not military man enough to see where the treachery was, especially as Admiral

Seymour had announced that he would understand a white flag to mean the evacuation of the forts." (This charge of having violated the white flag was made a special count against Arabi at his trial, and absurdly insisted upon by Gladstone, because he, Gladstone, had committed himself to a statement that to retire while under the white flag was a violation of the laws of war. This was persisted in after other graver charges were abandoned, until it was discovered that in Lord Wolseley's "Soldier's Pocket Book," a text book in our army, it is distinctly laid down that the contrary is the rule.)

"I was in two minds about going to Marlborough House, but decided it would be best to show loyalty. So went. Everybody cordial enough except old Houghton, who all but cut me. The Malets were there—poor old people—but I did not venture speaking to them. Robert Bourke came to me in great glee at the mess the Government found themselves in. Such are the amenities of party political life. Everybody else nearly was there that I had ever seen. The Prince of Wales shook hands with me, but he said nothing. Her Majesty was looking beaming—I suppose elated at her bombardment. Gladstone is said to have announced in the House that he would not send an army to Egypt. He declares he is not at war with anybody. However Button, with whom I dined, assures me troops are going and that they mean annexation. Dined with him and Lord Bective.

"*July* 14.—Breakfasted with De la Warr. I showed him Arabi's letter to Gladstone, and he advised me not to send it, but offered to propose to the Prince of Wales to speak to me about it. I think this will be a good plan. I dare not let the Government have such a document in their hands until it is settled what form intervention is to take."

The letter here referred to is one that Arabi dictated to Sabunji at Alexandria and sent to me, desiring me to communicate it to Gladstone as from him. It was not signed or sealed by him, and was sent by Sabunji in English, not in Arabic; for which reason Arabi afterwards, when charged with having written it, among other charges made against him at the time of his arrest, denied having written at all to Mr. Gladstone. I was consequently taunted by my enemies with having forged the letter, though I had stated that it was "dictated" in my enclosing letter of two days later. The letter as sent to Mr. Gladstone was as follows:

"Alexandria, *July* 2, 1882.

"SIR,

"Our Prophet in his Koran has commanded us not to seek war nor to begin it. He has commanded us also, if war be waged against us, to resist and, under penalty of being ourselves as unbelievers, to follow those who have assailed us with every weapon and without pity. Hence, England may rest assured that the first gun she fires on Egypt will absolve the Egyptians from all treaties, contracts, and conventions; that the Control and debt will cease; that the property of Europeans will be confiscated; that the Canals will be destroyed; the communications cut; and that use will be made of the religious zeal of Mohammedans to preach a holy war in Syria, in Arabia, and in India. Egypt is held by Mohammedans as the key of Mecca and Medina, and all are bound by their religious law to defend these holy places and the ways leading to them. Sermons on this subject have already been preached in the Mosque of Damascus, and an agreement has been come to with the religious leaders of every land throughout the Mohammedan world. I repeat it again and again, that the first blow struck at Egypt by England or her allies will cause blood to flow through the breadth of Asia and of Africa, the responsibility of which will be on the head of England.

"The English Government has allowed itself to be deceived by its agents, who have cost the country its prestige in Egypt. England will be still worse advised if she attempts to regain what she has lost by the brute force of guns and bayonets.

"On the other hand there are more humane and friendly means to this end. Egypt is ready still—nay, desirous to come to terms with England, to be fast friends with her, to protect her interests and keep her road to India, to be her ally; but she must keep within the limits of her jurisdiction. If, however, she prefers to remain deceived and to boast and threaten us with fleets and her Indian troops, it is hers to make the choice. Only let her not underrate the patriotism of the Egyptian people. Her representatives have not informed her of the change which has been wrought among us since the days of

Ismaïl's tyranny. Nations, in our age, make sudden and gigantic strides in the path of progress.

"England, in fine, may rest assured that we are determined to fight, to die martyrs for our country, as has been enjoined on us by our Prophet, or else to conquer and so live independently and happy. Happiness in either case is promised to us, and a people imbued with this belief, their courage knows no bounds.
"AHMED ARABI."

"Went to see Gregory. He is frightened at Alexandria's being burnt, and will have it that Arabi did not order it. I say he ordered it, and was right, to do so. This is the policy of the Russians at Moscow, and squares with all I know of their intentions. I cannot think it will do any harm in the long run, and it will get more completely rid of the Greeks and Italians. Of course, he was not responsible for the massacre, which is doubtless exaggerated. To fire the town, cut off the water supply and take up a strategical position on the railway is what any determined general would have done." (And so I say still. The burning of Alexandria gave Arabi just the time to entrench himself at Kafr Dawar. If he had carried out the other part of his program and blown up and blocked the Suez Canal, he might have made a good and long fight of it, and even possibly have won the campaign. I will return to this, however, when I come to treat of the war.)

"*July* 15.—Button writes that the Prince of Wales wants a copy of Arabi's letter, and I have sent word to say I shall be happy to read it to His Royal Highness. I will not let it out of my hand as yet. . . . Sir Donald Currie came to see the horses. He is sensible about Egypt, as many people are individually. But the newspapers are raising a universal howl. I am depressed in mind, thinking of the future. Egypt can hardly not be ruined, and it is little consolation to think that the Europeans there and the bondholders will be ruined too. Still, there is a God in heaven for those who trust Him.

"*July* 16.—It seems as if the Turks had at last consented to send troops. Button gave me the conditions yesterday. They are to come and go and catch Arabi, all in a month. The thing is absurd. If they go, they will go to stay. They will also make terms with Arabi, and all England will have gained will be that the Sultan will declare war. All things considered, this is the best solution I could have expected. Otherwise it must have been annexation. . . . Wrote letter enclosing Arabi's letter for Gladstone.

"*July* 17.—Went to London and saw Button. I have agreed to send the letter to Gladstone and to the Prince of Wales, and have accordingly done so. . . . I wish Gladstone to be warned of all the consequences of his action in Egypt, as on Saturday he stated that the destruction of Alexandria was a result which it was impossible to foresee, of bombarding it! Now, if Cairo is destroyed, he will be without excuse. Bright has resigned. At least *he* is an honest man. He made his statement to-night saying he considers the bombardment a breach of international law and the moral law." [1] (I have some reason to believe that Gladstone had shared Bright's delusion that the Alexandrian forts could be bombarded without serious consequences of bloodshed, conflagration, and war. The difference between the two men was this: that Bright, when he saw he had betrayed his principles by consenting to it 'went out and wept bitterly'; Gladstone stifled his remorse and profited as largely as he could by the popularity which war always brings to the Ministry that

---

[1] I met Bright more than once in later years, and his language was strong to me as to the way he had been misled into complicity with the bombardment of Alexandria. I find the following in my journal of 1885:

"*June* 9.—To the Howards. She (Mrs. Howard) dined last night with Hartington and Granville and Bright. . . . Bright told her that he was at the Cabinet which decided on the bombardment of Alexandria, but Lord Granville had assured him it would not really take place, and it had long ago been settled that he was to leave the Cabinet on the first shot fired in any war. It had been a cause of grief and tears to him to watch the slaughter which had since occurred, but he had not had the heart to stand up and denounce his former friends. He had, however, written to Mr Gladstone after the war to say that if he allowed Arabi to be tried by the Egyptian Government it would be a *lasting infamy.*"

"*March* 16.—At night to dine with the Howards. It was a very interesting dinner, John Bright, John Morley, Frederick Leveson, and Mr. Wright, etc. . . . At first we were all rather stiff. . . . However, Wright broke it up by asking Bright *à propos of boots,* who it was that caused the bombardment of Alexandria. Whereupon Bright broke in denouncing the war strongly and the injustice of keeping Arabi a prisoner in Ceylon. He also explained that Beauchamp Seymour had telegraphed to ask permission to bombard some time before but had been refused. At last it was Chamberlain who had insisted on his being allowed to do it. . . . Hartington, Bright said, had not urged it."

makes it.)   ". . . Home late and in low spirits.   I have done what I could to avert this war, and war is now the only solution."

Here, unfortunately, my diary of 1882 ends. [1]

[1] The allusions to an expected Mohammedan rising in India, here and elsewhere quoted from my diary, seem now, in the light of events, somewhat exaggerated. They were, however, justified by the ideas prevalent at the time; and the dread of a general conflagration in the East is perhaps the best excuse that can be made for our Government's action in pressing on in July an immediate violent solution of its difficulty in Egypt.

CHAPTER XVI

THE CAMPAIGN OF TEL-EL-KEBIR

It now remains for me to give an account of the chief incidents of the brief campaign in which for two months native Egypt stood up in arms against her English enemy. No true description of it will be found in the works of any English writer, and still less are the French versions of the story true. The reign of terror, which under the protection of the English garrison for a year or more followed the re-establishment of the Khedive and the Turco-Circassian *régime* at Cairo, effectually stopped the mouths of native Egyptians as to what had happened there during the Khedive's absence, and though a momentary light was shed on the facts by the publicity of Arabi's trial, no organ of the vernacular press was found bold enough to allude to them otherwise than according to the official version; while later, when under French protection the organs of native opinion had gained courage, time had been given for certain legends to grow up which still to a large extent influence the educated Egyptian mind.

The first point to make clear, for it is denaturalized in the Blue Books and has been ignored by all English writers, is the essentially National character of the defence offered by native Egypt to the English invasion. The official version, of course, is that it was the army alone that offered resistance to Seymour's impossible demands at the time of the bombardment, and afterwards to Wolseley's land invasion. This was merely a continuance of the diplomatic fiction which had been built up at the Foreign Office to excuse its determination to intervene in financial interests, and may be read in its most grotesque form of untruth in Lord Dufferin's opening speech to the European Conference at Constantinople. According to the English Ambassador, Egypt—and this was before the bombardment—was

in a state of anarchy, where neither life nor property was secure and where massacres were taking place, through the action
of the army headed by Arabi and other mutinous colonels,
which was making it impossible to carry on the government or
secure order and financial stability. How gross an exaggeration this statement of the political case was, and how it had
been gradually put together on a basis of lies and inventions,
I have already sufficiently shown. What needs still to be explained is the precise share of responsibility for the acceptance
of Seymour's challenge to the artillery duel at Alexandria, which
commenced the war, assignable to Arabi, on whom the whole
of it has been unjustly laid. [1]

That Arabi had been, from the date of the publication of
the Joint Note of 6th January, a chief advocate of self-reliance
and preparedness for war is undoubted, but at the same time
he had always been for conciliation, if possible, rather than war.
Resistance had always been his political platform, but on it he
by no means stood alone, and the arrival of the fleets at Alexandria in May had immensely strengthened his position with
all sections of civilian opinion. With the example of Tunis

[1] "It is no exaggeration," Lord Dufferin asserted, "to say that during the last
few months absolute anarchy has reigned in Egypt. We have seen a military
faction, without even alleging those pretences to legality with which such persons are wont to cloak their designs, proceed from violence to violence, until in-
subordination has given place to mutiny, mutiny to revolt, and revolt to a usurpation of the supreme power. As a consequence the Administration of the country
has been thrown into confusion; the ordinary operations of the merchant have
come to a standstill; the fellahin, no longer finding purchasers for their produce,
are unable to pay the land-tax, and the revenues of Egypt are failing. This
state of things has placed in extreme jeopardy those commercial interests in
which the subjects of all the Powers are so deeply concerned. Not only so, but
those special engagements into which the Governments of France and England
had entered with Egypt have been repudiated; the officers appointed to carry
them into effect have been excluded from the control they were authorized to exercise, and the system which had begun to work so greatly to the advantage of the
industrious cultivators of Egypt has been broken up and overthrown.

"But these effects form only a portion of the deplorable situation which has
excited the anxiety of Europe. It is not merely the public creditor who has
suffered extensive damage. The life and property of every individual European
in the country have become insecure. Of this insecurity we have had a most
melancholy and convincing proof in the brutal massacre by an insolent mob of a
number of unoffending persons at Alexandria, and in the sudden flight from
Cairo and the interior (a flight which implies loss to all and ruin to many) of
thousands of our respective citizens.

"It is evident that such a condition of affairs requires a prompt and energetic
remedy."

before Mohammedan eyes it was indeed impossible not to see what was being prepared for Egypt by the European Powers, the creation of a fictitious condition of anarchy and rebellion which should justify intervention for the protection of the life and property of Europeans, the seizure by persuasion or constraint of the person of the ruler on the plea that he needed protection from his rebellious subjects, and the forced acceptance by him of a military protectorate. This had been effected by the French army in Tunis. It was to be repeated now exactly on the same lines by the English in Egypt. Egyptian patriotism, therefore, was not difficult to persuade that at last, with the dire alternative before them, it was a less ignoble fate to yield after a defeat than at once, at the first summons.

Arabi's voice was an important element in the decision arrived at on the 10th of July to reject the admiral's demands, but it had no need of his insistence and still less of being imposed by menace. All the members of the general Council convened to consider the answer declared themselves equally of opinion that it was beyond the legal power of the Khedive to yield any portion of Egyptian territory to the demand of a foreign commander without striking a blow or at least without direct orders to that effect having been received from the Sultan. Nor was the Khedive himself of any other opinion. It included many representative men besides the members of the Government—and the spectacle was witnessed of all alike pressing the view that the forts must be defended, and of the Khedive taking a specially prominent part in the patriotic talk and being supported in it by Sultan's representative, Dervish Pasha. No Moslem present, not even Sultan Pasha, who had definitely thrown in his lot with the English, dared make the public declaration that another answer than refusal was possible to Seymour's demands.

Arabi, as the result of their unanimous decision, received from the Khedive precise orders as Minister of War and Marine to prepare the forts for action and to reply with their artillery as soon as the English fleet should have opened fire, while urgent instructions the same evening, of the 10th, were sent to the Under-Secretary of War at Cairo to proclaim throughout the provinces that war had been resolved on, and to hasten the calling in of the reserves and the formation of new battalions

of recruits.　It may be said that the Khedive was insincere in
the warlike attitude he adopted at the Council.　Of course he
was insincere.　No public action of his life showed Tewfik
otherwise than a double dealer.　In all probability both he and
Sultan Pasha, who had spoken in the same sense, had agreed to
make this show of patriotism so as to cover themselves with
public opinion in case it should so happen that the forts should
prove stronger than the fleets, nor must it be forgotten that the
Sultan's envoys were present at the Council, and the avowed
policy of the English Government at the moment was still to get
the Sultan to intervene.　Tewfik, therefore, as usual was playing for the double chance, and was resolved clearly on one thing
only, to side with the strongest party.

There is a curious despatch in the Blue Books which shows
what he said to his English advisers.　As early as the 6th of
July he was made acquainted with Seymour's intention to bombard, and had apparently been urged to place himself for safety
on board one of the English ships.　But this did not suit his
personal fears or the waiting game he was resolved on, and he
sent to Colvin to acquaint him with what his plan was in regard
to his safety during the firing.　He could not do otherwise—
so we read—than remain in Egypt.　He could not desert those
who had stood by him faithfully in the crisis, or abandon Egypt
when attacked by a foreign Power, merely, as it would be said,
to secure his personal safety.　He would, therefore, retire to a
palace on the Mahmoudieh Canal with Dervish Pasha.　And
he remarked that the more rapidly the whole affair was conducted, the less would be the danger to himself personally.
And this was the program he adhered to, except that he
finally decided on retiring, not to the Mahmoudieh Palace, but
to his country palace at Ramleh, eight miles farther from Alexandria, as a still safer place from the chance firing of Seymour's
guns.

Shortly after the war I had a curious confirmation of Tewfik's indecision from no less authoritative a source than Lord
Charles Beresford, who had commanded the Condor at the bombardment and had acted as Provost-Marshal in Alexandria
after it, and who told me that in a moment of unusual frankness the Khedive had one day explained to him the reason of
his remaining ashore during the fight, as being nothing else

than his extreme perplexity as to which of the combatants would prove the better fighter. The general belief in Egypt had been that the English ships would be sunk, and he had been in a state of panic doubt all day at Ramleh, running every half hour to the roof of the palace to see how it fared with them. It was only when he discovered in the evening that they remained intact, while the forts had been silenced, that he finally made up his mind to place himself under Seymour's protection. Beresford's experience of the weeks he had then spent at Alexandria, I may explain, had given him a profound contempt of Tewfik, and a certain sympathy with Arabi and the fellahin who had carried on the war in spite of their prince's defection.

Be this, however, as it may, the conduct of the Khedive at the Council and the fact that he had given his name to the orders issued for a war *à outrance* imposed a perfectly legal aspect on the subsequent National defence, and invalidated, according to all Mohammedan rule and practice, the Khedive's counter orders when he had passed over to the enemy's side. This must be remembered if we are rightly to understand the Nationalists' legal case, and the view taken of the position by plain patriotic minds when their prince's perfidy gradually became known. The Mohammedan view about war is a simple one. When blows have been struck and war publicly announced by the Chief of the State, it is his duty and the duty of all his people to continue it until some definite victory has been achieved or reverse sustained. A prince made captive during the war by the enemy is by the fact incapacitated from giving any further valid orders, and *à fortiori* a prince who has turned traitor; and it was in this light that Tewfik was considered by his subjects until brought back by the force of English arms as their restored, but unloved lord to Cairo. Nothing of this aspect of the case will, of course, be found in any English narrative, but, in place of it, absurd laudations of a prince to be admired as "loyal" for the sole illogical reason that he showed himself loyal to England and served her through the war as her unashamed accomplice. But I will return to these matters later.

A second point which it is necessary should be insisted on is the proper apportionment of responsibility for the maintenance of law and order throughout Egypt, and for the strategical conduct of the war, between Arabi and the other Nationalist leaders who worked with him during those eventful two months. The facts as I have been able to ascertain them are these. With regard to the government of the country, as soon as it was clearly demonstrated at Cairo that the Khedive could be no longer looked upon as Chief of the State, exercising freely his right of issuing orders, a General Council was assembled to consider the position of affairs and decide what should be done. In this the lead was taken by the religious and other civilian dignitaries, rather than by the military element. Arabi was not himself present at the general meeting, being absent with the army at Kafr Dawar, nor did he once during the war pay any visit to Cairo or intervene personally in the management of affairs there. The Council, however, was very fully attended, there being present, besides the great religious sheykhs, the Turkish Grand Cadi, the Grand Mufti, the Sheykh el Islam, and the heads of the four orthodox sects. All the most representative Moslems of the country were there, including four princes of the Viceregal House who had openly espoused the National cause, many of the provincial Governors who had been expressly summoned to Cairo for the occasion, and the chief country Notables, and also, representating the non-Mussulman population, the Patriarch of the Copts and the Chief Rabbi. The Council was, therefore, fully entitled to any claim of validity in its decisions which universality can give, for it comprised all sections of political opinion and class divergency. Many of the chief men were of Circassian origin, but endowed with sufficient patriotism as Moslems to see that, now it had come to fighting against a European invader, no honest choice was left but to defend Egypt against him irrespective of party feuds.

It was, accordingly, resolved by the Council, without a dissentient voice, that the Khedive was no longer in a position legally to command, and that his decrees, while he remained in English hands, were from that very fact invalid. Tewfik's first announcement of his new attitude had been to dismiss Arabi from his post of Minister of War. The Council resolved that Arabi should be maintained in it, and instructed him as such to continue the defence of the country. A permanent Council, or rather it should perhaps be called "Committee of Defence," was named to assist him in his work, and this under the able presidency of Yakub Pasha Sami, the Under-Secretary for War, continued throughout the campaign to organize the details of recruitment, provisioning and the supply of military material. Similarly, with regard to the civil administration of the country it was resolved that in the absence of Ragheb and the other Ministers at Alexandria—for these had been detained more or less under compulsion by the Khedive and his English guard— the business of government should be carried on by the separate departments without any change in the ordinary routine, nor did this lead to the smallest confusion, seeing that the Ragheb Ministry had never been a working one. Indeed, the Administration gained considerable in efficiency, and it may safely be said that no Egyptian Government was ever better managed in its details than was the National one during the campaign. The Ministry of the Interior fell to the charge of the Under-Secretary, Ibrahim Bey Fawsi, and the police, in its most important section, to Ismaïl Eff. Jawdat, both very able administrators, who, in spite of the excitement of the time, succeeded in maintaining perfect order throughout the country. Two or three Circassian Mudirs, who had sought to ingratiate themselves with Tewfik by imitating Omar Lutfi and inciting to disturbance, were by them arrested and detained in prison to the end of the war, and after this no further rioting occurred. Such Europeans as remained at Cairo were carefully protected, and all who wished to leave were forwarded under police escort to Port Saïd.

Nothing could have been more untrue than Lord Dufferin's repeated assertions at the Conference at Constantinople that massacres of Christians were occurring daily in Egypt. And so, too, with the other departments. There was no interruption in the regular gathering in of the taxes, or in the regular distribution of civil expenditure. At the end of the war the Treasury showed a perfectly clean balance, without the smallest deficit, when its coffers were delivered over to the Khedive's officers after Tel-el-Kebir. No smallest sum had been extracted and the books were in their usual order. The ordinary course of justice had been regularly maintained, and there was no visible sign of the country having passed through any unusual crisis. Four months' provision for the army remained in the magazines of the War Office when Wolseley took possession of them.

As to Arabi, his position continued to be essentially a political one, and it was as Minister of War that he worked with the supreme direction of the forces and as popular leader till Wolseley's advance on Tel-el-Kebir hurried him suddenly from the scene. His great prestige with the country sheykhs and the fellahin of the Delta made it easy for him to inspire these with enthusiasm for the war, and at his pleading supplies flowed in gratuitously from all sides, and also volunteers for the army. In this respect he proved himself of great service to the national defence, and he was probably well advised in making no attempt from first to last to take any personal part in handling troops in the field. His abstention on this head has been attributed by his detractors to physical cowardice, and it is difficult to avoid the conclusion that there was some truth in this. Arabi was too pure and unadulterated a fellah to have any of the strong fighting instincts which are found in some races but are conspicuously absent in his own. His courage was of another kind than that which prompts to daring action in war, and in spite of his soldier's training he had never been present at any actual battle. He was probably conscious of his deficiency on this head as he certainly was of his complete lack of all the higher scientific knowledge which modern warfare requires. He was absolutely without military education of a modern type, or experience beyond that of the common barrack-yard routine, and he would, I imagine, have been quite unable to manœuvre a division had he been called upon to do so even on parade. The true explanation, however, of his personal inaction, I think, is that Arabi, being for the moment practically Head of the State, was not expected to lead the army in person. This does not, however, excuse him altogether in my eyes, nor has it excused him in those of his fellow countrymen who rightly blame him for not having personally crossed swords with the enemy, at least in the last days of the campaign.

With regard to the actual military operations I do not profess to have full knowledge, but nevertheless will venture a short account of them as I have been able to obtain them from Egyptian, and not English, sources. My admirable correspondent, Sabunji, had unfortunately left Egypt with the other fugitives just before the bombardment, and I remained without knowledge of what was passing in the country till the end of the war. Nor do the documents of the trial throw much light on this. What I have been able to learn has been gathered piecemeal in after years from those who took part in them, and accounts of this kind are never very accurate as to dates or figures. The only European present with the army was that excellent Swiss patriot and friend to Egyptian freedom, John Ninet, who was in a position to know much of what went on, as he spent the first month of the war with Arabi at Kafr Dawar, helping him with his foreign correspondence; and with Ninet I have had many talks. But his enthusiastic character injures him as a quiet safe historical witness, and the book he published in 1884 is so carelessly written and so controversial in its style that it is impossible for one to have full confidence in regard to the details he records. Moreover, Ninet had ceased to be at head-quarters before the real campaign began, having remained on at Kafr Dawar when these were transferred to Tel-el-Kebir. Such knowledge as I have of the war I will nevertheless briefly give.

On the day of the bombardment the Egyptian artillerymen fought well, and for a far greater number of hours than either Sir Beauchamp Seymour or any of his officers had thought possible. They were, however, at a terrible disadvantage through the antiquated character of the forts they were called upon to defend. These dated from the reign of Mohammed Ali and were faced as the fashion had then been with stone, a most dangerous material for their defenders when exposed to modern shell fire, as the stone work splinters and so increases the explosive effect of the hostile missiles. The defect had not been foreseen even by so able an engineer as was Mahmud Fehmi, and the loss among the defenders was great. The total Egyptian garrison of Alexandria is given in the Blue Books as from 8,500 to 9,500 men, and this figure corresponds fairly well with native accounts, while a thousand has been named as the number of the killed and wounded. If the figures are anything near correctness the proportion is a very large one. The honour of the garrison was in any case amply saved, and was the beginning of a reaction of opinion against the war in England which in the following weeks became more and more pronounced. Arabi's part in the defence was as on subsequent occasions not a prominent one. He remained during the day at the Ministry

of Marine which is not far from Ras-el-Tin and so within the
range of the enemy's fire, but he made no personal inspection
of the defences until the bombardment was over, and contented
himself with being at hand to receive the news of the fight and
give the necessary orders.   In the evening he went to Ramleh
to announce the result to the Khedive, where Tewfik, to hide
his satisfaction, made a fool's quarrel with him because he had
not brought with him a detailed report of the day's fight *in
writing.*

It is difficult to understand that Arabi should not have seen
which way the Khedive's mind was already set.   In all probability he did so, and the danger there was of treachery, for in
the morning he sent a strong guard nominally for the Khedive's
protection, but really to keep him under surveillance, with a
message informing him that as Seymour threatened a renewal
of the bombardment he should have to withdraw the garrison,
and inviting him to retire with them beyond range of the English guns and so to Cairo.   Arabi without doubt ought to have
gone himself a second time to see that the invitation was not
on any pretext evaded and have carried Tewfik, if necessary,
by force as a prisoner away with him, for the example of the
Bey of Tunis was before him, and he had sufficient experience
of the Khedive's craft to make it impossible to trust anything
to his honour.   Arabi's negligence in this matter was a fatal
error.   Arabi was, however, apparently too occupied that morning in arranging the military evacuation to give the time necessary for another visit to Ramleh, and in the course of the
afternoon, by dint, according to Tewfik's account to his English
friends, of *bakshish* and a liberal distribution of orders, he
managed to slip away from his guards to Alexandria in the
train sent to convey him to Cairo, and there placed himself,
without any more disguise, under Seymour's protection.   He
carried away with him, too, as all were in the same train, both
Dervish and his Ministers, and so secured them as in some
measure partners of his treachery.   Once at Ras-el-Tin with
a guard of seventy English bluejackets the whole party were
practically prisoners.   Dervish, five days later, having a swift
steam yacht of his own, and having received peremptory orders
from Constantinople, put an end to the disgrace for himself of
the situation, and managed to evade the English fleet which tried

to stop him. But Ragheb and his fellow Ministers, hopelessly compromised, ended by accepting the situation and remained on at Ras-el-Tin as Tewfik's servants till such time as having served their purpose as a simulacre of legal government, they had to make room for a stronger and more decidedly English administration. Arabi, in the meanwhile, ignorant how he had been befooled, was wholly engrossed in the business of withdrawing the troops from their position of danger, and taking up a new and better line of defence at Kafr Dawar.

The choice of this very strong post upon the Cairo railway, lying as it does flanked by the shallow lake of Mariut and a series of marshes, was due, I believe, to Mahmud Fehmi's engineering skill, and Arabi could not have done better than he did by adopting it as the site of his new camp. It lay well beyond the reach of Seymour's guns, and could not be approached by a hostile army, except along the narrow causeway of the railway line, and so was practically impregnable from the side of Alexandria, while on the land side all the Delta lay open to the troops, with its inexhaustible supplies and free communication with Cairo. Here the Egyptian army was able to hold its own against the English successfully for nearly five weeks, repulsing all attacks, and even harassing the enemy with counter attacks almost to the gates of Alexandria. Had there been no other gate of entry into Egypt than Kafr Dawar the National game would have been won.

With regard to the burning of Alexandria I have never been able to make up my mind exactly what part, if any, the Egyptian army took in it. Arabi has always persistently denied having ordered it, and an act of such great energy stands so completely at variance with the rest of his all too supine conduct of the war that I think it may be fairly dismissed as improbable. At the same time it is equally clear that he could not but regard it as a fortunate circumstance, for without it it is very doubtful whether he could have made good his retreat to Kafr Dawar. His army was a beaten army, and though not exactly demoralized might easily have become so, had even a very small force been landed from the fleet to hold the railway line and bar their retreat. It certainly was in the English plan to entrap the army if possible, and only the unexpected valour of the defence, and perhaps the *ruse* of the white flag seems to have prevented some attempt at a landing with this purpose from being made by Seymour. As it was, the burning of Alexandria made it possible for Arabi to establish himself quietly at Kafr Dawar and gain those few days' breathing time needed by his army to recover completely its *morale*.

Ninet, who was present at the whole affair, attributes the conflagration primarily to Seymour's shells, and this is probably a correct account, for without it it would be difficult to account for the panic which on the 12th of July, made the whole population of Alexandria abandon their homes and fly from the city. Had the artillery attack been restricted, as was pretended, to the forts this hardly would have been the case, and it is quite certain that it was not so restricted. Whether by intention or by mistake the city received its share of the shell fire, and Ninet speaks as an eyewitness in regard to its destructive effect. At the same time it is equally certain that the conflagration was increased, and especially in the European quarter, with purpose and intention, and that this was the work to some extent of the rearguard of the army, which left Alexandria in a state of disorder and shared in the plunder, already begun by the Bedouins of the city. Nor is it less certain that Suliman Pasha Sami, who commanded the rearguard, was called to account in no way by Arabi for what his men had done. I do not consider the question of any great importance as affecting the moral aspect of the case, it being clearly a military measure which any commander would be justified in adopting, thus to cover his retreat and make useless, as far as in him lay, the enemy's base of operations on shore. Historically, however, it is of importance, and I therefore say that on a balance of evidence I am of opinion that the retreating army had its share in it, not in consequence of any order, but as an act of disorder. As there was a strong wind blowing at the time, the conflagration soon spread, and by midnight the whole city was in a blaze. The fact, however, in no way lessens the prime responsibility of our Government for the destruction, every detail of which, but for the gross miscalculation of our agents, might have been easily foreseen and ought certainly to have been provided for.

Once established at Kafr Dawar, which was occupied on the 13th, the Egpytian army was in clover and could wait events. Arabi established his headquarters at Genjis Osman, one station farther on in the direction of Cairo, and Mahmud Fehmi laid out the lines of defence, and all worked heartily and confidence was restored. The mass of the Alexandrian fugitives were gradually despatched by train to the interior, where for awhile they gave great trouble, being in a state of fanatical anger and despair, and ready to revenge their troubles on any European or native Christian who might cross their path. At Tantah especially, where the Circassian Mudir, Ibrahim Adhem, was an adherent of the Khedive, and who knew that disturbances between Mohammedans and Christians had been looked on favourably by the Court, something which was almost a massacre occurred, and but for the timely intervention of the great local magnate and friend of Arabi's, Ahmed Bey Minshawi, who put it down in spite of the Governor with a band of his fellah adherents, the disorder might have spread to other places. But the Mudir was summarily arrested and sent a prisoner to Cairo, as were two other Mudirs equally untrustworthy, and the trouble ended, nor was internal peace again disturbed during the whole of the war.

On the evening of the 14th, a first communication reached Arabi from the Khedive, the text of which is given by Ninet, but which will not be found in the Blue Books. It is a valuable document, dictated evidently by Colvin or some other of Tewfik's English advisers, as it is based in every phrase on the English official view of the situation. It begins by stating the cause of the quarrel, that the bombardment was the simple consequence of a refusal to comply with the English admiral's demand for the dismantling of the forts, and that he, the admiral, had no intention of imposing a state of war on Egypt, that he now wished to renew friendly relations with the country, and was ready to hand back the city to any Egyptian army which should be disciplined and obedient, and in default of such to Ottoman troops. In order to make the necessary arrangements for their transfer, the Khedive invites his Minister of War to return at once to Ras-el-Tin, there to confer with Ragheb Pasha and the rest of his colleagues, and in the meanwhile to suspend all warlike preparations, now become useless. We know from the Blue Books that this friendly invitation to Arabi was merely a trap to lure him back into English reach, and so secure his person, for on the 15th Cartwright telegraphs to

Granville, "The Khedive has summoned him [Arabi] here. If
he comes he will be arrested, if not, declared an outlaw." The
incident shows how entirely Tewfik had already made himself
the unresisting mouthpiece of English policy, and how entirely
the English Government had adopted as its own the treacherous
methods of the Ottoman Government in dealing with "rebels."
Arabi's answer was to remind the Khedive that it was His
Highness himself and Dervish Pasha who had urged that the
admiral's demands should be rejected and that his menaces, if
followed by acts, should be answered with war; that as a matter
of fact a state of war existed, and that until the British fleet
should have left Alexandria it was impossible that the army
could return to the city. The refusal was followed a few days
later by the receipt, at Kafr Dawar, of a number of printed
proclamations bearing the Khedive's signature, in which it was
announced to the various Mudirs, Notables, and others whom
it might concern, that Arabi, having refused to obey the Khedive's order to go to Alexandria and confer with him, he was
deprived of his functions as Minister of War. It was the
publication of these three documents at Cairo, whither Arabi
forwarded them, that led to the summoning of the Great National Council already described, with the result we have seen.

The month that followed was one full of hope and enthusiasm
for the Egyptians. Relieved by his strange defection to the
enemy from all doubt as to their allegiance to the Khedive, the
citizens and country Notables were able to display their patriotism without disguise, and the whole country was aware that it
was a war now in which, as Moslems, they were concerned no
less than a war for liberty. With the mass of the fellahin so
deeply in debt, it was understood besides as a war against their
Greek creditors, and there is no doubt that this was the chief
motive power that sent volunteers to the standard, and that
unloosed the purse strings of the Notables. A very few days
proved that in establishing the army at Kafr Dawar a wise
choice had been made, for the English, under General Alison
who had landed with several thousand men, though often attacking it, were always repulsed, and it was fondly hoped that the
resistance might thus be indefinitely prolonged.

At Genjis Osman, Arabi, now the chief personage in the
state, though still holding rank only as War Minister, held daily

a kind of court, to which the provincial magnates, the Cairo Ulema, and the great merchants thronged. A huge tent, formerly belonging to the Viceroy Saïd, received them, Saïd's widow having presented it to her husband's once A. D. C. as a national offering, while Nazli Hanum and others of the princely ladies showed also their enthusiasm by gifts to the hero of the day.[1] It cannot be denied that Arabi's head was somewhat turned by these flatteries, and that they were the occasion of military jealousies which proved detrimental to the cause when soon after the pinch came. If Arabi should succeed in repelling the English attack to the point of their having to come to terms with him, it was felt that he would remain master of Egypt; and officers far better educated than himself, and with a better knowledge of the art of war, and who knew Arabi for what he was—a very poor soldier—felt aggrieved at the thought of his future fortunes and his present pre-eminence. Arabi himself was doubtless quite unaware of this, and in his dreamy way followed where fortune led him, and with an ever-growing superstitious belief in his high destiny and his providential mission as saviour of his people. His religious tastes led him to surround himself especially with holy men, and much of the time which he should have given to the secular duty of organizing the defence was wasted with them in chaunts and recitations. This seems to have been continued by him to the very end. What his ultimate military plan was it is difficult to determine. According to Ninet his calculation was that if he could prolong the resistance for a few months, Europe would be obliged to come to terms with him. The Conference was sitting at Con-

---

[1] The following is from my journal of 1887: "*January* 31, Cairo.—Called on Princess Nazli. She is at least as clever as she is pretty Her conversation would be brilliant in any society in the world. She told us a great deal that interested us about Arabi, for whom she had, and I am glad to see still has, a great *culte,* talking of his singleness of mind and lamenting his overthrow. 'He was not good enough a soldier,' she said, 'and has too good a heart. These were his faults. If he had been a violent man like my grandfather, Mehemet Ali, he would have taken Tewfik and all of us to the citadel and cut our heads off —and he would have been now happily reigning, or if he could have got the Khedive to go on honestly with him he would have made a great king of him. Arabi was the first Egyptian Minister who made the Europeans obey him. In his time at least the Mohammedans held up their heads, and the Greeks and Italians did not dare transgress the law. I have told Tewfik this more than once. Now there is nobody to keep order. The Egyptians alone are kept under by the police, and the Europeans do as they like.'"

stantinople, and the Sultan was being urged on all sides to intervene, and the worst that could happen was that Ottoman troops
would be landed, who were as likely as not to fraternize with
his own. He knew himself to be regarded throughout the
Mohammedan world as the champion of Islam, for the pilgrims
just returning from Mecca had brought the news, and it would
be difficult for the Sultan to take real part with England against
him. He had, too, a remnant of his trust in Gladstone, and of
the traditional belief in Englishmen's sympathy with liberty,
which he believed might still prevail if only the truth could be
brought home to them by the spectacle of Egyptian patriotism
—dreams, of course, and most delusive ones, but shared in by
many others, and not altogether inexcusable, considering the
events of the past six months.

Nevertheless, on the 16th August, Wolseley, with the first
instalments of the British land expedition, disembarked at Alexandria, and, as it was not to be supposed that he would confine
himself to the thankless task of bombarding the impregnable
lines of Kafr Dawar, it became urgent with the military committee sitting at Cairo to decide on providing new lines of
defence on the far more easily assailable side of the Suez Canal.
An Eastern army under Ali Fehmi was consequently got together at Cairo, which occupied the Canal in force; and the
lines of Tel-el-Kebir, which, in spite of the warning I had sent
through Sheykh Mohammed Abdu in April, had never been
more than traced, began to be dug in earnest. It became also
a question of imminent importance to block the Suez Canal
towards its northern extremity, lest British ships should be
beforehand with the defence and should land at Ismaïlia. The
opinion was unanimous among the military chiefs that this was
a strategic necessity, and that at any cost of quarrel with the
French Canal authorites it should be done. Arabi, however—
and this was his second great mistake—could not make up his
mind to the act. His hesitation was due to French influence.
M. de Lesseps had arrived at Alexandria towards the end of
July and, having learned something of the English design of
using the Canal for an attack on Egypt, became alarmed for
its safety, and he had gone on to Port Saïd and set himself to
work to prevent, as far as in him lay, this design by appealing
to Arabi's sense of honour. De Lesseps was a man of great

self-confidence, and believed himself able, by the mere fact of
his presence, to intimidate our Government, and represented
that the Canal was neutral ground and excluded from the operations of belligerents. After the war, when I was carrying on
the defence of Arabi, I wrote to M. de Lesseps to obtain from
him what evidence he might be able to give in the prisoner's
favour as a humanitarian and friend of progress, and he placed
in my possession copies of the letters he had received from
Arabi in relation to this matter, though not of those he had
himself written.[1] From this it is clear how Arabi was misled.

After some preliminary correspondence, we find Arabi on the
4th of August giving his decision plainly. Several English men-
of-war, under the command of Admiral Hewett, were in the
Canal between Ismaïlia and Suez, and Lesseps had written to
complain that they were giving orders and issuing proclamations
to the inhabitants on shore. Their right to do this Arabi
repudiates, saying, that it is by direction of the Council that he
sends him the answer, and adds, apparently in reply to some
further appeal made to him personally by Lesseps, to respect
the Canal's neutrality: "As I scrupulously respect the neutrality
of the Canal, especially in consideration of its being so remarkable a work, and one in connection with which your Excellency's
name will live in history, I have the honour to inform you that
the Egyptian Government will not violate that neutrality, except at the last extremity, and only in the case of the English
having committed some act of hostility at Ismaïlia, Port Saïd,
or some other point of the Canal." Here the principle is
clearly and well laid down, but the weak point of it is to be
perceived in its leaving to the enemy to commit the first act of
hostility instead of forestalling and preventing him.

Nevertheless we have Ninet's assurance, which has been confirmed to me from other quarters, that every preparation was
made secretly·for the blocking of the Canal at a certain point
between Ismaïlia and Port Saïd, and that it was only due to
Arabi's extreme personal unwillingness to sign the final order
that, in opposition to the opinion of all his colleagues in the
Council, the hour of grace was allowed to slip by. Lesseps, on
the arrival of the British fleet at port Saïd conveying Wolseley
and the army, had sent Arabi a last bombastical telegram, which

[1] See Appendix.

Ninet quotes as follows: "Ne faites aucune tentative pour intercepter mon Canal. Je suis là. Ne craignez rien de ce côté. Il ne se débarquera pas un seul soldat anglais sans être accompagné d'un soldat français. Je reponds de tout." This occasioned a final council of war at Kafr Dawar on the 20th at which all but Arabi were resolved to disregard Lesseps' message. Arabi, however, suffered himself to be deceived still by the boast about the French troops, and argued against it, and though orders were given that evening for the "temporary" destruction of the Canal, the delay caused by the discussion had already been fatal, and Wolseley had steamed through the Canal before they had been executed. Arabi's weakness in this matter is a most serious blot on his strategic fame, and stamps him also with political inefficiency. Wolseley alluding, long after, to it in a speech made by him in connection with the proposed Channel Tunnel between England and France, said. "If Arabi had blocked the Canal, as he intended to do, we should be still at the present moment on the high seas blockading Egypt. Twenty-four hours delay saved us."

The date of Wolseley's occupation of Ismaïlia was the 21st of August, and from this point the defence of Egypt entered into a new and practically hopeless phase, though the campaign was not so wholly a walk over for the English as has been pretended. The British army was over 30,000 strong, and though probably of no great fighting value had it been opposed to European troops, was sufficient to deal with the scanty forces at Arabi's command. The whole strength at Kafr Dawar had never been more than 8,000 regulars, with 80 Krupp guns, nor in all Egypt could it be counted at more than 13,000 disciplined men, while the new levies got together within a month were unfit as yet for any service except that of manual labour at the trenches. Wolseley, therefore, had a comparatively easy job before him when once he found himself ashore with no obstacle between him and Cairo, except the unfinished lines of Tel-el-Kebir. The English intelligence department had, however, to make assurance doubly sure, already taken secret measures for success of a kind which is always employed in modern warfare but never avowed, and which it is right that I should here put on record, having by a curious accident the details of the most important of them in my possession. That Wolseley's advance was helped by bribery has always been indignantly denied by English writers, but it is time the truth should be authoritatively told.

The attack on Egypt from the side of the Suez Canal had been resolved on by our War Office and Admiralty early in the year, and it was determined about the middle of June to prepare the way betimes by a large operation of bribery, especially among the Eastern Bedouins. The credit of the particular *modus operandi* belongs personally to Lord Northbrook, who, as I heard at the time of its first supposed success from Gregory, took a special pride in it, and the more so because it was based upon a hint I had originally thrown out, with no thought when I did so that it might be ever seriously acted upon or used against any who were to be my friends. It will be remembered that in the spring of 1881 I had travelled through the desert east of the Canal, and had interested myself in certain unfortunate Sheykhs of the Teyyaha and Terrabin tribes held in captivity at Jerusalem, and that in order to persuade our Embassy at Constantinople to solicit their release I had represented that it might one day be found of importance to have these Bedouins friendly to England. Lord Northbrook had heard of this, and, now that I was in such disfavour with the Government, thought it would be amusing to "hoist me with my own petard," and by using my name in addition to more solid inducements to get the help of these Arabs against Arabi.

At that time hardly any Englishman could speak a word of Arabic, and it was difficult to discover an emissary capable and willing to undertake the job. Northbrook consequently called into his counsels the then professor of Oriental languages at Cambridge, Edward Palmer, a distinguished Arabic scholar, who also had some personal acquaintance with the district intended to be operated in, as he had been connected at one time with the Palestine Exploration Society. Palmer was then living in London, an impecunious man, making a poor living by journalism, and weighted in his struggle for life by a recent marriage. When, therefore, on the 24th of June he received an invitation, through Captain Gill, R. E., of the Intelligence Department, to breakfast the next morning with Lord Northbrook at the Admiralty, and was met there with an offer from Lord Northbrook that he should undertake the task, represented to

him as an honourable and patriotic one, of ascertaining the
bribable character of the Bedouins east of the Canal, and securing their services for the British Army, and with it the further
offer of £500 down for preliminary expenses, and promises of
large pecuniary reward in case of success, poor Palmer did not
hesitate and agreed to start at once.   Just before his departure,
however, on the 26th, he called on me, representing himself to
be on his way to Alexandria, where he had been appointed correspondent of the "Standard" newspaper, and asking introductions
to my Nationalist friends there for whom he felt, he said, a
strong sympathy and would favour in his writings.   This, of
course, was a cover to his real business, as to which he was
silent, and inclined me to granting his request, and, though I did
not trust his countenance, which was far from sincere, I gave
him introductions to Sabunji and one or two others, though not,
I think, to Arabi.

Palmer's true programme traced out for him at the Admiralty
was to go first to Alexandria, where he was to discuss his plans
with Admiral Seymour, and then without delay to proceed to
Jaffa where he should assume an Eastern disguise and visit
the desert south and west of Gaza, and put himself into communication with precisely those Teyyaha and Terrabin tribes
whose interests I had espoused eighteen months before.   His
journals, portions of which have been published, are on this
point very instructive.   In them the details of his arrangement
with Lord Northbrook are constantly alluded to.   He describes
going on board Admiral Seymour's yacht at Alexandria, where
he was told to proceed at once to the desert and begin work,
the Admiral giving him "a revolver, a rifle, and plenty of cart-
ridges," and where he finds it "expected there will be war at
once, and perhaps it may begin tomorrow."   "I am glad," he
says, "there is really to be fighting, because, though I shall be
a long way off, I shall be able to get a great deal of good out of
it and do something towards winning it for our side. . . . The
Admiral said to me he "congratulated the country on finding so
able a man to undertake such a difficult task."   Palmer also
sees "Sir Sidney Auckland [*sic*] the political agent"; and we
learn later in the journal that the Admiral told him Alexandria
was to be bombarded soon.   Then he goes, much elated, in the
Admiral's steam launch, on board the steamer for Jaffa, with

the British flag flying, and "two sailors to carry the gun and revolver."

At Jaffa he lodges with the British Consul, the Jew Shapira, who sends his son down to Gaza to help his preparations for the desert journey and find an Arab to go with him, and he buys himself Arab dress and other things he may require. He laments the heat and the difficulty of his mission, but consoles himself with dreams of rich rewards and possible honours. On the 15th, just before leaving for the desert, he hears secretly of the bombardment, and decides to go through to Suez where he writes for a ship's boat to take him off at a safe place.

On the 16th he sees a number of the Terrabin tribe: "They were very curious to know who I was and what I wanted. My man said I was a Syrian officer on the way to Egypt. Of course I am dressed in full costume like a Mohammedan Arab of the towns. I found out more about them than they did about me. I now know where to find and get at every Sheykh in the desert, and I have already got the Teyyaha, the most warlike and strongest of them all, ready to do anything for me. When I come back I shall be able to raise 40,000 men. It was very lucky that I knew such an influential tribe. . . . I get on capitally with my mission, and am longing to get instructions from Suez and know if our troops have landed. I did not expect to find out as much as I have done this first trip. I think our fortune will be made." On the 18th "I had an exciting time, having met the great Sheykh of the Arabs hereabouts. I, however, quite got him to accept my views."

And again, 19th July, "It is wonderful how I get on with them. I have got hold of some of the very men Arabi Pasha has been trying in vain to get over to his side, and when they are wanted I can have every Bedawi at my call from Suez to Gaza. . . . Of course I know nothing of what has been done in Egypt since I left, except that Alexandria was bombarded as the Admiral told me it would be soon. But I hear from the Arabs that the Egyptian military party are still in arms, so I suppose our troops must have landed by now." On the 20th "The Sheykh, who is the brother of Suliman, is the one who engages all the Arabs not to attack the caravan of pilgrims which goes to Mecca every year from Egypt, so that he is the *very man* I wanted. He has sworn by the most solemn Arab oath that, if I want him to, he will guarantee the safety of the Canal even against Arabi Pasha, and he says that if I can get three Sheykhs out of prison, which I hope to do through Constantinople and our Ambassador, all the Arabs will rise and join me like one man."

On the 21st, I am anxious to get to Suez, because I have done all I wanted by way of preliminaries, and as soon as I can get precise instructions I can settle with the Arabs in a fortnight or three weeks and get the whole thing over. As it is, the Bedouins will keep quite quiet and will not join Arabi, but will wait for me to give them the word what they are to do. They look upon Abdallah Effendi, which is what they call me, as a very grand personage indeed!" On the 22nd, "I hear from a Bedouin, who has just come on from Egypt, that Arabi Pasha has got 2,000 horsemen from the Nile Bedouins and brought them to the Canal. But when they get to Suez they will soon go back, for my men know them, and if fair means won't do I shall send 10,000 of the Teyyaha and Terrabin fighting men to drive them back. I have got the man who supplies the pilgrims with camels on my side, too, and as I have promised my big Sheykh £500 for himself, he will do anything for me. I am very glad that the war has actually come to a crisis because now I shall really have to do my big task, and *I am certain of success.* I shall know almost directly what I am to get. Lord Northbrook told me I was to have the £500 for this first trip, and that as soon as I began negotiations with the Arabs they would enter on a fresh arrangement with me. I shall save at least £280 out of this, which is not a bad month's work! . . . I don't think they can give me less than £2,000 or £3,000 for the whole job. . . ." And again on the 26th, "I find it is possible to get to the ships near Suez, and I start to-morrow, and hope to be on board in four or five days. I have been so successful that I shall write for more money, saying I have been obliged to spend all mine on presents—a few hundred pounds is a great deal to us and nothing to the Government, who would, I know, have given thousands for what I have already done—of course I shall make the most of the difficulties and they have been really great. I will send you a hundred or so as soon as I get the chance from Suez. . . . I have had to give away a great deal,

but have still nearly £300 left after paying my journey to Suez!
That is better than newspaper work, £300 in a month!" "I
have had a great ceremony to-day, eating bread and salt with
the Sheykhs in token of protecting each other to the death!"
On the 28th, "I have got the great Sheykh of the Haiwath
Arabs with me now, and get on capitally with him. In fact I
have been most wonderfully successful throughout. I have
been sitting out in the moonlight repeating Arabic poetry to
the old man till I have quite won his heart."

At last Palmer reaches Suez, August 1. "I am safe on
board the P. and O. boat," he writes, "and have got your letter. I got here by going to a part of the coast above Suez,
and got on board at midnight. It cost me a lot of money,
nearly £10, but I escaped the Egyptian sentries. The troops
are coming on Thursday, and this is Tuesday! . . . I have just
seen the Admiral. He is delighted with the result of my work
and has telegraphed to Lord Northbrook. He had three boat
crews watching the coast for me, but I got here by myself."
August 2, "I am off again to the desert for a short trip in
about two days. I have been asked to go to the coast and cut
the telegraph wires and burn the poles on the desert line so as
to cut off Arabi's communications with Turkey! Captain Gill
arrived at Port Said yesterday and will be here this morning.
Yesterday I had a most interesting day. I called on the cap-
tains of all the men-of-war and met with a most pleasant reception. They all insisted upon my drinking iced champagne with
them, and in the evening the Admiral gave a dinner party on
board the flagship in my honour. It was a beautiful dinner
and I did not get back to my ship until one this morning."
August 4, "On Monday I was ordered to accompany the commanding officer and take Suez. We landed with three guns and
500 men. The Egyptian soldiers ran away, so we had no
fighting to do. I was in the first boat which landed. We then
made the Governor give us up the town and £50,000 which he
had, and we took possession. The day before yesterday Lord
Northbrook telegraphed to the Admiral to congratulate me on
my safe arrival, and informing me that I was appointed 'Interpreter in Chief to Her Majesty's Forces in Egypt,' and placed
on the Admiral's Staff. I am here [Suez] in great state at
the hotel at Government expense, and have all my meals with

the Admiral.   I am going up to Ismaïlia the day after to-morrow on a gunboat, and the Admiral here said, 'Don't let the
other Admiral keep you—you are on the books of the "Eurya-
lus," his flagship.'   I have got a staff of about forty men working under me.   The Admiral told me the other night that I
was sure of the Egyptian medal and the 'Star of India.'   They
won't let me go to the desert, for the present at least, as they
want me here. . . . I am one of the Chief Officers of the Expedition and an awful swell.   The 72nd regiment are coming
to-morrow and I have got to see about camels for them. . . .
The pay is to be what I suggest, but I haven't settled it yet."
And then suddenly the splendid climax, "Captain Gill has just
come, and placed twenty thousand pounds at my disposal for
the Arabs."

The rest is a mere dream of gold and glory.   August 6,
"Suez . . . I start to-morrow for a few days in the desert to
buy camels.   Captain Gill and the Admiral's Flag Lieutenant
go with me, and we shall be all safe and jolly.   My position
seems like a dream.   The Admiral said as I preferred leaving
the Government to settle my pay, that in the meantime I might
draw *to any amount* for private expenses—so I will send you
another £500 as soon as I come back.   I could do it now, but
do not want to look hard up.   I have got £260 left, after paying all expenses of my journey, etc., in hard money in my despatch box, and to-day *twenty thousand pounds in gold were
brought by ship and paid into my account here!*   I have *carte
blanche* to do everything.   I give passes to the sentries.   If I
see a dozen horses I buy them off-hand.   Yesterday I found
thirty camels and gave a man £360 for them by just writing
on a slip of paper.   To-night I have been interpreting while
the Governor dined with the Admiral.   I have servants, clerks,
and interpreters at my beck and call, and in short I could
not be in a higher position.   We are very securely entrenched
here and the enemy is eighty miles off, and to-morrow the Indian troops are coming.   Of course it is war time, but as I
am on the staff of the Commander-in-Chief, I am not likely to
get into risky places.   I have seen active service though, having
been one of the first to land when Suez was taken.   The Admiral is such a nice man, and I am told he never forgets his

officers, but pushes them on to promotion. He *told me* I should get the 'Star of India'! good-bye."

This is the last pathetic entry in a very human document. The next day Palmer started with Gill and Charrington for Nakhl in the eastern desert, Gill's mission and Charrington's being to destroy the telegraph wire between Egypt and Syria, for which purpose they took with them a box of dynamite, while Palmer's mission was announced as that of "buying camels." The two officers, like Palmer, were dressed in Arab costume, but they had with them uniforms to add dignity to their proceedings when they should reach the friendly tribes. The amount of money taken with them out of Palmer's £20,000 has been variously stated at £3,000 to £8,000. Gill has recorded his dissatisfaction at the nature of the mission on which he was called to serve. It cannot have been the purchase of camels, an official euphemism which now that Palmer had become a high officer of Her Majesty he seems to have adopted, but beyond a doubt to carry out his original avowed purpose and fulfil his promises to his Bedouin friends, by paying them the large sums agreed on. He would have taken all the £20,000 for his 40,000 fighters but that the Admiral expostulated.

The party, however, was foredoomed to disaster. The Bedouin escort, men of the Haiwat and Howeytat, got scent of the gold they were carrying, and were determined to be beforehand with the Teyyaha, for whom it was intended—the Egyptian governor of Nakhl, an isolated fort halfway between Suez and Akabah, there is good reason to believe, being their accomplice and instigator. They had hardly therefore, got more than a few miles on their way before they were attacked, made prisoners, despoiled, stripped and bound, and finally shot at the edge of a ravine in the Wady Sudr. And so poor Palmer's dreams of fortune ended. The catastrophe was too conspicuous a one to save the Government from questions asked in Parliament, and that worthy gentleman, Sir Henry Campbell-Bannerman, as Under-Secretary, was put up in the House of Commons to give answer and to deny roundly the whole affair of Palmer's secret mission, or of any dealings on his part with the Bedouins, except as buyer of camels.

Nor does Professor Palmer's journal stand alone as docu-

mentary evidence. Captain Gill also left a diary amply confirming the main facts. His business under the Intelligence Department was of the same nature west of the Suez Canal as
Palmer's had been east of it. The diary begins at Alexandria
and the writer speaks of having gone to see Sir Frederick Goldsmid, the head of his department, and he expresses his hope
to be soon at work among the Bedouins west of the Canal. He
describes having received, in the Khedive's own handwriting, a
list of the principal Sheykhs between the Canal and the cultivation, of whom he mentions two by name, Saoud el Tihawi at
Salahieh, and Mohammed el Baghli at Wady Tumeylat. He
understood the Bedouins to be waiting to side with whomever
they found it their best interest to follow. At Port Saïd Gill
hears from the ex-Governor that these Bedouins can be bought
at from £2 to £3 per man. On 4th August he mentions reading Palmer's report to Sir B. Seymour. He says, "Had I
known the report would go direct to the Admiral, I would
have asked Hoskyns whether he had the money for Palmer."
He adds, "Palmer says he can buy fifty thousand Bedouins for
£25,000, and I shall certainly urge that the money be given
him." He mentions a report of his own as to blocking the Canal, which he says could only be effectively done by the Egyptians at one point, which he names, and gives as his reason the
want of stones elsewhere to sink the barges with. He talks of
Lesseps as having it in his power to do real mischief, as he has
all the dredges and boats belong to the Canal at his disposal.
August 5th: Gill goes down the Canal with another officer to
Suez, taking with them £20,000 in gold for Palmer. They stop
at Ismaïlia, and he sees there Mr. Pickard, with whom he dis-
cusses the best route to choose for cutting the telegraph. He
says there are three ways: (1) from the coast near el Arish,
which both agree would be dangerous, (2) from Gisr or Kan-
tara, objectionable as violating the neutrality of the Canal, and
(3) from Suez, the only practicable route. He does not seem
to trust Pickard, and decides to cut the wire himself from Suez.
August 6th: He mentions the fact that he is glad to get rid
of the £20,000 on its being made over to Palmer. He talks
of going with Palmer to a great meeting of Shekyhs he is to
attend at Nakhul, and remarks that if he goes so far with him
he shall be able to judge how far "Palmer's rather rose-col-

oured expectations" are justified.   These two documents between them amply prove the reality of the bribery resorted to before Tel-el-Kebir.

I was much connected with this affair at the time it occurred, as I was applied to by members of the families of all the three victims of it, to aid in their researches, and to make the matter public and in one instance to obtain from the Government a proper recognition of services rendered and as yet unacknowledged.   The case, after being denied in the House of Commons, was at my instance brought on by my brother-in-law, Lord Wentworth, in the House of Lords, and was the occasion of much anger among the Ministerial peers, and an astonishing display of untruth.   Lord Granville, Lord Northbrook, and their colleagues, got up one after the other and roundly denied the whole story of Palmer's mission, and of his having received any money for the purpose of bribery among the Arabs. It is a curious fact that Lord Salisbury, to whom I went just before the debate to try to enlist his aid in opposition to the Government, excused them in some measure to me on the ground that in cases where secret service money was concerned, it was conventionally permitted to Ministers to lie.   He nevertheless aided Lord Wentworth to the extent of securing him a fair hearing, which the others would have prevented.

Palmer's and Gill's were nevertheless but crude dealings, and would by themselves, I think, have done little to further Wolseley's objects but for the far more efficacious intervention in support of them given by the Khedive.   Saoud el Tihawi was the only Arab Sheykh who systematically or at all efficiently betrayed Arabi, and it was the Khedive who procured his defection.   Saoud received in payment for his work as spy in Arabi's camp 5,000 Austrian crowns, and betrayed him throughout, from the date of the removal of the Egyptian headquarters from Kafr Dawar to Tel-el-Kebir.   Saoud was an Arab of a naturally superior type, and with a good head on his shoulders, but he had long been perverted by his association with Lesseps and the French, having his land and permanent camp within a day's journey only of the Suez Canal, and had been accustomed to hunt the gazelle with them, and play the part of fine gentleman, which is the ruin of Bedouin morality.   That he did indeed play the part of spy and traitor in the English interest I have his own half admission, for passing by Salahieh in the spring of 1887, I stopped a night at his tents, and he seeing me to be English, and knowing nothing of my political sympathies, spoke of his doings during the war in terms there was no mistaking. Acting as scout for Arabi, it was easy for his men to pass from camp to camp, and so convey intelligence. There was nothing specially to be ashamed of in this treachery, according to Bedouin morals, for to the Arab tribes Egyptians and Turks and Franks are equally outside the sphere of their allegiance, and in serving them it is merely a question of what suits their interest best. On the east of the Nile the Bedouins have exceedingly little religious feeling to prevent their siding with the infidel, if their advantage lies that way, and no love was ever yet lost between Bedouin and Fellah.

What did Arabi infinitely more harm than this and facilitated the rapidity of Wolseley's advance, was the tampering with his officers through the instrumentality of certain emissaries despatched in disguise to Cairo and Tel-el-Kebir, who, armed with money and promises of promotion and advancement when the "rebellion" should have been put down, succeeded in detaching not a few from their loyalty. This was not done directly by Wolseley or the English intelligence Department, though, perhaps the funds were furnished by them, but by the Khedive, who was far better aware whom to approach with success than any Englishman could be. His most intelligent and active agent in this work was his A. D. C., Osman Bey Rifaat, who knew well the temper of most of the officers, and the jealousies which inspired them. To these, especially to those of Circassian origin, he represented the futility of the National resistance and the advantage there would be for them in being beforehand in reconciling themselves to the Khedive instead of awaiting the punishment which would certainly follow. Wolseley and the English were only acting as the Khedive's servants and in concert with the Sultan, who also was about to send troops, having declared Arabi a rebel. With the Circassians this line of argument naturally had weight, and with the baser class of Egyptian officers the money argument was added. Arabi, for the reasons already stated, although enthusiastically followed by the rank and file of the army, had incurred no little jealousy among the superior officers, who judged themselves to be all better soldiers than he, and his procrastination in the matter of blocking the Canal had still further increased their dissatisfaction. All confidence in his military leadership was destroyed among them from the day of the landing of the English at Ismaïlia without the promised opposition of the French, and without adequate preparations to oppose them on that side having been made.

With the civilian chiefs of the Nationalists another agent was employed, also not without effect. This was none other than the old leader of the fellah movement, Sultan Pasha, who, having thrown his lot in now wholly with the English, was not ashamed to lend himself to the work of spreading disunion among those who still retained their patriotism. To the new generation of the Egyptians it seems difficult to understand how a man of such initial high conduct as a lover of his country should have sunk to so mean a pass. But I think it is not really difficult to explain. Sultan was a proud man of great wealth and importance, and used to being given the first place everywhere—the "king," as he was called, of Upper Egypt, the first and foremost of the great fellah proprietors—and with what seemed to him a natural right to leadership in the fellah party. Arabi he had patronized as a younger man and one of no social standing, who might help him in his ambitions, but who should never have presumed to supplant him in the popular affections. He was disappointed on the formation of the Sherif Ministry in September, 1881, that he was given no place in it, and was only half consoled with the presidency assigned him of the new Parliament. Still less was he pleased when on the formation of the more purely fellah administration of February, 1882, he was again left out, and the lack of what he considered the due consideration shown him caused him to drift gradually into opposition. Then came the arrival of the fleets at Alexandria, and, as we know, he was partly cajoled, partly frightened by Malet into declaring himself in favour of the English demands, and threw in his lot finally with the Court party against his former associates. There is nothing difficult to understand, more than in the Khedive's case, in the downward grade he was obliged to follow. It became with him, I imagine, a matter of obstinacy rather than any longer of ambition, and his patriotic scruples had been allayed by the promise made him that the

English intervention was intended only to restore the condition of things previous to the Mahmud Sami Ministry, and that Egypt should still have her claim to Constitutional government respected. In this sense he addressed letters to his numerous former friends at Cairo, putting forward the explanation that the alliance between the Khedive and the English was a merely temporary necessity, as the English troops would not stay in Egypt when once the Khedive's authority had been re-established; and that Arabi had lost the confidence of the Sultan, and that the continued resistance at Cairo was generally condemned by Moslems. These letters, distributed carefully, were not without their influence, and money again played its powerful part. Sultan indeed seems to have advanced the money out of his own pocket, for the very first financial act of the restored Khedivial Government after Tel-el-Kebir was to make him a public present of £10,000 under the title of an indemnity for losses sustained by him during the war, while he also received an order of English knighthood. The sums actually given away by Sultan were not, as far as I can learn, very large, being supplemented with more considerable promises, which after the war remained unfulfilled, and very likely the £10,000 more than covered the sums Sultan actually disbursed. Be this as it may, there is no question that with the Khedive's help Wolseley's path of victory was made a very easy one.[1]

In spite, however, of all these disadvantages of internal intrigue, the National defence might still have been prolonged, if the end could not be averted, but for the bad luck which from this point throughout attended the army. As soon as

---

[1] I find the following in my diary of 1887: "*February* 13.—A visit from Abd-el-Salaam Moëlhy (one of the original Constitutionalists, and member of the Chamber of 1882). He told me that he had been an intimate friend and partisan of Sultan Pasha's, and had been one of those who joined Sultan in his quarrel with Arabi, but they were all very sorry now for not having held together; and he did not approve Sultan's conduct during the war. Sultan had been deceived by Malet, who induced him to act as he did on a distinct promise that the Egyptian Parliament should be respected in its rights. Malet gave this verbally, and Sultan asked to have it in writing, but was dissuaded from insisting by the Khedive, who assured him that the English Agent's word was as good as his bond. The old man, when he found out after the war how much he had been deceived, took it to heart and died expressing a hope that Arabi would forgive him, and that his name would not be handed down to posterity as the betrayer of his country. It was jealousy and anger at Arabi having become Minister that caused the quarrel."

it was quite clear that Egypt would be attacked from the East, Mahmud Fehmi, the engineer, the ablest of all Arabi's lieutenants, was despatched to Tel-el-Kebir, to carry out and finish the lines there, which had never been more than lightly traced. Had they been finished as they ought to have been, they should have proved a formidable obstacle to the advance of the English army, but by an extraordinary fatality, which was hardly within the range of the common hazards of war, the General, within a few days of his arrival, was captured and made prisoner by a small party of English Life Guards, who, far in advance of the English position, happened to be passing near. The accident was a strange one. Mahmud Fehmi, attended only by an A. D. C., and having put off his uniform on account of the heat, had passed one evening to the other side of the Wady Tumeylat, and partly to get a breath of air, partly, too, for a better view of the desert in the direction of Ismaïlia, had climbed alone, on foot, a low sandhill, of which there are several, running into the cultivated land, when suddenly the small English party pounced on him. As Mahmud was not in uniform, Colonel Talbot, in command of the party, was doubtful how to treat him, and was near accepting his explanation that he was an Effendi with property in the neighbourhood, but finally decided to carry him off with them, which they accordingly did, the A. D. C., having remained in a village hard by not knowing what had happened, nor had Talbot any notion of the value of his capture until some time after the return of the party to the English headquarters. As a matter of fact, however, it was one of the greatest possible importance, and a blow to the defence of Tel-el-Kebir for which there was no remedy. [1]

The second misfortune was the disabling at Kassassin of the two generals, first and second in command, at a critical moment of that not altogether unequal combat. These were Ali Fehmi, Arabi's tried companion, and Rashid Pasha, two officers who were both good soldiers, with courage and some experience of war, and who took the initiative against Wolseley first by a reconnaissance, and then by a renewed attack on him in force at Kassassin. It was the best and last chance the

[1] I give this version of the capture as being that of Mahmud Fehmi himself, but some have recounted it otherwise, accusing him of desertion. This is, however, not credited by those who knew him personally.

Egyptians had of checking the English advance, and it was not very far from being successful. According to the Egyptian account of the affair, the enemy was taken by surprise, and for a long time the issue remained doubtful, the Duke of Connaught being at one moment near being made prisoner. Had this happened and had the Egyptians maintained their advantage, there is no knowing what terms might not have been granted them of recognition and peace, for already public opinion had veered round in England, and people were becoming ashamed of a war waged against peasants fighting for their freedom from an ancient tyranny. Two things, however, failed them in their plans, first Mahmud Sami was to have advanced from Salahieh with a couple of thousand men to join them in the morning and take the enemy on his right flank, but misled by Saoud's Bedouins in the night he missed the point of rendezvous; and secondly, it is certain that Arabi, if he had had any soldierly instincts, ought to have taken the field in person with them, if not in the front line of attack, at least as commanding a strong reserve. As it was, the whole force employable did not appear on the battlefield, and by a still further stroke of ill fortune both the commanders were wounded, and put for the rest of the campaign *hors de combat*. It is also certain that one of the Egyptian generals, Ali Bey Yusuf, purposely betrayed his comrades.

From this point all was confusion at Tel-el-Kebir, and the pitiful end became certain. Arabi had lost his best generals and knew not where to replace them. There were not many he could trust, and those men only of quite inferior ability. One man indeed there was who might still have given consistency to the defence, but for some inexplicable reason he was left away from the field of action. This was the third of the original "three colonels," Abd-el-Aal Helmi, a valiant fighting man as any in the army. For some time past he had been employed in what was at one moment the important duty of defending Damietta from a possible British landing, and he had with him some of the very best troops, notably the Soudanese regiment which had been Abd-el-Aal's own. Had these, with their commander, been brought at once to Tel-el-Kebir, they might have saved at least the honour of the army, for Abd-el-Aal was one who could be relied upon for forward action, and his troops were full of spirit and undiscouraged by defeat. It seems, however, still to have been thought that Damietta needed its garrison, for I cannot find that the Military Committee so much as suggested Abd-el-Aal as Ali Fehmi's successor. I have sometimes thought that Yakub Pasha Sami, the President of the Military Committee at Cairo, good service as he had done in organizing the war, had at this time been tampered with by the Khedive's agents. He was a Mussulman, of Greek origin, and so one of the ruling class, and there are documents in my possession which show him, though Arabi's right-hand man at the War Office, as always a Khedive's man rather than a Nationalist. The Khedive seems to have counted him as such, and as in other instances after the war, treated him for that reason with exceptional rigour, and he was one of the seven Pashas exiled to Ceylon, though the attitude he adopted before the Judges had been one of servile repentance and protestations of loyalty. Of his deep jealousy of Arabi the papers give ample evidence, and it is quite possible that after the disabling of Ali Fehmi, he did his best to isolate Arabi and hasten his ruin at Tel-el-Kebir. Instead of Abd-el-Aal the command was given to a very worthy but quite incompetent man, Ali Pasha Roubi, one of Arabi's old companions of the early days of the National movement, but who had no other qualification for so responsible a post.

Arabi himself meanwhile, in spite of the imminence of the English attack, remained stolidly on in camp surrounded, as always, by the country Notables, who still flocked to see him, and by religious men, with whom he passed the time in prayers and recitations. He relied implicitly on Saoud el Tihawi to give him news of any further advance by Wolseley, and Saoud always lured him into security. The army at Tel-el-Kebir was the most incoherent one imaginable. Of regular, well-disciplined troops, infantry of the line, there cannot have been more than 6,000 to 7,000, with, perhaps, 2,000 cavalry and a corresponding number of guns served by good artillerymen. This was all the really reliable force. The rest were a half-clothed and wholly undisciplined rabble of recruits and volunteers, good, honest fellahin, hardworking as labourers in the trenches, but of no fighting value whatever. Their total number may have been 20,000, but I have no accurate statistics to go by. Day and night they worked valiantly to complete the unfinished lines, but this was all the military service they possibly could render.

Stone Pasha, the American, after the war stated it freely at his opinion that not one of the whole number had even as yet fired a ball cartridge, and this was probably true.

The end came suddenly at dawn on the morning of the 13th of September. There has been much romance written by English military writers of the silent and hazardous night march from Mehsameh under guidance of the stars and of a young naval officer, and doubtless to those who took part in it it seemed that the English army was groping its way blindly to the un-known, but in reality the road had been made plain for them by the secret means I have alluded to. Two of Arabi's minor officers, both holding responsible positions, had accepted, a few days before, the bribes offered them by the Khedivial agents. The names of these two deserve, to their eternal shame, to be put on record. The first was Abd-el-Rahman Bey Hassan, com-mander of the advanced guard of cavalry, who was placed with his regiment outside the lines in a position commanding the desert road from the east, but who on the night in question shifted his men some considerable distance to the left, so as to leave the English advance unobstructed. The second was the already mentioned Ali Bey Yusuf, in command of a portion of the central lines where the trenches were so little formidable that they could be surmounted by any active artillery. By the account generally given, and Arabi's own, he not only left the point that night unguarded, but put out a lantern for the guid-ance of the assailants. Other names have been mentioned to me, but not with the authority of these two, and I therefore pre-fer not to put them down. As to the two I have given, their position as traitors was notorious for years at Cairo, as little secret was made of it by them, especially by Ali Bey Yusuf, who complained freely of the scurvy treatment he had received for his services. £1,000 indeed had been paid him down in gold before the battle, but a further promise of £10,000 had never been kept to him, nor did he succeed in obtaining more from the Government, when he had spent his first round sum, than a poor pension of £12 a month, which was paid him to his death.

Arabi and the rest of the army, deluded by Saoud into a false security as to that night at least, slept profoundly, the poor men in their trenches and Arabi at his headquarters, about a mile to the rear. Thus, without any warning, they suddenly found the enemy upon them, the lines crossed at their weak point by the English, and a little later artillery in their rear. The vast number of the recruits fled without firing a shot, half-naked as they were sleeping, worn out with their constant labour of entrenchment, and having thrown their arms away across the open plain, and were cut down in hundreds as they ran. It was a mere butchery of peasants, too ignorant of the ways of war even to know the common formulas of surrender. This was in the centre and to the right of the position. To the left a more gallant stand was made, especially where Mohammed Obeyd was in command, and here and there all along the lines by the Egyptian artillery. The whole thing lasted hardly more than forty minutes. Mohammed Obeyd fell gallantly fighting, and with him the flower of the regular army, and many gunners too who had stuck obstinately to their guns. But at the end of an hour the fighting was wholly over, and what remained of the National army was a mere broken rabble.

As to the part played personally by Arabi that fatal morning, I have the evidence, besides his own, of a very worthy man, Mohammed Sid Ahmed, his body-servant, who in 1888 entered my service as manager at Sheykh Obeyd and remained two years with me. From him I have over and over again heard the events narrated. According to Sid Ahmed, the whole camp that night was in profound slumber, having been assured by the scouts that the English were making no movement, his master's headquarters at about the centre of the whole camp, but more than a mile in rear of the front line of trenches, as undisturbed as the rest. The Pasha had undressed and gone to bed as usual and slept soundly through the night, nor was any one awake before the sound of the guns announced the attack. Arabi then threw hastily on his uniform and got on horseback and rode towards the firing, followed, among others, by his servant, also mounted. They had not, however, got far when they were met by a crowd of fugitives, who declared that all was lost, while Saoud's Bedouins also were galloping wildly about, adding to the general confusion. The Pasha, Sid Ahmed assured me, did his best to rally the men, and continued to advance towards that part of the lines where Mohammed Obeyd was still holding out, but was gradually borne away with the rest, and yielded to his (Sid Ahmed's) prayers that he would seek his safety in flight. The idea that his master had any duty of dying on the field of battle was always wholly absent from Sid Ahmed's mind, and he prided himself on having succeeded in persuading him. They were both well mounted on horses, which had been sent to Arabi by one of the Bedouins of the Western Fayoum, and reached the Tel-el-Kebir station just before it was occupied by the English, and though unable there to take train, got across the small canal bridge before it closed, and so by the causeway to the other side of Wady Tumeylat, whence they galloped their best for Belbeis. They were alone, Arabi having been separated from his staff in the confusion. Arabi's one idea now was to get to Cairo before the news of the disaster should arrive and prepare the city for defence. At Belbeis they took train and reached the capital not long after noon. [1]

Arabi, on his arrival in Cairo, seems to have had hopes still of continuing the patriotic struggle by defending the city. He went straight to the Kasr el Nil and assisted at a council being held there by the members of the War Committee, but a compromise of opinion was all that he could obtain, namely, that while it was decided in principle to make submission to the Khedive, the question of defending Cairo against the English army was reserved. Nor had the matter got any forwarder next day when Drury Lowe with his Indian cavalry arrived at Abbassiyeh. The truth is all heart had been taken out of the official resistance by the intrigues of the Khedive's agents, and by Arabi's proclamation by the Sultan as a rebel having become known. Only the rabble of the streets, as yet ignorant of all, were still in favour of a defence. The military circumstances of Cairo were that it possessed nominally a large garrison, but these were all the newest of new recruits, and although they would probably have been sufficient to hold the citadel and so dominate the town, they could not have made a long defence without great destruction of property in the lower city. For

---

[1] In 1884 I received an account of Arabi's conduct at Tel-el-Kebir, almost identical with Sid Ahmed's, from his army doctor, Mustafa Bey, who was sleeping near him that night. His own account of his flight will be found in the Appendix.

this no one was prepared, and the sudden arrival of Drury Lowe decided the question with the War Committee for capitulation, and it was resolved to send him, according to his demand, the keys of the citadel. Arabi then seeing that all was over, and on the advice of John Ninet, with whom he had spent the night in anxious debate at the house of Ali Fehmi, drove to Abbassiyeh, and there surrendered his sword as prisoner of war to the English general. [1]

[1] I find in my journal of 1884 that on the 29th October the Egyptian princes, Osman and Kiamyl, came to see me, and that they talked patriotically about the late war, and gave me much information. "Osman was not actually there. He was too fat a prince to do anything physically, but he sympathized with the cause, and behaved with some dignity after it was over. Kiamyl was a member of the provisional government, and saw a good deal of Arabi during the war, and while bearing testimony to his honest patriotism, blamed him for his too easy conduct of affairs. He ought, he said, to have shot Ali Yusuf after Kassassin, for it was perfectly well known he was a traitor, having received five thousand pounds before the battle, which was thus lost. At one moment there were 18,000 Egyptians close to 2,500 English, who had with them the Duke of Connaught. If Ali Yusuf, who commanded the centre, had advanced then, the English must have been crushed and the prince taken, but he left the field of battle, and allowed the wings to be broken. The money paid by the English was most of it false St. George sovereigns and Egyptian pounds with lead inside. Cairo was full of them after Tel-el-Kebir, but they were bought up for the Government by the bankers at five and ten francs apiece in a few days. The money orders were also mostly forgeries, but Ali Yusuf insisted upon having an order with a signature he knew. Abd-el-Ghaffar was paid in false St. George sovereigns, some of which his wife took to Ismail Jawdat's wife to change. Prince Kiamyl had himself broken open some of these pieces and found them to contain lead. The Bedouins would not be taken in thus, and Saoud el Tihawi had told him after the war that he had received—I forget the sum—in silver dollars from one of the English generals. The whole state of things was very disgracful, and Kiamyl was under orders to go in three days to Tel-el-Kebir to arrest Ali Yusuf when the collapse came. Arabi was betrayed by all about him, some for gold, others for jealousy. Mahmud Sami was jealous of Arabi, and spoilt the second battle of Kassassin because he was not in chief command. He was to advance from Salahieh, and did not keep his rendezvous with Ali Fehmi—the latter was an honest and good soldier, but most of them were very worthless. Arabi would not put any Turk into high command, and the fellah officers were incapable and cowardly. Mahmud Sami was the only Turk, and he was playing a selfish game throughout. Kiamyl was present at the council at the Kasr-el-Nil when Arabi returned and when he explained the destruction of the army with floods of tears. He said he had fought till he was alone, which was hardly true, and that all was over. Kiamyl then reproached him, saying, 'A man who embarks in a great enterprise ought first to count the cost.' 'Arabi ought never,' he said, 'to have been at the head of the army. If he had hanged or shot a dozen men in the early part of the war, all would have gone well.' Prince Kiamyl would not hear of the campaign having been a complete walk over for the English."

According to Mohammed Sid Ahmed Arabi had with him a body of about

1,000 encamped near him at Tel-el-Kebir, most of whom were slain before his master left the field. But I do not attach full credit to this, at least as to numbers. There seem to have been some 10,000 Egyptians in all killed or wounded in the battle—mostly killed, for little quarter was given—but I do not pretend to answer for any of the figures named. The immense mounds of the buried dead tell their own tale perhaps best.

CHAPTER XVII

THE ARABI TRIAL

While these great events were happening on the Nile, I at my home at Crabbet spent the summer sadly enough.   My sympathies were, of course, still all with the Egyptians, but I was cut off from every means of communication with them, and the war fever was running too strongly during the first weeks of the fighting for further words of mine to be of any avail.   Publicly I held my peace.   All that I could do was to prepare an "Apologia" of the National movement and of my own connection with it—for this was now being virulently attacked in the press [1]—and wait the issue of the campaign.

Nevertheless, though in dire disgrace with the Government, I did not wholly lose touch with Downing Street.   I saw Hamilton once or twice, and submitted proofs of my "Apologia" to him and Mr. Gladstone before it was published, and this was counted to me by them for righteousness.   It appeared in the September number of "The Nineteenth Century Review," and

[1] One of the matters principally laid to my charge was due to a Reuter's telegram announcing that my country house near Cairo had been broken open by Arabi's order, and that seventeen cases of firearms had been found in it.   The foundation of this story was as follows: In 1881, when I was on my way, as I intended, to Arabia, I had brought with me some Winchester rifles and revolvers for the journey, amounting to seventeen rifles in all, as well as a small brass cannon of the kind used on yachts, as a present, if I could find a way to send it to him, to Ibn Rashid at Hail.   These were still stored in my house, and some one having announced the fact to the provincial authorities, they had taken possession of them, and removed them to the Cairo citadel.   In the confusion after the war I could gain no intelligence of what had become of my property except the story which was afloat in London that my brass cannon had been taken there as a trophy of war, and was forming an ornament at the Admiralty.   It was not till some ten years afterwards that having lunched one day with my cousin, Colonel Wyndham, at the citadel at Cairo, he took me afterwards to visit the arsenal, where I soon recognized my cannon and other property intact.   As the box containing the rifles had my name on it, no difficulty was made in restoring all to me.

at a favourable moment when the first sparkle of military glory had faded, and reasonable people were beginning to ask themselves what after all we were fighting in Egypt about. Written from the heart even more than from the head, my pleading had a success far beyond expectation and, taken in connection with an anti-war tour embarked on in the provinces by Sir Wilfrid Lawson, Mr. Seymour Keay and a few other genuine Radicals, touched at last what was called the "Nonconformist" conscience of the country and turned the tide of opinion distinctly in my favour. This encouraged me. About the same time, too, a letter reached me from General Gordon, dated "Cape Town, the 3rd of August," in which he avowed his sympathy with the cause I had been advocating, and which elated me not a little. It was as follows:

"Cape Town, 3, 8, 82.

"My Dear Mr. Blunt,

"You say in 'Times' you are going to publish an account of what passed between you and the Government. Kindly let me have a copy addressed as enclosed card. I have written a MS. bringing things down from Cave's mission to the taking of office by Cherif, it is called 'Israel in Egypt,' and shall follow it with a sequel, 'The Exodus.' I do not know whether I shall print it, for it is not right to rejoice over one's enemies. I mean *official* enemies. What a fearful mess Malet and Colvin have made, and one cannot help remarking the *finale* of all Dilke's, Colvin's, and Malet's secretivenes. Dilke, especially, in the House evaded every query on the plea that British interests would suffer. Poor thing. I firmly believe he knows no more of his policy than the Foreign Office porter did; he had none. Could things have ended worse if he had said everything? I think not. No more Control—no more employés drawing £373,000 a year—no more influence of Consuls-General, a nation hating us—no more Tewfik—no more interest— a bombarded town, Alexandria—these are the results of the grand secret diplomacy. Colvin will go off to India, Malet to China—we shall know no more of them. All this because Controllers and Consuls-General would not let Notables see the Budget when Cherif was in office. As for Arabi, whatever may become of him individually, he will live for centuries in the people; they will never be 'your obedient servants' again.

"Believe me, yours sincerely,

"C. G. GORDON."

The value to me of this letter I saw at once was great, for, though out of favour with the Foreign Office, Gordon's name was one to conjure with in the popular mind, and especially with that "Nonconformist conscience" which, as I have said, was beginning now to support me, and consequently I knew with Gladstone; and it was on the text of it that I began a fresh correspondence with Hamilton. Mr. Gladstone had stated in Parliament that I was the "one unfortunate exception," among Englishmen who knew Egypt, to the general approval of the war; and I sent him, through Hamilton, a copy of Gordon's letter, and at the same time invited his attention to accounts which had begun to appear in the newspapers of certain atrocities of vengeance which had been indulged in by Tewfik and his new Circassian Ministers at Alexandria on Nationalist prisoners made during the war. Torture had, it was related, been inflicted on Mahmud Fehmi, the engineer General, and the thumbscrew and kurbash were being used freely. I asked whether such was the state of things Mr. Gladstone had sent troops to Egypt to re-establish. The letter brought a prompt and interesting answer, and one which proved of value to me a few days later when it came to my pleading that Arabi should not be done to death by the Khedive without fair trial.

"10, Downing Street, Whitehall,
"*September 8th,* 1882.

"I need hardly say that Mr. Gladstone has been much exercise in his mind at the rumours about these 'atrocit.es.' I can call them by no other name. Immediate instructions were sent out to inquire into the truth of them, and to remonstrate strongly if they were confirmed. I am glad to say that, as far as our information at present goes, the statements appear to be unfounded. The strictest orders have been given for the humane treatment of the prisoners. There seems to be some doubt as to whether thumbscrewing was not inflicted on a spy in one case; and searching inquiries are to be instituted with peremptory demands of explanation and guarantees against recurrence. You may be quite sure that Mr. Gladstone will denounce 'Egyptian atrocities' as strongly as 'Bulgarian atrocities.'

"I cannot help thinking that your and Chinese Gordon's opinion of Arabi would be somewhat modified if you had seen some of the documents I have read.

'Some months ago (this, please, is quite private) certain inquiries were made about Chinese Gordon. He had suggestions to make about Ireland, and the result of these inquiries were, to the best of my recollection, that he was not clothed in the rightest of minds."

The last paragraph is historically curious. The proof Gordon had given Mr. Gladstone's Government of his not being clothed in his right mind was that he had written, during a tour in western Ireland, to a member of the Government, Lord Northbrook, recommending a scheme of Land Purchase and, if I remember rightly, Home Rule as a cure for Irish evils.

I was thus once more in a position of semi-friendly intercourse with Downing Street and of some considerable influence in the country when the crowning glory of the war, the news of the great victory of Tel-el-Kebir, reached England, and soon after it of Arabi's being a prisoner in Drury Lowe's hands at Cairo. The completeness of the military success for the moment turned all English heads, and it was fortunate for me that I had had my say a fortnight before it came, for otherwise I should have been unable to make my voice heard, either with the public or at Downing Street, in the general shriek of triumph. It had the immediate result of confirming the Government in all its most violent views, and of once more turning Mr. Gladstone's heart, which had been veering back a little to the Nationalists, to the hardness of a nether millstone. The danger now was that in order to justify to his own conscience the immense slaughter of half-armed peasants that had been made at Tel-el Kebir, he would indulge in some conspicuous act of vengeance on Arabi, as the scapegoat of his own errors. His only excuse for all this military brutality was the fiction that he was dealing with a military desperado, a man outlawed by his crimes, and, as such, unentitled to any consideration either as a patriot or even the recognized General of a civilized army. I have reason to know that if Arabi had been captured on the field at Tel-el-Kebir, it was Wolseley's intention to give him the short benefit of a drum-head court martial, which means shooting on the spot, and that it was only the intervention of Sir John Adye, a General much older in years and in length of service than Wolseley, that prevented it later— Adye having represented to Wolseley the disgrace there would be to the British army if the regular commander of an armed force, whom it had needed 30,000 troops to subdue, should not receive the honourable treatment universally accorded to prisoners of war. At home, too, I equally know that Bright, in indignant protest, gave his mind on the same point personally to Gladstone. It must not, however, at all be supposed that anything but the overwhelming pressure of public opinion brought to bear, as I will presently describe, frustrated the determination of our Government, one way or other, to make Arabi pay forfeit for their own political crime with his life. Mr. Gladstone was as much resolved on this as was Lord Granville, or any of the Whig lords in his Cabinet. To explain how their hands were forced in the direction of humanity I must go into detail.

The capitulation of Cairo and Arabi's surrender to Drury Lowe were announced in the "Times" of the 16th, and with it a telegram from its Alexandria correspondent, Moberley Bell, who represented the Anglo-Khedivial official view, demanding "exemplary punishment" on eleven of the National leaders, whom he named, including Arabi. I knew that this could only mean mischief resolved on of the gravest kind, and I consequently telegraphed at once to Button, asking him what the position in official circles was. His first answer was reassuring. "I can't think there is the least danger of their shooting anybody. You should, however, take immediate steps to appeal for merciful treatment." Two hours later, however, a second message from him came. "I don't like official tone with regard to your friends. Write me privately such a letter as I can show to my chief." By his "chief" he, of course meant Chenery, the "Times" editor, with whom, as I have said, he was on very intimate terms. I consequently wrote at once to Hamilton:

"I cannot think there should be any danger of death for the prisoners taken at Cairo, but should there be, I trust you will let me know in time, as I have certain suggestions to make regarding the extreme difficulty of obtaining them a fair trial just now, and other matters."

To this it is significant that I received no answer for two days, and then an off-hand one, to the effect that Hamilton was about to leave London for the country, "and so would be a bad person to depend upon for any intimation such as I wished." But I was not thus to be put off, and passing beyond Hamilton, I wrote once more direct to Mr. Gladstone. I did this after consultation with Button and with Broadley, whom I met at his house on the afternoon of the 19th. We decided that the latter would be the man for our purpose, and that the best chance of saving Arabi's and the other prisoners' lives would be for me to take Broadley out with me at once and produce him as their legal defender. Button, who knew the ins and outs of most affairs, was certain there was no time to lose, and we half engaged Broadley at a fee of £300, afterwards increased to £800 with refreshers. In the meantime Button rendered the cause a great service in the immediate crisis by managing that it should be announced next morning in the "Times" that Arabi and his companions were not to be executed without the consent of the English Government, and that they were to be defended by efficient counsel. Of course, we had not a shadow of authority to go upon for this statement, but the "Times" having announced it made it very difficult for the Government to go back upon a humane decision so publicly attributed to them.

My letter to Mr. Gladstone, sent in the same evening, was as follows:

"Sept. 19, 1882.

"MY DEAR SIR,

"Now that the military resistance of the Egyptians is at an end, and Arabi and their chief leaders have surrendered to Her Majesty's forces, I venture once more to address you in the interests of justice no less than of those whom the fortune of war has thus suddenly thrown into your hands. It would seem to be contemplated that a Court Martial should assemble shortly to try and judge the military leaders for rebellion, and, in the case of some of these, and of civil tribunal to inquire into their alleged connection with certain violent proceedings. If this should be the truth, I would earnestly beg your attention to certain circumstances of the case which seem to demand careful consideration.

"1.   The members of the proposed Court Martial, if Egyptians and appointed by the Khedive, can hardly be free agents or uninfluenced in their feelings towards the prisoners.   They would be chosen from among the few officers who espoused the Khedive's cause, and would of necessity be partisans.

"2.   Even were this not the case, native false witness is so common in Egypt, and the falsification of Arabic documents so easy, that little reliance could be placed upon the testimony adduced.   The latter would need to be submitted to experts before being accepted with any certainty.

"3.   Native evidence, if favourable to the prisoners, will be given under fear.   There will be a strong inducement to withhold it, and as strong an inducement in the desire of Court favour to offer evidence unfavourable.   The experts charged with examining documents will, if natives, be equally subject to these influences.

"4.   The evidence of Europeans settled in Egypt, though given without fear of consequences, may be expected to be strongly coloured by resentment.   These Europeans are, it would seem, themselves in some measure parties to the suit. They will many of them have lost property or have been injured in their trade during the late troubles or have personal insults to avenge.   The vindictive tone of the English in Egypt is every day apparent in their letters published by the English Press.

"5.   It will be insufficient, if full justice for the prisoners is to be secured, that the ordinary form of Her Majesty's representative being present through a dragoman or otherwise, at the proceedings, should be the only one observed.   Political feeling has probably run too high at Cairo during the last six months for quite impartial observation.

"6.   Should English officers, as it may be hoped will be the case, be added to the native members of the Court Martial, they will be ignorant or nearly ignorant of the language spoken by the prisoners, and will be unable themselves to examine the documents or cross-examine the witnesses.   They will necessarily be in the hands of their interpreters, who, if unchecked, may alter or distort the words used to the detriment of the prisoners. Nearly all the dragomans of the Consulates are Levantine Christians violently hostile to the Mussulman Arabs, while it may safely be affirmed that there are no Englishmen in Egypt both fully competent and quite unbiassed who could be secured in this capacity. Arabic is a language little known among our officials, and their connection with the late troubles is too recent to have left them politically calm.

"It would seem, therefore, that unless special steps are taken there is grave danger of a miscarriage of justice in the trial.

"To remedy this evil as far as possible I have decided, at my own charge and that of some of my friends, to secure the services of a competent English counsel for the principal prisoners, and to proceed with him to Cairo to collect evidence for the defence. I shall also take with me the Rev. Mr. Sabunji as interpreter, and watch the proceedings on behalf of the prisoners. My knowledge of Arabic is too imperfect for me to act alone, but Mr. Sabunji is a friend of the chief prisoners, and is eminently capable of speaking for them. He knows English, French, Turkish, and Italian well, and is probably the first Arabic scholar now living. The prisoners have full confidence in him, and I believe also that they have full confidence in me. Thus alone, perhaps, they will obtain, what I submit they are entitled to, a full, a fair, and—to some extent—even a friendly hearing.

"In conclusion, it may not be unnecessary that I should promise you that while thus engaged I, and those with me, would scrupulously avoid all interference with contemporary politics. I shall esteem it a favour if I can be informed at as early a date as possible what will be the exact nature of the trial and what the principal charges made. I hope, too, that every facility will be accorded me and those with me in Egypt to prosecute our task, and I cannot doubt that your personal sense of justice will approve it.

"I am, &c.,

"WILFRID SCAWEN BLUNT."

This letter, which I knew it would be difficult for Mr. Glad-

stone to answer with a refusal, especially after his recent assurances about "Egyptian atrocities" and "Bulgarian atrocities,"
I sent at once to Downing Street, having previously called there
and seen Hamilton, to whom I explained my plan. He did not,
however, give me much encouragement, as his answer to a
further note I sent him next morning proves. My note was
that I was writing to Arabi, and to ask him how the letter
should be sent, and expressing a hope to have an answer from
his Chief before Friday, the next mail day. Hamilton's answer suggests procrastination:

"Your letter, I am sorry to say, just missed the bag last night.
It reached me about three minutes too late; but in any case I
don't think you must count on a very immediate reply. Mr.
Gladstone is moving about, and moreover will most likely have
to consult some one before he gives an answer. I am absolutely
ignorant myself as to questions which your intended proceedings
may raise; and therefore I have no business to hazard an opinion. But is it not open to doubt whether according to international law or prescription a man can be defended by foreign
counsel? I am equally ignorant about the delivery of letters
to prisoners of war; but I should presume that no communication could reach Arabi except through and with the permission
of the Khedive and our Commander-in-Chief. In any case Malet will probably be your best means of communication."

According to this suggestion I wrote a letter to Arabi telling
him of our plans of legal defence and enclosed it, with a draft
of the letter, to Malet, and for more precaution sent both by
hand to the Foreign Office, to be forwarded, with a note to
Lord Tenterden commending it to his care. By a singular accident, however, both note and letter were returned to me with
the message that His Lordship had died suddenly that morning, and I was obliged, as the mail was starting, to send it by
the same hand, Button's servant Mitchell, to Walmer Castle
where Lord Granville was, and it was only just in time. In
the sequel it will be seen that the packet, though despatched to
Cairo, was not delivered farther than into Malet's hands and
then with the instruction that my letter to Arabi should be returned to me. Malet's official letter to me performing his duty
is sufficient evidence, if any were needed, to show how far the

Government was from co-operating at all with me in my design of getting the prisoners a fair trial. It is very formal and unmistakable:

"S<small>IR</small>,   "Cairo, *Oct.* 4, 1882.

"Acting under instructions from Her Majesty's Principal Secretary of State I return you herewith the letter for Arabi Pasha which you sent to me to be forwarded in your letter of the 22nd ultimo.

                       "I am, etc., E<small>DWARD</small> B. M<small>ALET</small>."

My letter to Arabi had been as follows:

"*To My Honourable Friend H. E. Ahmed Pasha Arabi.*

"May God preserve you in adversity as in good fortune.

"As a soldier and a patriot you will have understood the reasons which have prevented me from writing to you or sending you any message during the late unhappy war. Now, however, that the war is over, I hope to show you that our friendship has not been one of words only. It seems probable that you will be brought to trial, either for rebellion or on some other charge, the nature of which I yet hardly know, and that, unless you are strongly and skilfully defended, you run much risk of being precipitately condemned. I have therefore resolved, with your approval, to come to Cairo to help you with such evidence as I can give, and to bring with me an honest and learned English advocate to conduct your defence; and I have informed the English Government of my intention. I beg you, therefore, without delay, to authorize me to act for you in this matter—for your formal assent is necessary; and it would be well if you would at once send me a telegram, and also a written letter, to authorize me to engage counsel in your name. Several liberal-minded Englishmen of high position will join me in defraying all the expenses of your case. You may also count upon me, personally, to see, during your captivity, that your family is not left in want. And so may God give you courage to endure the evil with the good.

                       "W<small>ILFRID</small> S<small>CAWEN</small> B<small>LUNT</small>.

"*Sept.* 22, 1882.

"Crabbet Park, Threebridges, Sussex."

Gladstone's answer, which came sooner than I expected, shows as little disposition to favour any idea of a fair trial as was that of the Foreign Office. It came in this form from Hamilton:

"10 Downing Street,
"*Sept.* 22, 1882.

"Mr. Gladstone has read the letter which you have addressed to him about Arabi's trial and your proposal to employ English counsel. All that he can say at the present moment is that he will bring your request under the notice of Lord Granville with whom he will consult, but that he cannot hold out any assurance that it will admit of being complied with."

This was very plain discouragement, though short of a direct refusal, and a few words added by Hamilton in a separate note were even more so: "I confess," he says, "that the more I think of it the greater is the number of difficulties which present themselves to my mind involved by such a proposal as yours. You will, I presume, hear further on the subject in a day or two but not from me, because I am off as you know."

I was left, therefore, still in doubts while the situation was daily becoming more critical. I dared not leave for Egypt without having received a definite answer, for I knew that at Cairo I should be powerless, if unarmed with any Government authority, and should probably not even be allowed to see the prisoners, while Broadley, tired of waiting, had gone back to Tunis. The Parliamentary session was over and every one was leaving London, the work of the Ministers being left to Under-Secretaries, and all business practically at a standstill. Meanwhile the question of Arabi's death was being keenly debated in the Press, and all the Jingo papers were clamouring for his execution, only here and there a feeble voice being raised in protest. Sir Wilfrid Lawson's Egyptian Committee, which had done such good work during the summer, had become silent, and from Lawson himself I received just then a most desponding letter: "I greatly doubt," he said, "whether they will allow Arabi to have anything like a *fair* trial. They know well enough that if they do it will end in their own condemnation, and 'Statesmen' are too crafty to be led into anything of that sort. At any rate you are right in *trying* to get fair play for him." All I could do was to stay on in London and still worry Downing Street for an answer and go on prompting the "Times." Therefore, after waiting five more days, I wrote again to Gladstone for a definite answer, the situation having become to the last degree critical at Cairo.

"*Sept.* 27, 1882.

"I wrote to you about ten days ago, stating my intention of engaging competent English counsel for Arabi Pasha and the other chief Egyptian prisoners in case they should be brought to trial, and of going myself to Cairo to procure evidence for them and watch the proceedings; and I begged you to give me early notice of any decision that might be come to regarding them.

"Your reply, through Mr. Hamilton, though giving me no assurance that English counsel would be allowed seemed to suggest that my proposal would be considered; and I accordingly retained, provisionally, a barrister of eminence to act for the prisoners, should it be decided they should be thus defended. In view also of the legal necessity of gaining the prisoners' consent to the arrangement, I wrote, under cover to Sir Edward Malet, to Arabi Pasha, begging his authorization of my thus defending him, a letter to which I have as yet received no answer; nor have I received any further communication from yourself or from Lord Granville, to whom you informed me the matter would be referred.

"Now, however, I see it reported in the 'Times,' from Cairo, that a Military Court to try all offenders will be named no later than to-morrow, the paragraph being as follows:

" 'The Military Court to try all offenders will be named to-morrow. The Khedive, Sherif, and Riaz all insist strongly on the absolute necessity of the capital punishment of the prime offenders, an opinion from which there are few, if any, dissentients. Sherif, whose gentleness of character is well known, said to me to-day: "It is not because I have a feeling of spite against any of them, but because it is absolutely necessary for the security of all who wish to live in the country. An English expedition is an excellent thing, but neither you nor we want it repeated every twelve months." ' [1]

[1] Telegram from Moberly Bell,

"If this statement is true it would seem to confirm my worst suspicions as to the foregone decision of the Khedive's advisers to take the prisoners' lives, and to justify all my arguments as to the improbability of their obtaining a fair trial. I therefore venture once more to urge a proper legal defence being granted them, such as I have suggested; and, in any case, to beg that you will relieve me of further doubt and, if it must be so, responsibility in the matter, by stating clearly whether English counsel will be allowed or refused in the case of Arabi Pasha and the chief prisoners, and whether proper facilities can be promised me in Egypt of communicating with the prisoners, and obtaining them competent interpretation.

"In the present state of official feeling at Cairo, it would be manifestly impossible for me, and those I have proposed to take with me, to work effectually for the prisoners without special diplomatic protection and even assistance.

"The urgency of the case must be my excuse with you for begging an immediate answer."

This last letter, however, never reached its destination. Gladstone had left London, and Horace Seymour, his secretary in charge of his correspondence, under cover to whom I had sent it, handed it on, whether by order or not I do not know, to the Foreign Office. "Mr. Gladstone," he explained, "is out of Town, so upon receipt of your letter yesterday I sent the further communication which you addressed to him straight to the Foreign Office. . . . I did so because he had placed your former letter in Lord Granvillle's hands, as Hamilton informed you, and also because I gathered from your note that this would meet your wish and save time. I understand that you will shortly receive an official reply from Lord Granville conveying to you the view of the Government on the matters to which you refer." Gladstone therefore, had shifted his responsibility of saying "yes" or "no" on to Granville, and Granville being of course also out of town it was left for the Foreign Office clerks to deal with according to their ways. In spite of Seymour's promise that the view of the Government would shortly be conveyed to me, all the answer I received was one signed "Julian Pauncefote," stating that Mr. Gladstone had referred my two letters of the 19th and 27th to Lord Granville, and that Lord Granville regretted that he did not feel justified in entering into correspondence with me on the subject. It was thus that Gladstone, who had made up his mind that Arabi should be executed no less than had the Foreign Office, finally evaded the responsibility with which I had sought to bind him. I give the incident in detail as an illustration of official craft no less than as one of historical importance.

This "Pauncefote" reply decided us to waste no more time. In consultation with Button and with Lord De la Warr, who had come to London and had been working to get an answer from Lord Granville on independent lines, and who now offered to share with me the costs of the trial if we could secure one (a promise which I may note Lord De la Warr failed to redeem), it was agreed that we should telegraph at once to Broadley at Tunis to hold himself in readiness to proceed to Egypt, and that in the meanwhile we should send out to Cairo by that very night's mail the first briefless barrister we could lay our hands on as Broadley's junior till his arrival, and be on the spot to act as circumstances should suggest. Lord Granville had not agreed, nor had he at that time the least intention of agreeing, to the appearance of English counsel on behalf of the prisoners. But the "Times," as we have seen, had already committed the Government to a statement that Arabi was not to be executed without its consent, and that he was to be defended by efficient counsel; and this they had not had not the face publicly to disavow. And now Button's influence was so great with Chenery that he was confident he could again force Lord Granville's hand in the matter of English counsel through the insistence of the "Times" on a fair trial.

All that day, therefore, we searched the Inns of Court, which were almost empty, it being holiday time, and it was only at the last moment that we were fortunate enough to light upon the man we wanted. This was Mark Napier, than whom we could not have found a better agent for our purpose, a resourceful and determined fighter with a good knowledge of the law and one difficult to rebuff. He had the immense advantage, too, through his being the son of a former British Ambassador, of understanding the common usages and ways of diplomacy as also of speaking French fluently, a very necessary qualification at Cairo. Having agreed to go he received our short instructions, which were that he was to go straight to Malet and say that he had arrived as Arabi's counsel, and insist on seeing his client. This was all he could hope at present to achieve, and if he could do this he would do much. If Malet should refuse he was to protest and take advantage of every opening given him to emphasize the refusal. Above all he was to keep us constantly informed by telegram of what was going on, while we on our side would fight the battle no less energetically at the Foreign Office and in the Press. Mark, as I have said, had the great advantage of having had a diplomatic training and so could not be imposed upon by the prestige and mystery with which diplomacy is invested for outsiders, and which gives it so much of its strength. We could not possibly have lit upon a better man. He started, as proposed, that night by the Brindisi mail, taking with him a cipher code and two or three letters of introduction. That, with a hand-bag, was all his luggage.

As to myself, De la Warr, who knew the temper of the Foreign Office and their personal rage against me, was very insistent that I should not go to Cairo and to this I assented. At Cairo I should have been only watched by spies, possibly arrested and sent home, while here I could continue far more effectively the Press campaign which, of course, could only really win our battle. Button that very night managed a new master-stroke in the "Times." De la Warr had succeeded in getting from Granville an assurance that all reasonable opportunities would be given by the Khedive for the defence. This assurance was of course illusory as far as a really fair trial went, as the only legal assistance procurable at the time by the prisoners at Cairo was that of the various Levantine lawyers who practised in the international Courts, and these could be no better depended upon than were the terror-stricken native lawyers themselves to serve their clients honestly by telling the whole truth, though a defence of this perfunctory kind would be sufficient to serve our Government's purpose of being able, without risk of a conflict with English popular opinion, to ratify the intended sentences of death. It was intended to have the trial in the Egyptian Court over in a couple of days, and having proved "rebellion," to proceed at once to execution; and

English counsel would, no doubt, have been ruled out of the proceedings as a preposterous intervention of foreigners with no legal status in the country.

Granville's words to De la Warr had been no more than this: "I have no reason to doubt that the Khedive, with whom the proper authority rests, will give all reasonable opportunities for Arabi's defence which may not involve any extraordinary or unnecessary delay, and it devolves on the prisoners and their friends to take such measures as they may think fit on their own responsibility." This Button cleverly reproduced next morning in the "Times" as follows: "Lord Granville has written that every reasonable facility will be afforded the prisoners in Egypt and their friends for obtaining counsel for their defence. Mr. Broadley has therefore been telegraphed to to go at once to Cairo." It is clear from Lord Granville's angry expostulation with Lord De la Warr (see Blue Book) how little intention he had of having his words thus interpreted. But, once published in the "Times," he could not with any decency back out of the position; and thus by a very simple device we again forced his hand and this time on a point which, in the event, gained for us the whole battle. [1]

Nevertheless, we were very nearly being tricked out of our fair trial after all, and a singularly ugly circumstance of the position in our eyes was the sudden reappearance, just then at Cairo, of Colvin, the man of all others most interested, after the Khedive, in preventing publicity. The Foreign Office object clearly now was to hurry on the trial, so as to get it over before Broadley should have time to arrive, for Tunis was and still is without any direct communication with Egypt, and it was probable that ten days would elapse before he could be there. Of Napier's sending they had no knowledge. Orders, therefore, were at once given as a first step that Arabi should be transferred from the safe keeping of the British Army to the ill-custody of the Khedivial police, where communication with

---

[1] I have been recently asked to explain that the true reason why the "Times" so strongly supported us in our attempt at this critical juncture to obtain for Arabi a fair trial was the Machiavellian one of forcing the British Government to undertake responsibilities which would entail their assumption of full authority in Egypt. I heard, however, nothing of this at the time, and I prefer still to believe that it was a generous impulse more worthy of the "Times's" better tradition and of Chenery's excellent heart.

the outside world would be effectually barred for him without the English Government incurring thereby any odium. This was done on the 4th of October, two days before Napier's arrival; and the trial was fixed for the 14th, while Broadley did not succeed in reaching Cairo till the 18th. Nothing but Napier's unexpected appearance at the English Agency disarranged the concerted plan.

A further step taken to hasten the end and make an English defence difficult was to select the French criminal military code for use in the court martial, a form which under an unscrupulous government gives great advantages to the prosecution. According to it a full interrogatory of prisoner and witnesses is permitted before these have seen counsel and they are thus easily intimidated, if they take a courageous attitude, from repeating their evidence at the trial. Thus both Arabi and others of his fellow prisoners were during the interval between the interrogatory and the day fixed for trial secretly visited by a number of the Khedive's eunuchs, who brutally assaulted and ill-treated them in their cells with a view of "breaking their spirit." Lastly, the Egyptian Government were permitted to declare that no counsel should be allowed to plead except in Arabic, thus excluding those we were sending to the prisoners' help. These particulars were telegraphed me by Napier soon after his arrival and made us anxious.

All that the English Government had done in some measure to protect the prisoners from the Khedive's unregulated violence was to appoint two Englishmen who had a knowledge of Arabic to be present at the proceedings. These by a great stroke of good fortune were both honest and humane men, and, as it happened, old friends of my own, Sir Charles Wilson, whom I had travelled with in 1881 from Aleppo to Smyrna (not to be confounded with Sir C. Rivers Wilson), and Ardern Beaman, whom I had known at Damascus, and who now was Malet's official interpreter at the Agency. Both these men had been favourably impressed by Arabi's dignified bearing during the days of his detention as English prisoner of war, and now willingly gave Napier what little private help they could.

With Malet himself Napier succeeded at least so far as to get his status and that of the solicitor Eve, whom he had fortunately found at Cairo, recognized as legal representatives of

Arabi's friends, though he could not obtain from him any definite promise or more than a vague assurance that English counsel would be allowed to represent Arabi himself. His applications to see his client were constantly put off by Malet by referring him to Riaz Pasha, the Khedivial Minister of the Interior, who as constantly refused, and in the meanwhile the trial was being pushed forward with all haste, so that it was clear to Napier that he was being played with and that the trial would be over before the question of the admissibility of English counsel had been plainly decided.

Things were standing thus when on the 12th of October I received a sudden warning from De la Warr, who was still in communication with the Foreign Office: "From what I hear, unless vigorous steps are taken, Arabi's life is in great danger. You have probably received information from Mr. Napier." With this ill news I rushed off immediately to Button's rooms and there fortunately found him, and as all his information tallied with mine we agreed that a supreme appeal must be made to the public, and that the Foreign Office must be directly and strongly attacked and Gladstone compromised and forced into a declaration of policy. I consequently sat down and wrote a final letter to Gladstone, in which I spared nothing in my anger of accusation against Granville and was careful to insist on his own connection with the matter, and his early sympathies with the Nationalist leader, and, without troubling ourselves to ask for an answer in Downing Street, Button "plumped" it into next morning's "Times," Chenery generously giving it full prominence and directing attention to it in a leading article. He had ascertained that the intention of the Government was that the trial should commence on Saturday, that sentence should be pronounced on Monday, and that Arabi's execution should instantly follow. It was already Friday, so we only had three days (one of them a Sunday when no newspapers are published) in which to rouse English feeling against this *coup de Jarnac*. Fortunately it was enough. I believe it was on this occasion that Bright, learning from my letter how things stood, went down to Gladstone and told him personally and plainly that he would be disgraced through all history as a renegade from his humaner principles if he allowed the perpetration of so great a crime. Be this as it may, the Foreign Office capitulated to us there and then, and, admitting our plea of the necessity of a fair trial, gave instructions to Malet to withdraw his opposition and treat the counsel sent to Arabi favourably. The following telegram from Napier announces our success: "Granville has directed Malet to require that Arabi shall be defended by English counsel. Proceedings expected to be lengthy."

I have thought it necessary to go into very minute detail in narrating these early phases of Arabi's trial, because in this way only is it possible to refute the false and absurd legend that has sprung up in Egypt to the effect that there was from the first some secret understanding between Gladstone and Arabi that his life should be spared. I can vouch for it, and the documents I have quoted in large measure prove it, that so far from having any sentiment of pity for, or understanding with, the "arch rebel," Gladstone had joined with Granville in the design to secure his death, through the Khedive's willing agency, by a trial which should be one merely of form and should disturb no questions, as the surest and speediest method of securing silence and a justification for their own huge moral errors of the last six months in Egypt. It was no qualm of conscience that prevented Gladstone from carrying it through to the end, only the sudden voice of the English public that at the last moment frightened him and warned him that it was dangerous for his reputation to go on with the full plan. This is the plain truth of the matter, whatever glosses Mr. Gladstone's apologists may put on it to save his humane credit or whatever may be imagined about it by French political writers desirous of finding an explanation for a leniency shown to Arabi after the war, which has seemed to them inexplicable except on the supposition of some deep anterior intrigue between the English Prime Minister and the leader of the Egyptian rebellion.

This supreme point of danger past, it was not altogether difficult to foresee that the trial could hardly now end otherwise than negatively. A fair trial in open court with the Khedivial rubbish heap turned up with an English pitchfork and ransacked for forgotten crimes was a thought not to be contemplated by Tewfik without terror, while for the British Government as well there would be revelations destructive of the theory of past events constructed on the basis of official lies and their own necessity of finding excuses for their violence. The Sultan, too, had to be safeguarded from untimely revelations. The danger for the prisoners' lives was not over, but there seemed fair prospect of the thing ending in a compromise if we could not gain an acquittal. The changed state of things at Cairo is announced by Napier as early as the 16th October; and I will give the rest of my story of the trial mainly in the form of telegrams and letters.

Napier to Blunt, Oct. 20th:
"It is believed the Egyptian Government will try to quash the trial altogether, and that the chief prisoners will be directed to leave the country. I have not sufficient facts at my command to form a judgment on this point, but I think it not unlikely."

And again from Broadley, just arrived at Cairo:

Broadley to Blunt, Oct. 20th:
"Borelli Bey, the Government prosecutor, admitted frankly that the Egyptian Government had no law or procedure to go by, but suggested we should agree as to a procedure. He admitted the members of the Court were dummies and incompetent. He hoped I should smooth the Sultan and let down Tewfik as *doucement* as possible."

Napier to Blunt, Oct. 20th:
"I think now we can guarantee a clean breast of the whole facts. It is as much as the Khedive's throne is worth to allow the trial to proceed."

The chief danger we had to face was a desire, not yet extinct at the Foreign Office, till by hook or crook to establish some criminal charge against Arabi which should justify his death. Chenery writes to me 21st October: "Among important people there is a strong feeling against him [Arabi] on the alleged ground that he was concerned with, or connived at, the massacre in Alexandria. The matter will almost certainly come up at the trial." This danger, however, did not at Cairo seem a pressing one, and certainly it was one that the prosecution was least likely to touch, the Khedive himself being there the culprit. Nothing is more noticeable in the interrogatories than the pains taken by the members of the Court to avoid questions tending in that direction and the absence on that point of all evidence which could incriminate any one. It was one, however, of great political importance to our Government that it should be proved against Arabi, for on it they had based the whole of their wilful insistence in forcing on a conflict, and without it their *moral* excuse for intervention fell flatly to the ground. The same might be said in regard to another absurd plea, insisted upon personally by Gladstone, that there had been an abuse of the white flag during the evacuation of Alexandria, a supposition which he had caught hold of in one of his speeches and made a special crime of, though in truth withdrawal of troops while a white flag is flying is permitted according to all the usages of war. Otherwise the coast seemed clear enough of danger, for it was evident that the British public would no longer allow our Government to sanction Arabi's death for mere political reasons.

Meanwhile at Cairo things were going prosperously. On the 22nd Broadley and Napier were admitted to Arabi's cell and speedily found in what he could tell them the groundwork of a strong defence. Arabi's attitude in prison was a perfectly dignified one, for whatever may have been his lack of physical courage, he had moral courage to a high degree, and his demeanour contrasted favourably with that of the large majority of those who had been arrested with him and did not fail to impress all that saw him. Without the smallest hesitation he wrote down in the next few days a general history of the whole of the political affairs in which he had been mixed, and in form which was frank and convincing. No less outspoken was he in denouncing the ill-treatment he had received since he had been transferred to his present prison from those scoundrels, the Khedive's eunuchs, who had been sent at night by their master to assault and insult him. Not a few of the prisoners had been thus shamefully treated; yet by a singular lack of moral courage the greater number dared not put into plain words a crime personally implicating the cowardly tyrant who had been replaced as master over them. Nothing is more lamentable in the depositions than the slavish attitude assumed by nearly all the deponents towards the Khedive's person, hated as he had been by them and despised not a month before. A more important event still was the recovery from their concealment of Arabi's most important papers, which had been hidden in his house and which he now directed should be sought out and placed in Broadley's hands. It was with great difficulty that his son and wife in their terror could be brought to allow the search—for they, too, had been "visited" by the Khedive's servants—but at last the precious documents were secured and brought to Broadley by Arabi's servant already mentioned, Mohammed Sid Ahmed. The proved of supreme value—including as they did the letters written by order of the Sultan to Arabi and others of a like compromising kind. The news of the discovery struck panic into the Palace and there seemed every chance that the trial would be abandoned.

Napier writing to me October 30th says: "The fact is I believe we are masters now, and that the Khedive and his crew would be glad to sneak out of the trial with as little delay as possible. The fidelity of Arabi's servant and the constancy of his wife enabled us to recover all his papers but one. They are now in a safe deposited in Beaman's room at the Consulate. . . . The Government cannot face our defence. They will offer a compromise, banishment with all property reserved. What better could be got? . . . This question will probobly soon have to be considered."

It will be understood that the changed aspect of affairs at Cairo found its echo, and more than its echo, in the London Press. Cairo was full of newspaper correspondents, and Broadley, who was a past master in the arts of journalism, soon had them mostly on his side. His hospitality (at my expense) was lavish, and the "chicken and champagne" were not spared. Malet and Colvin, supreme in old days, were now quite unable to stem the torrent of news, and revelation followed revelation all destructive of the theory they had imposed on the Government, that Arabi and the army had been alone in opposing the English demands and that the National movement had been less than a universal one. Colvin was now become discredited at the Foreign Office as a false guide, and Malet's incapacity was at last fully recognized. Lord Granville, furious at our success, and seeing the political situation in Egypt drifting into a hopeless muddle, did what was probably his wisest course in submitting

the whole matter to Lord Dufferin for a settlement. I had
early notice from Button of this new move and that Dufferin's
first business on arriving at Cairo would be to bring about a
compromise of the trial. My letter of instructions to Broadley in view of the situation thus created is worth inserting here:

Blunt to Broadley, Nov. 2, 1882.

"I wish to state over again my ideas and hopes in undertaking Arabi's defence and that of his companions, which if
they are realized will repay me for the cost even though larger
than I had originally thought probable. Or course the main
object was to save the prisoners' lives, and that I think we may
consider already accomplished, for public opinion has declared
itself in England, and, the preliminary investigation having so
entirely failed in the matter of the June riots and the burning of
Alexandria, no evidence that now could be produced and no verdict given by the judges could any longer place them in jeopardy.
Since your arrival, however, and through your skill and good
fortune, a flush of trumps has come into our hands. Instead
of Arabi's papers being locked up in the Foreign Office they are
in our possession, and, as you tell me to-day, our defence is
perfect while we hold such a commanding position over the
enemy that we can fairly dictate them terms. We cannot, therefore, be content with anything less than an honourable acquittal
or the abandonment of the trial. At present the latter seems
the most probable. Lord Dufferin has been ordered to Egypt;
the Premier yesterday threw out a feeler for a compromise, and
from everything I hear proposals will shortly be made for some
arrangement of the affair by which the scandal and discredit
of an exposure will be avoided. It depends, therefore, entirely
on us to save not only Arabi's life but his honour and his freedom and also I believe the lives and freedom of all the political
prisoners inculpated with him.

"I believe a strong attempt will be made by Lord Dufferin
to get Arabi to agree to a detention in the Andaman Islands,
or some part of the British Empire where he would remain a
political prisoner treated with kindness but not suffered to be at
large. I believe also he will endeavour to get from him a cession
of his papers. Neither of these attempts must be allowed to
succeed, and all proposals including them must be rejected. It

is no business of ours to save the Sultan's or the Khedive's honour nor to save Lord Granville from embarrassment, and I shall consider our failure a great one if we do not get far more. I think Arabi should, in the first place, state that he demands a trial in order to clear his honour, and especially to demonstrate the innocence of those who acted with him during the war, viz., the whole nation, or, if not brought to trial, that the charges against them should be withdrawn as well as against himself. There should, in fact, be a general amnesty, also he should retain his papers, though probably he might give an understanding that they should not be published for a term of years. We cannot, under the circumstances, object absolutely to exile, because I suppose it would be argued the Khedive could exile him by decree, but even this I should make a matter of favour, because the Constitution of February, 1882 (which I hope you have closely studied, and which is a most valuable document from the fact of its having been confirmed by the Sultan as well as granted by the Khedive) forbids such exiling. Still the point would have to be conceded. We should, however, refuse anything like imprisonment. The Khedive might exile him from Egypt, and the Sultan from the Ottoman Empire, but neither would have a right to fix the place or nature of his abode beyond them.

"Nor could the English Government, having handed Arabi to the Khedive for trial, let him be taken back untried to be dealt with as a criminal by England. The English Government has recognized this by refusing so to take him back. Still less could it imprison him if so taken without trial. It is, therefore, clear that unless tried and convicted he must leave Egypt a free man. Nor can he legally be deprived in Egypt of his rank and pay. But I should suppose that he will agree to retiring with military rank only, and a small maintenance to save him from actual poverty and the necessity of working with his hands. I think these terms would be dignified, and they are terms we can insist upon. Otherwise I urge the necessity of a defence tooth and nail, and I sincerely trust that you will not listen to any proposal which may be made of a *pro formâ* trial and letting the Khedive down *doucement,* as Borelli proposed. There should either be a real honest exposure of *all* the facts, or an honourable withdrawal of *all* the charges. I trust in you to co-operate with me fully in obtaining this result, without regard for the feelings of Consuls or Ambassadors or Viceroys. They are nothing to us, and our client's honour and cause are everything. Your diplomatic skill is, I have no doubt, a match for Lord Dufferin's, and it will be a great game to win. You have made Malet do what you wanted, and so you will make Dufferin do. If you achieve this we will not talk more about the fee. I enclose a letter of introduction to Lord Dufferin."

The following from Mr. Beaman, Malet's official interpreter, and a witness of unimpeachable authority, is of the highest historical importance. Beaman had been in charge of the Agency at Cairo during the last weeks before the bombardment, and being a good Arabic scholar knew more of the true state of affairs than any one employed there. He had been appointed a few days before the date of his letter to superintend, on Malet's part, the trial:

Beaman to Blunt, Cairo, Nov. 6, 1882.
". . . This is our last day before the adjournment. . . . The Palace people here are in a great stew at the advent of Lord Dufferin, who arrives to-morrow. Broadley's arrival has been an agony to them, but this is the last blow. I believe Dufferin is a man who will quickly see through our friend 'Twefik, and as I hear that his ears are open to everybody the temporary Embassy will be better informed, I expect, than the Agency has ever been. I had a great deal of intercourse with natives before the bombardment of all classes and parties, and knew the whole of the game from the four sides, English, Turkish, Arabi, and Tewfik. They were each quite distinct. As I could not have given my authorities, and as people would not have accepted my word for things I could have told, I kept my information for myself, but I have given some good hints to Sir Charles Wilson, who now has a fairer idea of the Egyptian question than any of our officials here. He is an extremely cautious man, with a great share of shrewdness and true judgment which he does not allow to be warped. Through him I have been able to get facts to Malet which I should never have told Malet himself. I think now that Malet has quite lost any respect he could ever have had for the Khedive. Throughout our proceedings he has acted with the greatest fairness to us, although dead against his own

interests. . . . You know how deeply he was pledged to the Khedive, and it is quite bitter enough a cup to him to see his idol come down from the card house which is breaking up. . . . I think the Ibrahim Agha business alone is quite enough to show the Khedive in his true colours. I heard the whole story direct from the Palace, how the *titunji,* the Khedive's pipe bearer, had kissed the Khedive's hand, and asked permission to spit in the faces of the prisoners, and it was on this that Sir Charles Wilson made inquiry and found it all true. Nevertheless, because it was evident that the Khedive had a very dirty piece of linen to be washed in the business, it was left alone. I suggested when all the witnesses swore falsely that the oath of triple divorce should be administered to them, and Sir Charles Wilson was in favour of it too, but it was hushed up. His Highness's own family now no longer pretend to deny it among themselves. And this is the man for whom we came to Egypt.[1]

"If I was not bound by my position here not to advise Broadley, I could give him hints enough for his cross-examination to turn out the Khedive to-morrow. I hope it will come out nevertheless. The first man to be got rid of is Riaz. He is playing the very devil through Egypt. The other day he said: 'The Egyptians are serpents and the way to prevent serpents from propagating is to crush them under foot. So will I crush the Egyptians.' And he is doing it."

Matters stood thus in the first week of November, the date of Lord Dufferin's arrival at Cairo. It was a fortunate circumstance for us who were defending the cause of justice in England that Parliament that year happened to be holding an autumn session. It brought to our aid in the House of Commons several Members of first rate fighting value—Churchill, Wolff, Gorst, Lawson, Labouchere, besides Robert Bourke, Lord John Manners, W. J. Evelyn, and the present Lord Wemyss, of the regular Tory opposicion, with two or three Irish Members. Percy Wyndham, to his credit, was the only Tory who had voted with the minority of twenty-one against the war.

[1] The fact of Tewfik's having sent his eunuchs to insult the Nationalist leaders in prison is attested by Sheykh Mohammed Abdu, who was among the earliest arrested, and was himself one of its victims. He recorded his prison experience in a declaration submitted to Sir Charles Wilson 29th October, but which is absent from the Blue Books.

CHAPTER XVIII

Lord Dufferin's arrival at Cairo on the 6th November placed matters there on an entirely new footing. Up to that point Riaz Pasha and the rest of the Khedive's Ministers had been doing pretty much as they liked, subject only to Malet's weak supervision. But Dufferin was a man of another mould, and soon showed the Khedive that his position while in Egypt was to be that of master, not adviser. He paid little attention to his tales, and not much, I believe, to Malet's, but opened the doors of his Embassy to every one who could give information. Mackenzie Wallace, his chief assistant, in a very few days acquired a good general knowledge of what had been going on in Egypt during the last two years, and his book about it gives more of the truth than any other yet published in English. Dufferin, though an idle man, was a rapid worker, and where he had something serious to do, knew how easiest to do it.

Nevertheless, for the first fortnight after Dufferin's arrival, and until he had quite assured himself of his ground, the prosecution of Arabi was allowed to work on in its own casual way, swayed by the Khedive's ever shifting impulses of a desire to conceal the truth on the one hand, and an unwillingness on the other to let go his prey. These will be best recorded by simply reproducing the letters and telegrams which now passed almost daily between me in London and Messrs. Broadley and Napier at Cairo, as will the successive steps by which a compromise of the trial was eventually come to.

Broadley to Blunt, November 6th (in answer to his letter of November 2nd):

"I entirely concur in all you say, and shall exercise the greatest prudence. I am completing a perfect case for defence, showing:

"(1) Purity, honesty of Arabi's inspirations.

"(2) Perfect concurrence of Tewfik till July 12.

"(3) Perfect concurrence of the Sultan throughout.

"(4) Universality of the movement.

"(5) Wholly illegal constitution of the Court Martial.

"(6) Absurdity of the white flag (on which subject Napier has secured A 1 deposition from Lambton).

"(7) Abnormal humanitarian character of Arabi.

"(8) Abnormal iniquity of all proceedings until our arrival.

"(9) Torture of prisoners.

"(10) Letters from Tewfik to Constantinople against England.

"(11) Systematic falsification of the 'Moniteur.'

"Shall demand release of all the accused. *Keep this private.*

"Now all I fear is the enormous expense of a protracted trial of eight or nine months. Arabi *alone* calls 400 witnesses. . . . I spend freely. I entertain the correspondents. I have wheedled the 'Egyptian Gazette' into being our special organ. I have turned public opinion here quite in favour of Arabi. We are obliged to employ a dozen interpreters at salaries varying from £1 to £2 10s. a week. . . . My absence from Tunis means utter loss of *all* there. All my pending cases have been given up, including some of great magnitude. Bourke will tell you I have one retainer alone of £250 a year, and another of £100. . . . I hope you will take all this into consideration. . . . I only say I believe all will depend on liberal if not lavish expenditure. Remember we have every one against us, and people don't work without a reward here. . . . An Arabi fund should be raised. The nine months' Tichborne trial is a specimen. But I don't think we should exceed *one-tenth* of that at the worst. . . . All I say hinges on expenses. Don't think of me but only of incidental expenses. . . . I work sixteen hours a day. . . . Napier is invaluable."

Napier to Blunt, November 6th:

"You seem to be doubtful about the *acte d'accusation.* We have not had it officially communicated. It is not proposed by the prosecution to frame it until the close of the evidence. But in substance it is fairly stated in a telegram I think to the 'Times':

"(1) The abuse of the White Flag.

"(2) Complicity in massacres and pillage, June 11.

"(3) Complicity in destruction by fire of the city.

"(4) Carrying war into territory of the Sultan.

"(5) General acts of mutiny and rebellion against the Khedive and the Sultan."

Broadley to Blunt, November 7th (telegraphed):

"If you don't mind expense great success sure—see my yesterday's letter. I shall crush Tewfik and his crew past hope of redemption."

Napier to Blunt, November 10th:

"I have seen Dufferin to-day. He received me most kindly, though he declined to enter on business at once. He had only just received his instructions. Broadley and I are to meet him to-morrow.

"There seems to be a desire to burk inquiry into the rebellion question. The Government and all the papers are pledged to the ridiculous rebel cry, the one of all others that incenses me most. It is an old trick that has been played in Afghanistan, the Cape, and elsewhere. Any one can see that it may be smashed into a cocked hat at once. . . . Proposals for a compromise must come from the other side, must be put in writing, and must contain all that you claim—indeed I think they ought to amount to unconditional surrender. Of this of course more fully afterwards. You may be assured that we will not consent to anything without communication with you, and fullest deliberation."

Napier to Blunt, November 15th:

"I suppose you can guess the innumerable difficulties with which we have to deal. In the first place since we were not permitted to be present at the examination of the witnesses, it is necessary for us not only to have the whole of the evidence copied, but also to submit the whole of it to each of the prisoners for his observation and consideration. . . . There are 136 witnesses who will be brought against us. Besides these, 125 prisoners have been interrogated, and their answers will be used against each other. Then anybody who pleases seems to have been allowed to write letters to the Court, among others, H. H. the Khedive and, I believe, the Ministers, or some of them. . . . Not one word of the evidence is on oath, and most of it consists of hearsay and opinion. . . . 'In your opinion is Arabi a rebel?" 'I don't know.' 'You bad, wicked man, why don't you know?' 'I can't tell why I don't know.' 'Then think it over, and to-morrow bring a written statement of what you do know.' To-morrow the wretch arrives with a written statement that the prisoner in question is a rebel and incendiary.

"Then again the translations afforded us are not correct translations from the originals, and the originals are not true records of the evidence of the witnesses themselves. . . .

"Thank Heaven they have imprisoned a man named Rifaat. [He had been Secretary to the Government and Director of the Press.] They could not have done anything so destructive to their own case. Not only does he know French well, but he has good literary ability, and a very fair knowledge of all these tortuous and involved intrigues rolled up one within another the untanglement of which is a business enough to make the head reel. How if it were to appear that the Abdin, Sept. 9, demonstration had been got up by the Khedive as the best means of ridding him of the disagreeable tutelage of Riaz and his Ministry! And how if the dark deeds of June 11 were plotted in the Palace to force the English and French to crush the now uncontrolled and uncontrollable National movement!

"I have been in hopes all along that the Government would not face the trial, and that they would find some means to put an end to the scandal that must ensue. But I begin to think that that will not be so. Many people in high places are prompted by motives of revenge, and still hope to wreak it upon their enemies. Others hope that by the unworthy devices of the Court a fair trial may yet be prevented. And I have no doubt they will in a great measure succeed. Again, perhaps it is the policy of the English Cabinet to insist upon the matter being threshed out, so as to give them time to meet the storm, and an opportunity of throwing over the Turks and perhaps Tewfik. If the trial is to go on I cannot tell what the expense will be, but I fear it will be very great."

Napier to Lady Anne Blunt, November 16th:

"Lord Dufferin began at once by lending us his assistance. Broadley and I called a day or two after his arrival. Broadley made a very masterly statement which put him in possession of the whole of our numerous causes of complaint. He has also been given copies of our formal protests, and I believe will indirectly assist us to defeat the Court of imbeciles with whom we have to deal. . . . The correspondents, with the exception of Bell, are all, I believe, favourable. The 'Daily News' especially. Wallace of the 'Times' has just arrived, and I believe his influence will go far to counteract Bell's extraordinary correspondence. Bell will particularly be called to account for his 'Arabi's head-in-a-charger' policy. I think he seems a little uncomfortable on the prospect of being examined on his telegrams in Court."

Mackenzie Wallace, here alluded to, arrived with Dufferin from Constantinople, where he was "Times" correspondent, and afterwards became Dufferin's private secretary when His Lordship went to India as Viceroy. He was an able man, and acted while in Egypt entirely in concert with Dufferin, and has written the only English narrative of the events of 1882 which has any historical value.

What follows is in connection with the final attempt made by the prosecution to get evidence against Arabi on a point which might be treated as a capital one, namely, the arrest of Suliman Sami, who had been in command of the Egyptian rear-guard at the evacuation of Alexandria, and who, having been subjected to the usual intimidation treatment in prison, was now said to be ready to give evidence that Arabi had ordered him to burn the city. It was this sudden desperate attempt to obtain a capital verdict that brought matters to a crisis at Cairo, and resulted, as we shall see, in the compromise effected by Dufferin of the trial.

Broadley to Blunt, November 17th:

"An attempt has been made to force Suliman Bey to implicate Arabi. It has been done so clumsily that Suliman has contradicted every other witness called to prove the same thing, *but* I believe it was done at a midnight or secret sitting when Wilson was absent. . . . Try and make your peace with the Foreign

Office, Dufferin is square, and we could get a lot by soft words."

Beaman to Blunt, November 17*th:*
"I just write a line . . . to say that things are going on
very well.   The evidence of Suliman Sami, which seems to have
rejoiced the prosecution, is not worth a straw, having been
palpably invented for the occasion, and not supported by any of
the preceding testimony.   The only question seems to be if the
prisoners will get off without a trial, or if they will have a chance
of being fairly heard in their own defence.   I am convinced that
the Government here is using every effort to quash the proceedings, as the facts that would come out in cross-examination would
be compromising to every man almost now in power, and would
lay bare some very unpleasant facts about the Khedive.   For
this last reason it is just possible that our Government may feel
inclined to propose terms to Arabi, as it will be a rough *exposé*
if the trial proves the biggest scamp in Egypt is the man whom
we brought an army here to uphold.   Personally I have very
little doubt that the Khedive and Omar Loutfi arranged the
Alexandrian massacre in order to aim a blow at Arabi, who had
just declared himself responsible for public safety.   I hold
proofs which carry me half way to conviction, but the time has
not yet come to produce them."

Broadley to Blunt.   Telegram.   November 18*th:*
"Believe excellent compromise possible.   Do not attack the
Foreign Office.   Absolute secrecy necessary."

Broadley to Blunt.   Telegram.   November 20*th:*
"London parleys Dufferin.   Egyptian Government's desire
to compromise lessened by thinking public opinion in England
changed owing to Suliman Sami's perjury."

Broadley to Blunt, November 21*st:*
"Important crisis imminent.   The friends of the Egyptian
Government assert intention of hanging Arabi.   Remain in
London."

Broadley to Blunt, November 21*st:*
"Nothing I could say could give you an idea of the infamous
conduct of the Egyptian Government.   They set our procedure

rules at defiance, and say they do not care a curse, as they are treating diplomatically for the hanging of Arabi."

Napier to Blunt, November 21st:
"We are simply fighting all the force of the Egyptian Government single-handed, though I believe Lord Dufferin will come to the rescue. They are striving to procure the judicial murder of these prisoners, and it takes all our time to meet their many wiles. Wilson and Dufferin are helping us, but they, the Egyptian Government, are quick and unscrupulous. We are necessarily more slow and cautious."

Broadley to Blunt. Telegram. November 26th:
"Egyptian Government proposes to try Arabi alone. Telegraph your opinion."

Broadley to Blunt. Telegram. November 27th:
"Letters explaining situation fully posted. Reason to believe if Arabi, Mahmud Sami and Toulba consent to admit formal charges of rebellion or continuing war against orders of the Khedive, the Egyptian Government will consent to exile or internment at the Cape of Good Hope, or elsewhere, some of the accused simple exile, the majority amnesty. I implore absolute secrecy. Napier and myself favourable to compromise seeing difficulty of proving efforts to prevent burning, etc."

Blunt to Broadley, November 28th:
"Cannot approve terms named—certainly not Cape, but am consulting friends to-night about funds. Our political position immensely strong. Definite answer later."

Broadley to Blunt. Letter. November 27th, 1882:
("Private and most urgent.)
"MY DEAR BLUNT,
"I invite *all* your prudence, calm consideration and tact to the subject of this letter. I have had a long interview [with] Dufferin to-day. He is most friendly. The dossier is before us. *Nothing* presents difficulties but the burning of Alexandria. As regards this I believe the proof will fail as to Araby's orders, but many ugly facts remain, viz.: no efforts to stop conflagration

and loot. (2) Continued intimacy with Suliman Sami *after-wards*. (3) No punishment of offenders. (4) Large purchases petroleum. (5) Systematic manner of incendiarism by soldiers.

"This is *the rub*. Could Arabi have not stopped the whole thing? Besides, some of his former speeches, etc., have a very burning appearance.

"If Arabi will plead *guilty formally to* one *of the charges of rebellion* (*i. e.,* his continuing war after Khedive's orders) he will be exiled.

"Cape of Good Hope under certain conditions with sufficient allowance. I think I can secure these terms for him, Mahmud Sami and Toulba. Rest, simple exile or pardon. Can I think secure *allowance* or with forfeiture property—retention military rank.

"Against this we have enormous length trial—chances of turn public opinion—expense *and* the five facts which I allude to above.

"If a word of this transpires you will do me incalculable injury. Think over all this and remember our great and grave responsibility. Dufferin is charming. Please at once telegraph as follows: If you say 'I accept the principle. Make best possible terms,' say *pax. I advise* this course as best. If you say, 'Go on—no sort of compromise can be accepted,' say *bellum*.

"I am prepared to fight manfully to the bitter end strongly as ever. I leave all to you—but think well over *all* the contingencies.

"Very faithfully yours,
"A. M. BROADLEY."

Napier to Blunt. Letter. November 27th:
"Cairo, *Nov. 27th,* 1882.

"DEAR BLUNT,

"It is much to be regretted that the Post Office people have found out our correspondence, for they have, to my knowledge, opened your last letter to me registered and received last Friday. It contained the Borelli charges returned, and a short note from you. I do not think anything was abstracted. I shall send this by ordinary post under cover to H. H. Asquith, Temple, E. C., in the hope that it may escape their vigilance. I, of course, protested at once, but do not suppose that they will mend their ways. I also greatly regret that I have no time to keep copies of my own letters to you for reference. You must not be surprised therefore if you sometimes meet with repetition. I cannot tell you of all the tricks they have played upon us, as they would fill volumes. The letter had been obviously opened by being slit across above the seal, and gummed up again. It had been cleverly done, and I might not have discovered it but for the fact that the gum used was not quite set. It therefore opened along the line of the slit, and I at once found the gum where no gum should have been. I will send you a short note by the direct mail so that you shall not be surprised at the delay in the delivery of this. Although we have been hard at work since last mail, I do not know that anything of much importance has occurred except that we have been admitted to the defence of Mahmud Sami, with whom we have had several long conferences. Toulba is ill, suffering from nervous excitement, I think, and asthma. I do not know whether he will die, but I have done everything in my power to get him proper medical assistance, a change of room, a companion, and, if possible, a raised bed.

"The last evidence in the question of the burning of Alexandria has not been communicated to us except through the medium of the Egyptian Gazette, which may or may not be correct. It is not formidable in itself, but it is quite sufficient to give colour to a finding against the prisoner on that charge. It becomes, therefore, of the most vital importance to consider whether there is no way out other than through the portals of the court martial. There is no doubt that we could discredit the evidence, and even smash it up in cross-examination. And besides, on the other charges of Rebellion and Massacre of June 11th I feel sure we could make it hot for the prosecution, but there is an opinion in a very high quarter that there is a strong determination to execute if the Court should find guilty. Assume, therefore, that the Court Martial find the prisoner (for I am only speaking of the chief now) guilty, it will be for the English Government to reverse the sentence. I am of opinion that it would be dangerous to trust them to carefully examine the evidence and the manner in which it has been obtained. I think it possible that that matter would be hastily disposed of in the Foreign Office, and that they might leave the prisoner to the Court, declaring that everything had been done to secure a fair trial, and that they could not interfere with a verdict deliberately arrived at after the fullest opportunity given to the defence.   And besides, it is more than probable that they would allow *some* sentence to pass—any sentence suffered here would be most dangerous to the prisoner.   After careful consideration I dare not advise the prisoner to trust to the trial if he have an alternative.   If terms of banishment are offered, with proper safeguards and provision for maintenance, I shall be strongly in favour of accepting them.   To sum up: If found guilty by the Court, some punishment, perhaps death, certainly a serious one, will be inflicted: If acquitted, either voluntary banishment without means, or remaining in the country at the mercy of the Government here.   If he leaves the country under a compromise all charges except that of rebellion would have to be withdrawn, and provision for his life in a suitable place would have to be accorded.   I have reason to believe that the course of a compromise finds favour with all but Riaz, and is also favourably regarded by Dufferin.

"Give us your opinion, and believe me ever very sincerely yours,

"MARK NAPIER.

"P. S.—As far as the case goes nothing could be better.   In law, in fact, and in the infamous manner it has been conducted. *But* there are the dangers and considerations I have alluded to. Broadley has in my opinion conducted all the different discussions with the Court and Dufferin with the greatest energy, skill, and judgment.   The law of the case is perfect for us, *but* it is a case which will be decided in the Cabinet and not in the Court.   It is impossible to rebut hearsay, and as I have had no opportunity to consider the whole evidence, I will not offer an opinion on that now."

Broadley and Napier to Blunt.   Telegram.   November 28th, 7.42 p. m.:
"Long interview with Dufferin.   I entreat you give us discretion to obtain best terms possible.   We know delay fatal. Rely on our judgment.   Foreign Office's support unreliable.

Dufferin disposed to exceed his instructions on our behalf. Dufferin rules Egyptian Government. Defense case burning Alexandria suspicious. Hence anxiety. Embrace present moment. Dufferin's good offices absolutely necessary. Telegraph instantly full discretion. Interview Dufferin ten to-morrow.
"BROADLEY, NAPIER."

Napier to Blunt. Same date:
"I give you my honour I most strongly concur in our telegram herewith. Strongest cause for full immediate discretion. Every personal interest contrary to our request. NAPIER, private."

Blunt to Broadley, November 28th midnight:
"Cannot approve terms less than honourable exile—not internment—Aden, Malta, Cyprus. Within these limits use discretion."

Broadley to Blunt. Telegram. November 29th:
"Arabi gives us written authority to act with discretion in concert with Dufferin, who proposes Arabi pleads guilty on formal charge of rebellion—others abandoned. Sentence read commuting punishment to exile—exile simple on parole—good place which you can settle with the Foreign Office—perhaps Azores. Suitable allowance granted and compensation for loss of property entailed by sentence. You probably fail to realize difficulty of rebutting case of burning Alexandria and obtaining evidence for defence. Foreign Office certainly indisposed to interfere in any Egyptian sentence short of death—for example, long detention in an Egyptian prison. Am convinced ultimate result inevitably worse, dreading great responsibility, having full knowledge of the position of affairs. I trust you will leave us discretion, to avoid possible disaster."

Blunt to Broadley. Telegram. November 29th, 3 p. m.:
"Have consulted De la Warr. We approve full discretion on basis of telegram just received."

Broadley to Blunt. Telegram. November 30th:
"All progressing well. Try to negotiate in concert with De la Warr the place of exile—Fiji suggested. Gratified at your confidence."

Blunt to Broadley. Telegram. November 30th, 2.30 p. m.:
"Reject Fiji or Azores. Insist on Moslem country for religious life. They cannot refuse. Will consult Chenery. De la Warr away."

Broadley to Blunt. Telegram. December 1st:
"Dufferin's conduct admirable. Suggests De la Warr's arranging place of exile with Foreign Office. Prisoners entirely satisfied."

Broadley to Blunt. Telegram. December 3rd:
"Arabi's trial over. For correct account see 'Standard.' Egyptian Government fulfilled all engagements to the letter."

Broadley to Blunt. Telegram. December 4th:
"Arabi delighted at result and sends thanks—inclined to Cape. Dufferin brick [sic]."

Broadley to Blunt. Telegram. December 4th, 4.50 p. m.:
"Surprised your not wiring. Success complete. Anglo-Egyptian colony furious."

Blunt to Broadley. Telegram. December 4th:
"Congratulate all. De la Warr says place of exile in English territory left to Dufferin. I don't fancy Cape. How about Gibraltar or Guernsey. Consult Arabi."

Broadley to Blunt. Telegram. December 4th:
"Many thanks kind telegram."

It will be perceived by these telegrams that it was not without reluctance that I agreed to the compromise proposed by Dufferin. We had at the moment the full tide of English opinion with us, and I knew that the Foreign Office could not do otherwise than agree to almost any terms we chose to impose, and I was most unwilling that the charge of rebellion should be admitted by us. At the same time it was not possible for me in the face of Broadley's, and especially Napier's, telegrams to withhold my assent. The responsibility was too great. I had also the question of costs to consider. It is true that a public subscription had been opened which had brought us valuable names. But the actual sums subscribed did not yet amount to £200, while Broadley's bill was running already to £3,000. A continuation for another month of the trial would have meant for me a larger expenditure than I was prepared to face in a political quarrel which was not quite my own. I therefore took counsel with De la Warr, and especially with Robert Bourke, of whom I have already spoken, and who warned me how frail a thing public opinion was to rely on, and advised me strongly to consent. I remember walking up and down with him in Montagu Square, where he lived, in indecision for half an hour before I was finally convinced and yielded. I consequently sent the telegram of approval, and eventually, after much argument, we succeeded in obtaining as Arabi's place of exile the Island of Ceylon, the traditional place of exile of our father Adam when driven out of Paradise. No more honourable one could possibly have been fixed upon.

The exact terms of the arrangement come to with Dufferin were unfortunately not committed by him to writing, an oversight on Broadley's part, who ought to have insisted on this and thus saved us much after trouble and misunderstanding. The negligence allowed the Egyptian Government to inflict degradation of rank on the prisoners, which was certainly not in the spirit of Lord Dufferin's arrangement, though, perhaps, legally following the *pro formâ* sentence of death for rebellion. Room, too, was left for dispute as to what was the amount of the allowance intended as compensation for the confiscations. Broadley seems to have exaggerated to his clients the promises on this head. Personally I consider that they were not illiberally death with, as the property of most of them was insignificant, and they were allowed to retain property belonging to their wives. The only considerable sufferer pecuniarily was Mahmud Pasha Sami, who had a large estate which he forfeited. As to Arabi, his sole worldly possessions, besides what furniture was in his house at Cairo, a hired one, and some horses in his stable, consisted of the eight acres of good land he had inherited from his father in his native village, to which he had at various time added parcels of uncultivated land on the desert edge, amounting to some six hundred acres, paid for out of his pay in prosperous days. These at the time of the confiscation cannot have been worth much over £2,000 or £3,000, for barren land was then selling for only a few reals the acre, and he had not had time to reclaim or improve them. [1]

A point, too, which was long disputed, but which is no longer of importance, was whether the *paroles* of the prisoners were given to the Egyptian or the English Governments. But with these matters I need not trouble myself more than to say that the English Government, having gained its end of getting the rebellion admitted by us, and so a title given for their intervention in Egypt, gave little more help to the defence of certain unfortunate minor prisoners who on various pretexts found themselves excluded from the amnesty, and were subjected to all the injustices of the Khedive's uncontrolled authority. These, however, belong to a period beyond that of which I now propose to write, namely, that of the permanent Occupation, and cannot be detailed in my present memoir, which now, I think, has made clear at least my own part in the events of the revolution to the last point where that part was personal.

Looking back at my action in Egypt during that period, with its early successes and its final failure to obtain for the National Government fair treatment at English hands, I cannot wholly regret the course I took. I made, of course, many mistakes, and I feel that I am in considerable measure responsible for the determination the Nationalists came to to risk their country's fortune on the die of battle. But I still think their fate would have been a worse one if they had not fought, tamely surrendering to European pressure. They at least thus got a hearing from the world at large, and if any attention since has been paid to fellah grievances it has been won wholly by Arabi's persistence, which I encouraged, in accepting the logic of their political principles even to the point of war. It obliged England to listen to their complaints and, if it could not prevent her from depriving them of their political liberty, it has forced her since to remedy most of their secular material wrongs.

---

[1] A claim made recently in his name for a large indemnity in regard to these lands, and embodied in a petition addressed to our King Edward, is an entire illusion on Arabi's part, and marks the fact, otherwise very apparent to those who know him, that he has fallen into a condition of senile decay for which there is no remedy.

The worst oversight was that the promised general amnesty was not exactly defined. Hence the later prosecutions on so-called "criminal" charges.

What the future may bring to Egypt I know not. She has grown rich under English tutelage, and though I do not consider riches synonymous with the well being of a nation, they have been in Egypt of at least this value, that they have enabled the native Nile population so far to hold its own against foreign intrusion as owner of the soil. While this is, the Nation will remain alive, and the day may yet come for the fellah race when self-government will be restored to them, and the armed struggle of 1882 will appear to them in its true light as the beginning of their national life, and one, as such, glorious in their annals. To that day of final emancipation I still pin my hopes, though it is not likely I shall live to see it.[1]

If my life is prolonged for a few years, it is my intention to continue the writing of my memoirs, and this will include much that is of importance to Egypt, though nothing of such high historical value as the recital already made. The present volume may well stand by itself, and so with regret I leave it. I should have wished to include in it an account of Lord Dufferin's mission of reconstruction, and the weak efforts made by Gladstone to undo the wrong he had inflicted on the cause of liberty, and on his own reputation as a man of good. But this would lead me too far, and I prefer to end my actual narrative at the point where we have now arrived, the close of the eventful year, 1882. On one of the last days of it I received a second characteristic letter from Gordon in which, speaking of the war and the suppression of liberty in Egypt, he quotes the following appropriate verse:

"When thou seest the violent oppression of the poor, or the subversion of justice, marvel not at it, for the Higher than the Highest regardeth it."

[1] This was written in 1904.

APPENDICES

APPENDIX I

I was born in the year 1840 at Horiyeh, near Zagazig, in the Sherkieh. My father was Sheykh of the village, and owned eight and a half feddans of land, which I inherited from him and gradually increased by savings out of my pay, which at one time was as much as £250 a month, till it amounted to 570 feddans, and that was the amount confiscated at the time of my trial. I bought the land cheaply in those days for a few pounds a feddan which is worth a great deal now, especially as it was in a poor state (*wahash*) when I bought it and now is in good cultivation. But none of it was given me by Saïd Pasha or any one, and the acreage I inherited was only eight and a half. I invested all the money I could save in land, and had no other invested money or movable property except a little furniture and some horses and such like, which may have been worth £1,000.

As a boy I studied for two years at the Azhar, but was taken for a soldier when I was only fourteen, as I was a tall well grown lad and Saïd Pasha wanted to have as many as possible of the sons of the village Sheykhs, and train them to be officers. I was made to go through an examination, and what I had learned at the Azhar served me well, and I was made a *boulok-amin,* clerk, instead of serving in the ranks, at sixty piastres a month. I did not, however, like this, as I thought I should never rise to any high position, and I wished to be a personage like the Mudir of our province, so I petitioned Ibrahim Bey, who was my superior, to be put back into the ranks. Ibrahim Bey showed me that I should lose by this as my pay would then be only fifty piastres, but I insisted and so served. I was put soon after to another examination, out of which I came first, and they made me *chowish,* and then to a third and they made me lieutenant when I was only seventeen. Suliman Pasha el Franzawi was so pleased with me that he insisted with Saïd Pasha on giving me promotion, and I became captain at eighteen, major at nineteen, and Lieutenant-Colonel, *Caimakam,* at twenty. Then Saïd Pasha took me with him as A. D. C. when he went to Medina, about a year before he died. That was in A. H. 1279 (1862?).

Saïd Pasha's death was a great misfortune to me and to all, as he was favourable to the children of the country. Ismaïl was quite otherwise. In his time everything was put back into the hands of the Turks and Circassians, and the Egyptians in the army got no protection and no promotion. I went on serving as Caimakam for twelve years without much incident till war came with Abyssinia. I was not sent to the war with Russia, but when the war with Abyssinia broke out all available troops were wanted, and the garrisons were withdrawn from the stations on the Haj Road, and I was sent to do this. I was sent quite alone without a single soldier or a single piastre and had to get there as best I could on a camel. I went in this way to Nakhl and Akaba and Wej collecting the garrisons and putting in Arabs to take charge of the forts there as *ghaffirs*. Then we crossed over the sea to Kosseir and so by Keneh to Cairo. I was not paid a penny for this service or even my expenses. The country was in a fearful state of oppression, and it was then I began to interest myself in politics to save my countrymen from ruin. I was sent on to Massowa from Cairo and took part in the campaign of which Ratib Pasha was commander-in-chief, with Loringe Pasha, the American, as Chief of the Staff. I was not present at the battle of Kora, being in charge of the transport service between Massowa and the army. It was a disastrous battle, seven *ortas* being completely destroyed. Loringe Pasha was the officer mostly in fault. The Khedive's son, Hassan, was there, but only as a boy, to learn soldiering. He was not in command nor is it true that he was taken prisoner by the Abyssinians.

After this I thought much about politics. I remember to have seen Sheykh Jemal-ed-Din, but not to speak to, but my former connection with the Azhar made me acquainted with several of his disciples. The most distinguished of them were Sheykh Mohammed Abdu, and Sheykh Hassan el Towil. The first book that ever gave me ideas about political matters was an Arabic translation of the "Life of Bonaparte" by Colonel Louis. The book had been brought by Saïd Pasha with him to Medina, and its account of the conquest of Egypt by 30,000 Frenchmen so angered him that he threw the book on the ground, saying "See how your countrymen let themselves be beaten." And I took it up and read all that night, without sleeping, till the morning. Then I told Saïd Pasha that I had read it and that I saw that the French had been victorious because they were better drilled and organized, and that we could do as well in Egypt if we tried.

You ask me about the affair of the riot against Nubar Pasha in the time of Ismaïl and whether I had a hand in it. I had none, for the reason that I was away at Rashid (Rosetta) with my regiment. But the day before the thing happened I was telegraphed for by the War Office with my fellow Caimakam, Mohammed Bey Nadi, to deal with the case of a number of soldiers that had been disbanded by the new Ministers without their arrears of pay or even bread to eat, and who were at Abbassiyeh. But I knew nothing of what was being arranged against Nubar. That was done by order of the Khedive, Ismaïl Pasha, through a servant of his, Shahin Pasha, and his brother-in-law, Latil Eff. Selim, director of the military college. These got up a demonstration of the students of the college, who went in a body to the Ministry of Finance. They were joined on the way by some of the disbanded soldiers and officers, not many, but some. At the Ministry they found Nubar getting into his carriage, and they assaulted him, pulled his moustache, and boxed his ears. Then Ismaïl Pasha was sent for to quell the riot and he came with Abd-el-Kader Pasha and Ali Bey Fehmy, the colonel of his guard, whom he ordered to fire on the students, but Ali Fehmy ordered his men to fire over their heads and nobody was hurt. Ali Fehmy was not with us at that time. He was devoted to Ismaïl, having married a lady of the palace, but he did not like to shed the blood of these young men.

Ismaïl Pasha, to conceal his part in it and that of those who got up the affair, accused Nadi Bey and me and Ali Bey Roubi of being their leaders and we were brought before a *mejliss* on which were Stone Pasha and Hassan Pasha Afflatoun with Osman Rifki, afterwards Under-Secretary of War, and others. I showed, however, that its was impossible we could be concerned in it as we had only that very night arrived from Rosetta. Nevertheless we were blamed and separated from our regiments, Nadi being sent to Mansura, Roubi to the Fayum, and I to Alexandria where I was given a nominal duty of acting as agent for the Sheykhs of Upper Egypt, whose arrears of taxes in the shape of beans and other produce were to be collected and sent to Alexandria in security for money advanced to Ismaïl by certain Jews of that place. But before we separated we had a meeting at which I proposed that we should join together and depose Ismaïl Pasha. It would have been the best solution of the case, as the Consuls would have been glad to get rid of Ismaïl in any way, and it would have saved after complications as well as the fifteen millions Ismaïl took away with him when he was deposed. But there was nobody as yet to take the lead, and my proposal, though approved, was not executed. The deposition of Ismaïl lifted a heavy load from our shoulders and all the world rejoiced, but it would have been better if we had done it ourselves as we could then have got rid of the whole family of Mohammed Ali, who were none of them, except Saïd, fit to rule, and we could have proclaimed a republic. Sheykh Jemal-ed-Din proposed to Mohammed Abdu to kill Ismaïl at the Kasr-el-Nil Bridge and Mohammed Abdu approved.

Ismaïl collected the money of the Mudiriehs six months before his deposition. Latif afterwards avowed his part in the affair. Latif was put in prison but released on application of the freemasons to Nubar.

Tewfik Pasha, when he succeeded Ismaïl, by his first act made public promise of a Constitution. You ask me whether he was sincere in this. He never was sincere, but he was a man incredibly weak, who never could say "no," and he was under the influence of his Minister, Sherif Pasha, who was a sincere lover of free forms of government. Tewfik, in his father's reign, had amassed money, which was what he cared for most, by receiving presents from persons who had petitions to make, and who thought he could forward their ends. He had no wish for a Constitution, but he could not say "no" when Sherif pressed him. So he promised. Two months later he fell under the stronger influence of the Consuls, who forbade him to decree it. On this Sherif called the Ministers together, and they all gave him their words of honour that they would resign with him if he resigned. And so it happened. But some of them, notwithstanding their promise, joined Riaz Pasha when he became Prime Minister in Sherif's place. In order to persuade them Riaz engaged that each Minister should be supreme in his own department, and that they would not allow Tewfik to interfere in any way with the administration. Mahmud Sami joined him as Minister of the *Awkaf,* Ali Mubarak as Minister of Public Works, and Osman Pasha Rifki, a Turk of the old school, who hated the fellahin, was made Minister of War. The new government was a tyrannical one. Hassan Moussa el Akkad, for signing a petition against the breaking of the Moukabala arrangement, was exiled to the White Nile, and Ahmed Fehmi for another petition, and many other people were got rid of who incurred the displeasure of the Ministers. Of all the Ministers the worst was Osman Rifki.

We colonels were now once more with our regiments, and as native Egyptians subject to much oppression. On any pretext a fellah officer would be arrested, and his place filled by a Circassian. It was the plan to weed the whole army of its native officers. I was especially in ill favour because I had refused to allow my men to be taken from their military duty and put to dig the Tewfikieh Canal, which it was the practice to make them do without extra pay. Plans were made to involve me in some street quarrel with the view to my assassination, but through the love of my soldiers I always escaped. All officers who were not Circassians were in danger, and all were alarmed. It was thus that Ali Fehmy, who was a fellah born, though through his wife connected with the Court, came to join us, for he feared he, too, would be superseded. He was Colonel of the 1st Regiment of Guards, and stationed at Abdin; I was at Abbassiyeh with the 3rd Regiment, and

Abd-el-Aal Helmi was at Toura. Ali Roubi commanded the cavalry.

Matters came to a crisis in January, 1881. I had gone to spend the evening with Nejm ed Din Pasha, and there were at his house some pashas talking over the changes Osman Rifki had in hand, and I learned from them that it had been decided that I and Abd-el-Aal should be deprived of our commands, and our places given to officers of the Circassian class. At the same moment a message arrived for me from my house to say that Ali Fehmy had come there with Abd-el-Aal and was awaiting me. So I went home and I found them there, and from them I learned the same evil news. We therefore took council what was to be done. Abd-el-Aal proposed that we should go in force to Osman Rifki's house and arrest or kill him, but I said, "No, let us petition first the Prime Minister, and then, if he refuses, the Khedive." And they charged me to draw the petition up in form. And I did so, stating the case, and demanding the dismissal of Osman Rifki, and the raising of the army to 18,000 men, and the decreeing of the promised Constitution. [N. B.—I think Arabi makes a mistake here, confusing these last two demands with those made on the 9th of September. But he insisted on it the three proposals were first made in February, and made in writing then.] This we all three signed, though knowing that our lives were at stake.

The following morning we went with our petition to the Minister of the Interior and asked to see Riaz. We were shown into an outer room and waited while the Minister read it in an inner room. Presently he came out. "Your petition," he said, "is *muhlik*" (a hanging matter). "What is it you want? to change the Ministry? And what would you put in its place? Whom do you propose to carry on the government?" And I answered him, *"Ye saat le Basha,* is Egypt then a woman who has borne but eight sons and then been barren?" By this I meant himself and the seven ministers under him. He was angry at this, but in the end said he would see into our affair, and so we left him. Immediately a council was assembled with the Khedive and all his Court, and Stone and Blitz also. And the Khedive proposed that we should be arrested and tried, but others said, "If these are put on trial, Osman Pasha also must be tried." Therefore Osman was left to deal with it alone. And the rest you know.

You ask did the Khedive at that time know of our intention to petition. He did not know that nor that Ali Fehmy came to us. But afterwards he knew. You ask did I know the Baron de Ring. I did not know him, nor any one of the Consuls, but I heard that the French Consul had the most influence, and I wrote to him telling him what our position was, and begging him to let the other Consuls know that there was no fear for their subjects. You ask if I knew Mahmud

Sami. I did not know him yet. But he was friends with my friend Ali Roubi, and I had heard a good account of him as a lover of freedom. He was of a Circassian family, but one that had been 600 years in Egypt.

As to the second demonstration of September 9th, we knew then that the Khedive was with us. He wished to rid himself of Riaz, who disregarded his authority. I saw him but twice to speak to that summer, and never on politics. His communication was through Ali Fehmy, who brought us word to the following effect: "You three are soldiers. With me you make four." You ask me whether he was sincere. He never was sincere. But he wished an excuse to dismiss Riaz. We therefore demanded next time the dismissal of Riaz, as well as the rest, knowing he would be pleased. On the morning of the 9th September we sent word to the Khedive that we should come to the *asr* to Abdin to make demand of the fulfilment of his promises. He came, and with him Cookson, and it was with Cookson that I debated the various proposals made. He asked if we should be content with Haidar Pasha, but I said "we want no relation of the Khedive." There were no written demands the second time, only a renewal of the three demands of the 1st February, the Chamber of Notables, the raising of the army to 18,000 men, according to the firmans, and the dismissal of Riaz. They agreed to all. The Khedive was delighted. I know nothing of Colvin having been there, or of any advice he gave to the Khedive. The only ones I saw were Cookson and Goldsmid. It was Cookson who talked to me. If the Khedive had tried to shoot me, the guns would have been fired on him, and there would have been bad work. But he was entirely pleased with the whole of the proceedings.

You ask about Abu Sultan (Sultan Pasha). He was disappointed, because when the Ministry was formed under Sherif Pasha he was not included in it. It was thought, however, that the post of President of the Chamber of Deputies was more honourable and more important. Only he did not take this view, and was put out at being omitted from the Ministry. That was the beginning of his turning against us.

To your question about the ill-treatment of the Circassians arrested for a plot while I was Minister of War, I answer plainly, as I have answered before, I never went to the prison to see them tortured or ill-treated, I simply never went near them at all.

About the riots of Alexandria there is no question but that it was due to the Khedive and Omar Pasha Loutfi, and also to Mr. Cookson. The riots were certainly planned several days beforehand, and with the object of discrediting me, seeing that I had just given a guarantee of order being preserved. The Khedive sent the cyphered telegram you know of to Omar Loutfi, and Omar Loutfi arranged it with Seyd Kandil, the chief of the Alexandria *mustafezzin*. Seyd Kandil kept the thing from us who were at Cairo. Mr. Cookson's part in it was that a number of cases of firearms were landed, and sent to his consulate, obviously with the intention of arming somebody. The moment I heard of what had happened, I sent Yakub Sami to Alexandria with orders to make a full inquiry, and the facts were abundantly proved. Much of what has been said however was incorrect. It is not true that the bodies of Christians were found dressed as Moslems. The riot began with a Maltese donkey boy, but that was only the excuse. Omar Loutfi, as you say, was a strong partisan of Ismaïl's. You ask why a man so dangerous was left in a post where he could work so much mischief. I can only say that he was not under the orders of the Minister of War, but of the Interior. It was a misfortune he was left there. Neither Nadim nor Hassan Moussa el Akkad went to Alexandria on any business of that kind. Hassan Moussa went there on a money errand.

What you ask me is true about Ismaïl Pasha. He made us an offer of money. The circumstances of it were these. We had ordered a number of pieces of light artillery from Germany, but they would not deliver them without payment, and we had none. Ismaïl Pasha offered to let us have £30,000 to pay this, on condition that we would allow it to be said that we were acting in his interests. The offer was made through M. Mengs [Max Lavisson], Ismaïl's Russian agent, and Hassan Moussa had some hand in it. But it was never produced, and if Ismaïl really sent it to Alexandria, it remained there in their hands. We never touched it.

I do not remember to have heard of any offer such as you speak of having been made by the Rothschilds [this was an offer made as I heard at the time by the Paris Rothschilds of a pension to Arabi of £4,000 (100,000 francs) yearly, if he would leave Egypt], but I received soon after the leyha [the note sent in by the Consuls demanding the dismissal of the Mahmud Sami Ministry], a visit from the French Consul, during which he asked me what my pay then was, and offered me the double—that is to say, £500 a month from the French Government if I would consent to leave Egypt and go to Paris and be treated there as Abd-el-Kader was treated. I refused, however, to have anything to do with it, telling him that it was my business, if necessary, to fight and die for my country, not to abandon it. I never heard of the Rothschilds in connection with this offer.

I will now give you an account of how Tel-el-Kebir was lost. Some days before, when the English were advancing, we made a plan to attack them at Kassassin. Mahmud Sami was to advance on their right flank from Salahieh, while we were to advance in front, and a third body was to go round by the desert, south of the Wady, and take them in the rear.

The attack was tried and put partly in execution, but failed because the plan had been betrayed by Ali Bey Yusuf Khunfis, who sent the original sketch made by me to Lord Wolseley. He and others in the army had been corrupted by Abou Sultan acting for the Khedive. When Mahmud advanced, he found artillery posted to intercept him and retreated, leaving us unsupported, and the battle was lost. Sir Charles Wilson, while I was in prison at Cairo, brought me my plan, and asked me whether it was in my own hand, and I said "yes," and he told me how they had come by it. "It is a good plan," he said, "and you might have beaten us with it."

This was our first misfortune. At Tel-el-Kebir we were taken by surprise and for the same reason of treachery. The cavalry commanders were all seduced by Abou Sultan's promises. They occupied a position in advance of the lines, and it was their duty to give us warning of any advance by the English. But they moved aside and gave no warning. There was also one traitor in command within the lines, Ali Bey Yusuf Khunfis. He lit lamps to direct the enemy, and then withdrew his men, leaving a wide space open for them to pass through. You see the marks upon this carpet. They just represent the lines. That is where Ali Yusuf was posted. Mohammed Obeyd was there, and I was at this figure on the carpet a mile and a half to the rear. We were expecting no attack as no sound of firing had been heard. I was still asleep when we heard the firing close to the lines. Ali Roubi, who was in command in front, sent news to me to change my position as the enemy was taking us in flank. I said my prayer and galloped to where we had a reserve of volunteers, and called to them to follow me to support the front line. But they were only peasants, not soldiers, and the shells were falling among them and they ran away. I then rode forward alone with only my servant Mohammed with me, who, seeing that there was no one with me and that I was going to certain death, caught hold of my horse by the bridle and implored me to go back. Then seeing that the day was lost already, and that all were flying, I turned. Mohammed continued with me and we crossed the Wady at Tel-el-Kebir, and keeping along the line of the Ismaïlia Canal reached Belbeis. There I had formed a second camp, and I found Ali Roubi arrived before me, and we thought to make a stand. But on the arrival of Drury Lowe's cavalry none would stay, and so we abandoned all and took train for Cairo. Ali Roubi made mistakes by extending the lines too far northwards, but he was loyal. The traitors were Abdul Ghaffar, I think, and certainly his second in command of the cavalry, Abd-el-Rahman Bey Hassan, and Ali Yusuf Khunfis. You say Saoud el Tihawi, too. It may be so. Those Arabs were not to be trusted. His grandfather had joined Bonaparte when he invaded us a hundred years ago.

Now I return home after twenty years of sorrowful exile, and my own people I laboured to deliver have come to believe, because the French papers have told them so, that I sold them to the English!

THE GRAND MUFTI'S REMARKS ON THE ABOVE

[N. B.—On March 18th, 1903, I read the foregoing account to Sheykh Mohammed Abdu at his house at Aïn Shems. He approved most of it as correct, but made the following remarks:

1. *As to the riot against Nubar.*—Arabi's account of this is correct, except that the order given to Ali Femy to fire on the students was not intended to be obeyed and was part of the comedy. Ali Fehmy fired over their heads by order. Latif Bey was arrested and imprisoned after the riot by Nubar, but was released on an application made to Nubar by the freemasons, Latif being a member of that body. Latif in after days freely acknowledged his share in the affair. As to what Arabi says of his having proposed at that time to depose Ismaïl, there was certainly secret talk of such action. Sheykh Jemal-ed-Din was in favour of it, and proposed to me, Mohammed Abdu, that Ismaïl should be assassinated some day as he passed in his carriage daily over the Kasr el Nil bridge, and I strongly approved, but it was only talk between ourselves, and we lacked a person capable of taking lead in the affair. If we had known Arabi at that time, we might have arranged it with him, and it would have been the best thing that could have happened, as it would have prevented the intervention of Europe. It would not, however, have been possible to establish a republic in the then state of political ignorance of the people. As to Ismaïl's having taken away fifteen millions with him to Naples, nobody knows the amount. All that is known is that it was very large. For the last few months of his reign Ismaïl had been hoarding money, which he intercepted as it was sent in to the Finance Office from the Mudiriehs.

2. *As to Tewfik in his father's time.*—What Arabi says of Tewfik having taken presents for presenting petitions to Ismaïl may be true, but the thing was not talked of, nor is it in accordance with Tewfik's conduct when in power. I do not believe it.

3. *As to Riaz' tyranny.*—Riaz was tyrannical, but not to the point of shedding blood. This he was always averse to. I do not remember any talk about the people being made away with secretly by him. There was no danger of such at any rate before the affair of the Kasr-el-Nil. During the summer, however, of that year, 1881, there was talk of attempts against Arabi and the other colonels.

4. *As to the affair of the Kasr-el-Nil, February 1st, 1881.*—Arabi's account is confused and incorrect. The first petition made by Arabi and the officers was simply one of injustice being done them. It was made by Osman Rifki, and it drew down upon them the anger of the Minister of

War, who determined to get rid of them, and first brought Arabi under the notice of the Consuls. Baron de Ring, who had a quarrel with Riaz, interested himself in their case, but only indirectly. The petition talked of by Arabi as having been drawn up in January by him and taken to Riaz, certainly contained no reference to a Constitution or to the increase of the army to 18,000 men. These demands were not made until the September demonstration. The petition of the Kasr-el-Nil time was simply a strong complaint to Riaz of Osman Rifki's misdoings, and demanding his dismissal from the Ministry of War. Riaz, at the council after the demonstration, was in favour of its being made the subject of an inquiry, which would have necessitated the trial by court-martial not only of the petitioners, but also of Osman Rifki. Riaz was not in favour of violence. But it was pointed out to him, privately, that if he opposed the more violent plan it would be said he was seeking to curry favor with the soldiers as against the Khedive, and he, therefore, left the matter to Osman Rifki, to be dealt with as he pleased.

5. *As to the demonstration of Abdin, September 9th,* 1881.—The seven months between the affair of Kasr-el-Nil and the demonstration of September were months of great political activity, which pervaded all classes. Arabi's action gained him much popularity, and put him into communication with the civilian members of the National party, such as Sultan Pasha, Suliman Abaza, Hassain Shereï, and myself, and it was we who put forward the idea of renewing the demand for a Constitution. The point of view from which he at that time regarded it was as giving him and his military friends a security against reprisals by the Khedive of his Ministers. He told me this repeatedly during the summer. We consequently organized petitions for a Constitution, and carried on a campaign for it in the press. Arabi saw a great deal of Sultan Pasha during the summer, and Sultan, who was very rich, made much of him, sending him presents, such as farm produce, horses, and the rest, in order to encourage him, and to get this support for the constitutional movement. It was in concert with Sultan that the demonstration of Abdin was arranged, and it is quite true that Sultan expected to be named to a Ministry after the fall of Riaz. But Sherif Pasha, who became Prime Minister, did not think of him and overlooked him. Afterwards Sultan was pacified and pleased when he was offered the presidency of the new Chamber of Notables. It was not till after the *leyha,* ultimatum, that he had any quarrel with Arabi. Then it is true that Arabi drew his sword in Sultan's presence and that of other members of the Chamber when they hesitated and were afraid to oppose the leyha. Up to this they had acted together. Arabi's account of the Khedive's message, "You three are soldiers. With me you are four," is excellent, and exactly shows the situation as between him and the officers. Colvin certainly was with the Khedive at Abdin, but as he knew

no Arabic he probably was not noticed by Arabi. It was Cookson who did the talking. Baron de Ring had been recalled by his government on the request of Riaz, who complained of his encouragement of the officers.

6. *As to the riots of Alexandria.*—Arabi is correct in his account as regards Omar Loutfi and the Khedive, who had been arranging the riot for some weeks. But it is not true as regards Seyd Kandil, who was only weak and failed to prevent it. He is also wrong about Cookson. The firearms introduced into the Consulate were for the defence of the Maltese and other English subjects. Seyd Kandil was exiled for twenty years, but was allowed quietly to come back, and is now at his country place in Egypt, and I have often talked over the affair with him. If you like we will go together and pay him a visit next autumn. Arabi is right in saying that neither Hassan Moussa nor Nadim were concerned in the riot. Nadim went down to Alexandria to deliver a lecture and Hassan on money business.]

[The Mufti also added the following remarks on March 20th, 1903.

There was an attempt to introduce freemasonry into Egypt in the later years of Ismaïl Pasha. The lodges were all connected with lodges in Europe. Sheykh Jemal-ed-Din joined one, but he soon found out that there was nothing of any value in it and withdrew. Ismaïl encouraged it for his purposes when he began to be in difficulties, but freemasonry never was a power in Egypt.

Mohammed Obeyd was certainly killed at Tel-el-Kebir. There were rumours for a long time of his having been seen in Syria, and we used to send from Beyrout when we were living there in exile to try and find him for his wife's sake, who was at Beyrout, but they always turned out to be false reports.

Mahmud Sami was one of the original Constitutionalists, dating from the time of Ismaïl. He was a friend of Sherif and belonged to the same school of ideas. It is most probable that he gave warning to Arabi of his intended arrest, as he was one of the Council of Ministers and must have known. After the affair of Kasr-el-Nil he was altogether with Arabi and the Colonels. That was why Riaz got rid of him from the Ministry and appointed Daoud Pasha in his place.

Riaz, at the beginning, underrated the importance of Arabi's action. Afterwards he was afraid of it. He began by despising it as he did all fellah influence in politics.

Sherif Pasha resigned in February, 1882, not on account of any quarrel with Arabi, but because he was afraid of European intervention. He was opposed to an insistence on the power of voting the budget claimed by the Chamber of Notables, and he retired so as not to be compromised.

Ragheb Pasha is (as mentioned by Ninet) of Greek descent, though a

Moslem. He had been Minister under Ismaïl, but was a Constitutionalist. After the leyha he was named Prime Minister, with Arabi for Minister of War. He acted honestly with Arabi, and remained with the National Party during the war.

Butler gives May 20th, 1880, as the date of the first military petition. That is probably correct.

Ibrahim el Aghany was one of the best and ablest of Jemal ed Din's disciples at the Azhar. He is still living and employed in the Mékhemeh (?).

When the Council was summoned to consider Arabi's petition asking for Osman Rifky's dismissal, the Khedive was with Osman Rifky for having Arabi arrested and sent up the Nile, but Riaz at first was for an inquiry. During an adjournment, however, of the Council, Taha Pasha persuaded Riaz that if he was for lenient measures it would be thought he was intriguing with the soldiers against the Khedive—to make himself Khedive—and Riaz thereupon made no further opposition. This I learned afterwards from Mahmud Sami who, as one of the Ministers, was present at the Council.

Ibrahim Eff. el Wakil with Hassan Shereï and Ahmed Mahmud were the leaders of the liberal party in the Chamber of Notables.]

Further Account given by Sheykh Mohammed Abdu, December 22nd, 1903

[When Sheykh Jemal-ed-Din was exiled a few days after the Sherif's dismissal in 1879, I was told to leave Cairo where I was professor in the normal school, and to go to my village. My successor at the school was Sheykh Hassan the blind. I was soon tired of being in my village and went to Alexandria where I was watched by the police, so I went secretly to Tantah and wandered about for a long while. Then I came back to Cairo hoping to see Mahmud Sami, who was my friend, and at that time Minister of the Awkaf, but he was away, so I went to Ali Pasha Mubarak's, Minister of Public Works, who was also a friend, but he received me badly, and everybody advised me not to stay, as it would be thought I came in connection with a secret society which had been recently formed by Shahin Pasha and Omar Lutfi and other Ismaïlists against Riaz, so I went to my village again. But again I grew tired of it, as the villagers were always quarrelling and resolved to return once more and lecture at the Azhar. Riaz Pasha was at that time in difficulty to find any one who could write good Arabic in the Official Paper, and he consulted Mahmud Sami, who told him that if there were but three more like me Egypt could be saved. And my successor, Sheykh Hassan, gave him the same opinion of me.

So I was appointed at the end of Ramadan (October, 1880), third

Editor of the Journal. But my two senior Editors were jealous and would give me no work to do. So the Journal was no better written. At this Riaz was displeased, and made inquiry, and as the result I was made Editor, and a little later Director of the Press. This was before the end of 1880. The first time I saw you was when I called on you with Rogers Bey at the Hôtel du Nil, and it was I who recommended to you Mohammed Khalil, and afterwards he brought you to see me at my house. I criticized the Government strongly in the Official Journal, and as Director of the Press allowed all liberty. But I was not in favour of a revolution, and thought that it would be enough if we had a Constitution in five years' time. I disapproved of the overthrow of Riaz in September, 1881, and, about ten days before the military demonstration at Abdin, I met Arabi at the house of Toulba Ismat, and Latif Bey Selim had come with him, and there were many there. And I urged him to moderation, and said, "I foresee that a foreign occupation will come and that a malediction will rest for ever on him who provokes it." On this Arabi said that he hoped it would not be he. And he told me at the same time that Sultan Pasha had promised to bring petitions from every Notable in Egypt in favour of the Constitution. This was true, for all the Omdehs were angry with Riaz for having put down their habit of employing forced labour. Suliman Abaza would not join in the revolution as he thought it premature, and Shereï Pasha was also against it. But when once the Constitution was granted we all joined to protect it. But Arabi could not control the army, where there were many ambitions.

I did not know of the intended demonstration at Abdin, as I was known to be friendly to Riaz, but it was arranged with Sultan Pasha and Sherif Pasha. The Khedive was in a constant change of mind about Arabi at that time, and joined Riaz and Daoud Pasha in their attempt to crush Arabi, but the day before the event they told the Khedive, who, to overthrow Riaz, approved.]

CONVERSATION WITH ARABI AT SHEYKH OBEYD, JANUARY 2ND, 1904

You ask me at what date the Khedive Tewfik put himself first into communication with us soldiers. It was in this way. Shortly before the affair of the Kasr-el-Nil he encouraged Ali Fehmy to go to us, with whom we were already friends, his intention being to use him as a spy on us, he being Colonel of the Guard. But Ali Fehmy joined us in our petition to Riaz Pasha, and was involved with us in our arrest. After the affair of the Kasr-el-Nil, and seeing the position we had gained in the minds of the people, the Khedive thought to make use of us against Riaz, and he sent Ali Fehmy to us with the message, "You three are soldiers. With me you make four." That was about a month after the affair, and we knew he was favourable to us also through Mahmud Sami, who was then Minister of War. And Mahmud Sami told us, "If ever you see me leave the Ministry, know that the Khedive's mind is changed to you, and that there is danger." In the course, therefore, of the summer (1881) when trouble began to begin for us through the spies of Riaz Pasha, who was Minister of the Interior, and who had us watched by the police, we had confidence in Mahmud Sami.

And I was specially involved in displeasure through my refusal to allow my soldiers to be taken from their military work to dig the Tewfikieh Canal, they being impressed for the labour by Ali Pasha Moubarak as Minister of Public Works. For this and for other reasons the Khedive turned from us, and resolved, with Riaz Pasha, to separate and disunite the army; and the regiments were to be sent to distant places so that we should not communicate one with the other. And Mahmud Sami was called upon, as Minister of War, to work their plan against us, the Khedive at that time being at Alexandria with the rest of the Ministers. And when Mahmud Sami refused, Riaz Pasha wrote to him, "The Khedive has accepted your resignation." And both he and the Khedive notified Mahmud Sami that he was to go at once to his village in the neighbourhood of Tantah, and remain there, and not to go to Cairo, and on no account to have communication with us. He nevertheless came to Cairo to his house there, and we called on him, but he refused to see us. Then we knew that evil was intended against us. And the Khedive appointed Daoud Pasha Yeghen in his place, and the vexation on us increased, and we knew that attempts were to be made against us. At the beginning of September the Khedive returned to Cairo with Riaz and the Ministers, and it was resolved to deal with us. Then I took counsel with Abd-el-Aal and Abd-el-Ghaffar, the commander of the cavalry at Gesireh, and Fuda Bey Hassan, *Caimakam* in command at the Kaláa. The miralaï in command at the Kaláa had been dismissed by Mahmud Sami shortly before leaving office, and had not been replaced. This miralaï was of us but *khaïn* (a traitor), and we agreed that we would make a demonstration and demand the dismissal of the whole Ministry, and that a Ministry favourable to the Wattan should replace them, and that a Mejliss el Nawwab should be assembled, and that the army should be raised to 18,000 men. But we did not tell Ali Fehmy of our design, for we did not wholly at that time trust him. And the next morning I wrote stating our demands, and sent it to the Khedive at Ismaïlia Palace, saying that we should march to Abdin Palace at the *asr,* there to receive his answer. And the reason of our going to Abdin and not to Ismaïlia, where he lived, was that Abdin was his public residence, and we did not wish to alarm the ladies of his household. But if he had not come to Abdin we should have marched on to Ismaïlia.

When, therefore, the Khedive received our message he sent for Riaz Pasha and Khairy Pasha and Stone Pasha, and they went first to Abdin Barracks, where both the Khedive and Riaz Pasha spoke to the soldiers, and they gave orders to Ali Fehmy that he should, with his regiment, occupy the Palace of Abdin. And Ali Fehmy assented, and he posted his men in the upper rooms out of sight, so that they should be ready to fire on us from the windows. But I do not know whether they were given ball cartridge or not. Then the Khedive with the Generals went on to the Kaláa, and they spoke to the soldiers there in the same sense, calling on Fuda Bey to support the Khedive against us, the Khedive scolding him and saying, "I shall put you in prison"; but the soldiers surrounded the carriage, and the Khedive was afraid and drove away, and he went on by the advice of Riaz to Abassiyeh to speak to me, but I had already marched with my regiment through the Hassaneyn quarter to Abdin. They asked about the artillery and were told that it also had gone to Abdin, and when the Khedive arrived there he found us occupying the square, the artillery and cavalry being before the west entrance, and I with my troops before the main entrance, and already when I arrived before the palace I had sent in to Ali Fehmy, who I had heard was there, and had spoken to him, and he had withdrawn his men from the palace, and they stood with us.

And the Khedive entered by the back door on the east side, and presently he came out to us with his generals and aides-de-camp, but I did not see Colvin with him, though he may have been there, and he called on me to dismount, and I dismounted, and he called on me to put up my sword, and I put up my sword, but the officers approached with me to prevent treachery, about fifty in number, and some of them placed themselves between him and the palace, but Riaz Pasha was not with the Khedive in the square, and remained in the palace. And when I had delivered my message and made my three demands to the Khedive, he said, "I am Khedive of the country and shall do as I like" (*"and Khedeywi 'l beled wa 'amal zey ma inni awze"*). I replied, "We are not slaves, and we shall never more be inherited from this day forth" (*"Nahnu ma abid wa la nurithu ba'd el yom"*). He said nothing more, but turned and went back into the palace. And presently they sent out Cookson to me with his interpreter, and he asked me why, being a soldier, I made demand of a parliament, and I said that it was to put an end to arbitrary rule, and pointed to the crowd of citizens supporting us behind the soldiers. He threatened me, saying, "We shall bring a British army," and much discussion took place between us, and he returned six or seven times to the palace, and came out again six or seven times to me, until finally he informed me that the Khedive had agreed to all, and the Khedive wished for Haidar Pasha to replace Riaz. But

I would not consent, and when it was put to me to say I named Sherif Pasha, because he had declared himself in favour of a Mejliss el Nawwab, and I had known him a little in former times, in the time of Saïd Pasha, when he served with the army. And in the evening the Khedive sent for me and I went to him at Ismaïlia Palace, and I thanked him for having agreed to our request, but he said only, "That is enough. Go now and occupy Abdin, and let it be without music in the streets" (lest that should be taken as a token of rejoicing).

And when Ali Pasha Nizami came to Cairo with Ahmed Pasha Ratib from the Sultan, the Khedive was alarmed lest an inquiry should be made, and Mahmud Sami being again Minister of War ordered us to leave Cairo, and I went to Ras-el-Wady and Abd-el-Aal to Damiata, but Ali Fehmy remained at Cairo. And I saw nothing of Ali Nizami. But being at Zagazig on a visit to friends, Ahmed Eff. Shemsi and Suliman Pasha Abaza, as I was returning by train to Ras el Wady, it happened that Ahmed Pasha Ratib was on his way to Suez, for he was going on to Mecca on pilgrimage. And I found myself in the same carriage with him, and we exchanged compliments as strangers, and I asked him his name, and he asked me my name, and he told me of his pilgrimage and other things, but he did not speak of his mission to the Khedive, nor did I ask. But I told him that I was loyal to the Sultan as the head of our religion, and I also related to him all that had occurred, and he said, "You did well." And at Ras el Wady I left him, and afterwards he sent me a Koran from Jeddah, and later, on his return to Stamboul, he wrote to me, saying that he had spoken favourably of me to the Sultan, and afterwards I received a letter dictated by the Sultan to Sheykh Mohammed Dhaffar telling me what I know.

As to Yakub Sami, he was of family originally Greek from Stamboul. He went by my order to Alexandria to inquire into the affair of the riot, but they would not allow a true inquiry to be made into it. It was Yakub Sami who, with Ragheb Pasha, proposed that we should cut off the Khedive's head. You say we should have done better to do so, but I wished to gain the end of our revolution without the shedding of a drop of blood.

APPENDIX II

Programme of the National Party of Egypt, forwarded by
Mr. Blunt to Mr. Gladstone, Dec. 20th, 1881,
with Mr. Gladstone's Answers

1. The National party of Egypt accept the existing relations of Egypt with the Porte as the basis of their movement. That is to say: They acknowledge the Sultan Abd el Hamid Khan as their Suzerain and Lord, and as actual Caliph or Head of the Mussulman religion; nor do they propose, while his empire stands, to alter this relationship. They admit the right of the Porte to the tribute fixed by law, and to military assistance in case of foreign war. At the same time, they are firmly determined to defend their national rights and privileges, and to oppose, by every means in their power, the attempts of those who would reduce Egypt again to the condition of a Turkish Pashalik. They trust in the protecting Powers of Europe, and especially in England, to continue their guarantee of Egypt's administrative independence.

2. The National party express their loyal allegiance to the person of the reigning Khedive. They will continue to support Mohammed Towfik's authority as long as he shall rule in accordance with justice and the law, and in fulfilment of his promises made to the people of Egypt in September 1881. They declare, however, their intention to permit no renewal of that despotic reign of injustice which Egypt has so often witnessed, and to insist upon the exact execution of his promise of Parliamentary government and of giving the country freedom. They invite His Highness, Mohammed Towfik, to act honestly by them in these matters, promising him their cordial help; but they warn him against listening to those who would persuade him to continue his despotic power, to betray their national rights, or to elude his promises.

3. The National party fully recognize the services rendered to Egypt by the Governments of England and France, and they are aware that all freedom and justice they have obtained in the past has been due to them. For this they tender them their thanks. They recognize the European Control as a necessity of their financial position, and the present continuance of it as the best guarantee of their prosperity. They declare their entire acceptance of the foreign debt as a matter of *national honour*—this, although they know that it was incurred, not for Egypt's benefit, but in the private interests of a dishonest and irresponsible ruler—and they are

ready to assist the Controllers in discharging the full national obligations. They look, nevertheless, upon the existing order of things as in its nature temporary, and avow it as their hope gradually to redeem the country out of the hands of its creditors. Their object is, some day to see Egypt entirely in Egyptian hands. Also they are not blind to the imperfections of the Control, which they are ready to point out. They know that many abuses are committed by those employed by it, whether Europeans or others. They see some of these incapable, others dishonest, others too highly paid. They know that many offices, now held by strangers, would be better discharged by Egyptians, and at a fifth of the cost; and they believe there is still much waste and much injustice. They cannot understand that Europeans living in the land should remain for ever exempt from the general taxation, or from obedience to the general law. The National party does not, however, propose to remedy these evils by any violent action; only it would protest against their unchecked continuance. They would have the Governments of France and England consider that, having taken the control of their finances out of the hands of the Egyptians, they are responsible for their prosperity, and are bound to see that efficient and honest persons only are employed by them.

4. The National party disclaim all connection with those who, in the interest of Powers jealous of Egypt's independence, seek to trouble the peace of the country—and there are many such—or with those who find their private advantage in disturbance. At the same time they are aware that a merely passive attitude will not secure them liberty in a land which is still ruled by a class to whom liberty is hateful. The silence of the people made Ismaïl Pasha's rule possible in Egypt, and silence now would leave their hope of political liberty unfulfilled. The Egyptians have learned in the last few years what freedom means, and they are resolved to complete their national education. This they look to find in the Parliament just assembling, in a fair measure of freedom for the press, and in the general growth of knowledge among all classes of the people. They know, however, that none of these means of education can be secured except by the firm attitude of the national leaders. The Egyptian Parliament may be cajoled or frightened into silence, as at Constantinople; the press may be used as an instrument against them, and the sources of instruction cut off. It is for this reason and for no other that the National party has confided its interests at the present time to the army, believing them to be the only power in the country able and willing to protect its growing liberties. It is not, however, in the plans of the party that this state of things shall continue; and as soon as the people shall have established their rights securely the army will abandon its present political attitude. In this the military leaders fully concur.

They trust that on the assembling of the Parliament their further interference in affairs of State may be unnecessary. But for the present they will continue to perform their duty as the armed guardians of the unarmed people. Such being their position, they hold it imperative that their force should be maintained efficient, and their complement made up to the full number of 18,000 men. They trust that the European Control will keep this necessity in view when considering the army estimates.

5. The National party of Egypt is a political, not a religious party. It includes within its ranks men of various races and various creeds. It is principally Mohammedan, because nine-tenths of the Egyptians are Mohammedans; but it has the support of the Moors, of the Coptic Christians, of the Jews, and others who cultivate the soil and speak the language of Egypt. Between these it makes no distinction whatever, holding all men to be brothers and to have equal rights, both political and before the law. This principle is accepted by all the chief Sheykhs of the Azhar who support the party, holding the true law of Islam to forbid religious hatred and religious disabilities. With Europeans resident in Egypt the National party has no quarrel, either as Christians or as strangers, so long as these shall live comformably with the laws and bear their share of the burdens of the State.

6. Finally, the general end of the National party is the intellectual and moral regeneration of the country by a better observance of the law, by increased education, and by political liberty, which they hold to be the life of the people. They trust in the sympathy of those of the nations of Europe which enjoy the blessing of self-government to aid Egypt in gaining for itself that blessing; but they are aware that no nation ever yet achieved liberty except by its own endeavours; and they are resolved to stand firm in the position they have won, trusting to God's help if all other be denied them.

December 18, 1881.

MR. GLADSTONE'S ANSWER

Hawarden Castle, Chester,
Jan. 20th, 1882.

MY DEAR SIR,

You will I am sure appreciate the reasons which disable me from offering anything like a becoming reply to your very interesting letter on Egyptian affairs, which occupy, I am sorry to say, an insignificant share of my daily attention.

But I am sensible of the advantage of having such a letter from such an authority, and I feel quite sure that unless there be a sad failure of good sense on one or both, or, as I should say, all sides, we shall be enabled to bring this question to a favourable issue.

My own opinions about Egypt were set forth in the "19th Century" a short time before we took office, and I am not aware as yet of having seen any reason to change them.

I remain, my Dear Sir,
Faithfully yours,
W. E. GLADSTONE.

Wilfrid S. Blunt, Esq.

10, Downing Street, Whitehall,
Jan. 21st, 1882.

MY DEAR WILFRID,

I feel I owe you a great apology for your not having received an earlier acknowledgment of your most able and interesting communication on the Egyptian movement. Holiday making must be my excuse; but my absence from Downing Street did not prevent the prompt submission of your letter to Mr. Gladstone, from whom I enclose a note. He is sorry that it is somewhat tardy in its despatch.

It is difficult, if not impossible, to write on the present critical state of affairs, when the situation may alter from day to day.

You may imagine that the alleged national character to the movement necessarily commends itself to Mr. Gladstone with his well-known sympathy with young nationalities struggling for independence. The great crux (I am of course only speaking for myself, and with a strong consciousness of ignorance) seems to be, how to favour such a movement with due regard to the responsibilities in which we have been involved, and the vested interests which are at stake. Every alternative seems to be beset with insuperable objections and insurmountable difficulties. I can only say that if you can do anything towards finding a solution for these difficulties you will be doing a great work for Egypt, for the country, and for the present Government. I know that you have already been of great service, and are entitled to speak on this question with greater authority than almost any one else.

With special regards to Lady Anne, and apologies for such a cursory uninteresting note in return for your information,

Always yrs. affectionately
E. W. HAMILTON.

MR. GLADSTONE'S ANSWER TO MR. BLUNT'S SECOND LETTER
DATED CAIRO, FEBRUARY 7TH, 1882

10, Downing Street, Whitehall,
2nd March, 1882.

MY DEAR WILFRID, .

Mr. Gladstone has read with much interest your further letter, for which he is much obliged. He hopes that you will have felt, or will feel, assured from the language in the speech from the Throne, of which I enclose by his desire a copy, that the British Government, while intending firmly to uphold international engagements, have a sympathy with Egyptian feelings in reference to the purposes and means of good government.

Yours always,
E. W. HAMILTON.

EXTRACT FROM THE QUEEN'S SPEECH FORWARDED TO MR.
BLUNT BY MR. HAMILTON

In concert with the President of the French Republic, I have given careful attention to the affairs of Egypt, where existing arrangements have imposed on me special obligations. I shall use my influence to maintain the rights already established, whether by the Firmans of the Sultan or by various international engagements, in a spirit favourable to the good government of the country and the prudent development of its institutions.

APPENDIX III

TEXT OF THE EGYPTIAN CONSTITUTION OF FEBRUARY 7TH,
1882

(*N.B.*—This occurs in Blue Book, Egypt, No. 7 (1882), but is given there in French only. The clauses embodying the amendments or explanations obtained at Sir Edward Malet's and Sir Auckland Colvin's instance by the author on January 19th, 1882, are marked with an asterisk.)

LETTER FROM MAHMOUD SAMY PASHA ON TAKING OFFICE,
FEBRUARY 2ND, 1882, TO HIS HIGHNESS THE KHEDIVE

MONSEIGNEUR,

Your Highness has condescended to entrust to me the care of forming a new Cabinet; I consider it as the first of my duties to submit to you the principles which will guide my conduct and inspire that of the Ministry over which I am to preside.

The events which have succeeded each other in Egypt for some years past have prejudiced public opinion in various ways here, and in foreign countries. These prejudices relate to two orders of ideas: our financial expenditure and our internal reforms.

The general debt of the country was definitely regulated by a series of Decrees which was itself completed by the Law of Liquidation of 19th July, 1880.

These laws have acquired the character of International Conventions. Your Highness's Government has never ceased to respect them. The Ministry will watch over their exact and faithful execution.

The liquidation of the floating debt is an accomplished fact for all those interested (and they are immensely in the majority) whose rights have been recognized up to now by the competent authorities; it will continue to be actively proceeded with.

The service of the Consolidated Debt, which includes the special administrations of the Daïra and the Domains employed to guarantee the Loan of 1878 is being regularly performed. The administrations which were created to secure this service, the General Control, the Commission of the Debt, the Control of the Daïra, the Commission of Domains, are institutions which must be always loyally supported by the Government; they have always been so up to the present day.

Nothing will be changed in this state of things in the future: the Ministry will endeavour to consolidate these institutions and to facilitate their action. It considers harmony in all these public services as an essential condition to the regular course of affairs, and it thinks that the general administration of the country owes incontestable advantages to this policy.

Your Highness has always been convinced that, to accomplish internal reforms with wisdom and security, the co-operation of a Chamber of Deputies was necessary, and it is with this idea that the present Chamber has been convoked.

The Ministry share these sentiments. They will concentrate all their attention upon the reorganization of the Tribunals, the reform of the administration, the improvements necessary to public education to aid the country to advance in the path of progress and civilization. They will study measures suitable for the development of agriculture, commerce, and industry, as well as all the other projects of reform which have been the object of your Highness's constant solicitude. But before all they believe it necessary to determine the powers of the Chamber of Deputies, in order to enable it to give to the Government the co-operation which it expects, and to realize the hopes of the people.

This is why the Cabinet's first act will be to sanction an Organic Law for the Chamber of Deputies.

This law will respect all rights and obligations of a private or international character, as well as all engagements relating to the Public Debt and to the charges which the latter imposes upon the State Budget. It will determine wisely the responsibility of the Ministers before the Chamber, as well as the mode of discussing the laws.

Far from being a source of anxiety, this Organic Law will unite all the conditions necessary for securing the interests of the public.

Such is, Monseigneur, the programme of the new Ministry, conformable to the wishes of the country.

The High Powers—and particularly the Sublime Porte, whose friendly support has never failed us in the exercise of the rights and privileges which it has granted us—will continue, I confidently hope, to lend to your Highness's Government, as in the past, that valuable co-operation which has always been beneficial to Egypt.

I also hope that the authority of your Government will be devoted solely to safeguarding individual rights and the maintenance of order, and that it will guide the nation in the way of progress and prosperity.

The day on which your Highness took in hand the reins of power you promised to Egypt a new era of progress. We come to assure your Highness of our absolute unanimity for the realization of that promise. The goal you would attain, Monseigneur, is the same which we are striving for. Full of confidence in you, we have faith in the future.

If your Highness deigns to consent to the programme which I submit, I have the honour to beg your Highness to sanction the decrees which I present for signature, to constitute the Ministry.

MAHMOUD SAMY.

LETTER FROM HIS HIGHNESS THE KHEDIVE TO HIS EXCELLENCE
MAHMOUD SAMY PASHA

15, Rabi-Awel, 1299.
(February 4, 1882.)

MY DEAR MAHMOUD SAMY PASHA,

In accepting the task of forming a new Cabinet, without being ignorant of the importace of this undertaking, you give a new proof of your devotion and of your patriotism. If I have charged you with this mission, it is because I knew these your noble sentiments of which you have given many proofs, by the numerous services you have rendered in the various offices you have already filled. I approve of your programme, and of the principles which you develop in it. These principles are the foundation of justice. They are calculated to maintain and assure order in the country as well to give security to all those who inhabit it.

I share your opinion that my Government should take the necessary measures to ensure judicial and administrative reforms, and that it should promulgate for the Chamber of Deputies the Organic Law in conformity with the ideas explained in your programme.

My Government ought also to take upon itself the task of developing public instruction, agriculture, commerce, and industry. My loyal and sincere co-operation shall always be yours in the accomplishment of this object.

I pray God to crown our common efforts for the benefit and prosperity of the people.

MEHEMET TEWFIK.

DECREE

We, Khedive of Egypt,

In view of our Decree of the 4th October, 1881 (11 Zilcadé, 1298),

In view of the decision of the Chamber of Delegates, and conformably with the advice of our Council of Ministers,

Have decreed and decree,

Art. 1. The Members of the Chamber of Deputies are elected. An ulterior and special Law will make known the conditions of electorability and of eligibility for election, and at the same time the mode of election to the Chamber of Deputies.

Art. 2. The Members of the Chamber of Deputies are elected for a period of five years. They receive an annual payment of £E.100.

Art. 3. The Deputies are free in the exercise of their mandates They cannot be bound either by promises or by (government) instructions, or by an (administrative) order, or by menaces of a nature to interfere with the free expression of their opinions.

Art. 4. The Deputies are inviolable. In case of crime or misdemeanour committed during the course of the Session, they cannot be put under arrest except with the leave of the Chamber.

Art. 5. The Chamber may also, after its convocation, demand, provisionally and for the duration of the Session, that any one of its Members who has been imprisoned shall be set at liberty, or that all action directed against him shall be suspended during the Chamber's recess, if for a criminal matter, where no judgment has yet been pronounced.

Art. 6. Each Deputy represents not only the interests of the constituency which has elected him, but also the interests of the Egyptian people in general.

Art. 7. The Chamber of Deputies shall sit at Cairo. It is convoked each year by Decree of the Khedive, and according to the advice of the Council of Ministers.

Art. 8. The ordinary annual Session of the Chamber of Deputies shall be for three months, viz., from the 1st November to the 31st January. But if the work of the Chamber is not finished by the 31st January, it may then demand a prolongation of fifteen to thirty days. This prolongation will be accorded by Decree of the Khedive.

Art. 9. In case of necessity the Chamber will be convoked in Extraordinary Session by the Khedive. The duration of the Extraordinary Session will be fixed by the Decree convoking it.

Art. 10. The Sessions of the Chamber shall be opened in the presence of the Ministers either by the Khedive or by the President of the Council of Ministers, acting by delegation of the Khedive.

Art. 11. At the first sitting of each annual Session an opening Speech shall be pronounced by the Khedive, or in his name by the President of the Council of Ministers. It shall have for its object to make known to the Chamber the principal questions to be presented to it in the course of the session. Afer the reading of the opening speech the sitting shall be adjourned.

Art. 12. During the three following days, the Chamber, having named a Committee for the purpose of preparing a reply to the opening speech, shall vote its reply, which shall be presented to the Khedive by a deputation chosen from amongst its members,

Art. 13. The reply to the opening speech may not treat of any question in a decisive sense, nor contain any opinion which has been the object of previous deliberations.

Art. 14. The Chamber shall submit to the Khedive a list containing the names of three Members whom it may propose for the office of President. The Khedive shall name by Decree one of the Members, thus designated, President of the Chamber of Deputies. The office of President shall continue for five years.

Art. 15. The Chamber shall elect two Vice-Presidents which it shall choose from among its Members, and shall name the Secretaries of its Bureau.

Art. 16. An official report of the sittings of the Chamber shall be drawn up under the direction of the Bureau of the Chamber, composed of its President, Vice-President, and Secretaries.

Art. 17. The official language for the Chamber shall be Arabic. The proceedings and reports of the Chamber shall be drawn up in the official language.

Art. 18. The Ministers shall have the right of being present at the sittings of the Chamber, and of speaking there, when they shall think fit. They may cause themselves to be represented there by high state officials.

Art. 19. If the Chamber decides that there is reason for summoning one of the Ministers to appear before it to give explanations on any question, the Minister shall apear in person or cause himself to be represented by another official to give the required explanations.

**Art.* 20. The Deputies shall have the right to supervise the acts of all public functionaries during the Session, and through the President of the Chamber they may report to the Minister concerned all abuses, irregularities, or negligences charged against a public official, in the exercise of his functions.

Art. 21. The Ministers are jointly and severally responsible to the Chamber for every measure taken in Council, which may violate existing rules and regulations.

Art. 22. Each Minister is individually responsible, in the cases foreseen in the preceding article, for his acts occurring in the exercise of his functions.

**Art.* 23. In case of persistent disagreement between the Chamber of Deputies and the Ministry; when repeated interchanges of views and motives shall have taken place between them, if then the Ministry does not withdraw, the Khedive shall dissolve the Chamber of Deputies, and decree that new elections shall be proceeded with, within a period of time not exceeding three months, counted from the day of dissolution to that of reassembly. All Deputies thus dismissed shall be eligible for reelection.

Art. 24. If the new Chamber confirms by its vote that of the preceding Chamber which had provoked the disagreement, this vote shall be accepted as final.

*Art. 25. The Bills and Regulations emanating from the initiative of the Government shall be brought into the Chamber of Deputies by the Ministers, to be examined, discussed and voted. No Law shall become valid until it has been read before the Chamber of Deputies, Article by Article, voted clause by clause, and consented to by the Khedive. Each Bill shall be read three times and between each reading there shall have been an interval of fifteen days. In case of urgency a single reading shall, by a special vote of the Chamber, be declared sufficient. If the Chamber judges it necessary to demand the introduction of a Bill from the Council of Ministers, it shall make the demand through the intermediary of the President of the Chamber, and in case of the approval of the Government, the Bill shall be prepared by the Ministry and introduced to the Chamber according to the forms fixed by this Article.

Art. 26. The Chamber shall choose from amongst its Members a Committee, charged to examine all Bills and Regulations submitted to it. This Committee may propose to the Government amendments of such bills as it has been charged to examine; in which case, the bill and the amendments proposed shall be sent back, before any general discussion, by the President of the Chamber, to the President of the Council of Ministers.

Art. 27. If the Committee does not propose any amendments or if those proposed are not adopted by the Government, the original text of the Bill shall be placed for discussion before the Chamber. If the amendments proposed by the Committee are accepted by the Government, then the text thus amended shall be placed for discussion before the Chamber. In case the Government should not accept the amendments proposed by the Committee, then the latter shall have the right of submitting its opinion and observations to the Chamber.

Art. 28. The Chamber of Deputies may adopt or reject all Bills submitted to it by the Committee. It may also return them to the Committee to be examined a second time.

Art. 29. The President of the Chamber shall convey to the President of the Council of Ministers the Laws and Regulations voted by the Chamber.

Art. 30. No fresh tax—direct or indirect—on movable, immovable or personal property may be imposed in Egypt without a Law voted by the Chamber. It is therefore formally forbidden that any new tax shall be levied, under whatever title or denomination it may be, without having been previously voted by the Chamber of Deputies, under penalty, against the authority which shall have ordered it, against the employés who shall have drawn up the schedules and tariffs and against those who shall have effected the recovery of the amounts, of being prosecuted as peculators. All contributions thus unduly levied shall be returned to those who have paid them.

Art. 31. The Annual Budget of the Receipts and Expenditures of the State shall be communicated to the Chamber of Deputies not later than the 5th of November of each year.

Art. 32. The General Budget of Receipts shall be presented to the Chamber, accompanied by notes explanatory of the nature of each receipt.

Art. 33. The Budget of Expenditure shall be divided Department by Department, and shall be subdivided into sections and chapters, corresponding to the various branches of the public service depending upon each Ministry.

Art. 34. The following cannot on any account be objects of discussion in the Chamber:

The service of the Tribute due to the Sublime Porte.

The service of the Public Debt.

Also all matters relating to the Debt and resulting from the Law of Liquidation, or Conventions existing between the Foreign Powers and the Egyptian Government.

*Art. 35. The Budget shall be sent to the Chamber, to be examined and discussed there (under reserve of the preceding Article).

A Committee composed of as many Deputies, and having the same number of votes as the Members of the Council of Ministers and its President, shall be named by the Chamber to discuss, in common with the Council of Ministers, the Budget Estimates, and to vote them either unanimously or according to the majority.

Art. 36. In case of an exact division of votes between the Commission of the Chamber and the Council of Ministers, the Budget shall be returned to the Chamber and, should the Chamber confirm (by its vote) that of the Council of Ministers, this vote shall become executory *(executoire)*. But if the Chamber should maintain the vote of its Committee, then the procedure shall be according to Articles 23 and 24 of the present Law. In this case, the credits of the Budget Estimates which shall have caused the division of votes, if they figured in the Budget of the preceding year, and if they are not affected to any new object of expenditure, such as public works or others, shall be employed provisionally and until the meeting of the new Chamber, according to Article 23.

Art. 37. If the new Chamber confirms the vote of the preceding

Chamber, on the Budget, this vote shall become definitely executory, in conformity with Article 23.

Art. 38. No Treaty or contract between the Government and third parties and no farming concession shall acquire a final character without having been first approved by a vote of the Chamber, provided that such Treaty, contract or concession does not relate to an object for which a sum has already figured in the approved Budget, corresponding to the year for which the Treaty, contract or concession shall have been proposed. Likewise no concession for public works, the execution of which shall not have been foreseen by the Budget, and no sale, or gratuitous alienation of the State domains, nor concession of privilege of any kind shall become definitive until it shall have been approved by the Chamber.

Art. 39. All Egyptians may address a petition to the Chamber of Deputies. The petitions shall be sent to a Committee chosen by the Chamber from among its Members. Upon the report of this Committee the Chamber shall take into consideration or reject the petitions. The petitions taken into consideration shall be sent back to the Minister concerned.

Art. 40. All petitions relative to personal rights or interests shall be rejected if they are outside the competence of the Administrative and Civil Tribunals, or if they have not been previously addressed to the competent administrative authority.

Art. 41. If during the recess of the Chamber grave circumstances shall demand that urgent measures be taken to avoid a danger menacing the State, or to assure public order, the Council of Ministers may, then, upon its own responsibility and with the sanction of the Khedive, order those measures to be taken, even if they should be within the competence of the Chamber, supposing the time to be too short for the convocation of the latter. Nevertheless, the affair should be submitted for examination, at its next sitting, to the Chamber.

Art. 42. No one may be admitted to explain or discuss questions or to take part in the deliberations of the Chamber other than its Members, with the exception of the Ministers or of those who are assisting or representing them.

Art. 43. The votes of the Chamber shall be given by the holding up of hands or by calling over of names or by ballot.

Art. 44. The vote by calling over of names shall only be on the demand of at least ten Members of the Chamber of Deputies. All votes which may affect the provisions of Article 47 shall be made openly.

Art. 45. The naming of the three candidates for the Presidency of the Chamber, as well as the election of the two Vice-Presidents and the nomination of the first and second Secretaries to the Chamber shall be made by ballot.

Art. 46. The Chamber of Deputies may not validly deliberate unless at least two-thirds of its Members are present at the deliberation. All decisions shall be taken absolutely according to the majority of votes.

Art. 47. No votes entailing Ministerial responsibility shall be given without a majority of at least three-quarters of the Members present.

Art. 48. No opinion shall be given by proxy.

Art. 49. The Chamber of Deputies shall elaborate its own internal Regulations. These shall be made executory by Decree of the Khedive.

*Art. 50. The present Organic Law may be amended after agreement between the Chamber of Deputies and the Council of Ministers.

*Art. 51. The interpretation of all Articles and phrases of the present law which it may be necessary to make clear shall be made on agreement between the Chamber of Deputies and the Council of Ministers.

Art. 52. All provisions of Laws, Decrees, Superior Orders, Regulations, or Usages contrary to the present Law are and shall remain revoked.

Art. 53. Our Ministers are charged, each in what concerns him, with the execution of the present Law.

> Done in the Palace of Ismaïlieh, 7th February, 1882
> (18 Rabi Awel, 1299).
> *(Signed)* MEHEMET TEWFIK.

By the Khedive:

The President of the Council of Ministers, Minister of the Interior.
(Signed) MAHMOUD SAMY.

The Minister of Foreign Affairs and of Justice.
MOUSTAPHA FEHMY.

The Minister of War and Marine.
AHMED ARABI.

The Minister of Finance.
ALI SADIK.

The Minister of Public Works.
MAHMOUD FEHMY.

The Minister of Public Instruction.
ABDALLAH FIKRY.

The Minister of the Wakfs.
HASSAN CHÉRÉY.

APPENDIX IV

LETTER RECEIVED BY MR. BLUNT FROM BOGHOS PASHA NUBAR AS TO HIS FATHER NUBAR PASHA'S POLITICAL CONNECTION WITH THE KHEDIVE ISMAÏL. (TRANSLATED FROM THE FRENCH.)

Paris, *September 26th,* 1907.

SIR,

I have just read in the *Egyptian Gazette* of the 14th instant your reply to Mr. Lucy about the Cyprus Convention, and I was very glad to observe the offer you made in it of correcting in your book any errors which might be pointed out to you. It has decided me to appeal to your loyalty in regard to a mistake about my father which has found its way into it. I do not know from what sources you have drawn your information, nor do I doubt your good faith, which has certainly been misled.

You say that Nubar Pasha was Ismaïl's Minister of Finance, and that in virtue of this office he was responsible for the ruinous loans contracted by the latter. This is evidently a complete mistake, my father never having been Minister of Finance, and having had nothing to do directly or indirectly with any of the loans.

The only offices which he filled during Ismaïl's reign were the Ministry of Public Works and the Ministry of Foreign Affairs. He was never, I repeat, Minister of Finance, for this very good reason that, in spite of his great intelligence and qualities as a statesman, he recognized that he did not understand financial questions, and the Khedive, who also knew it, would never have thought of confiding a Ministry to him, which he himself felt he was incapable of directing.

Ismaïl's Minister of Finance was the Moufettish Ismaïl Pasha Sadek, whom you speak of on pages 18, 39 and 40 of your book. He was the sole collaborator and confidant of the Khedive upon financial matters, and it was he who organized the loans.

As to my father, I think what will best show you how entirely he was a stranger to financial administration, is a simple *resumé* of his career, under Ismaïl, which I shall try to condense into a few lines.

"In the very first year of Ismaïl's accession, 1863, Nubar Pasha was sent on a mission to Paris to regulate the differences relating to the Suez Canal. He remained there two years, and upon his return to Egypt he was appointed, first, Minister of Public Works, and then, Minister for Foreign Affairs. A year later, in 1866, he went once more on a

397

mission to Europe, and remained three years absent. It was during this period that he obtained the Firman of 1867, granting to Egypt administrative autonomy, the right of making Customs Conventions with the Powers, and the title of Khedive for the Viceroy. It was at this time, too, that he commenced the first negotiations for Judicial Reform with the Powers. He did not return to Egypt until 1869, and then for six months only, in order to assist at the opening of the Suez Canal, and preside at the Commission of Inquiry for Judicial Reform which was sitting at Cairo, and he returned to Paris in 1870 to continue there the negotiations for the Reform. These negotiations, begun in 1867, lasted until 1875, about eight years, during which time Nubar Pasha lived almost entirely in Europe, with the exception of short intervals of a few months in Egypt. In 1874 he was dismissed by the Khedive on account of a difference of opinion relative to the said negotiations, and he remained in Europe without employment for a year. He was recalled by Ismaïl to the Ministry for Foreign Affairs in June, 1875. Six months later, he was again dismissed, January, 1876. He then remained two years in Europe, exiled, and did not return until 1878, when recalled by the Khedive to form the Mixed Ministry in conjunction with Sir Rivers Wilson."

My father declares in his memoirs, which I hope one day to be able to publish, that during the fifteen years of Ismaïl's reign, he spent twelve in Europe on missions, on leave of absence, or in exile. The dates and facts which I have recited above prove the accuracy of this statement. During all these absences from Egypt, Nubar Pasha, exclusively occupied with his negotiations, could not take any part in the interior affairs of the country, about which he was not even consulted. Thus, while in Paris in 1869, he learnt from M. Béhic, Minister of Public Works to the Emperor Napoleon III, in the course of a conversation with him relative to the Judicial Reform, that the Khedive had just arranged a loan of ten millions sterling, of which my father had not even been informed; and again, at Constantinople in 1873, where he was pursuing his negotiations for the Reform, it was indirectly that he learned that the Khedive was negotiating a fresh loan of thirty millions.

You see, Sir, by these facts, which it will be easy for you to verify, that not only was my father never Minister of Finance, nor connected with the Khedive's loans, but that all his energy, his talents and the influence which he had acquired were employed in negotiations abroad: (1) for the regulation of the question of the Suez Canal, which culminated in the arbitration of Napoleon III, through which Egypt obtained a verdict for the abolition of forced labour in the making of the Canal; (2) for obtaining Firmans from the Sublime Porte; (3) for the Judicial Reform which was his conception and his work, and to which he consecrated all his energy, his intelligence, and the best years of his life. I must also add that he continued to work zealously for the abolition of forced labour while Director of Railways and at the Ministry of Public Works. This we owe in large measure to him, as Sir W. Wilcocks so courteously testifies in his book on the Irrigation of Egypt.

Do you not think, Sir, that I have a right under these circumstances to appeal to your courtesy in asking you to rectify in the new edition of your book the erroneous passages which I have mentioned? You cannot fail to see the importance which I attach to these corrections, for it would not be just, in a work bearing upon history, for my father to be held responsible for government measures to which he was altogether a stranger.

My father in the course of his laborious career made many friends, but also many enemies, as all politicians do. His enemies have not failed to spread calumnies about him and to invent stories. I will only cite two: First, that concerning his nationality. His political adversaries, in the interest of their cause, successively reproached him with being an English and a German subject! These allegations, the object of which was to discredit him in the course of his negotiations for Judicial Reform by contesting, though he was a Minister of the Khedive, his Egyptian nationality, have been since recognized as being without any foundation. Another legend relates to his supposed immense fortune. The most calumnious and fantastic assertions have been made with regard to this, generally by people who were interested in tarnishing the memory of an adversary by leaving it to be understood that such great wealth could only have been acquired by unlawful means. They did not hesitate to say and write that he possessed more than four millions sterling. Although I have not condescended up to now to reply to calumnies which have appeared in newspapers, there is no reason why I should not give you, for your personal information, the precise facts and figures.

At his death my father left a fortune of £155,000, having settled upon my mother during his lifetime a personal fortune amounting to an equal sum. Thus the four millions, at which the most moderate estimators valued what he possessed, were not in reality more than about £300,000. This is a fact which can easily be verified, for the Deed of Partition of his inheritance—there being children who were minors among the heirs— was registered at the Mixed Tribunal at Cairo.

It is equally easy to show the sources from which this fortune was derived. It consisted of donations, which he had received from the Khedive in recompense for services rendered, and of an exceptionally fortunate investment of a part of these donations.

By the *resumé* which I have given of his career, you will see the importance of the services he rendered to his country and the results obtained by his various negotiations. The Khedive did not fail to recompense him, as he had recompensed others of his Ministers, and as the British Parliament has recently done for Lord Cromer by voting him a donation of

£50,000. Thus he received, upon the successful result of the negotiations relating to the Suez Canal, the Firman of 1867 and the Judicial Reform, various recompenses consisting of sums of money, of a property of nine hundred acres, and of a house in Alexandria—the whole being of the value of about £80,000.

My father had the fortunate inspiration, at the creation of the Cairo Water Company, of which he was President, to invest an important part of this sum, £25,000, in shares of the Company; and this investment alone sufficed to raise his fortune to the sum I have indicated, for it is a matter of public knowledge that the Cairo Water Company's shares had gone up to ten times their value at the date of Nubar Pasha's death.

I will end by begging you to excuse my having written you so long a letter, but your offer of rectification proves your anxiety to be impartial and has authorized my doing so. Thanking you in advance, therefore, for the corrections which my information will enable you to make, I beg you will accept, Sir, etc.,

BOGHOS NUBAR.

Note.—I am glad to have obtained Boghos Pasha's permission to publish the whole of this interesting letter, and regret that I cannot, at the late date of my receiving it, make any alteration in the text of this edition, such as he at first suggested. I think, however, that the letter, published in full, will be found more satisfactory than a mere omission of the passages it corrects could possibly have been.

W. S. B.

APPENDIX V

NOTE AS TO THE BERLIN CONGRESS.

It has been pointed out by Mr. Lucy, in the *Westminster Gazette,* that the account given in the text, page 34, of the quarrel between M. Waddington and Lord Salisbury, at the Berlin Congress, is manifestly incorrect, inasmuch as it was the Anglo-Russian agreement of 31st May, not the Cyprus Convention with Turkey of 4th June, that was published by the *Globe* newspaper through the instrumentality of Marvin, the Cyprus Convention being issued in the ordinary way. The confusion between the two instruments in the text is undeniable and needs correction. At the same time the result of as full an enquiry as I have been able to make into the affair, by a reference to contemporary documents, is not such as to make me doubt the substantial truth of the story. What seems precisely to have happened is this:

Lords Beaconsfield and Salisbury, before entering the Congress, had concluded two separate agreements, both secret, regarding Ottoman affairs—the one with Russia, the other with Turkey. These while conceding something to Russia, would, they thought, conjointly secure the integrity of the Sultan's dominions on the Asiatic side against further aggression. The agreement with Russia recognized her permanent possession of Batum, but was more than counterbalanced, in their opinion, by the second Convention, unknown to the Russian Government as to the rest of the world, guaranteeing the remainder of his Asiatic dominions under English protection to the Sultan. The two treaties were drafted at the Foreign Office almost simultaneously, and by accident or negligence that with Russia became known, the very day it was signed, to M. Charles Marvin, a poor journalist and teacher of languages, who had been taken on as extra Writer for his knowledge of Russian in the Treaty Department at the Foreign Office. Marvin, who was wretchedly underpaid at the rate of tenpence an hour, had been intrusted with the copying of the agreement, and yielded to the temptation of betraying a summary of it to his employers in the Press. This was on the 31st May, a fortnight before the Congress met.

For some days after this Marvin seems to have remained on unsuspected at the Foreign Office, it being imagined at first that it was perhaps Count Schouvalof himself, the Russian ambassador in London, who had given the information to the Press. Later, seeing that the summary was no more than a summary, and had appeared in one newspaper only, the *Globe,* it was resolved to deny it; and Lord Salisbury had little difficulty in persuading the House of Lords and the country that it lacked authenticity. In answer to a question put to him about it by Lord Grey, Lord Salisbury declared roundly "the statement to which the noble Earl refers, and other statements that have been made that I have seen, are wholly unauthenticated and are not deserving of the confidence of your Lordship's House."

Nevertheless, the incident raised a suspicion of England's good faith abroad, and, doubtless was the cause of the declaration, mentioned in the text, being demanded of the Ambassadors at the first sitting of the Congress. This must have been subscribed to by Lords Beaconsfield and Salisbury on the 13th June, the other dates being:

The Agreement with Russia, signed in London, 31st May.

The *Globe* summary, published in the evening of the same day, 31st May.

Lord Salisbury's denial in the House of Lords, 3rd June.

First sitting of the Berlin Congress, 13th June.

Publication by the *Globe* of the full text of the Agreement, on evening
of 14th June.

Lord Beaconsfield's and Lord Salisbury's discomfiture must consequently have been still more sudden than in my account of it when the
news became public property at Berlin on the 15th; and doubtless the
sensation caused there was primarily on account of the Agreement, not of
the Convention, which latter was not published till 8th July. All the
same I still adhere to my recollection of the letter shown me at Simla
that it was the Cyprus Convention that was the main cause of M. Waddington's resentment, and of Lord Salisbury's concession to him about
Tunis and the rest. That it was so is confirmed to me by a passage in
my diary of 1884, when, being at Constantinople and having just had a
conversation with Count Corti on the subject, I made the following entry.
It must be remembered that the Count had been Italian ambassador at the
Berlin Congress, and was actually ambassador to the Sultan at the date
of the conversation; nor was he other than a friendly witness, for he
was always regarded as an *Anglomane* and ally of our British diplomacy.

"*October* 26. Count Corti came to take us in a steam launch to The-
rapia. We had luncheon with the Wyndhams, and called on the Noailles
(at the English and French Embassies). . . . On our way back to Constantinople Count Corti entertained us with stories of the Berlin Congress
and of Lord Salisbury's antics there. Disraeli and Salisbury had gone
there quite on their high horse to curb the territorial ambitions of Russia,
and the publication of the secret convention for the acquisition of Cyprus
was a great shock to everybody. Salisbury broke it gently to Waddington
before the news was published, and Waddington consulted his colleagues, it
being generally agreed that there was no middle course between going to war
and saying nothing. 'Il faut la guerre ou se taire.' But the publication
was a great blow to Disraeli, who took to his bed and did not appear for
four or five days. Lord Salisbury, however, brazened it out, and came
to the Congress with an air of defiance. There was no rupture between
him and Waddington, and they remained on apparently friendly terms,
but Waddington had his revenge. He was sitting one day with Salisbury,
and, the conversation leading that way, Waddington asked what the
English Government would say to France taking Tunis, and Salisbury
said he did not see the harm. Whereupon Waddington communicated
this to Paris, and on his return the French ambassador in London was
instructed to write to Lord Salisbury reminding him of his words. Thus
Salisbury was caught. 'But,' said Corti, 'if he had known anything of
his business he would have declined to answer the note officially and would

have pleaded a private conversation.' He did not believe that any arrangement of *condominium* was come to between Salisbury and Waddington at that time, though I told him, without mentioning names, of the letter Lytton had shown me. Corti is interesting diplomatically, as he has been to more congresses than any man in Europe."

This entry, which is a contemporary record of Count Corti's recollection of the incident, five years after it happened, shows that the two secret agreements had remained closely connected in his mind as the cause of Waddington's displeasure. They certainly were present in the Duke of Richmond's mind when, representing the Foreign Office on 17th June, in answer to a further question about the authenticity of the full text of the Anglo-Russian Agreement, he said "as an explanation of the policy of Her Majesty's Government it is *incomplete* and therefore inaccurate," for this *incompleteness* can only be understood as an allusion to the Cyprus Convention in 1878, and the seizure of Tunis by France in 1881, which after all is the important matter. Some day, no doubt, the whole incident will be made clear by a publication of the secret records at the Foreign Office or at the Quai d'Orsay. In the meantime we may accept it as probable that, finding the Russian Agreement divulged, Lord Salisbury resolved to make a clean breast also of the other Agreement, and, in Count Corti's words, broke gently to M. Waddington the existence also of a Convention with Turkey. One thing I am certain of in my recollection, that the letter shown me at Simla described the quarrel and the terms obtained in the reconciliation with M. Waddington.

The Cyprus Convention was published in London on the 9th July, having been signed on the 4th June, but there is evidence of its having been in Lord Beaconsfield's thoughts at least three months earlier, for Lord Derby, speaking in the Lords, 18th July, gave it as his reason for leaving the Cabinet in March that the policy of the Government had become such, that it was already, at that date, being considered necessary "to seize and occupy the island of Cyprus."

W. S. B.

APPENDIX VI

THE WIND AND THE WHIRLWIND

A POEM BY WILFRID SCAWEN BLUNT
PUBLISHED 1883

I

I have a thing to say. But how to say it?
  I have a cause to plead. But to what ears?
How shall I move a world by lamentation—
  A world which heeded not a Nation's tears?

How shall I speak of justice to the aggressors,—
  Of right to Kings whose rights include all wrong,—
Of truth to Statecraft, true but in deceiving,—
  Of peace to Prelates, pity to the Strong?

Where shall I find a hearing? In high places?
  The voice of havock drowns the voice of good.
On the throne's steps? The elders of the nation
  Rise in their ranks and call aloud for blood.

Where? In the street? Alas for the world's reason!
  Not Peers not Priests alone this deed have done.
The clothes of those high Hebrews stoning Stephen
  Were held by all of us,—ay every one.

Yet none the less I speak. Nay, here by Heaven
  This task at least a poet best may do,—
To stand alone against the mighty many,
  To force a hearing for the weak and few.

Unthanked, unhonoured,—yet a task of glory,—
  Not in his day, but in an age more wise,
When those poor Chancellors have found their portion
  And lie forgotten in their dust of lies.

And who shall say that this year's cause of freedom
  Lost on the Nile has not as worthy proved
Of poet's hymning as the cause which Milton
  Sang in his blindness or which Dante loved?

The fall of Guelph beneath the spears of Valois,
  Freedom betrayed, the Ghibelline restored,
—Have we not seen it, we who caused this anguish,
  Exile and fear proscription and the sword?

Or shall God less avenge in their wild valley
  Where they lie slaughtered those poor sheep whose fold
In the gray twilight of our wrath we harried
  To serve the worshippers of stocks and gold?

This fails. That finds its hour. This fights. That falters.
  Greece is stamped out beneath a Wolseley's heels.
Or Egypt is avenged of her long mourning,
  And hurls her Persians back to their own keels.

'Tis not alone the victor who is noble.
  'Tis not alone the wise man who is wise.
There is a voice of sorrow in all shouting,
  And shame pursues not only him who flies.

To fight and conquer—'tis the boast of heroes.
  To fight and fly—of this men do not speak.
Yet shall there come a day when men shall tremble
  Rather than do misdeeds upon the weak,—

—A day when statesmen baffled in their daring
  Shall rather fear to wield the sword in vain
Than to give back their charge to a hurt nation,
  And own their frailties, and resign their reign,—

—A day of wrath when all fame shall remember
  Of this year's work shall be the fall of one
Who, standing foremost in her paths of virtue,
  Bent a fool's knee at War's red altar stone.

And left all virtue beggared in his falling,
  A sign to England of new griefs to come,

Her priest of peace who sold his creed for glory
  And marched to carnage at the tuck of drum.

Therefore I fear not. Rather let this record
  Stand of the past, ere God's revenge shall chase
From place to punishment His sad vicegerents
  Of power on Earth.—I fling it in their face.

II

I have a thing to say. But how to say it?
  Out of the East a twilight had been born.
It was not day. Yet the long night was waning,
  And the spent nations watched it less forlorn.

Out of the silence of the joyless ages
  A voice had spoken, such as the first bird
Speaks to the woods, before the morning wakens,—
  And the World starting to its feet had heard.

Men hailed it as a prophecy. Its utterance
  Was in that tongue divine the Orient knew.
It spoke of hope. Men hailed it as a brother's.
  It spoke of happiness. Men deemed it true.

There in the land of Death, where toil is cradled,
  That tearful Nile, unknown to Liberty,
It spoke in passionate tones of human freedom,
  And of those rights of Man which cannot die,—

—Till from the cavern of long fear, whose portals
  Had backward rolled, and hardly yet aloud,
Men prisoned stole like ghosts and joined the chorus,
  And chaunted trembling, each man in his shroud.

Justice and peace, the brotherhood of nations,—
  Love and goodwill of all mankind to man,—
These were the words they caught and echoed strangely,
  Deeming them portions of some Godlike plan,—

A plan thus first to their own land imparted.
  They did not know the irony of Fate,

The mockery of man's freedom, and the laughter
   Which greets a brother's love from those that hate.

Oh for the beauty of hope's dreams! The childhood
   Of that old land, long impotent in pain,
Cast off its slough of sorrow with its silence,
   And laughed and shouted and grew new again.

And in the streets, where still the shade of Pharaoh
   Stalked in his sons, the Mamelukian horde,
Youth greeted youth with words of exultation
   And shook his chains and clutched as for a sword.

Student and merchant,—Jew, and Copt, and Moslem,—
   All whose scarred backs had bent to the same rod,—
Fired with one mighty thought, their feuds forgotten,
   Stood hand in hand and praising the same God.

III

I have a thing to say. But how to say it?
   As in the days of Moses in the land,
God sent a man of prayer before his people
   To speak to Pharaoh, and to loose his hand.

Injustice, that hard step-mother of heroes,
   Had taught him justice. Him the sight of pain
Moved into anger, and the voice of weeping
   Made his eyes weep as for a comrade slain.

A soldier in the bands of his proud masters
   It was his lot to serve. But of his soul
None owned allegiance save the Lord of Armies.
   No worship from his God's might him cajole.

Strict was his service. In the law of Heaven
   He comfort took and patient under wrong.
And all men loved him for his heart unquailing,
   And for the words of pity on his tongue.

Knowledge had come to him in the night-watches,
   And strength with fasting, eloquence with prayer,

He stood a Judge from God before the strangers,
   The one just man among his people there.

Strongly he spoke: "Now, Heaven be our witness!
   Egypt this day has risen from her sleep.
She has put off her mourning and her silence.
   It was no law of God that she should weep.

"It was no law of God nor of the Nations
   That in this land, alone of the fair Earth,
The hand that sowed should reap not of its labour,
   The heart that grieved should profit not of mirth.

"How have we suffered at the hands of strangers,
   Binding their sheaves, and harvesting their wrath!
Our service has been bitter, and our wages
   Hunger and pain and nakedness and drouth.

"Which of them pitied us? Of all our princes,
   Was there one Sultan listened to our cry?
Their palaces we built, their tombs, their temples.
   What did they build but tombs for Liberty?

"To live in ignorance, to die by service;
   To pay our tribute and our stripes receive:
This was the ransom of our toil in Eden,
   This, and our one sad liberty—to grieve.

"We have had enough of strangers and of princes
   Nursed on our knees and lords within our house.
The bread which they have eaten was our children's,
   For them the feasting and the shame for us.

"The shadow of their palaces, fair dwellings
   Built with our blood and kneaded with our tears,
Darkens the land with darkness of Gehennem,
   The lust, the crime, the infamy of years.

"Did ye not hear it? From those muffled windows
   A sound of women rises and of mirth.
These are our daughters—ay our sons—in prison,
   Captives to shame with those who rule the Earth.

"The silent river by those gardens lapping
  To-night receives its burden of new dead,
A man of age sent home with his lord's wages,
  Stones to his feet, a grave-cloth to his head.

"Walls infamous in beauty, gardens fragrant
  With rose and citron and the scent of blood.
God shall blot out the memory of all laughter,
  Rather than leave you standing where you stood.

"We have had enough of princes and of strangers,
  Slaves that were Sultans, eunuchs that were kings,
The shame of Sodom is on all their faces.
  The curse of Cain pursues them, and it clings.

"Is there no virtue? See the pale Greek smiling.
  Virtue for him is as a tale of old.
Which be his gods? The cent. per cent. in silver.
  His God of gods? The world's creator, Gold.

"The Turk that plunders and the Frank that panders,
  These are our lords who ply with lust and fraud.
The brothel and the winepress and the dancers
  Are gifts unneeded in the lands of God.

"We need them not. We heed them not. Our faces
  Are turned to a new Kebla, a new truth,
Proclaimed by the one God of all the nations
  To save His people and renew their youth.

"A truth which is of knowledge and of reason;
  Which teaches men to mourn no more and live;
Which tells them of things good as well as evil,
  And gives what Liberty alone can give,

"The counsel to be strong, the will to conquer,
  The love of all things just and kind and wise,
Freedom for slaves, fair rights for all as brothers,
  The triumph of things true, the scorn of lies.

"Oh men, who are my brethren, my soul's kindred!
  That which our fathers dreamed of as a dream,

The sun of peace and justice, has arisen
  And God shall work in you His perfect scheme.

"The rulers of your Earth shall cease deceiving,
  The men of usury shall fly your land.
Your princes shall be numbered with your servants,
  And peace shall guide the sword in your right hand.

"You shall become a nation with the nations.
  Lift up your voices, for the night is past.
Stretch forth your hands. The hands of the free peoples
  Have beckoned you—the youngest and the last.

"And in the brotherhood of Man reposing,
  Joined to their hopes and nursed in their new day,
The anguish of the years shall be forgotten
  And God, with these, shall wipe your tears away."

IV

I have a thing to say. But how to say it?
  How shall I tell the mystery of guile—
The fraud that fought—the treason that disbanded—
  The gold that slew the children of the Nile?

The ways of violence are hard to reckon,
  And men of right grow feeble in their will,
And Virtue of her sons has been forsaken,
  And men of peace have turned aside to kill.

How shall I speak of them, the priests of Baal,
  The men who sowed the wind for their ill ends?
The reapers of the whirlwind in that harvest
  Were all my countrymen, were some my friends.

Friends, countrymen and lovers of fair freedom—
  Souls to whom still my soul laments and cries.
I would not tell the shame of your false dealings,
  Save for the blood which clamours to the skies.

A curse on Statecraft, not on you my Country!
  The men you slew were not more foully slain

Than was your honour at their hands you trusted.
    They died, you conquered,—both alike in vain.

Crime finds accomplices, and Murder weapons.
    The ways of Statesmen are an easy road.
All swords are theirs, the noblest with the neediest.
    And those who serve them best are men of good.

What need to blush, to trifle with dissembling?
    A score of honest tongues anon shall swear.
Blood flows. The Senate's self shall spread its mantle
    In the world's face, nor own a Cæsar there.

"Silence! Who spoke?" "The voice of one disclosing
    A truth untimely." "With what right to speak?
Holds he the Queen's commission?" "No, God's only."
    A hundred hands shall smite him on the cheek.

The "truth" of Statesmen is the thing they publish,
    Their "falsehood" the thing done they do not say,
Their "honour" what they win from the world's trouble,
    Their "shame" the "ay" which reasons with their "nay."

Alas for Liberty, alas for Egypt!
    What chance was yours in this ignoble strife?
Scorned and betrayed, dishonoured and rejected,
    What was there left you but to fight for life?

The men of honour sold you to dishonour.
    The men of truth betrayed you with a kiss.
Your strategy of love too soon outplotted,
    What was there left you of your dreams but this?

You thought to win a world by your fair dealing,
    To conquer freedom with no drop of blood.
This was your crime. The world knows no such reasoning.
    It neither bore with you nor understood.

Your Pharaoh with his chariots and his dancers,
    Him they could understand as of their kin.
He spoke in their own tongue and as their servant,
    And owned no virtue they could call a sin.

They took him for his pleasure and their purpose.
  They fashioned him as clay to their own pride.
His name they made a cudgel to your hurting,
  His treachery a spear-point to your side.

They knew him, and they scorned him and upheld him.
  They strengthened him with honours and with ships.
They used him as a shadow for seditions.
  They stabbed you with the lying of his lips

Sad Egypt! Since that night of misadventure
  [Which slew your first-born for your Pharaoh's crime,
No plague like this has God decreed against you,
  No punishment of all foredoomed in Time.

V

I have a thing to say. Oh how to say it!
  One summer morning, at the hour of prayer,
And in the face of Man and Man's high Maker,
  The thunder of their cannon rent the air.

The flames of death were on you and destruction.
  A hail of iron on your heads they poured.
You fought, you fell, you died until the sunset;
  And then you fled forsaken of the Lord.

I care not if you fled. What men call courage
  Is the least noble thing of which they boast.
Their victors always are great men of valour.
  Find me the valour of the beaten host!

It may be you were cowards. Let them prove it,—
  What matter? Were you women in the fight,
Your courage were the greater that a moment
  You steeled your weakness in the cause of right.

Oh I would rather fly with the first craven
  Who flung his arms away in your good cause,

Than head the hottest charge by England vaunted
  In all the record of her unjust wars.

Poor sheep! they scattered you. Poor slaves! they bowed you.
   You prayed for your dear lives with your mute hands.
They answered you with laughter and with shouting,
   And slew you in your thousands on the sands.

They led you with arms bound to your betrayer—
   His slaves, they said, recaptured for his will.
They bade him to take heart and fill his vengeance.
   They gave him his lost sword that he might kill.

They filled for him his dungeons with your children.
   They chartered him new gaolers from strange shores.
The Arnaout and the Cherkess for his minions,
   Their soldiers for the sentries at his doors.

He plied you with the whip, the rope, the thumb-screw.
   They plied you with the scourging of vain words
He sent his slaves, his eunuchs, to insult you.
   They sent you laughter on the lips of Lords.

They bound you to the pillar of their firmans.
   They placed for sceptre in your hand a pen.
They cast lots for the garments of your treaties,
   And brought you naked to the gaze of men.

They called on your High Priest for your death mandate.
   They framed indictments on you from your laws.
For him men loved they offered a Barabbas.
   They washed their hands and found you without cause.

They scoffed at you and pointed in derision,
   Crowned with their thorns and nailed upon their tree.
And at your head their Pilate wrote the inscription—
   "This is the land restored to Liberty."

Oh insolence of strength! Oh boast of wisdom!
   Oh poverty in all things truly wise!
Thinkest thou, England, God can be outwitted
   For ever thus by him who sells and buys?

Thou sellest the sad nations to their ruin.
   What hast thou bought? The child within the womb,

The son of him thou slayest to thy hurting,
  Shall answer thee "an Empire for thy tomb."

Thou hast joined house to house for thy perdition.
  Thou hast done evil in the name of right.
Thou hast made bitter sweet and the sweet bitter,
  And called light darkness and the darkness light.

Thou art become a bye-word for dissembling,
  A beacon to thy neighbours for all fraud.
Thy deeds of violence men count and reckon.
  Who takes the sword shall perish by the sword.

Thou hast deserved men's hatred. They shall hate thee.
  Thou hast deserved men's fear. Their fear shall kill.
Thou hast thy foot upon the weak. The weakest
  With his bruised head shall strike thee on the heel.

Thou wentest to this Egypt for thy pleasure.
  Thou shalt remain with her for thy sore pain.
Thou hast possessed her beauty. Thou wouldst leave her.
  Nay. Thou shalt lie with her as thou hast lain.

She shall bring shame upon thy face with all men.
  She shall disease thee with her grief and fear.
Thou shalt grow sick and feeble in her ruin.
  Thou shalt repay her to the last sad tear.

Her kindred shall surround thee with strange clamours,
  Dogging thy steps till thou shalt loathe their din.
The friends thou hast deceived shall watch in anger.
  ｛Thy children shall upbraid thee with thy sin.

All shall be counted thee a crime,—thy patience
  With thy impatience. Thy best thought shall wound.
Thou shalt grow weary of thy work thus fashioned,
  And walk in fear with eyes upon the ground.

The Empire thou didst build shall be divided.
  Thou shalt be weighed in thine own balances
Of usury to peoples and to princes,
  And be found wanting by the world and these.

They shall possess the lands by thee forsaken
  And not regret thee. On their seas no more
Thy ships shall bear destruction to the nations,
  Or thy guns thunder on a fenceless shore.

Thou hast no pity in thy day of triumph.
  These shall not pity thee. The world shall move
On its high course and leave thee to thy silence,
  Scorned by the creatures that thou couldst not love.

Thy Empire shall be parted, and thy kingdom.
  At thy own doors a kingdom shall arise,
Where freedom shall be preached and the wrong righted
  Which thy unwisdom wrought in days unwise.

Truth yet shall triumph in a world of justice.
  This is of faith. I swear it. East and west
The law of Man's progression shall accomplish
  Even this last great marvel with the rest.

Thou wouldst not further it. Thou canst not hinder.
  If thou shalt learn in time thou yet shalt live.
But God shall ease thy hand of its dominion,
  And give to these the rights thou wouldst not give.

The nations of the East have left their childhood.
  Thou art grown old. Their manhood is to come;
And they shall carry on Earth's high tradition
  Through the long ages when thy lips are dumb,

Till all shall be wrought out. O Lands of weeping.
  Lands watered by the rivers of old Time,
Ganges and Indus and the streams of Eden,
  Yours is the future of the world sublime.

Yours was the fount of man's first inspiration,
  The well of wisdom whence he earliest drew.
And yours shall be the flood time of his reason,
  The stream of strength which shall his strength renew.

The wisdom of the West is but a madness,
  The fret of shallow waters in their bed.

Yours is the flow, the fulness of Man's patience
  The ocean of God's rest inherited.

And thou too, Egypt, mourner of the nations,
  Though thou hast died to-day in all men's sight,
And though upon thy cross with thieves thou hangest,
  Yet shall thy wrong be justified in right.

'Twas meet one man should die for the whole people.
  Thou wert the victim chosen to retrieve
The sorrows of the Earth with full deliverance.
  And, as thou diest these shall surely live.

Thy prophets have been scattered through the cities.
  The seed of martyrdom thy sons have sown
Shall make of thee a glory and a witness
  In all men's hearts held captive with thine own.

Thou shalt not be forsaken in thy children.
  Thy righteous blood shall fructify the Earth.
The virtuous of all lands shall be thy kindred,
  And death shall be to thee a better birth.

Therefore I do not grieve. Oh hear me, Egypt!
  Even in death thou art not wholly dead.
And hear me, England! Nay. Thou needs must hear me.
  I had a thing to say. And it is said.

THE END

VERMONT COLLEGE
MONTPELIER, VERMONT.

DATE DUE

GAYLORD			PRINTED IN U.S.A.